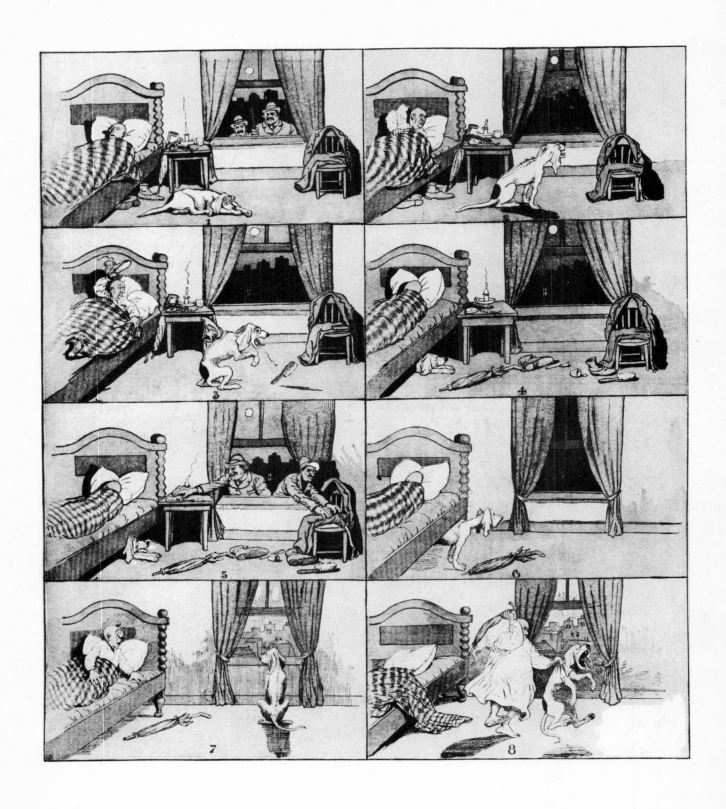

WALT McDougall and Mark Fenderson: "The Unfortunate Fate of a Well-Intentioned Dog," from the New York *World* of February 4, 1894. One of the first Sunday comics in color.

Comic Art in America

A SOCIAL HISTORY OF THE FUNNIES, THE POLITICAL
CARTOONS, MAGAZINE HUMOR, SPORTING CARTOONS
AND ANIMATED CARTOONS

BY STEPHEN BECKER

WITH AN INTRODUCTION BY RUBE GOLDBERG AND
WITH NEARLY 400 ILLUSTRATIONS

SIMON AND SCHUSTER   NEW YORK
1959

THIS BOOK IS GRATEFULLY DEDICATED TO THE NATIONAL CARTOONISTS SOCIETY, OVER FOUR HUNDRED CREATIVE GENTLEMEN WHO ARE BOTH THE HEIRS AND THE PERPETUATORS OF THE GREAT TRADITIONS OF COMIC ART.

ACKNOWLEDGMENTS

CERTAINLY MY FIRST AND GREATEST DEBT is to the National Cartoonists Society. Its members were unfailingly generous with time and information, and many of them helped to dig up rare illustrations and remote reminiscences. Often where introductions were needed— to cartoonists, syndicates, or editors — the Society supplied them. I was privileged to watch several cartoonists at work and to spend long hours in discussion with scores of them.

And all this was in spite of the fact that the Society— more specifically, the Boards of Governors under the presidencies of John Pierotti and Mort Walker— knew that it would have no control over my judgments and prejudices. The responsibility for those is all mine; but without the help of the Society and of many individual cartoonists, only the skimpiest of histories would have been possible. To Marge Duffy Devine, the Society's secretary, an extra word of thanks.

Practically all the 396 illustrations are under copyright, most of them by syndicates, some by individuals. Nowhere did we encounter any reluctance to grant permission. Several of the syndicates were particularly generous, throwing open their files and supplying learned guides who unearthed dozens of original drawings.

Full credit to the owners of copyright accompanies each illustration. With some of the older drawings copyright confusion still exists; and a few individuals and organizations seem to have dropped out of sight altogether. If in our credits we have fallen short of legal perfection, we extend apologies. Our efforts to trace copyright owners were strenuous, and if errors or omissions exist we shall be happy to correct them in later editions.

There are not many books on comic art. These six were helpful in one area or another, and our gratitude goes to their authors:

The Comics, by Coulton Waugh, The Macmillan Company, 1947. An entertaining survey of comic strips from the 1890s on.

Comics and Their Creators, by Martin Sheridan, Hale, Cushman and Flint, 1942. Informal biographies of many leading comic-strip artists.

Cartoon Cavalcade, by Thomas Craven, Simon and Schuster, 1943. A survey of humorous panels, comic strips, and other periodical cartooning.

The American Past, by Roger Butterfield, Simon and Schuster, rev. ed. 1957, which includes an excellent treatment of the late nineteenth-century editorial cartoon.

The Lines Are Drawn, by Gerald Johnson, J. B. Lippincott Company, 1958, an extended examination of the Pulitzer Prize cartoons.

A History of American Graphic Humor, by William Murrell, published for the Whitney Museum of American Art by The Macmillan Company © 1938. Quotations from this book are used by permission of The Macmillan Company. A witty, learned and thoroughly enjoyable history, in two volumes, with little discussion of comic strips but extended treatment of other forms of comic art. A book so well done as to be momentarily discouraging to later chroniclers.

The drawings of Farmer Al Falfa and the sequences from Mighty Mouse, Heckle and Jeckle and Tom Terrific and his Wonder Dog appear herein through the courtesy of Terrytoons, a division of CBS Films, Inc.

To Messrs. Waugh and Sheridan, thanks for permission to quote briefly from their books.

Thanks also to Miss Toni Mendez, artists' and writers' representative, who was the original catalyst between author and publisher; and for their kind assistance, thanks to the Newspaper Comics Council.

To the following syndicate executives and employees, many thanks: Maurice T. Reilly and Lloyd Jones; Sylvan Byck and James Ryan; James Hennessy and Stuart Hawkins; Harold Anderson and Philip Steitz; Robert A. Cooper; Sumner P. Ahlbum; John Osenenko and Don LaSpaluto; and Helen Staunton.

A special word of thanks to Mr. Ernest McGee of Philadelphia, owner and fond curator of probably the largest private collection of old comics pages in the country. The many hours spent leafing through his bound volumes, and absorbing some of his apparently limitless knowledge of the period from 1890 to 1915, were highly rewarding.

My thanks to Burton W. Marvin, Dean of the School of Journalism at the University of Kansas, and Curator of the Albert T. Reid cartoon museum. Dean Marvin opened the museum to me during a vacation period and permitted me to work in seclusion and to examine the files freely.

Writers of non-fiction customarily thank their wives, without whose help, etc. The gesture is no less valid for being hackneyed and sentimental, and I have a special reason for making it. This book took two years to write, and for the last six months of that time I was hospitalized (first dying, then thoroughly paralyzed, then slowly recovering). My wife, Mary, took over the tedious jobs of assembling manuscript, deciphering old notes (some of them actually on shirt cardboards), rounding up scores of illustrations, corresponding with cartoonists and syndicates, and maintaining friendly relations with the publishers. She did it all with the aplomb, taste and skill of a veteran editor— which she is not; even more, she ran a household, kept our three small children healthy and happy, and gave me the affection and confidence I needed, which only she could supply.

So I hope no one minds this note of loving thanks. Without Mary the book would not have come to an end, and the writer would have.

STEPHEN BECKER

CONTENTS

INTRODUCTION

by Rube Goldberg

M*y waking hours (and, indeed, many of the dream-sodden sleeping moments of my life) have been so saturated with cartooning that I could not wish for a greater privilege than the task of writing the foreword to this comprehensive history of the profession by Stephen Becker.*

It has been an exhaustive job for this brilliant young writer, and I am sure the members of my craft will be grateful to him. Here is an almost endless parade of cartoonists sitting on glittering floats alongside their characters and creations of happy memory for the public to watch, as well as giving inspiration to present-day cartoonists who have, up to now, been denied a glimpse of the pioneers who paved the way for their thrills, their disappointments and their rewards.

Stage people love to dwell affectionately on the "smell" of grease paint. There is a pungent aroma to every art. One of my earliest thrills was the "smell" of cartoons. My brother at the age of twelve earned a few extra pennies on Saturdays delivering magazines to barber shops. On days when he was indisposed he turned his route over to me. I shall never forget the excitement I experienced when I first took hold of a bundle of those magazines, among which were Puck, Judge, Life, *and* Collier's, *and inhaled the fragrant aroma of printer's ink, galloping over the shiny pages in the intriguing shapes of humorous figures by T. S. Sullivant, Zim, Albert Levering, Keppler, Gillam, Gibson and others. I literally held the magazines close to my face so that I might inhale the talents of those cartoonists whose work I admired with an adolescent ecstasy.*

Later, when I was studying mining engineering at the University of California (which profession has as much to do with cartooning as a head of lettuce has with a high silk hat), I'd sneak back to San Francisco and buy copies of the New York World *and* Journal *at an out-of-town newsstand in front of the old* Chronicle *building. Then I'd put aside my books on graphostatics and study the work of Tad, Bob Edgren, Tom Powers and Opper.*

No one but a born cartoonist can understand the isolation of a young hopeful with nobody close to him who really sympathizes with his hopes and ambitions. He must literally wallow in the work of established cartoonists to find vicarious companionship. His friends are the cartoon figures he can find on the printed page.

While there are some cases where a talent for cartooning is handed down from father to son, in most instances the great urge to draw comes like an unpredicted hurricane that has completely fooled the weather forecaster. It is God-given. It just happens. You cannot explain it any more than the blooming of a flower on a desert cactus. It strikes men of all shapes and sizes. Homer Davenport and H. T. Webster were physical giants. Billy DeBeck and Clare Briggs were on the short side. Sidney Smith was tall. George McManus short. There was no similarity in any of their features.

But to me, at least, there was a striking similarity in their characters. Of course, they all had a keen sense of humor. They had a fine feeling for human values, being critically aware of the emptiness of pomposity. They had an innate modesty, although some of them tried to hide it under a cloak of self-assurance and loud vests. Even Bud Fisher, who was about the cockiest of all the cartoonists on my sprawling tapestry of affectionate specimens, was blessed with some humility. He exhibited a glimpse of tenderness when he saw me forty years ago wheeling a baby carriage containing the chubby form of my eldest son. He actually kissed the baby!

During the existence of the National Cartoonists Society over the last thirteen years I have met the successors to the idols of my youth— young men whose brilliant careers are described later in this book. They have the same human traits, the same boyish freedom from guile and affectation. True, they have a greater sense of financial responsibility than their progenitors, perhaps due to the demands of syndication and taxes. But they otherwise belong to that special breed which I have chosen to call, on previous occasions, "a race apart."

On a recent trip to Tokyo I met the leading Japanese cartoonist, Taizo Yokoyama. Although the language barrier frayed the entente cordiale *slightly around the edges, we had little trouble in finding a real level of happy understanding. He wore a beret to cover his balding dome, which he called attention to with a mischievous smile of self-deprecation. It was startlingly like the smile I had often seen on the face of Billy DeBeck.*

Russia's two leading cartoonists— Ivan Semenov of Krokodil Magazine *and Vitali Goriaev of U.S.S.R. Magazine— were brought to my home by Bill Crawford, one of our best editorial cartoonists, when they were visiting this country some months ago. I started bombarding them with provocative questions about Russia while serving Scotch highballs, which they emphatically requested instead of the obvious vodka. The questions and answers were quite perfunctory, as you might imagine. The conversation got nowhere until we managed to assault the subject of cartoons and art. I say "assault" advisedly. They became animated and warm. They were surprisingly well informed about our cartoonists. Talking shop with them was not unlike talking shop with our American fellows.*

They stayed till half past two in the morning. Before they left the Iron Curtain had dissolved in the sweet fluid of cartoonists' affinity for one another. Of course, I don't know what they said when they got back home. But I was convinced that these two cartoonists, working under rigid Russian discipline, were essentially the same inside as ourselves.

In this book Steve Becker has pulled aside the portieres of anonymity behind which cartoonists have labored over the years. You will meet sober-faced men whose humorous drawings touch off an explosion of laughter; jovial men whose characters are forever on the brink of impending disaster; mousy men whose cartoon figures are bulging with power and muscle; and lumbering individuals who sit daily at their drawing boards concocting pictures of cute babies, nuzzling puppies and darling mice. The popularity of cartoon characters seems endless, although many of their oddly assorted creators have long since been gathered to their reward.

Many strips are self-perpetuating. The comic strip is the only form of entertainment that is not susceptible to the ravages of time. There is always a capable young cartoonist waiting around to carry on, often sustaining the high quality of the original. This is a tribute to the fundamental vitality and general appeal of the cartoon form. It can be said that a cartoonist is never a dead duck. There is always a good loud quack in his remains.

The Pulitzer Prize is awarded for "the best editorial cartoon of the year." It seems distressingly ironic that this distinguished award is denied to the vast army of talent that keeps millions of Americans laughing and crying as they reach greedily for the comic page each day. Of course, Joseph Pulitzer had no psychic powers to foresee the great impact all forms of cartooning were to have on the American scene. But present-day cartoonists keep attending imaginary séances where they hope the spirit of Pulitzer will materialize and give a signal that eligibility for the Prize be extended far beyond the limits of the editorial page.

Just as laws are meant to be broken, so are the definitions of the cartoon form meant to be spilled on the floor and mopped up with the towel of misunderstanding. Cartooning today has developed so many facets since the time of Doré and Daumier that a concise definition is impossible.

This book is cartoon's best definition— ranging from straight illustrative strips through sports, politics, caricature, social comment and fantasy. Steve Becker's inexhaustible interest in the subject brings you a lively comprehension that can never be spelled out in pedantic words.

We cartoonists may be a "race apart" in our approach to our work. But we like to believe that the creatures of our pens bring us close to the hearts and minds of the great American public.

CHAPTER I

Comics: The First Draft

An ENGLISH WRITER once remarked that a good comic strip was worth a hundred bad novels. The compliment is dubious: practically anything is better than a hundred bad novels. The Englishman was simply varying one of the hoariest of clichés: that a good picture is worth so many words— by his estimate, roughly seven million. The cliché, like most clichés, is not entirely true. A couple of good graphs may be worth twenty pages of an industrial report, and one photograph of a grieving face may be worth all the melancholy literature since Homer; but illustrations are less helpful with Spinoza, or a form sheet at the race track, or a love letter.

What the sages undoubtedly meant is that man's primary contact with his universe is visual, which accounts for cave paintings, religious images, circus posters and most marriages. The impact of one image is a thousand times more *immediate* than the impact of a thousand words, and of course the image itself may be more coherent and graceful.

More important, reading requires previous training, while seeing is automatic. Most of us read now, but in the old days, before about 1800, most of us did not. In any one culture, drawing, sculpture and the spoken theater all preceded written literature by several hundred years. We, for example, have our war novels, most of which, seen under the aspect of eternity, die a-borning; the French of 1150 A.D. had the Bayeux tapestry, an embroidery two hundred thirty feet long by twenty inches high, on which were pictured, in color and with brief legends, the hostilities between

A scene from the Bayeux Tapestry, one of the first European examples of a long story told graphically. Courtesy of Penguin Books Limited.

1

TENNIEL: one of three illustrations to "The Wonderful Whalers," a poem in *Punch*, volume 21, 1851.

Harold of England and William the Conqueror, culminating in the Battle of Hastings. The tapestry is now thought of as a "work of art," which it has always been; but eight hundred years ago it was, above all, communication.

The cartoon is one kind of pictorial communication. The word "cartoon" was once applied to models and studies for frescoes, mosaics and tapestries; satirical drawings, in those days, were called caricatures or hieroglyphics. In 1843 London saw a great exhibit of "cartoons" for the Houses of Parliament: designs for the walls of Commons and Lords. *Punch,* the first regular illustrated comic weekly, which had begun publication on July 17, 1841, took a dim view of those designs, and published its own "cartoons" satirizing them. (One of the workhorses of the early *Punch* was John Tenniel, famous now for his illustrations of *Alice in Wonderland.*) From then on, a "cartoon" was any single drawing—generally accompanied by a caption (technically a title, above the drawing) or a legend (story; below)—which was self-contained—that is, which transmitted its message without further explanation. Roughly speaking, and allowing for exceptions, the editorial cartoon came first in this country, the sports cartoon next and the humorous cartoon, from which comic strips evolved, last. Editorial cartoons became regular features in American newspapers during the 1890s, though there had been many isolated examples (and thousands of political caricatures) previously. More than any other individual, Walt McDougall fathered the editorial cartoon as a regular feature. His "Belshazzar's Feast," in the New York *World* during the Presidential campaign of 1884, is credited, even more than the Reverend Samuel D. Bur-

THE ROYAL FEAST OF BELSHAZZAR BLAINE AND THE MONEY KINGS.

WALT MCDOUGALL's most famous cartoon: "Belshazzar's Feast," from the New York *World* of October 30, 1884—very shortly before Election Day. It was credited with helping to swing New York State—and consequently the Presidential election—away from Blaine, and to Cleveland.

chard's panicky allusion to "rum, Romanism, and rebellion," with having ensured Cleveland's victory over Blaine.

A comic strip is, broadly speaking, a series of boxes called "panels," telling one story at a time, in a day or a month. For purposes of that story the panels are peopled with one cast. They appear regularly. With occasional exceptions, they make use of dialogue in "balloons," or of a written narrative.

None of these components was suddenly "discovered" when comics began; it was their combination that led to the new form. Hogarth and Rowlandson had used balloons, as had prints published in America in the 1760s. Rowlandson had used "continuity"— one story with one cast, appearing regularly— in his *Tours of Dr. Syntax*. In the 1870s and 1880s American dailies and weeklies flirted with the comics form. In 1872 Augustus Hoppin was doing three daily drawings for *Jubilee Days*, a four-page quarto. The *Daily Graphic*, in the same decade, was more sophisticated, and in 1873 ran a series of comic pictures satirizing women's fashions. Frank Bellew, a real forerunner of the comic-strip artist, did a six-panel strip in 1881 called *Mr. Bowler's Midnight Encounter*; he was soon followed by Palmer Cox and his *Brownies*, in *St. Nicholas Magazine. Puck* and *Judge*, established in the late 1870s and early 1880s, were running strips of panels by 1890. In the nineties Bellew did a six-panel pantomime strip for the old *Life*, and E. W. Kemble began, for the same magazine, his drawings of Negro children, under the general title of "Blackberries," which later became a Sunday comics feature.

MAKING FUN

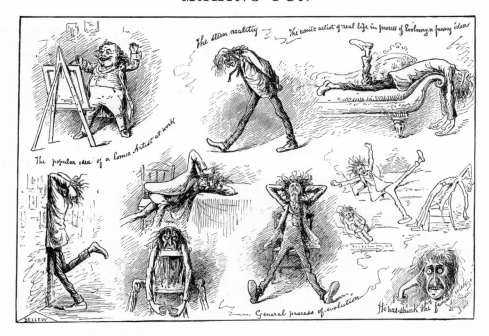

The cartoonist's daily labors, depicted by an old master, CHIP BELLEW, in *Harper's Weekly* of January 17, 1891. From the collection of Jay Irving.

3

Puck, Judge and the old *Life* were the seedbed of the comics. They ran thousands of funny cartoons, some of which required two or more panels. "Funny" is of course a relative word: most of the two-line jokes which served as legends were merely excuses for a well-executed drawing, and most of the cartoons fall flat today. The drawings were often elaborate; artists had time to draw, and the magazines had comfortable production schedules. Newspaper cartoons, on the other hand, had to be drawn more simply, had to be reproduced more quickly and had to convey an immediate message to a readership of varied intelligence.

Which brings us back to the basic truth: that pictures strike us more efficiently than words. That truth has stood up against time, education and various forms of society and government. When Rowlandson and Hogarth struck out against taxation or poor administration or general immorality, they worked in a medium that could reach everybody. They probably realized, too, that people believe illustrations more trustingly than they do prose. When Ben Franklin decided that the colonies would fail without unity, he refrained from long essays and drew a cartoon, and his world knew exactly and immediately what he meant. Frenchmen in the nineteenth century bought colorful penny sheets called *images populaires* which depicted, largely, the glory of French warriors, and by reflection the glory of all things French. Probably no historical reviews, no passionate pamphlets would so well have reassured the ordinary citizens of a nation disappointed in liberty, equality, fraternity and needing a dose of nationalistic consolation.

All art says *something* about the society that produces it; and often—cumulatively, over a period of years— the impress of an art alters the face

A mid-nineteenth-century Image Populaire. These were also called Images d'Epinal, after the name of the town in which they were printed. This one was titled "The Departure and Return of the Conscript." They were printed on cheap paper and sold for less than a penny each. Courtesy the print division of the New York Public Library.

DÉPART ET RETOUR DU CONSCRIT.

4

of its society. A precursor of the American comic strip was *Ferdinand Flipper,* which appeared in 1839 in a New York weekly. It was a continuous account of life in California illustrated by woodcuts. (This was before the gold rush, and California was still primitive and unknown.) To say that *Ferdinand Flipper* made any difference to the history of America would be an exaggeration, but it was surely read by many who would have ignored an on-the-spot reportage; it may have induced a stray reader to take his chances out west; and it probably added infinitesimally to a half-formed general conviction that the United States would ultimately extend from coast to coast. Early editorial cartoons affected politics in much the same casual manner: it was easy to look at a single unambiguous statement of opinion and to decide almost immediately whether or not you agreed with it. In the light of later events your decision might be wrong, but you had at least been prodded to a reaction. Considering the number of people — then as now— who ignore written editorials, any prodding at all was a minor triumph for the newspaper.

But, with rare and interesting exceptions, the comics have never tried to compete with the editorial spokesmen of their outlets. The first humorous pages declined to compete with humanity, for that matter: they portrayed animals in various states of frolic or temporary distress. James Swinnerton's *Little Bears and Tigers* started in the San Francisco *Examiner* in 1892; as Coulton Waugh says, they were not in themselves unusual or exciting, but they were amusing, and people looked for them regularly. Before long a page of funny drawings or even an illustrated section was an accepted part of the newspaper and possibly even a good reason for buying it. Swinnerton's were of course not the first humorous drawings; newspapers had been using black-and-white illustrations for years, and some small percentage of them was bound to be funny. (There was often humor in early advertising art.)

The original humorists were generally men who worked in a field where humor was secondary: engravers, woodcut artists and, later, lithographers. Throughout the nineteenth century in America there was a note of rough, almost backwoodsy humor in much of the advertising art, most of which was printed from woodcuts. But deliberate humor, humor for sale, was occasional until the emergence of the almanacks and humor magazines of the middle of the century. And newspaper humor— comic strips and their relatives— had to wait for the development of color, an innovation sufficiently spectacular to catch readers, hold their attention and make them habitués.

Joseph Pulitzer, probably the greatest of American newspaper publishers, took over the New York *World* in 1883, and within two years it had become the country's leading newspaper: the *Sunday World* in 1885 had a circulation of over two hundred thousand, and was of twenty pages; by 1892 Sunday editions ran to forty or forty-eight pages. Pulitzer has always

A full page of JAMES SWINNERTON's Tigers, about 1897, in the New York *Journal*. Courtesy of Ernest McGee.

A sample of T. S. SULLIVANT's work from the old *Life* Magazine. An all but forgotten genius, prime inspiration to a handful of current artists. Courtesy of Walt Kelly.

overshadowed Morrill Goddard, who is now all but forgotten; Goddard was the first great Sunday editor in American journalism, and most of what happened to comics in the 1890s was due as much to him as to Pulitzer or Hearst.

In May of 1890 Pulitzer's business manager for the *World*, George Turner, altered a Hoe press so that he was able to print a square of red in the center of the front page. The next year an unsung hero named Kohlsaat, publisher of the small Chicago *Inter-Ocean*, took a trip to Paris, where he presumably neglected both the Louvre and the Bal Tabarin in his excitement over the first color press, which he inspected in the offices of *Le Petit Journal*. When he returned to Chicago, he ordered a similar press from Walter Scott & Co.; it was in operation in 1892. Meanwhile Turner had left the *World* to manage the New York *Recorder*, a newspaper financed by the Duke tobacco fortune. Turner knew that the *World* was constantly experimenting with color, and he had R. Hoe & Co. design a color press for the *Recorder*. Professional larceny began at once: one of Pulitzer's men got wind of Turner's plans, sneaked a look at the new press and sketched it. He took the sketch to Walter Scott & Co., and the race was on.

Pulitzer decided that the *World* would use its color press to reproduce famous paintings from the art galleries of Europe. The *Recorder* selected a dismal feature called *Cosmopolitan Sketches— Annie, the Apple Girl*. Both the printing and the feature were so bad that the press was used for a total of only four issues. Still, the honor of printing the first newspaper color page in America goes to the New York *Recorder*, which had taken delivery of a color press exactly a week before the *World* did. The date was April 2, 1893.

But the first full-color page of any consequence appeared in the New York *World* of May 21, 1893, only twenty-eight years, remember, after the end of the Civil War. Called "The Possibilities of the Broadway Cable Car," it consisted of one highly populated drawing by Walt McDougall, carefully composed, inked and shaded, and printed in what can most charitably be described as vigorous pastels. In the same issue was a second page of color: the *Santa Maria*, lividly resplendent, reproduced for the *World's* readers from an original Spanish painting.

WALT McDOUGALL's "The Possibilities of the Broadway Cable Car." From the New York *World* of May 21, 1893. One of the first printed color pages in an American newspaper.

It was a time of change, all right. In Chicago in 1894 the first automobile race held on the North American continent was won by J. Frank Duryea, who covered 54.36 miles at an average speed of 7.5 miles per hour. And on Sunday, January 28, that same year, Mark Fenderson did a pantomime page in nine panels of full color, called "On the Tramp: A Song Without Words." A week later Fenderson and McDougall collaborated on an eight-panel color page, also in pantomime, entitled "The Unfortunate Fate of a Well-Intentioned Dog " (frontispiece).

In a sense Fenderson and McDougall opened the gates. The color pages of 1893 were certainly not "comics"; neither were those of 1894, if we specify dialogue and continuity. But these latter were in Sunday-strip form and told a story. They were enthusiastically received. A period of experiment had begun. Color illustrations were a novelty, and the public would, for some time to come, like practically anything in the form. Over the next few years Fenderson and McDougall turned out thousands of panels and strips, and they were joined by dozens of aspiring artists.

McDougall was, of course, already famous as an editorial cartoonist for the *World*. His work in the 1890s led him to a new and important career as a comic-strip artist after 1900, when the early syndicates became active. He produced *Fatty Felix* in 1903, *Strange Visitors from the Land of Oz* in 1904, *Peck's Bad Boy* in 1906, *Hank the Hermit* in 1911 and *Uncle Dockstader* in 1913. Most of his strips ran for years, and by 1927 (when we shall meet him again, sitting between Jimmy Walker and Al Smith) he was almost a demigod to American cartoonists.

Fenderson seems to have been the first comic-strip artist to use a brush for outlines and contours. His career was not as long or as brilliant as McDougall's. He turned out more "one-shot" strips— illustrative of an anecdote, with a cast and a setting used once only— than sustained continuities. He loved experiment: with composition, technique, color, story. He hopped from a boy-and-dog anecdote to a married-couple quarrel, and remained more a "feature" cartoonist, leaving the extended continuity to his colleagues. His fellows owed him a good deal: his panels were perfectly proportioned, his strokes were bold and his figures had force.

Pulitzer had always believed in the free use of illustration, and even his typography was varied and arresting. His features covered the range of human interest, and he had, for purposes of raising the *World's* circulation, the population of what would someday be the largest city of all. The *World* was popular, and Pulitzer's fortune enabled him to experiment. He had early sensed that the public was restless, and that a good newspaper would, over a period of time, vary its content, layout and emphasis.

By 1896 all the kinks had been ironed out of the color press save one: the yellow ink, on which depended greens and oranges, persisted in its refusal to dry properly. It ran and smudged incorrigibly. On the urgent advice of Morrill Goddard, Pulitzer had agreed to combine two experiments: the color presses and regular comics. The story goes that Charles Saalburgh, foreman of the color-press room, needed an open patch of white space which the presses could print yellow. Saalburgh would then have a clearly defined test area, and could experiment with quick driers. Saalburgh looked through the *World* and found a series of comic drawings from "Shantytown," by Richard Felton Outcault, formerly a draftsman for the *Electric World*. From a play by Edward Harrigan called *O'Reilly and the Four Hundred*, Outcault had adapted the opening words of the song "Maggie Murphy's Home," which were "Down in Hogan's Alley." On the *World* Outcault had used Hogan's Alley and its inhabitants to burlesque current events, among them the celebrated wedding of Consuelo Vanderbilt to the Duke of Marlborough. One of the residents of Hogan's Alley was a gap-toothed, jug-eared urchin who wore what looked like a white nightgown. Saalburgh chose that nightgown as the test area for his tallow-drying yellow.

The results astonished not only Saalburgh, but Pulitzer himself, most of New York City, certainly Outcault, a rival publisher named William Randolph Hearst and ultimately the entire world of journalism. Coulton Waugh imagines one of the first appearances of the Yellow Kid (the first had been on July 7, 1895):

So on February 16, 1896, when the readers of the New York Sunday *World* settled back in their crimson plush chairs and slacked their suspenders after dinner, they found in the large section devoted to funny drawings a three-quarter page in color entitled "The Great Dog Show in M'Googan's Avenue," and signed, "Outcault." It was a kind of panorama of the city's slum backyards, filled with cats and wash and a lot of tough children in high-society costumes, who were very busy exhibiting their pets. These kids framed a central figure, a strange creature who, though evidently a boy, appeared to have passed through the major experiences of life in the first six months. Though small, he was important-looking. His head, bald, with flap ears, had a wise, faintly Chinese face, and he looked directly into the reader's eyes with a quizzical, interrogative smile, half timid, half brash, as if he understood perfectly well the portentous event which was happening through him. The kid was dressed in a kind of nightgown on which was a smeary handprint, and this nightgown was colored a pure, light yellow, which made a vivid bull's-eye in the whole big page.

A month later another Yellow Kid appeared, and public reaction must have convinced Pulitzer that he had struck a nerve. Anything that might build circulation was valuable in itself. Pulitzer and Saalburgh could hardly have realized so early that their experiment would add a phrase— "yellow journalism"— to the American language, or that it would evoke that first, gentle wave of mass hysteria which accompanies the birth of popular art forms. The Yellow Kid was soon on buttons, cracker tins, cigarette packs and ladies' fans; eventually he was a character in a Broadway play.

Outcault, a native of Ohio, was only thirty-three years old at the time; he

One of the first *Yellow Kids* by RICHARD FELTON OUTCAULT. From the *World* of February 16, 1896. "The Great Dog Show in M'Googan Avenue." Courtesy of Ernest McGee.

had studied art in Paris, and had contributed frequently to *Judge* and the old *Life*. His drawings are crowded, full of flying figures and the whirling lines of action; in one of them we count thirty-one human beings and eight assorted animals. This is complicated stuff; we cannot simply glance at it once and then pass along. Outcault arrested attention: there was a whole short story in one of his drawings.

There had been simple short stories in Fenderson and McDougall—stories without words. But the Yellow Kid's nightshirt, the focal point of the drawing, stood out like a billboard, and almost from the beginning written messages appeared on it. The messages were often identification tags, or bad puns, or statements of malicious intent. But the written word had moved into the drawing; it was no longer simply a caption or a legend. The Yellow Kid was the first serious break in the ancient tradition that words had no place in the drawing itself. That tradition was partly responsible for the static quality of earlier comic drawings, and of magazine cartoons up to the 1920s: the drawing itself was usually no more than a still-life with figures, setting off the caption or the two-line joke. There might be talent in the drawing, but there was no visual wit; the wit, if any, lay in the

WHAT THEY DID TO THE DOG-CATCHER IN HOGAN'S ALLEY.

A tumultuous *Yellow Kid*, September 20, 1896, when OUTCAULT was still with the *World*.

ELEVEN OF THE GREAT EARLY COMIC ARTISTS.

words. (By and large, that is: we must except Marriner, Sullivant and Kemble, for example.) With the Yellow Kid the words began to reflect the humor of the drawing, and vice versa, to the point— and an important point it was— where *neither was satisfactory without the other*. The next steps now seem inevitable, though they were not taken immediately: the short story was broken down into its elements, so that the true strip form— a series of consecutive panels— became necessary; and the written messages became speech, enclosed in balloons.

If the Yellow Kid had not been funny, he would probably have died quickly. He did, after all, bring something new and upsetting into American homes: the slums, and slum kids, and ordinary cruelty, and slang, and the cockiness of poverty. Little bears and tigers, and cute old men with pooches, were innocuous enough; they stood for the sweet and amiable world of things-as-they-should-be. The Yellow Kid picked himself up out of the gutter of things-as-they-are, snarled cheerfully at his audience and hit a little Negro boy with a golf club, or sat at the curb nursing a hangover. If Outcault had drawn that world seriously and called it "Mickey, a Boy of the Slums" or "The Family with Four Hundred Dollars a Year," readers would have turned away uneasily, repelled by the reminder, outraged by the violation of their privacy and grossly deceived in their search for light entertainment.

But the Yellow Kid *was* funny, and he boosted circulation. This pleased Pulitzer, Saalburgh and Morrill Goddard.

It also pleased a man named William Randolph Hearst.

Hearst had already been successful in reviving his father's moribund San Francisco *Examiner*, where Swinnerton's bears and tigers had appeared as early as 1892. In 1895 Hearst invaded New York, buying the equally moribund *Morning Journal* from Albert Pulitzer, Joseph's brother and rival. Hearst was a proud man, but not too proud to admit that Joe Pulitzer was good; he emulated the *World* frankly. He took offices in the *World* building, and shortly began to buy up the *World's* staff— particularly its Sunday staff. By the fall of 1896 Hearst was ready to bid for Pulitzer's public. He made that bid through the comics.

He had felt for some time that color comics were one of the keys to high circulation. By 1896 he had surely realized that they were here to stay, and that their future was almost unlimited; he was a great publisher, and may have been able to visualize comics as the national institution they have become. His attack on the public would be led by a new supplement, an eight-page comic section called *The American Humorist*. The first public announcement was made in the *Journal* of October 4, 1896, and was embellished by this deathless lyric:

> *A Morning Glory, ablaze with light,*
> *I'm here, a bewitching, bewildering sprite,*
> *Fresh as the posies that come with the vernal;*
> *Discreet? Why, of course, but not too coy,*
> *Dainty, yet daring, a thing of joy,*
> *The latest advance of the* SUNDAY JOURNAL.

In the issue of October 17, Hearst ventured into even more rarefied realms of hortatory prose:

> AH! THERE! THE YELLOW KID
> TOMORROW! TOMORROW!

An expectant public is waiting for the "American Humorist," the NEW YORK JOURNAL'S COMIC WEEKLY— EIGHT FULL PAGES OF COLOR THAT MAKE THE KALEIDOSCOPE PALE WITH ENVY.

Bunco steerers may tempt your fancy with a "color supplement" that is black and tan— four pages of weak, wishy-washy color and four pages of desolate waste of black.

> But the JOURNAL'S COLOR COMIC WEEKLY!
> Ah! There's the diff!

EIGHT PAGES OF POLYCHROMATIC EFFULGENCE THAT MAKE THE RAINBOW LOOK LIKE A LEAD PIPE.

That's the sort of color comic weekly that the people want; and they shall have it.

And on October 18 the first issue of the *American Humorist* appeared. As Waugh says, the most iridescent of all the effulgence was Outcault's Yellow Kid.

Hearst had bribed Outcault away from Pulitzer earlier in the year; Pulitzer had bought him back; Hearst had upped the ante again, and Pulitzer had washed his hands of Outcault. Not, however, of the Yellow Kid, to which he still had a legal right. He hired George Luks, who later became a master American easel painter, to continue the Kid.

By 1898 the Yellow Kid had ceased to be the star of the *American Humorist*. Perhaps the public had tired of him; perhaps there had been a reaction in favor of respectability. Outcault had left Hearst to go over to the *Herald*, under James Gordon Bennett, in 1897. There he had experimented with *Li'l Mose* and *Buddy Tucker*, and in early May 1902 the first *Buster Brown* ran in the Herald. By 1906 Buster was in the *American*, because Hearst had bought Outcault back (!), and the *Herald* was running its own version; Outcault also did a biography of Buster in that year, largely in prose. Buster was a genteel version of the Yellow Kid, mischievous but beguiling, and a good deal more acceptable than his predecessor in most homes. He was popular enough to give a permanent name to a collar, and his name is part of the language; the strip kept appearing, in one form or another, until World War I; but there was something a shade pale, a shade too well-behaved and ultimately a shade snobbish about Buster. Most critics feel that it was his lack of true vulgarity that killed him off. To this we may add another supposition: that the Katzenjammer Kids had made him unnecessary.

Hearst had visited Europe for the first time as a boy of ten, and had returned with a small collection of *bilderbogen,* including Wilhelm Busch's *Max und Moritz,* the illustrated adventures of a pair of young pranksters who stole chickens, put gunpowder in the professor's pipe, sawed wooden bridges almost in two and laughed at the subsequent total immersion of the dignified. Max and Moritz were ultimately ground up for mash and fed to

WILHELM BUSCH'S creations, Max and Moritz, the inspiration for *The Katzenjammer Kids.*

15

geese, which may strike us as primitive child psychology but provided a rousing climax to the story. A man named Rudolph Block was comics editor of the *American Humorist* in 1897, and he or Hearst or both suggested to a young staff artist named Rudolph Dirks that he work up a strip based on *Max and Moritz*.

"Katzenjammer," literally "the yowling of cats," is German slang for "hangover." *The Katzenjammer Kids* was an instantaneous success, and the Slam-Bang-Pow school of comics was born. This was unabashed slapstick, on the middle-class level. There was no overtone of raucous slum life, and the groans, imprecations, threats, punishments and bursts of laughter were bizarre, hilarious, fantastic, somehow linked to reality but not actually of it.

In the first strip there were three kids, but in all subsequent strips only two. Hans, Fritz, Mama, der Captain, and der Inspector have outlived all their original contemporaries; they have survived wars and depressions, complicated litigations and abrupt, permanent changes in the American mood. They are, for comics, Tyl Eulenspiegel and Tom Sawyer: archetypes of the mischievous juvenile. And they are so perfectly representative that when, in 1912, the *World* and the *Journal* fought for them, two strips came into being with the same casts— both of which are alive, kicking and widely syndicated today.

Dirks's drawing owes nothing to Wilhelm Busch, who printed from wood blocks. Perhaps Dirks absorbed a simplicity and solidity of line from his European model, but his postures and grimaces are far more expressive, and he uses, perhaps surprisingly, less background and shading. His invention and imagination operate more freely than Busch's— necessarily when we remember that Busch contented himself with a book or two, while Dirks turned out a strip a week, and then a strip a day, for years.

Dirks's first strips were without dialogue, but the temptation to insert speech in the German dialect must have been great. (Perhaps this is a harmless offshoot of the traditional early cruelty to minority groups.) Soon he began to try balloons, and the reaction was encouraging, even sensational; before long a strip was disappointing without a bellowed "Donnerwetter!" from the Captain, or a gentle "Dot's gut" from Mama.

Dirks is important in several ways to the whole field of comics. He originated what has been the most long-lived and popular of strips; he echoed Outcault in continuing a set cast of characters; he used the sequence of panels consistently, rather than the single large drawing; and he stabilized the use of the balloon for speech. Later on he was a principal in a precedent-setting lawsuit; we meet him again in 1912.

The *Journal* had by now added two more supplements, each using some color: the *Woman's Home Journal*, eight pages, and the *American Magazine*, sixteen pages. But the most feverish activity— particularly when the Spanish-American War had ended and Hearst could retrench a bit—

THE KATZENJAMMER KIDS CHANGE GRANDPA'S GLASSES.
Everything seems bigger through these spectacles until Grandpa discovers the joke.

THEN THINGS BEGIN TO LOOK LIVELY FOR THE KIDS.

An early version of *The Katzenjammer Kids* by their originator, RUDOLPH DIRKS. From the New York *American* of May 22, 1898.

remained in the area of comics. The *World* had no intention of falling behind, and the *Herald* was holding its own. Competition was, in short, fierce; and Hearst must have been inordinately pleased when, in 1899, Frederick Burr Opper made his debut in the *Journal*. Opper had done a good deal of occasional cartooning, and was a staff artist on the *Journal*. He is remembered now for three strips: *Happy Hooligan, And Her Name Was Maud* and *Alphonse and Gaston*. The first is a classic, and the last has made excessive courtesy forever ludicrous.

Happy Hooligan wore a tin can for a hat. He had a round head, and the hat, his trade-mark, defied gravity. He had a button nose, an impossibly long upper lip and a slit of a mouth just above his neck. He had big feet, and a patch on each knee of his trousers. He was less bright, less confident and infinitely more kindhearted than the other inhabitants of his unjust world. Otherwise he was just like you and me: everything he touched turned to disaster. The Yellow Kid and the Katzenjammer Kids were, loosely speaking, aggressors: the world shrank from their cheerful sadism. But Happy Hooligan was the eternal butt. He was rejected by "nice people," arrested by the police, scorned and maltreated by animals, jostled and beaten by passers-by. And the incidents that gave rise to all this mayhem were never his fault; they began, usually, when he tried to do someone a good turn. Our laughing indignation at this cruel and inhuman punishment is a gentle channeling, probably, of the indignation we feel at our own defeats: Happy is the scapegoat, the dumb cluck, the man to whom we are all superior except in good nature. He is consequently funny. His body is limp and flexible; occasionally when fate has bowed him to the form of a parenthesis we are reminded of two of Frink's early characters, Circus Solly and Slim Jim. (Frink apparently had no first name; his many strips are all signed with the one surname.) Happy's face is utterly woebegone; his hands hang useless and empty. Gloomy Gus, another great creation, may admonish him quietly, but no good ever comes of it. Happy is doomed.

Happy Hooligan's relatives, by FREDERICK BURR OPPER. A strong family resemblance, of course. This was the heading of a Sunday page on October 14, 1906. ©1906 by the *American-Journal-Examiner*.

A *Happy Hooligan* of 1924, late in OPPER's career. (He was also a well-known editorial cartoonist by then.) The last panel is classic. © King Features Syndicate, Inc.

Opper did facial expressions beautifully, a valuable talent when we notice that all his heads and faces are roughly the same: round, neckless, with wide eyes and a shoe-button nose, the long upper lip and the slash of a mouth.

Maud was a mule. *And Her Name Was Maud* was an endless variation on an ancient and explosive theme: never let a mule turn his (her? its?) back to you. Maud was an amiable-looking creature, surrounded by men named Si and Ezra, and the plot varied only in nonessentials. The last panel of each strip was Maud's Revenge: a triumphant, double-barreled blast of the hind legs, with the innocent victim propelled clear out of the panel. Two conventions survived from Maud: the variation-on-a-theme, and the violation of the panel's boundaries when it served a purpose.

Alphonse and Gaston, like Happy, became national celebrities. Ultimately they became national symbols, and their names stood for their qualities. Their unbounded *politesse* carried them into spectacular difficulties which ordinary mortals, rude and aggressive, were spared. As they bowed and scraped, nature took its course and what might have been simple became catastrophic. One of their reactions to catastrophe was a sharp stab of homesickness, and Opper celebrated many American towns as the objects of Gastonian nostalgia.

Opper used his three strips as the occasion demanded. Some Sundays all three would appear; then he would run one alone, but with characters from the others. For two or more artists to work on the same strip was common; each would introduce his own characters. In the *American* of May 25, 1912, is an unsigned joint strip by Opper, Dirks and Charles Schultze, or "Bunny," who created *Foxy Grandpa*. On June 29 there is another, signed by Opper, Dirks, Bunny and Gene Carr, who contributed bumptious dogs to the comic world.

Like Dirks, Swinnerton and, later, McManus, Opper used patches of solid black effectively; there seems to be no character of importance in *Happy Hooligan* without a focal garment— hat, pants or jacket— of black. The technique "placed" characters within the panel and helped Opper to direct the reader's eye; it has since become standard.

Tumble Tom Fixed It.

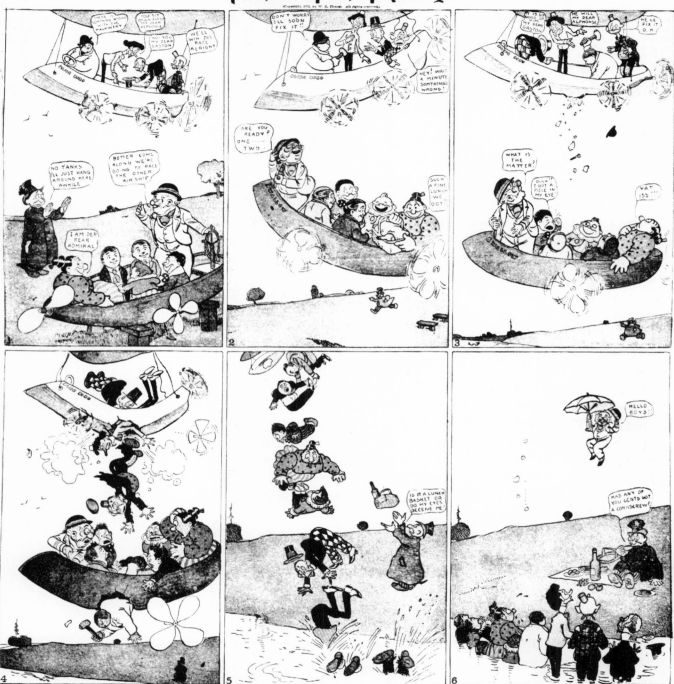

A rare Sunday page, from the New York *American and Journal* of May 25, 1902. Here on one page were Happy Hooligan, Gloomy Gus, Alphonse and Gaston (OPPER); Tumble Tom (SWINNERTON); Foxy Grandpa and his two young friends (BUNNY SCHULTZE); and the Katzenjammer Kids with Mama (DIRKS) — each character drawn by its creator. Courtesy of Ernest McGee.

Happy ran for over twenty-five years. Alphonse and Gaston had a shorter life, but may be remembered longer. Maud disappeared first. It may be that the growth of the syndicates increased rural readership, and that farmers, like the other butts of early humor, would take just so much and no more.

A newspaper syndicate was in operation on the North American continent before the United States came into being; it helped to create the United States. In 1768 a propaganda column called the "Journal of Occurrences," published by Boston patriots to promote revolt against Britain, was syndicated to several newspapers in Philadelphia, New York and other cities of the colonies. Syndication is, roughly, the preparation of material at one point for transmission to, and publication by, periodicals at other points. The "Journal of Occurrences" was doubtless transmitted in printed sheets; the copy was then set in type at its various points of publication and integrated to local news, economic predictions and essays on agriculture. In 1841 Moses Y. Beach of the New York *Sun* syndicated President Tyler's message to the Congress for New York State and New England newspapers. By 1850 the English publisher Cassell was syndicating material to provincial English newspapers.

But the large-scale syndicate owes its development to Ansel Nash Kellogg, publisher, during the Civil War, of the Baraboo, Wisconsin, *Republic,* a country weekly. Kellogg's hired hands had enlisted in the Union Army, and the exasperated publisher was unable to put out his newspaper alone. He ordered two pages of features and war news from the Wisconsin *State Journal* in Madison. Shortly other rural newspapers in Wisconsin were ordering these "patent insides"; the *State Journal* thrived on the trade. By the end of the war Kellogg had decided that syndication was a potentially lucrative field; he left for the big city, established a syndicate in Chicago in 1865 and sold printed matter and advertising to what soon became a regular list of fourteen hundred clients.

Competition became brisk immediately. Chicago was a railroad center, and transmission to a wide area was feasible. In time stereotyped plates as well as printed matter were sent out. These could be placed directly on the presses, and eliminated resetting or re-engraving.

By the 1880s syndication was an established enterprise. Irving Bacheller, novelist and journalist, organized a syndicate for the distribution of news, gossip columns, women's features and fiction. Within a year S. S. McClure, later editor of *McClure's Magazine,* was syndicating fiction and selling Rudyard Kipling, Robert Louis Stevenson, H. Rider Haggard and Arthur Conan Doyle, among others, to an appreciative audience.

Once it became possible to ship plates, it was inevitable that comic features would be syndicated. Among the first important comics syndicates were the St. Louis Color Process Syndicate, the Otis Wood Syndicate, the

C. J. Hirt Syndicate and the T. C. McClure Syndicate. Newspapers on which staff artists had produced salable strips soon began to syndicate their own creations. The Cleveland *Plain Dealer* seems to have been shortsighted at the turn of the century: J. H. Donahey did editorial cartoons, *Archie and Angie* and *Cunnel Moonshine* exclusively for that newspaper. But not for long.

With syndication, the Golden Age began. People in Zanesville and Omaha could spend Sunday morning over the same strips read by their fellow citizens in New York, Chicago and San Francisco. A comics character could be more than a funny fellow, and so could his creator: the one could become a national symbol, the other a national hero.

The poet of the early years was Winsor McCay. *Little Nemo in Slumberland* followed William Steinigans' *The Bad Dream That Made Billy a Better Boy* in capitalizing on the dream world of children; but McCay was a genius in his field, while Steinigans was simply a good journeyman. *Little Nemo* was probably the first strip to exploit color for purely aesthetic purposes; it was the first in which the dialogue, occasionally polysyllabic, flirted with adult irony. It heads a rather small category of what we may call "intellectual" comics. *Krazy Kat* and *Pogo* are two of its obvious companions, and, as they do now, *Little Nemo* appealed to all age groups on all levels of society. It was, in another sense, a further swing away from the Yellow Kid toward an area of gentle and harmless, though exciting and suspenseful, conflicts.

Nemo himself was a tousle-haired boy somewhere between six and eight, who is always shown in his long white nightshirt. He is accompanied, or tracked down, on his travels by Flip, a kind of diminutive Irishman— or overgrown leprechaun— in a tall plug hat and an ermine-collared black jacket. From his greenish face projects an outsized cigar. Flip, within his own outlandish limits, is the realist who tempers fantasy with horse sense. He rides a sway-backed, heavy-hoofed nag, and is unperturbed by the panoplied mounts of his acquaintances and adversaries.

Waugh has pointed out that Winsor McCay did not create within the usual comic conventions of the time. He is descended more from the ancient line of book illustrators, and is even reminiscent of the illuminators, medieval artisans who created labyrinthine capital letters and rubrics, and who painted, laboriously, Biblical and legendary scenes, before the invention of movable type. McCay recalls ornately illustrated editions of Grimm and Andersen, or of other tales in which the familiar limits of time and space are freely, bewitchingly distorted. His long, Byzantine backdrops, his majestic animals, his classical architecture and rococo landscaping take him far from the naturalistic world we know; yet his settings are familiar and evoke visual echoes from our own youth. He loved animals and mob festivities, exotic personalities and parades. His strips are what an eight-

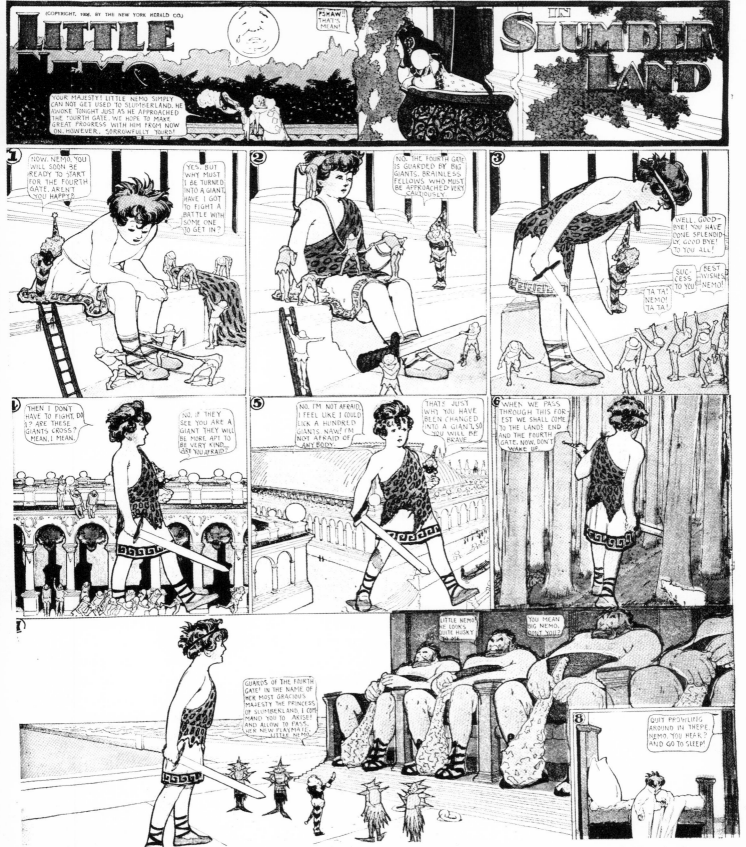

WINSOR McCAY's *Little Nemo in Slumberland*. Fantasy, exaggeration, and classic architecture— the stuff Nemo's dreams were made on. Reprinted by permission of Winsor McCay's family.

year-old's dream would be if a boy had any choice, and the bold, magnificent opulence of his color makes him almost unique among comic artists; only Feininger can be ranked with him.

Little Nemo began in 1905 in the New York *Herald* and ran for years. Old-timers among cartoonists recall it with an almost reverent mixture of affection and wistfulness. In 1947 it was revived, when the McCay Feature Syndicate was established; the Richardson Feature Syndicate of Indianapolis distributed many of the old sequences. The man who did the pasting, trimming and general refurbishing of the old strips was Little Nemo himself: Robert Winsor McCay, the artist's son, who inspired the first sequences back in 1905.

Little Nemo was not McCay's only contribution to comic art. When we meet him again, in 1915, he has a dinosaur with him.

In his time William F. Marriner was known to as wide an audience as Opper, Dirks, Outcault and McCay were; today he is forgotten, and neglected even by historians. He was syndicated from 1900 to 1914, and his children and animals entered homes all over the country. Like most of his contemporaries, he was versatile: strips and panels came off his drawing board in colorful profusion. Two of his less important strips were *Mary and Her Little Lamb* and *Sambo and His Funny Noises;* his real success came with *Wags, the Dog That Adopted a Man,* which ran weekly from 1904 to 1914. Billy Marriner's human characters, and particularly his children, have oversized heads, and hats to match. His line is delicate and crisp, and his shading meticulous. There is good humor in everything he did; he was one of the few cartoonists of the period who never displayed contempt for, or superiority to, the subject. He loved fishing, and loved to draw fishing scenes. "Charm" is almost a deadly word these days, but if we remember that it means "enchantment," there is more of it in one of Marriner's megalocephalic tots, dug in on a riverbank, blissfully ignorant of the gnarled state of his fishing pole and the snarled state of his line, than in anything published since. His influence was probably great: the oversized head, the wide eyes, the pitcher ears have become standard in our time. And his attitude toward children— that they are at once a bit more logical and a bit more fanciful than their elders— has been characteristic of all the best kid strips. Part of Marriner's technical excellence lies in his combination of careful fine-line solidity at the focal points of his panel and free, unembarrassed use of "white space"— i.e., blank areas— elsewhere.

Marriner's kids were much loved, and his *Wags* was much looked forward to for ten years. He died tragically in 1914 when his summer place in New Jersey burned to the ground. His work was ably carried on, for a time, by Pat Sullivan.

With Fenderson, McDougall, H. C. (Cornell) Greening, Ed Carey, and C. W. Kahles, Marriner belonged to a generation of comic artists whose

A BILLY MARRINER Sunday page, May 7, 1905. *Wags* was a regular feature. © 1905 by C. J. Hirt.

A BILLY MARRINER panel from
Judge. His rural kids are still
unsurpassed. This is undated,
but was probably drawn in
about 1907.

A REAL SPORTSMAN.
THE BOY ABOVE—"Is dere any game round here?"
THE OTHER—"Dere wuz, but I got it all."

careers ended during or before World War I, but who by then had indicated every direction, every form, that the comic strip has since taken.

Cornell Greening appeared as much in magazines as in newspapers; like
so many of the early greats— working, let us remember, for a relatively
uncritical audience— he was prolific and versatile. His panels in magazines suffer from the great fault of the times (a fault in retrospect only,
perhaps): they were simply well-drawn illustrations of one- or two-line
jokes. (Many of his panels satirized Jews in what today seems a disagreeable manner.) His strips, on the other hand, struck out in new directions.
Uncle George Washington Bings, the Village Storyteller was traditional:
development, sock at the end, rural satire. Opper and Frink had mined
the same vein. But Greening's *Prince Errant* used legends and no balloons,
and was an obvious predecessor of Harold Foster's *Prince Valiant*. Greening's *Percy the Robot* may be considered early pictorial science fiction; and
a strip called *The Troubles of Our First Family*, or *Adam's Troubles Raising Cain* opened a door to history and prehistory.

Ed Carey was another of the Protean ancestors. His *Simon Simple* ran
in the San Francisco *Chronicle* in 1905, and even before then he had taken
over *Brainy Bowers* from R. W. Taylor; he turned it out from 1902 to 1908.
He did many panels, and he filled comics supplements with a variety of

short-lived, episodic strips. Like many of his contemporaries, he could work in many styles; like them again, there was always *something*, perhaps indefinable to the non-artist, which marked his work as his own. In 1915, for the McClure Syndicate, he did a strip of which Charlie Chaplin, by then a national idol, was the hero; Gus Mager and Elzie Segar worked on the same idea.

Time usually distorts the past, which makes historians necessary. For those of us who can remember, or those of us who have heard, comics before 1910 were the work of four or five Old Masters: Opper, Outcault, Dirks, McCay. Some know that George Herriman drew his first strip in 1903; perhaps more are aware that George McManus was first published in 1900. But by 1906 there were major newspapers in every major city of the United States; by 1906 half a dozen vigorous syndicates were competing; by 1906 a town like Mansfield, Ohio, was running a weekly comics supplement in full color. Quantities of material were needed; and for every remembered founding father, there were a dozen competent, imaginative craftsmen now ignored.

There was Eddie Eks, who did *Billy the Bellboy* and *Alex the Cop.* And Frink's *Circus Solly*, which became *Slim Jim*— with an occasional repetition of episodes ten years apart! There was Dink, who did *Sammy Small* and *Mr. Pest, Book Agent* (and few of us remember even the vanished tribe of book agents, much less Dink himself); Clarence Rigby, who took time out from his magazine panels to do *Little Ah Sid, the Chinese Kid*, and who took over *Major Ozone, the Fresh Air Fiend* from George Herriman; A. D. Reed's *Uncle Pike*, which ran from 1902 to 1912 and was the most savage of the rural satires; Bertha Corbett's faceless *Sunbonnet Babies*; Lowry's *Man with the Elephant, Pete the Monkey, Barnacle Jim*; Howarth's *Lulu and Leander*; Hy Gage's *Mrs. Rummage* and *Mr. Grouch and His Wife*; Hugh Doyle's *John Poorjohn, Lazy Lew, Mr. Wiseguy the Detective* (Doyle was primarily a sports cartoonist); Robert Carter's *Coffee and Sinkers*, about a boy and a dog (Carter became one of the First World War's great editorial cartoonists).

There were dozens and perhaps hundreds of others, working part-time or full-time. There was space to be filled, and a future to be made, and circulation to be increased. There were healthy, hungry, growing syndicates. Most of all, there were men who liked to draw, and who enjoyed being funny.

There was space to be filled. Marriner could take a whole Sunday sheet and fill it with just six panels. Horina, of the Chicago *Tribune*, once did a whole four-page Sunday section for that newspaper. A panel could be composed, organized, drawn for color effect. There were few week-to-week continuities, and therefore few plot requirements. The drawing was all, and if the idea could be expressed in six panels, or even four, there were

ED CAREY's version of the Charley Chaplin Sunday page. It was also titled *Pa's Imported Son-in-Law*. From the Philadelphia *Press* of June 18, 1916. Courtesy of Ernest McGee.

FRINK's *Slim Jim* making his escape from martial difficulties. © 1915, the World Color Printing Co. Courtesy of Ernest McGee.

no objections. Modern comic-strip artists, seeing three full-length Sunday sequences squeezed into one sheet, twenty-four or more tiny panels, with the drawing minimized if not lost altogether and the balloons barely legible, turn away in professional anguish; they mumble bitterly at the sight of a fifty-year-old Chicago *Sunday Tribune* color section.

The old Chicago *Tribune* experimented as much as any newspaper, even the *World*, even the *Journal*. In 1906 the *Tribune's* Sunday supplement ran four imported strips, all sent on from Munich. Three of the artists, all Germans, are forgotten: Schramm, Pommerhanz, and Lothar Meggendorfer, all of whom did kid strips modeled more or less on the Katzenjammers. The fourth was an American, Lyonel Feininger, who had moved back to Germany, whence his parents came, when he was very young. His strips were signed "Your Uncle Feininger," and there were two of them: *The Kin-der-Kids* and *Wee Willie Winkie's World*. They were both splendid and more than a touch fantastic; in the jagged lines, the heroic colors and the fantastic, other-worldly, almost poetic sequences there is (now, looking back) more than a suggestion of the later George Herriman. Feininger, who died

F. M. HOWARTH's Leander leading Lulu and her parents into some mischief or other. From the San Francisco *Examiner*, 1903. Courtesy of Ernest McGee.

Lyonel Feininger unleashing his fancy in the Chicago *Tribune* of 1906. This page was drawn in Munich and sent along to Chicago. © 1906 by the Tribune Co. Courtesy of the Chicago *Tribune*– New York *News* Syndicate, Inc.

in 1956, spent most of his life, before Hitler, in Germany, and over the years he became a great expressionist, and then cubist, painter. Of course it is easy enough now to say that his comics work in 1906 showed huge talent. It did; but not because there was a technical similarity to the work of an easel painter. Very simply, he showed a talent for comics in 1906, and if that talent derived from the personality and training of a potentially great easel painter, so much the better. His line was the bold, slashing, careless line of the confident, or even overconfident, artist; his colors were vital and moody, clashing magnificently or blending subtly.

But by 1906 American comics were about to enter a new phase, and no one working in Germany, or anywhere outside the United States, would be able to follow. A large body of experiment lay behind the artists, the syndicates and the newspapers. Problems of color reproduction and circulation had largely been solved; vast audiences had been met and conquered. And the country was changing. Teddy Roosevelt had been busting trusts for four years. The Muckrakers— who, like the cartoonists, depended on the public press for outlets— had been attacking the evils that underlay, and to some extent made possible, the smug and cheerful America of the turn of the century. The Pure Food and Drug Act, a landmark in American legislation because it affected half the housewife's purchases, had occasioned stormy political battles; issues of the day were entering the American sitting room. Industrial expansion, punctuated by occasional panics, had happily swept away many of the attitudes and effects of Civil War days. There were the beginnings of an inkling, for example, that the Negro had not *really* been emancipated at all; and labor unions were entering their period of bitter growth. Minority groups, who had so often been the butts of cartoons published nationally, were becoming self-conscious and defensive, and not just the Irish and Negroes and Jews, either: Bryan's campaigns had left a mark on the American farmer, and the lavish and well-publicized banquets of the rich were becoming irksome to the workingman. In 1903 the Wright brothers flew. By 1906 the automobile was no longer a national joke: the average laborer and the average housewife were beginning to wonder when their turn might come. The panic of 1907, with its subsequent monetary reforms, added to a feeling of unity and participation among the general public. America was, in short, beginning to turn serious. Mankind in general had progressed fairly steadily since about 1000 A.D.; it would soon stumble over World War I, which marked the end of a millennium more truly than any other of man's wars. The sound of a different drum was becoming audible. Teddy bears and mischievous kids would not— will never, we hope— cease to be comic. But a new kind of democracy and a new kind of world were on the way, and they would inevitably be reflected in the funnies.

Unfortunately, we cannot ignore another event of importance which occurred in 1906: two natural disasters struck San Francisco. One lasted only a week and caused damage in the millions. The other is still in progress, and the damage may be too astronomical ever to be estimated at all. Its name is Reuben Lucius Goldberg, and it smokes cigars. There will be a good deal more about Rube Goldberg farther along; even in a friendly, heart-warming book like this one, reality must be faced. Doubts as to Rube Goldberg's reality can no longer be entertained by the serious student.

RUBE GOLDBERG strikes a blow for Franco-American solidarity. He drew this in Paris in 1919. Courtesy of Rube Goldberg.

CHAPTER II

The Beginnings
of a Big Business

Why should a horseplayer read the funnies? Why would he buy a newspaper for one comic strip if he weren't already buying it for its racing page? To answer those questions is, apparently, to have the editorial mind: the first two daily strips in America by-passed animals, kids, married couples, pretty girls and adventurers, and spotlighted horse players. Three reasons come to mind: for suspense and excitement, racing or betting on races is a good combination of emotion and finance; racing or betting on races is a six-day-a-week occupation; and readers who like horses and enjoy races, but feel that betting is morally wrong, can, through a comic strip, satisfy a legitimate appetite without danger of sin.

Another race was partially responsible for the first of these strips: a circulation race between the Chicago *Daily News* and the Chicago *American*. Editor of the *American* was Moses Koenigsburg, a man of great talent and drive, who later established King Features Syndicate. Cartoonist of the *American* was Clare Briggs. Koenigsburg was after a steady readership for his sports section, and wanted a day-to-day feature with some quality of suspense; he decided to use a racing strip. Briggs dreamed up a phony *nouveau riche* without money, and Koenigsburg decided that the point of the strip would be the man's complex, funny efforts to raise a daily stake. "A. Piker Clerk" was born. He was an instant hit, and Koenigsburg and Briggs sighed happily; but a message came down from Hearst himself, who thought the strip vulgar; and A. Piker Clerk was dead. It was only 1904, and Briggs went on to a great career in cartooning. Clerk was the first daily comic to appear in true strip form— that is, a strip of panels across the top of a page— yet no one picked up the idea for three years.

It was picked up— or originated independently— by Harry Conway Fisher, known to the ages as Bud Fisher. Born in Chicago in 1884, Fisher packed his bags and moved west after three months at the University of Chicago. He signed on as a sports cartoonist with the San Francisco *Chronicle* and bided his time for a couple of years.

He was an obstreperous young man in an expanding decade, and San Francisco was a bizarre kind of city: a civilized frontier town, in many ways. Before he was twenty-five Fisher had learned to put his feet on any desk and to preserve a haughty professional independence. At least once he resigned when his space was cut down. No one had informed him that he was to do five columns instead of six; so informed when he had finished his drawings, he calmly ripped them across, and just as calmly quit. Told that he had to give two weeks' notice, he answered that he would stay for two weeks without doing a lick of work, and so he did; he reported every morning, left every night, and spent the day chatting about great fights or sketching for his own amusement. On the last Saturday night he was given two fight tickets and an apology, and, fortunately for the *Chronicle*, went back to work. Paul Terry and Rube Goldberg knew him well— they have always shared with him that raffish independence characteristic of San Francisco at the time— and remember him then as an island of self-assurance in a sea of minor egos. Goldberg also began as a sports cartoonist, as did Tad (Thomas Aloysius Dorgan), Opper, T. E. Powers, Gus Edson. The sports department was a man's world, and it had one inestimable advantage for the developing cartoonist: the material was supplied by current events, and there were no great worries about "continuity," which left the artist free to concentrate his imagination on the drawing at hand. The material was also varied, and a cartoonist could toy with hundreds of characters a year; if he found a few that he and the public liked, he could use them more and more, to the point where he had the matter, if not the form, of a comic strip.

So it was with Augustus Mutt, Bud Fisher's version of the harried horse player. Fisher had used this checked-suited, felt-hatted, chinless, mustachioed proboscid in occasional daily "spots" as the prototypical bettor, eternally on the trail of a killing, eternally broke. In 1907 he composed a true strip; his editor approved; and on November 15 Augustus Mutt got a foot in the door of the Pantheon. In no time at all Fisher had been bought up by Hearst's *Examiner*; and within six months Mutt had met— in an

The first *Mutt and Jeff* by BUD FISHER, from the San Francisco *Chronicle* of November 15, 1907. A landmark: the first appearance of a successful daily strip. Courtesy of the Bell Syndicate, Inc.

Bud Fisher's *Mutt and Jeff* in 1921. Little Cicero has already joined the cast.
© H. C. Fisher.

institution for the feeble-minded— a pint-sized, silk-hatted illogician named
Jeff (for Jeffries: in 1908 the coming Jeffries-Johnson fight was the talk
of the sporting world).

Mutt and Jeff lived; and Fisher had the foresight, or ego, to copyright
the strip in his own name. The strip survived attacks from the public and
legal battles against imitation. In 1910 there was a serious but not fatal
public reaction against comics, partly because the medium itself seemed
vulgar to the "nice people," and partly because the sight of a man being
kicked off a dock into the ocean by his best friend was considered corrupting to juvenile morality. Fisher never bothered to fight back; he simply
continued drawing Mutt and Jeff. If Monday's and Tuesday's strips failed
to amuse Daddy, he would nonetheless— curious about his son's guffaws or
his wife's occasional giggle— continue to read the strip, and by Thursday
his own unexpected snickers would convert him. Then in 1913 Fisher left
Hearst for the Wheeler Syndicate, with a contract for a guaranteed $1,000
a week plus a percentage (80 per cent of the gross!) of syndicate sales.
Hearst had the strip imitated until Fisher won a court order restraining
Hearst and, for practical purposes, investing Fisher with perpetual rights

Mutt and Jeff in 1925, demonstrating the gap between appearance and reality.
© H. C. Fisher.

to the two characters. Within a few years, after the addition of a Sunday page, Fisher was making $4,600 a week from the syndicate alone, and adding to it by vaudeville appearances and by the books and toys featuring Mutt and Jeff.

The strip was always funny, but after Jeff's arrival the emphasis began to change. Originally the plot varied little: Mutt needed a stake, and used fair, foul or fantastic means to find it. By 1910 Mutt was still the horse player's horse player, but Jeff's complicity had begun to make the swindle an end and not a means; the comic situation was exploited for its own sake, and not for the sake of the two-dollar window. By 1915 the two were to be found in any of man's habitats, natural or unnatural, and Jeff was occasionally given a strip to himself.

The drawing changed, too. The original Mutt was identifiable always, but his face was generally lost in the detail of the panel, and his expressions counted for little. Slowly Fisher began to add patches of black, like Opper's (George McManus and Chic Young became the ultimate masters of this technique), and to reduce the shadings of clothes and background. He compressed his dark areas and let them stand out boldly against white, which clarified his outlines and brought features and expressions into higher relief.

Mutt and Jeff is still popular. Among other things, this means that it has tried to produce five laughs a week for over half a century. Naturally, Fisher drew his gags from any source: old (and clean) burlesque jokes, variations on the fly-in-the-soup joke, variations on a dozen race-track jokes, any physical situations, the sizes of his characters, Mutt's troubles with Mrs. Mutt or Jeff's successes with pretty girls (Jeff has been an ecstatic chaser for decades), folk stories, rich-and-poor stories, political anecdotes, Irish bulls, logical paradoxes. Early on, Jeff was the butt. When butts survive the worst, their tormentors tire of baiting them, and slowly Jeff's endurance has worn Mutt down. It is Jeff, now, with his unanswerable nonsense and his amatory triumphs, who dominates Mutt. The latter has, for that matter, been relatively subdued for thirty years. His son, Cicero, and his wife have burdened him with the melancholy of the married man, and Jeff has made of him a gloomy foil, a straight man.

When Fisher signed with the Wheeler Syndicate in 1915 he went to the New York *World*, and when the *World* shut down he went to the New York *Daily News* for a year. His strip was absent from New York for ten years, and reappeared in the *Post* in 1942; it was dropped again in 1943, but came back after the war. Fisher died in 1954, and Al Smith has been doing the strip since, with no change in the basic idea, but with a noticeable improvement in Mrs. Mutt's looks, which Mutt probably deserves after half a century.

Smith is a greatly talented cartoonist who chose deliberately to devote himself to Fisher's characters. He started with Fisher in 1932, during the

Mutt and Jeff in 1958, by AL SMITH. The same old Jeff, obviously. © the Bell Syndicate, Inc.

depression when the strip's circulation was at a low ebb. Smith was so good that Fisher decided to rest on his laurels, and almost from the beginning Smith was doing six strips and a Sunday page, ideas and drawing. Smith had previously created a two-column panel for the *World* in which Cicero's Cat first appeared as an office pet; Smith contributed his creation to Fisher, and a *Cicero's Cat* thenceforth ran as a tag to the Mutt and Jeff Sunday page.

As a pair, Mutt and Jeff are of course part of the American mythology. Fisher may or may not have been overjoyed to know that James Joyce added overtones of both America and eternity to a dialogue in *Finnegans Wake* between a primitive, incoherent inhabitant of England and an early invader from the mainland, by calling them Mute and Jute.

The years from 1907 to 1920 saw the first great crystallization in American comics, when the grand lines of the major categories became apparent: married couples; kids; adventure; girls; animals; slapstick. The categories were not, and are not now, clearly defined, of course. Married couples have kids; kids have adventures; adventurers have girl friends; and animals and slapstick appear everywhere.

Charles W. Kahles, a man of inventive imagination and almost compulsive industry, worked in many categories between 1900 and 1910. He sparked new lines of experiment and new drawing techniques; he was successful enough to be considered a founding father by many. And yet his career is anomalous. We can point to no resounding success, and to only one or two specific innovations, in the dozen or fifteen regular Sunday strips he created over ten years. We are left with the uneasy feeling that we have missed something. Perhaps it was his very versatility; there are only a handful of comic artists working on as many as two strips, in our day.

Two of his strips can make interesting claims. The first, *Sandy Highflyer*, started in the Philadelphia *North American* in 1903 (the year of Kitty Hawk). Sandy was a boy balloonist; the strip was a combination of kids and adventure, and it claims fame as the first of a long line of aviation strips. The second, *Hairbreadth Harry*, began in 1906 in the Philadelphia

Three panels from C. W. KAHLES' *Hairbreadth Harry*, the Boy Hero. These are from the Philadelphia *Sunday Press* of December 29, 1907. The narrative is an excellent parody of the melodramatic literary style in vogue a few years before.

Press as a take-off on the mustache-twirling melodrama of the American theater ("But I can't pay the rent!") and introduced cliff hanging, or day-to-day suspense, as a story device— and incidentally as a circulation builder. Among Kahles' other strips were *Billy Bounce* (1903–9), *The Teasers*, which ran for eight years, *Pretending Percy*, which hung on for six years, *Clumsy Claude, Captain Fibb* (which also ran in *Judge*), and the *Merry Nobles Three*, probably his funniest strip. In 1905 alone, in the New York *World*, Kahles created *Mr. Buttin, Tim and Tom the Terrible Twins*, and *Fun in the Zoo*; in 1906, *Billy Bragg* and *The Funny Side Gang*.

Kahles spans two periods, really: in time he belongs with the early Leonardos like Ed Carey and Marriner and Greening; but his effect, through *Sandy* and *Harry*, lingered as an influence into the 1920s. Unlikely as it seems, he bears some responsibility for a strip he would never have dreamed of doing, a strip which ran over a quarter of a century, added wit and character to American comics and destroyed forever the unprincipled ridicule of minority groups, once so popular.

The strip was Harry Hirshfield's *Abie the Agent*. Hirshfield had, in 1910, created a strip called *Desperate Desmond* (which also ran for years) imitative of but wittier than *Hairbreadth Harry*. Desmond's man Friday was Gomgatz, a cannibal chief, and Hirshfield needed a zany language for him. Almost as a private joke, Hirshfield slipped a little Yiddish into Gomgatz's balloons. According to Martin Sheridan, it was Nathan Straus, remembered for his generous philanthropies, who was so tickled by Gomgatz's jargon that he suggested to Arthur Brisbane, the *Journal's* great editor, that Hirshfield do a strip around a Jewish central character.

Brisbane may have felt that the problem was tricky. Minorities had been fair game twenty years before, or even ten; Greening was still satirizing Jews, Sullivant, the Irish, and any number of artists the Negro. *Abie* was something else. It had to be: Hirshfield, who is still one of our funniest citizens, has a sharp wit, but he is an utterly unmalicious man. Abie, as an up-to-date Jewish businessman, was dogged by all the problems of the warmhearted, generous family man with a deep distaste for violence, who lives in a business-is-business world of knavery, egotism, legal complexities and neighborhood disasters.

Abie— and Jews through him, if the reader wanted to see it that way— was kidded but not satirized. Satire usually depends on some salient and disagreeable trait. Jews had traditionally been satirized as money-grubbing; the Irish as ignorant and illogical; Negroes as lazy and linguistically pretentious; Germans as hopelessly practical and chained to their dialect; farmers as crafty, credulous and miserly. Submerge these imagined traits in qualities common to all mankind, and satire disappears, or at least ceases to be directed at a specific target.

Which was precisely Abie's effect. In a published speech Brisbane once said, *"Abie the Agent* is the first of the adult comics in America." He was right. Abie's troubles and aspirations were those of the middle-class paterfamilias in a business society, and since 1910 most Americans have been becoming just that. When your goals and another man's are identical, you understand him and identify with him; if you are an adult, so is he.

Hirshfield's career is worth a good comic strip in itself. He started out in the art department of the Chicago *Daily News*, and was fired, characteristically, not for philandering, laziness or toying with an expense account, but for straightening up an oddly tilted photograph of some old Italian building, which of course proved to be the Leaning Tower in Pisa. He moved to the San Francisco *Chronicle*, following Bud Fisher and Rube Goldberg in the sports-cartoon department. Brisbane, far off in New York, saw a new talent and hired Hirshfield for the *Journal*. It was with the *Journal*, and later through King Features Syndicate, that Hirshfield developed *Desperate Desmond* and *Abie*. In 1931 he broke with Hearst and King Features Syndicate over contractual difficulties; a court decision gave the syndicate the right to continue the strip if they could find a man to do different characters in Hirshfield's style. No such man could be found; and in 1935 Hearst renegotiated Hirshfield's contracts, whereupon *Abie* ap-

HARRY HERSHFIELD's *Abie the Agent.* The strip added several new dimensions (and emotions) to the dialect story. © King Features Syndicate, Inc.

Another *Abie* from October 10, 1930. The man's troubles were endless, but so was his ingenuity. © King Features Syndicate, Inc.

peared again, with the same cast and the same themes. The event was unprecedented.

Hirshfield lives in New York City. Being an accomplished wit, raconteur and master of ceremonies, he appeared for years with Joe Laurie, Jr., and Ed Ford on radio's *Can You Top This?* and he is in constant demand as M.C. or guest speaker. It is an article of firm belief in the cartooning trade that Hirshfield has not had to buy a meal for himself since sometime in the early thirties.

Woman came into her own in the 1920s. Constitutional amendments had been warping the very fabric of society, sir, for ten years. In 1909 a man could make all the money he wanted, help to appoint a Senator and celebrate his victory with good whisky, secure in the knowledge that no silly female would be permitted to tamper with reality by so much as casting a vote. By 1920 various devils had stormed this paradise. The Sixteenth Amendment established the income tax, striking directly at the breadwinners; the Seventeenth provided for the popular election of Senators, which was a dangerous grant of power to the public; the Eighteenth banned liquor, which meant that a woman who knew a bootlegger was of more value than a man who didn't; and the Nineteenth sapped the last bastion of a beleaguered civilization by granting the vote— one full vote, equal in importance to that of any man— to the ladies.

It is not to be believed that these upheavals were unrelated, or that they occurred suddenly. Women, for example, had been agitating for the vote since the Civil War, and a good many of them had been trying to get rid of liquor even further back. The First World War was naturally a major dislocation of American life, but the process of democratic ferment cannot be so neatly dated. The beginnings of change are, as usual, swathed in the mists of time. The casual historian might just as well blame the emancipation of American women on a man named Cliff Sterrett, and let it go at that.

Sterrett's academic training for this program was a year of art at the Chase School in Manhattan, in 1902. He accumulated experience freelancing and then as a staffer in the art department of the New York *Herald;*

and when he was ready, he began a strip in the old New York *Evening Telegram*, taking as his theme one of the burning topics of the time: the struggle between old-fashioned parents and comely daughters. His title: *For This We Have Daughters*.

"You have no idea of the strict censorship we were forced to work under in those days," he once complained to Martin Sheridan. (He seems to do a lot of complaining about censorship, probably to divert males from contemplation of the damage he has caused.) "In the first place, we couldn't show a girl's leg above the top of her shoe. Furthermore, a comic-strip kiss was unheard of, and all action had to take place and be completed before nine o'clock."

In time Sterrett would help change all that. He dropped *For This We Have Daughters*, started *When a Man's Married*, continued with *Before and After*. But the idea of a strip about a girl lingered, and in the *Journal* of 1912 Sterrett found his future with a strip called *Positive Polly*. Within the next year he had changed the title, first to *Polly* and then to *Polly and Her Pals*.

Polly is a doll. She is the saucer-eyed, snub-nosed, curly-haired, long-legged descendant of the healthy beauties of the 1890s. She is almost twice as tall, and more than twice as sensible, as Paw and Maw. (Paw's name, incidentally, is Sam Perkins.) Aunt Maggie is an old maid who has spent much of her time laying elaborate traps for a husband. The cast is rounded out by Ashur— ambitious and ineffectual— Lisha, Gertrude and Carrie. For years there was a Chinese family retainer, Neewah, who was simply an Oriental version of Paw (C. H. Wellington used the same device in *Pa's Son-in-Law*).

Polly's spirit and presence inform the strip, but most of the episodes revolve around the comic efforts of the others to accomplish minor but unreasonable goals. Sterrett never hesitated to burlesque fads or even national institutions; in one year he flailed away at Leap-Year brides, osteopathy, aphasia, Prohibition and women's fashions. "I still encountered many obstacles in the field of censorship even after the World War," he

CLIFF STERRETT's *Polly and Her Pals*. Paw never did get used to the younger generation. © 1928 King Features Syndicate, Inc.

said to Sheridan. "Many letters of condemnation arrived from clergymen who criticized the then-daring fashions. And all I did was show a girl's ankle." Sterrett naturally went right on showing a bit of ankle to his critics— presumably lascivious critics, to be so maddened by an inch and a half of tibia.

Other critics, however, pointed out that Sterrett's drawing is high art. In the art professor's terms, he composed beautifully; each of his daily panels is a delicate balance of black and white, and often one panel leads into another through the simple rhythm of the lines. Sterrett usually dresses his characters in striped or checked garments, and the play of line against square is masterly. If heads, hands and feet were removed, what remained would be pen-and-ink abstraction of a high order.

But heads, hands and feet are not removed, and Sterrett's strip is not abstract. Its heroine is Polly; its harassed hero is Paw. Strictly speaking, it is a family strip rather than a girl strip; even the family cat, reflecting Paw's triumphs and disasters, is a major character.

Polly was an instant success, and remained successful forty-five years later. Sterrett maintained— even improved— his excellence as a draftsman. His gags remained fresh; his spotting was a constant delight to the eye; and his harried, energetic family remained the prototype of that slightly zany bunch down the block who just can't seem to take modern life seriously. In 1958 Sterrett retired, and Polly came to an end. It was a real loss.

George McManus was one of the best-loved and most-praised of comic-strip artists. He is nevertheless vastly underestimated. His fame rests largely on *Bringing Up Father*, in which Jiggs has been coping with money and Maggie for forty-five years. But his achievements before 1915 were in themselves spectacular, and would alone have assured him of a place in the first rank.

The New York *World* called its Sunday comics section "The Funny Side of the World," and there are weeks, in 1905 and 1906, when McManus seems almost to have turned out the whole section himself. He was a native

Polly again, and a fine sample of CLIFF STERRETT's composition. © 1935 King Features Syndicate, Inc.

One of the earliest *Newlyweds* by GEORGE MCMANUS, June 19, 1904. Readers of *Bringing Up Father* can easily identify this as McManus' work. © King Features Syndicate, Inc.

of St. Louis, and his first strip had been *Alma and Oliver*, drawn for the St. Louis *Republic*. ("It was a terrible mess," he said later, "and wouldn't get by a high-school editor today.") It was a stroke of fate that brought him to New York: a bootblack gave him a tip on a thirty-to-one shot at the local track, and McManus, in a blaze of hope, put up a hundred dollars. He won three thousand. The horse's name was Hamburg Belle. McManus was not so lucky in New York, at first; the three thousand was just about gone when he landed a job with the *World*. He had been offered another job that same week, but went with the *World* because Pulitzer also owned a newspaper in St. Louis and McManus's drawings would appear in the old home town.

By 1905 his talents were flowering. Between that year and 1910 he stocked the *Sunday World* with these: *Snoozer*; *The Merry Marceline* (also drawn by F. M. Follett); *Nibsy the Newsboy in Funny Fairyland* (which was very close in approach, though not in style, to *Little Nemo*); *Cheerful Charley* (the deadpan Indian whom no one could induce to laugh); *Panhandle Pete* (who, with two cohorts and an invaluably aggressive goat, perpetuated swindle upon swindle, once annexing a cannibal kingdom); *Let George Do It*; *The Newlyweds* (which established a pattern: the pretty and capable wife with the oafish but goodhearted husband). Later on, in 1912 and 1913 on the *Journal*, McManus created *Their Only Child*,

PANHANDLE PETE CAPTURES THE SEA SERPENT

A daily *Jiggs* from 1919, when the strip was already entrenched as a national favorite. © King Features Syndicate, Inc.

Rosie's Beau and *Bringing Up Father*. The range of ideas is wide, and it was in the area of ideas that McManus needed time for experiment. His style was, by 1905, fully formed, and from that year on there was no chance of mistaking a McManus page for anyone else's. There are fleeting glimpses of Jiggs in all his early work: the bullet head, the long, round jaw, the circular nose. His line was already clean and sure; his backgrounds were open and uncluttered; he had begun to use the patch of black as a focal point. The facial expressions were beautifully simple: using the angle of the mouth and the level of the eyebrows, McManus ran his creations through a rainbow of emotions, and he carried the technique to its ultimate with Jiggs.

Rosie's Beau and *Bringing Up Father* started in the New York *American* in 1913. As late as 1916 *Rosie's Beau* was still the Sunday feature, while Maggie and Jiggs ran daily. McManus had been slowly working out the idea of Jiggs, and adding refinements and embellishments.

A play of the 1890s called *The Rising Generation*, about the effect of sudden wealth on a workingman's family, had impressed McManus as a source of potential humor. This was the specific stimulus to *Bringing Up Father*; but general stimuli existed everywhere. After 1848 the United States had absorbed wave upon wave of immigrants, mostly workingmen; and the country's industrial expansion in the last half of the century had naturally enriched all sorts of people. In every large city there *were nouveaux riches*; there *were* hideous imitations of Renaissance architecture; there *were* octagonal rooms, ornate chandeliers, eclectic interiors. All of which meant that there were suddenly respectable householders whose new shoes pinched, whose celluloid collars chafed, who were intimidated by their own servants, and who yearned for escape to the poolroom, the card game, the beer garden or Dinty Moore's, where the cabbage is steamy and the corned beef fat, and where a man only gets one fork, which saves him a lot of embarrassment.

Jiggs was a natural; but so was McManus, who had a vast sense of humor, liked cigars as well as Jiggs did, dressed elegantly and carried a

A *Panhandle Pete*, May 29, 1904. Notice the trading stamp in the upper right-hand corner; bonuses and premiums even then! © 1904 the Press Publishing Co.

One solution to domestic strife. Jiggs escapes the world of manners for the world that matters. © 1925 King Features Syndicate, Inc.

cane, and treated his syndicate, upon occasion, cavalierly. Having made his home with the *Journal* in 1912, he later signed his contracts with King Features Syndicate, which meant that he sent all his material to New York; he lived in California and had, like many cartoonists, deadline trouble. During the 1920s airmail was taken over by the government for several months, and the government planes were not suited to the job; many of them crashed in the Rockies. Twice, when McManus was late, he wired New York that his work had been on an unlucky plane; he checked the newspapers regularly for air crashes. The third time he outsmarted himself, inadvertently choosing a westbound plane. The syndicate, though not amused, was helpless: there was only one McManus.

McManus' elegance and polish were proverbial, but it is true, as his friends say, that he resembled Jiggs physically. His personal popularity was extraordinary, and so was Jiggs's. When Maggie and Jiggs passed their twenty-fifth anniversary, McManus was guest of honor at a Congressional dinner in Washington— a distinction never before granted to a comic-strip artist— and received an avalanche of wires and letters from old friends and fans, among whom were government leaders and Supreme Court Justices.

McManus worked, as Martin Sheridan reports, with a pen in one hand and a cigar in the other. His strip was syndicated all over the world, with interesting variations on the culinary theme: in Mexico, Jiggs flees the house for a dish of tortillas; in France for *choucroute garnie*. In Ireland, traditionally if not accurately the home of corned beef and cabbage, Jiggs is not published! This omission is perhaps balanced by the Eleventh Bombardment Squadron of the U.S. Air Force, which has been known since the First World War as the Jiggs Squadron, and which has borne the man's portrait on all its planes.

When George McManus died in 1954, the loss to his friends and profession was irreparable. Jiggs could be— and was— ably continued by another, but there was no replacing McManus, a man of great wit, heart and individuality who had been a giant in his chosen field all his life.

When *The Katzenjammer Kids* was only a couple of years old, Rudolph Dirks took some time off to enlist in the Army during the Spanish-American War. The strip was dropped during his absence and restored when he returned. By 1912 Dirks needed another vacation, and a good long one, preferably with time for travel and painting; but by 1912 journalistic pressure was too high, journalistic competition too fierce, for an extended layoff.

The *Journal* was sympathetic but businesslike: when Dirks had completed a year's worth of future strips, he could take a year off. Doing two years' work in one for the sake of a vacation is a self-defeating proposition; but Dirks tried. Complications and probably some ill will arose between him and the newspaper; feeling that his contract had been violated, he packed and left for Europe. The *Journal* followed him about by cable, and for several months he mailed off Sunday pages; but when the *World* went after him, sensing an opportunity, he was in a mood to listen. The *World* hired him; he would join them when his contractual difficulties with the *Journal* were settled.

Shades of 1896! The *Journal* immediately enjoined Dirks from working for the *World*. Dirks counterattacked. The case came to court, and was decided for the *Journal*. An appeal, however, brought about a reversal of part of the original verdict, and the final decision, announced in 1913, was that the *Journal* retained rights to the title and to a strip with the original characters, while Dirks retained the right to draw those same characters under another title. The case was, incidentally, big news for a whole year, and is still studied in law schools as a classic of its kind. During that year Hans and Fritz did not appear.

The supply of juvenile mischief is apparently inexhaustible. For thirty-five years the two strips have been appearing regularly. The man who continued *The Katzenjammer Kids* in the *Journal* was H. H. Knerr; Dirks retitled his own strip *The Captain and the Kids*. Knerr had worked for years in Philadelphia, doing several different comics for the *Inquirer* and an animal strip for the *Ledger*. (*Zoo-Illogical Snapshots*, animal parodies, ran in other papers as well.)

Comparisons of the two strips are useless, invidious and generally reflective only of personal likes and dislikes. One critic will prefer Dirks because there is more motion in his panels; another will prefer Knerr be-

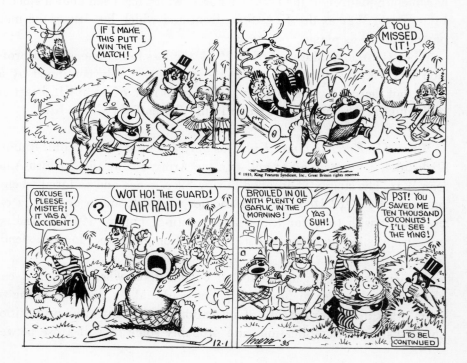

KNERR's *Katzenjammer Kids* twenty years after the copyright battle. Mischief everywhere. © 1935 King Features Syndicate, Inc.

The Captain and the Kids by Rudolph Dirks, who lost his original title *The Katzenjammer Kids,* but retained his rights to the characters. © 1956 United Feature Syndicate, Inc.

cause he draws more finely; another goes back to Dirks because his spotting is more emphatic; another votes for Knerr because his greater use of white space makes for a more open strip. Knerr took over the frame of mind from Dirks, and that was all-important. The same devilishness, the same domestic catastrophes, the same sadistic teamwork will tickle readers of both strips. The public likes them equally, and the public is the real judge of comic art.

After 1915 the major syndicates became big business, and daily comics became indispensable to all newspapers but the New York *Times*. The true proliferation of daily strips began between 1919 and 1925, when, for example, *Harold Teen, Little Orphan Annie, Gasoline Alley, Moon Mullins, The Nebbs, Toots and Casper, Boots and Her Buddies, Betty* and *Thimble Theater* all debuted, not to mention *Barney Google*. Many strips, like *Krazy Kat,* originated between 1910 and 1920 but belong, in mood and outlook, to the twenties; many artists, like Milt Gross, did their first work before World War I, but were not really at home before the twenties and thirties.

One of RUBE GOLDBERG's famous *Foolish Questions*, with the old sports cartoonist showing through. Courtesy of Rube Goldberg.

And the categories were taking shape. The family was established; the kids were running wild; animals were classic. Soon comic artists would settle on one aspect of a category, or on new variations of an old theme. C. H. Wellington's *Pa's Son-in-Law* was close on the heels of *Bringing Up Father; Moon Mullins* would be another version of the neighborhood butts trying to hold their own; Boots and Betty were highly original variants of Rosie.

And the poor, neglected hero would come into his own. So far, the tall, clean-cut doer of high deeds had been omitted entirely; but his time was coming.

One hero who deserves our immediate attention arrived in New York from the Far West in late 1906. Attired in a flamboyantly natty checked suit, a high-collared shirt with ruffles, yellow shoes, the latest in pearl-gray spats and a straw hat with a string on it, he stepped off the train clutching two suitcases, his dignity and a monstrous cigar. He was the hard-bitten ex-sports-cartoonist of the San Francisco *Chronicle*. Rube Goldberg was his name, and he could lick any man in the house; but he was about to undergo twelve consecutive days of unemployment (he still shudders at the memory) which would break his spirit and make him agreeable, even hilarious, forever after.

In 1905 San Francisco was a fairly wide-open town, but a man still had to make his own opportunities. Goldberg was fresh out of college, an admirer of Maurice Ketten, T. E. Powers, T. S. Sullivant and T. A. Dorgan. Tad had just left for New York, and Goldberg, by his own admission, made a pest of himself until in desperation the *Bulletin* gave him a job as sports cartoonist. His salary was nine dollars a week, which left little for long-range investment; after a couple of months he was raised to twelve dollars. But money was no object. Goldberg had loved drawing for years. He and his brother had kept themselves in small change by delivering *Puck* and *Judge* to barber shops; Rube read them all, and claimed later that he had been influenced by every contributor to either magazine. (Eugene Zimmerman, or Zim, who appeared in both, was another of his early idols.) In joining the *Bulletin*, though he may not have realized it at the time, Goldberg had achieved one of man's classic desires: he was being paid to do the kind of work he loved.

When the *Chronicle*, a morning newspaper, offered him a chance to do more work for less money, late in 1905, he took it eagerly, with characteristic illogic. Specifically, he could do sports sketches, along a strip at the top of the page, often seven columns wide, and he would be given ten dollars a week. He made the sacrifice. But his work was so good— there was already that sense of gentle exaggeration, or defiance of gravity— that by the middle of 1906 he had been jumped to fifty dollars.

This was no simple cartooning job. At the Hart-Root fight in Reno in

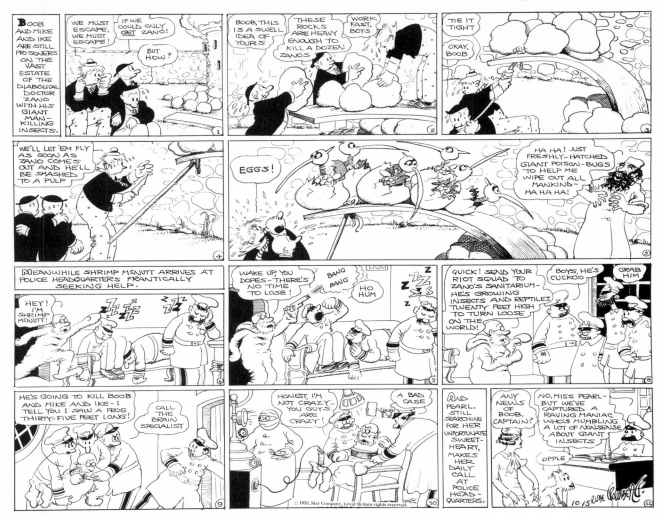

GOLDBERG'S *Boob McNutt* in his usual pack of trouble. The artist was never short on imagination. Courtesy of Rube Goldberg.

1905 the *Chronicle's* reporter drank himself senseless, and the paper wired Goldberg to do the story as well as the sketches. From then on he did short, funny pieces with his cartoons. And under the old boxing law on the West Coast there was no such thing as a referee's decision: if a fight ended without a knockout, the newspapers judged it, and bets were settled by reference to the sports pages. Goldberg became, before he was twenty-five, artist, writer and gambling czar.

He had subscribed to the *World* and the *Journal*. New York was the cartoonist's Mecca, and Goldberg frankly desired national fame. In those years Hearst scouted the country for talent, and Rube waited expectantly for a call that never came. Finally he took matters into his own hands and left for New York, with a diamond ring given to him by his father, Max, which was to be pawned when need arose. He never pawned it.

His life in New York began well. He had arranged to spend the first days with a friend named Harry Bunker, who played cards with an assortment of cartoonists. On Goldberg's first night in town he was awakened by the noise of the game, and found that one of the players was Tad. It was a good omen. Goldberg had faith and drive; he was shy, but determined and ambitious.

He had never liked letters of introduction, but the twelve days of unemployment unnerved him, and he finally dug out a note from H. L. Baggerly, sports editor of the *Bulletin,* to the city editor of a now defunct New York newspaper called the *Evening Mail,* which was backed by a Republican subsidy but otherwise in a shaky financial state. The city editor was polite but firm: there was nothing available. Goldberg went back to his furnished room on Thirty-fourth Street (by now he had his own place) and thought things over. The next day he dropped in on the *Mail's* sports editor, a former Olympic swimmer named Fred Wenck, who knew of Goldberg through his sporting friends. Wenck liked his work, and sent him out to cover an A.A.A. track meet that very night, at the old Madison Square Garden.

Goldberg worked all night, turned in a half-page and was overjoyed to see it printed. Wenck agreed to give him a three-month trial and went off to talk to the managing editor about pay. He came back shortly to report that "the s.o.b. will only give you fifty a week." Goldberg accepted with a straight face.

Within three months— by February 1907— he was running a series of "Foolish Questions," which caught on immediately. The classic example is the battered man beside a battered motor car who is asked, "Have an accident?" and answers, "No, thanks; just had one." (The colloquy, or the form of colloquy, became a staple of vaudeville.) The public took note of Rube Goldberg and began to phone in suggestions for the series.

Inevitably, Hearst also took notice, through Arthur Brisbane, who asked Goldberg to call upon him. Brisbane offered steady work with the *Journal* at fifty dollars a week. Goldberg protested; how was it that an empire like Hearst's could offer no more than a tottering little newspaper like the *Mail?* Brisbane was brusque: "Take it or leave it, but it's your last opportunity to work for Hearst."

Goldberg left it; out of loyalty and decency he went back to the *Mail.* And now he took on a full work load. He did sports, "Foolish Questions," *I'm the Guy, They All Look Good When You're Far Away, The Look Alike Boys, The Weekly Meeting of the Tuesday Ladies' Club.* He became more than the heart of the art staff; he became the heart of the newspaper.

His happiness was relatively unbroken until about 1915, when the *Mail* was sold to Edwin L. Rumely, Ph.D., whom the Rumely Plough Company of Laporte, Indiana, had made hugely rich. In the general upheaval Goldberg, whose salary had already risen to fancy figures, decided to attack. He was being syndicated in a small way, but any sudden change of owner-

Mike and Ike, They Look Alike, another RUBE GOLDBERG creation. Courtesy of Rube Goldberg.

A *Boob McNutt* heading from 1925. Everybody had heard kids shouting, "Get a horse," but only GOLDBERG would take it literally. Courtesy of Rube Goldberg.

ship creates uneasiness among employees, and men of independent talent choose these moments to strike out for clarification, status and more pay.

Rube had never liked business, but his father was good at it and was, moreover, tactful. Whenever a contract had to be renegotiated, Max came east, and so he did now in 1915. He started with an advantage: Rumely, with a new paper on his hands, wanted to keep its star performer, who happened to be Rube. Max knew that Bud Fisher was up to a thousand a week by then. "That's what you should be getting," he said to Rube, being fatherly. "You're crazy," Rube said, being filial.

Rumely and Max conferred, after which Rube and Max met for dinner. When Max ordered wine and laughed, Rube knew he had done it. It was a memorable dinner.

In 1916 business matters became too pressing even for a man with a diamond stickpin and two dozen detachable collars; so Goldberg asked an old friend, Virgil V. McNitt, to come east and help syndicate him. McNitt came on from Cleveland, and within the next couple of years he organized, with Charles McAdams, the McNaught Syndicate. One of their first products was Rube's famous strip *Boob McNutt*.

McNutt, McNitt and McNaught. It could only happen to Rube Goldberg.

CHAPTER III

Comics:
Here to Stay

THE TWENTIES. Bootlegging, graft in high places, flaming youth. Harding's speeches: vast, billowing, slumbrous waves of platitude. The apotheosis of the Stutz. Silent Cal and his war bonnet. The hip flask, of course. The raccoon coat, gang warfare, Babe Ruth, the stock market. Leopold and Loeb, the Kellogg-Briand Peace Pact (it ended war forever) and Charles A. Lindbergh. Bread and circuses.

There were 125,000,000 Americans in 1925, and probably 120,000,000 of them never saw a gangster, never wore a raccoon coat, never danced the Charleston. They were therefore not newsworthy at the time, and have since become a dull footnote to a lurid legend, stolid whipping boys to a generation of satirists. We find them in the comic strips of the twenties— families and kids, normalcy in its purest form— and we find no gangsters, footballers or (except for Carl Ed's *Harold Teen)* pioneer hot-rodders. If historians of the next century were to rely upon the comic strip, they would conclude that we were a peaceful lot of ruminant burghers from 1920 to 1929, with only occasional flashes of inspired insanity, and that our social conflicts and national crises were settled by family conferences at the dinner table. That view is, for the most part, correct: the flamboyance of the age was a surface phenomenon, and beneath the surface America was almost bewilderingly ordinary.

Which was natural: Harding, who stood for complacency and inaction, retrenchment and the weekly poker game, had been swept into office almost in spite of himself. ("We drew to a pair of deuces," he said humbly, "and filled.") True, America had been momentarily aroused by the First World War; true, much of the population was bitter about Prohibition; true, the younger generation may have been eager to taste the delights of petting and booze— but the torchbearers, the practitioners of the modern freedom, the "Lost Generation," were only a handful, and they were largely urban. Elsewhere the family had forgotten about the war because it wanted to. Mama approved of Prohibition; Papa grumbled, but Mama was boss anyway. Maybe Papa liked the looks of the Stutz, but the car for him was still the Ford: it was cheaper, and easier to service, and it was properly modest and substantial. The nearest thing to a gangster the family had seen was that fellow in a tight jacket who was hanging around the railroad station one day last week. And when Cal Coolidge said that the business of America was business, he was talking good sense. All the rest of this high living was the fault of Wall Street, Foreigners and Progressive Education.

Colonel Robert McCormick and Captain Joseph Patterson, cousins who had been publishing the Chicago *Tribune* since 1914, displayed journalistic brilliance during this period. Their news and editorial pages reflected the surface of America—— rum running, all-night orgies, lurid divorce scandals, sex murders, corruption in high places, the unreliability of non-Americans— yet their features and their comics pages were given over almost entirely to the American family and its natural concomitant, the American child. Page one was prurient and xenophobic; the comics page was modest and home-loving.

When Patterson invaded New York with the *Illustrated Daily News* (which rapidly became just the *Daily News)* in 1919, he brought the pattern east, and between them the *Tribune* and the *News* set a national tone for the next fifteen years. The *News* was, for one thing, a tabloid. Thirty-five years later the tabloid tradition was classic: it was the workingman's newspaper, the mass-circulation newspaper. But in 1919 Patterson was taking a chance; the tabloid was new and untried in America. (In London Lord Northcliffe's *Daily Mirror* had a circulation of more than a million; that fact had struck Patterson and McCormick. Northcliffe had met Joseph Pulitzer in 1900, and Pulitzer had been impressed; he had given the New York *World* to the Englishman to publish as he chose for just one day, and the *World* of New Year's Day 1901 appeared as a tabloid, which Northcliffe called "the newspaper of the twentieth century." Pulitzer did not approve, though he admired.)

The first issues of the *Daily News* carried one comic strip, *The Gumps*, and there has never been a less glamorized, more archetypical family in

The Gumps, 1935, by SIDNEY SMITH. The horizontal line near the bottom was for the benefit of newspapers— even then— which economized on space by trimming their strips. © 1935 Chicago *Tribune*– New York *News* Syndicate, Inc.

American comics. If Andy Gump were real he would be monstrous— he has no chin and no hair; his mouth is an aperture beneath a mustache which runs from ear to ear. He is not real; nor are the specific adventures of the Gump family. But the drives that animate the Gumps are real, all right; they are the drives that moved most American families back in the twenties, and that still do. We tend to think of them as the "early American virtues." Ambition is one of them, and pride is another. Andy may be funny-looking, but he bows to no man; he may be poor, but he is as clever and courageous as billionaire Uncle Bim. Andy's wife, Min, is (to put it as gallantly as possible) no beauty, but she has her own family, and she guards it with all the ferocity of a mother bear. Even young Chester has his own toughness: ambition and pride inherited from his father, plus the natural stubbornness of a young man proving himself among adults. Tilda, the old maid, is as repellent as Andy physically, and as fierce socially.

Well, look at them, and think about them. Min was homely, and so were a lot of female newspaper readers, because those who weren't homely were busy primping and dancing. Any American woman to whom beauty and frivolity were an affront— and there were many in the early 1920's— approved of Min Gump, and sympathized with her, and admired her for her stanchness. Andy got the men's vote because he was energetic and ugly and had an eye for the main chance. And even Tilda stood for something: the poor relation, or family retainer, technically lower in status than the rest of the family, but bound and determined to keep her independence. The Gumps undoubtedly meant little if anything to the sophisticated citizens who made the legend of the twenties; but to anyone caught up in the timeless process of making a livelihood, of "getting ahead," the Gumps were real. They were bread, potatoes and near-beer, and so was most of America.

Sidney Smith did not create the Gumps; but he made them great. He came out of the Midwest, and his first newspaper job was on the old Bloomington, Indiana, *Sun Eye*. He worked as a staff artist in Indian-

Another *Gumps* of 1935. The preoccupation with lost financial opportunities is typical of Andy. © 1935 Chicago *Tribune*– New York *News* Syndicate, Inc.

apolis, Toledo, Philadelphia and Pittsburgh; then he went to Chicago, with the *Herald* and *Examiner*; and in 1911 he settled down with the Chicago *Tribune*. His first strip for them was *Old Doc Yak*, but within a year Captain Patterson had switched him to a new strip, *The Gumps*, conceived and named by Patterson himself. (Patterson's proprietary, almost paternal, feeling for the Gumps persisted for many years; he retained editorial control of the strip until his death.)

The Gumps were triumphantly successful. Within five years of their debut Smith had been signed to his famous million-dollar contract— $100,000 a year for ten years. In 1935 he signed another, this one at $150,000 a year for five years, went downstairs and outside, stepped into his Ford sedan and started home. An hour later he was dead, victim of an automobile accident, and the first chapter in the Gumps' long history was ended.

Back before Prohibition many Chicago newspapermen had spent some (or all) of their spare time in a public house called Stillson's, just across the street from the old Chicago *Tribune* building. Here Smith spent many hours with Ring Lardner, Clare Briggs, Frank King and J. P. McEvoy. Another of their circle was a very funny man named Sol Hess, partner in the wholesale watch-and-diamond firm of Rettig, Hess, and Madsden, whose offices were a block away. Hess was a wit and raconteur of the old school; he could weave about the least significant event a hilarious tissue of alarums and excursions. He loved to deliver despairing accounts of his home life, and Smith found that he could use those accounts. Shortly Hess was supplying much of the dialogue for *The Gumps*, and soon out-of-town newspapers wrote in to ask for the right to republish the strip. Direct syndication by the *Tribune* was the result, and a good deal of the credit must go to Hess. He was never paid for his contribution to *The Gumps*, even after syndication; but when Smith signed the million-dollar contract in 1922, Hess realized that the comics could be a bigger business than diamonds. He hesitated to try collaborating with anyone but Smith, but when the Bell Syndicate made him a formal offer Hess and W. A. Carlson joined forces (Carlson had been doing animation on the West Coast for MGM). From the very beginning Hess and Carlson stuck to the idea of a family strip.

By May of 1923 the two men were ready to publish, and the Nebbs were born. Rudy Nebb, husband and father, differed from his predecessors in not being henpecked; *he* was the strong man, *he* wore the pants, *he* made the decisions. Usually he was found running a resort hotel— a setting with unlimited story possibilities. "The name Nebb had been used a number of times in *The Gumps* in referring to a character who was more or less browbeaten by his wife," Hess once explained to Martin Sheridan. "It comes from the Jewish word 'nebich,' a reference of contempt for a

Part of a *Nebbs* Christmas strip, by SOL HESS and WALLY CARLSON, 1925. Hess, the great storyteller, is now gone; Carlson, the artist, now does a panel, *Mostly Malarkey*. © the Bell Syndicate, Inc.

'poor sap.' The name Rudy was very popular at the time, at least its distinguished owner was, so we chose the famous movie idol Valentino's first name.

"All the regular characters are fictitious except for Max Guggenheim, who in real life is in the packing business and is our next-door neighbor." Guggenheim was the pessimist of the strip, the wet blanket, whose function was to reduce Rudy's ego to manageable proportions. "It is Max," Coulton Waugh wrote, "who is seldom wrong, and whose advice Rudy loudly disclaims, but secretly follows. Max is the man behind the drone."

Hess left the jewelry business two years after the Nebbs' debut. He was already a legend in the comic-strip profession: a generous, optimistic man who gave happily of himself and his talents. He blocked out a basic pattern for family strips, and if he had been marred by the slightest meanness he would never have been able to recognize that pattern: he thought of humanity not as idealized embodiments of vice and virtue, but as unadorned specimens of an imperfect species. His great ability was to know them and appreciate them for what they were, and to love them anyway. Sol Hess was not a retailer of romance, and even less a satirist of the ordinary. He saw warmth and humor in the worst of us, and he brought to the comic strip a wrangling family affection. He was folks, and not folksy.

The Gumps and *The Nebbs* were popular novels, in a sense, about real families. Their stories were continuous, and not day-to-day gags. In creating some illusion of life, Smith and Hess had to be careful not to trespass too far into the realm of exaggeration. It was left to another strip, Jimmy Murphy's *Toots and Casper,* to lay down the rules for a new kind of family: light-hearted, a little zany, and dedicated to the notion— a peculiarly and almost exclusively American notion— that Daddy is a well-meaning imbecile and that Mommy, being beautiful, deserves better but loves him anyway.

Murphy is a Chicago boy who moved to Omaha. In his late teens he had free-lance work in all three Omaha newspapers of the time, but not long afterward he was taken on by the Spokane *Inland-Herald,* where he drew front-page political cartoons. He moved on to the Portland *Journal* in Oregon, and then to the San Francisco *Call-Post*. Still in his mid-twenties, he had done eight years of political cartooning, had been syndicated and widely reproduced, and had been called to New York by Mr. Hearst himself. In December of 1918 he began *Toots and Casper* for Hearst's *American*. In 1920 he signed with King Features Syndicate, and *Toots and Casper* was distributed nationally.

They were not always what they are today. In 1919, and for most of 1920, there was no Buttercup (a boy baby, and future President). But Buttercup was necessary, because the funny-family strip is predicated on the husband's fatuousness; and what greater fatuity exists than the paternal? And until 1923 Toots was a bobbed flapper; in May of that year Casper— a boob at every opportunity— admired another woman's curls, and Toots yielded her bob, taking on her final curly-haired form as a Murphy creation.

Toots' attractiveness was new. Cliff Sterrett's Polly was a cute trick, but she was the daughter; Murphy initiated the almost sinful idea of the beautiful wife. In doing so, he gave fresh force to the thesis that women are noble and desirable, while men are at best tolerable; that man's role in life is to serve his lady, whatever trouble it lands him in. This thesis may be simply a fiction tailored to fit the facts: that men must work, and dig up money, and raise children, and refrain from vices like fishing and poker when those vices would upset life's imperative routines. If we must devote ourselves to others, how comforting to feel that our wives are goddesses, our children destined to greatness!

Between them, Hess and Murphy mapped out the terrain of the two family strips— one mundane and slightly unwashed, the other idealized and sweetened. Those who followed them were not imitators; *Blondie*, for instance, is the most popular of all strips, and Chic Young's techniques and imagination are unvaryingly perfect for his story. But the two forms of the family strip were established by 1925.

Part of a 1925 *Toots and Casper* by JIMMY MURPHY, showing the two title characters, who had changed considerably since their debut, and son Buttercup, who had only recently come along. © King Features Syndicate, Inc.

The trouble is that these strips keep eluding the categories we establish for them. *Gasoline Alley* is a family strip, and one of the great ones; what is it, exactly, that sets it apart from both *The Gumps* and *Toots and Casper*? For one thing, its characters are not caricatures, as the Gumps are; for another, its adventures don't partake of the fictional, as the Gumps' do; then, it makes no strenuous effort to be funny, which *Toots and Casper* often does. But the important difference is none of these: it is simply that Walt and Skeezix and their friends and relatives have been aging, day by day, as the strip progressed. The continuity is not limited to one sequence or episode; the continuity is permanent. The reflection of life is therefore not momentary; it is constant. The strip is, in a sense, one long sequence, which can be synopsized over a thirty-eight-year period.

Frank King, its author, grew up in Wisconsin, where he spent most of his spare time drawing. He broke into newspaper work as a staffer in Minneapolis, but, like most ambitious Midwesterners of the period, he was drawn to Chicago. He spent a year at the Academy of Fine Arts and won a scholarship for a second year, one advantage of which was that it gave him time to work for the Chicago *American* on Saturdays. He drifted into advertising art, and then shifted to the Chicago *Examiner*, doing sketches, diagrams and caricatures for three years. The *Tribune* eventually made him an offer, which he accepted; he soon found himself illustrating columns and Sunday features, and when John McCutcheon went overseas late in the war, King did the front-page cartoons. But a feature called the "Rectangle" was King's real springboard. It was a black-and-white Sunday page of graphic comment on current events, news highlights and popular fads; these were titled *Pet Peeves, It Isn't the Original Cost, It's the Upkeep*, etc. In one corner of the page was a panel called *Gasoline*

The first *Gasoline Alley*, a classic panel, dated August 24, 1919. Walt Wallet is instantly recognizable. © Chicago *Tribune*– New York *News* Syndicate, Inc.

Alley, depicting the weekly meeting of a few automobile enthusiasts in an alley behind their apartments. The automobile was not taken for granted in those days; there were millions of men whose passion in life was tinkering with valves or adjusting carburetors. *Gasoline Alley* caught the public fancy, and finally King was running it as a full page in color on Sundays and a daily black-and-white strip.

For the first year and a half the strip stuck to its internal combustion, but on Valentine's Day of 1921 it went off on a wild tangent from which it has not yet returned. On that day a foundling was left on Walt Wallet's doorstep.

The device was sure-fire. It introduced suspense, compassion and humor in one stroke. If King had tried to break away from cars by having Walt fall in love and start his own family, readers might have been drawn into the new story; then again, they might have deplored the passing of the automotif. But they were taken unawares, and for most of them the transition must have been inevitable; within three weeks they had shifted mental gears and were following the destinies of the baby— a boy, whom Walt kept and named Skeezix— with more enthusiasm than they had ever developed for the Maxwell.

From then on, *Gasoline Alley* reads like a popular novel— uncomplicated, the action well within everyone's ken, the attitude gentle, optimistic, warmhearted. Skeezix grew up; Uncle Walt yielded his bachelor's independence and married pretty Phyllis Blossom; Skeezix went through the usual juvenile adventures; Corky was born to the Wallets; and a daughter, Judy, rounded out the family. The years passed. Skeezix finished high school and married Nina; the war came and he enlisted; he returned a staff sergeant, and now he is busy re-creating the cycle that began so long ago. (Bill Perry now does the Sunday page.)

Nothing has ever happened to Skeezix that has not also happened to great segments of the American population. King has taken the norm, in all areas, and fitted Skeezix to it. Nina, for example, is pretty as many American women are pretty; she is not an exaggeration of the ravishing blonde. Uncle Walt is, and always has been, stout, and Aunt Phyllis is

FRANK KING's Skeezix in a typical scene of army life— griping and deploring officers. © 1942 Chicago *Tribune*– New York *News* Syndicate, Inc.

More army life by FRANK KING. These strips were authentic; what Skeezix went through, we all went through. © 1943 Chicago *Tribune*– New York *News* Syndicate, Inc.

pleasingly plump. Skeezix himself is neither sloppy nor elegant, neither stupid nor brilliant, neither lazy nor avaricious. The inhabitants of *Gasoline Alley* are what Americans like to think their fellow citizens might be if only this were a more reasonable world, with lower taxes, steady employment and less international nervousness. Skeezix does not have "adventures," but he makes an adventure of his life; and for the home-loving citizen who will never see Timbuctoo, that kind of adventure is flattering and comforting. Skeezix is as close to the real American as any character the comics have produced; he is a fixture of American journalism.

A couple, in our folklore, is not quite a family. Kids, being inevitable, have become indispensable. And kids, of course, preceded even families in the funny papers, simply because kids are funny in themselves. They inhabit a world of odd but self-consistent logic; a world, so to speak, of non-Euclidian geometry, in which the postulates violate the rules of experience, and in which the natives survive by creating their own common experience in defiance of those rules. Otherwise fatal activities, like the extreme consumption of delicatessen, the bouncing of rocks, baseball bats and coconuts off youthful skulls, or direct contradiction of parental orders not to jump off the barn with an umbrella-parachute, are staples in the world of the juvenile. Like nations, children are most interesting when they violate norms; unlike nations, children rarely know what the norms are, and live in a constant state of perilous anarchy. *Little Orphan Annie*, probably the most famous— and in some quarters the most irritating— of all comic-strip tykes, goes so far as to function without visual apparatus; her blank eyes (to which the reader himself imparts the suitable expression) are notorious, and have been parodied time and again. That her occasional protector is the richest man in the world, and that his assistant is a mysterious Oriental giant, reflect rather fact than fantasy in the world

A Sunday *Gasoline Alley* by FRANK KING. A domestic comedy of errors. © 1949
the Chicago *Tribune*– New York *News* Syndicate, Inc.

of the child. Until the age of disillusionment— seven or eight, probably— most children see their own fathers as omnipotent and omniscient, and Annie's environment is simply that of the fairy tale, made modern by the paraphernalia of the twentieth century. Daddy Warbucks, for example, is not a simple millionaire; he is quite frankly a munitions tycoon, a war profiteer, a thoroughly American Zaharoff.

But Daddy Warbucks and his millions are not usually at Annie's beck and call. For the most part she must make her own way out of scrapes and dangers, aided only by a startlingly intelligent dog named Sandy, whose eyes are also deficient. The scrapes and dangers range from gang warfare in big cities to sinister murder plots in isolated rural areas, and Annie's presence always tips the scales— of course in favor of virtue and courage. Her adversaries are unbelievably evil, and her friends are almost unbearably good. Which is as it should be in that absolute world of childhood.

Harold Gray, Annie's creator, came to the Chicago *Tribune* as an assistant in the art department not long after his graduation from Purdue University. He served in the First World War, came back to the *Tribune,* and introduced Annie to the world on August 5, 1924. Gray's experiences had apparently taught him one firm rule: that you cannot overestimate the public's attachment to traditional virtues. Gray's "good" characters are inevitably hard-working, pious, stanchly courageous, philosophically individualistic, and non-intellectual; there is the strong implication that if one is not *all* of these things, then one is none of them. They are also, it should be added, eminently successful as comic-strip characters.

Much has been written about Gray's free-swinging conservatism, and it is quite true that he has advanced his own views in the strip. His editorializing begins, however, not with flat statements about rationing, taxes or freedom of enterprise, but in his very cast of characters. The pattern of piety and virtue is not simply a literary convention; it is a reflection of the belief that the good life is the patient, unassuming, well-ordered life.

Harold Gray's Orphan Annie with her Sandy, in a formal pose, backed by a partial gallery of Gray's characters. © Chicago *Tribune*–New York *News* Syndicate, Inc.

A Sunday page of *Little Orphan Annie*, full of good drawing, suspense, and pathos. Switching from Annie to Daddy Warbucks and back again is highly effective; conceiving and laying out such a Sunday page is no easy task. © 1956 the Chicago *Tribune*– New York *News* Syndicate, Inc.

The ageless *Harold Teen*. This strip is dated 1951, and there are Harold and Shadow at the same old soda fountain, still dreaming. © the Chicago *Tribune*– New York *News* Syndicate, Inc.

Within that pattern lie safety, happiness and the good society; outside it lie danger and evil, corruption and damnation. Annie's adventures occur outside the pattern, and she is always saved or vindicated by the "good people," occasionally with an assist from the bad ones, whose bumbling leads to their self-destruction.

All that is well within the pattern of the traditional fairy tale, and inoffensive in itself. Most of Gray's critics sense, but fail to express, another source of uneasiness: Gray's implication that when all else fails, it is permissible to fall back on the free exercise of power by the virtuous— or by their leaders: e.g., Daddy Warbucks. In its simplest form this is severe Calvinism: the decisions and actions of the elect are unimpeachable. Daddy Warbucks has, in short, license, much as Mickey Spillane's hero has. The law turns out to be for the protection of the good, and not for the protection of all men. The assumption of moral superiority leads inevitably to the assumption of physical and social superiority; only the good have rights.

Defensible or not, Gray's thesis holds an audience. Many of his readers are simply compassionate; Annie has no home (to paraphrase Coulton Waugh), so her readers take her in. Others enjoy the feeling of righteousness that accompanies the defeat of the wicked; others simply follow an unending, constantly varying adventure.

A philosophical counterpoint to Annie's derring-do is occasionally furnished by *Maw Green*, whose aphorisms and homilies appear in a small three- or four-panel strip beneath Annie. Maw's dialogues always lead to a conclusion that may be expressed as a "thought for today," a homely statement of some eternal truth. Maw is the mature (and slightly acid) embodiment of many of the good folk in *Annie*.

Gray is not alone in employing a fairy-tale atmosphere, and within its limits he has a perfect right to say what he pleases. A more pertinent and legitimate criticism of his techniques is that he takes us into a world of fantasy, where good always triumphs, and then identifies specific modern events and theories— real, rather than fantastic— with the good and evil of his dream world. It is as though we were to see the story of Jack and the Beanstalk on television, and watch Jack climb the stalk and break through to the giant's castle, and then discover that the giant was William McKinley. The hullaballoo would be enormous; no newspaper would pass it over in silence. But Harold Gray has packaged his pill expertly. Annie belongs to her readers, who love her, and who respond by the millions to the illusions she creates.

Frank Willard, who created *Moon Mullins* for the Chicago *Tribune*-New York *News* Syndicate in 1923, died in 1957, having instructed a generation and a half in the niceties of social stratification. *Moon Mullins* is an intriguing strip. People, mostly of the middle class, keep popping up to say that they don't understand it. But workingmen and college professors rise to defend it. (It is now drawn, and very ably, by Ferd Johnson.)

Its theme has been defined as "the gap between aspiration and fulfill-

FRANK WILLARD's beautiful slapstick in a *Moon Mullins* of 1941. Emmy, as usual, bears the brunt. © 1941 the Chicago *Tribune*– New York *News* Syndicate, Inc.

A rare technique for WILLARD— a whole daily *Moon Mullins* in one long panel. The dialogue and facial expressions— especially Willie's— are Willard at his best. © 1944 the Chicago *Tribune*– New York *News* Syndicate, Inc.

ment," which is unnecessarily pretentious. More simply, the cast of *Moon Mullins* is the greatest collection of social pretenders ever assembled in four panels. Always, earthy reality wins out over the ideal, the pretension; beef stew defeats poetry. Moon is a roughneck; his brother Kayo is an apprentice roughneck, and the only realist in the strip. Moon himself is a romantic: he likes pretty girls and money, and his pursuit of both is reckless and devoted. In his secondary characters, though, Willard achieved greatness. Lord and Lady Plushbottom are, so to speak, peerless; they have set the nobility back a thousand years. Uncle Willie is Legion: he is the man in the undershirt, the subway rider who sprinkles cigar ash on the gorgeous blonde, the night watchman who falls asleep, the short-order cook who eats all day. Appropriately, he is bound, in this life, to Mamie, and lives always in the shadow of Behemoth. His despairing efforts to find comfort, if not dignity, are simply flights from Mamie.

Whether or not Plushbottom represents any specifically American nostalgia, he is the most pretentious of the family, and therefore the least puncture-proof. He is also the most pathetic, and in many ways the most admirable; he is, in his tenement dwelling, the equivalent of the British explorer dressing for dinner in the heart of the Congo. His dear wife Emma, formerly Emmy Schmaltz, is harder-headed, not taken in by his self-deception; yet she is as often a butt as he. Fate seems to single out this scrawny, irascible prisoner of circumstance for the most slapstick of punishments; it is always she who loses her shoes on a pebbled road, who falls off the pier, who is mistaken by the police for a gun moll. The others are scarcely sympathetic. Mamie has her own troubles with Willie; Plushbottom may, at best, expostulate gently; Moon is busy chasing down a card game; and Kayo is too cynical to be duped into sympathy.

Moon Mullins might be subtitled The Quest for High Life, or the Imitation of Glamour. The impulse is always upward— to fame, riches, dazzling lights. But the culmination is always a descent to reality, via the nightstick, the pratfall or the custard pie. Perhaps the key to the strip (and to its popularity) is this: nobody works. This family is a collection of con artists; that they con themselves, or each other, as often as they do anyone else, is the meat of the strip. It is also simple justice; we would be disappointed if Moon ever did come home with that thousand bucks, if Plushie ever did impress a young beauty, if Kayo ever did give up that derby hat and show mere human sympathy. What we admire is not this family's virtues; it is their tirelessness. They are the indefatigable pretenders to a shaky throne.

Another of the great kid strips is *Smitty*, which Walter Berndt has been drawing for the Chicago *Tribune*-New York *News* Syndicate since 1922. Smitty is not simply a juvenile; he is a workingman— a prototypical American office boy. The give-and-take between him and his boss, Mr.

WALTER BERNDT's *Smitty*. Adults underestimate Smitty, who often makes exactly the same mistake with little brother Herby. © 1952 the Chicago *Tribune*– New York *News* Syndicate, Inc.

Bailey, is reminiscent of the whole first-step-on-the-ladder tradition. Smitty, being enterprising, is occasionally almost impertinent; when there is a good ball game in town, it becomes necessary to outwit his boss for an afternoon off; and underlying the whole relationship is the certainty, known all along to Smitty and gradually communicated to the readers, that the indispensable man in this office is not the boss but the boy.

Smitty began as a boy of about twelve, and over almost forty years he has slowly matured to the age of perhaps seventeen. His dress has not varied much; we think of him always in a black suit, wearing a very small black bow tie. His brother Herby, whose adventures are more intriguing to some than those of Smitty, began as a real tyke, perhaps a precocious four years old, vastly undersized and wearing always the simplest of smocks, which bellied out before him like a spinnaker. Herby too has grown and is now perhaps seven. One of his more recent adventures involved him in a desperate course of dancing lessons, the objective of which was to help him win favor in the eyes of a girl his own age. Constant readers were treated to the spectacle of little Herby, confined to his frock for decades, blossoming forth in black tie and dinner jacket. Smitty himself is thoroughly involved with a cute trick from the office, and that situation has enabled Berndt to explore the vagaries of adolescent affection. Mr. and Mrs. Smith, the boys' parents, were once more prominent in the strip than they are now. Mr. Bailey seems to have replaced them as the adult influence.

Berndt has been very successful in combining the long continuity with the daily gag. Within each five- or six-week sequence— some longer, some shorter— each day's strip carries its own punch. The drawing style is more complex than we might think at first glance, seeing the free use of white space, straight lines and patches of black. The backgrounds are not complicated, but they contribute to the sense of reality in the strip. A woman walking along the street will not be entirely alone; an automobile chugs down the road behind her, a barrel leans against a wall. In Smitty's office the water cooler is the most common prop.

Berndt claims that he learned practically everything he knows about drawing from Tad Dorgan. Berndt had little formal education and only one art lesson; but in 1916 he became an office boy on the New York *Journal*, where he first met Dorgan. He threw himself into cartooning enthusiastically, and within a year was doing a panel called "Then the Fun Began," as well as an eight-column sports cartoon on Mondays, filling in for Dorgan. In 1921 Berndt drew a daily cartoon entitled "That's Different" for the Bell Syndicate; it was entirely unsuccessful, and soon Berndt was with the New York *World* doing a strip called *Bill the Office Boy*, which is the obvious precursor of *Smitty*. Unfortunately Berndt had to leave the *World* for personal reasons, and that was the end of Bill. The day he left, Berndt saw Captain Patterson, showed him *Bill* and was asked to sign a contract (contracts were unusual in Patterson's empire). As usual, Patterson added one personal touch: he did not like the name Bill and asked to change it. Berndt opened the telephone book at random, found himself among the Smiths and decided immediately that the use of such a common name would be no drawback at all. He has been doing *Smitty* since 1922, and has never tired of it. Neither have millions of readers.

Except for the *Nebbs* and *Toots and Casper,* these strips were offered to the world by Colonel McCormick and Captain Patterson. Willard once stated that the roughneck strip was Patterson's idea; the Gumps were, too, and it is probably true that no other publisher in history— not even Hearst — took as much interest in the comics he published as Patterson did. The *Tribune* and the *News* did not dominate the twenties; yet of the dozen enduring strips created in that decade, half are their products. They were as important in those years as Pulitzer and Hearst had been twenty years before, and their function was essential in the transition from comics as an adjunct to journalism to comics as a profession in itself.

But Patterson and McCormick were by no means the whole story. Via the family, they were bringing realism to the comic strip, and conditioning audiences to the "true adventure" which would come along in the thirties. Others, however, were tilling equally fertile fields. Kids, particularly, proliferated: there were Ad Carter's *Just Kids*, Gene Byrnes's *Reg'lar Fellers*, C. M. Payne's memorable *S'matter Pop?*, Merrill Blosser's *Freckles and His Friends*, R. M. Brinkerhoff's *Little Mary Mixup*, which had begun in the late 1910s, and Percy Crosby's inimitable *Skippy*.

No two of these cartoonists worked in anything like the same style, or with anything like the same attitude. Byrnes, who had been famous for

GENE BYRNES's *Reg'lar Fellers*, with Jimmy Dugan, Pudd'nhead, and Pinhead. © 1935 Gene Byrnes.

It's a Great Life If You Don't Weaken during the First World War, created a group much like the *Our Gang* of the early thirties. They were named Pudd'nhead and Pinhead and Jimmy Dugan, and they wore Basque shirts or beanies or caps, and they were never motionless. They even had a dog named Bullseye, much like *Our Gang's* canine companion. Their adventures were often in imitation of their elders', as most children's are— they established businesses, went to war, sought glory. Byrnes obviously liked to draw children, and he had the odd knack of distorting their movements in precisely the way children contort themselves, but exaggerating slightly: his creations lean just a little farther than standing children can, jump just a little higher than anybody can, and always run with both feet off the ground simultaneously.

Reg'lar Fellers remained popular for almost three decades. In 1941 a *Reg'lar Fellers* radio program replaced Jack Benny during the summer, and Hollywood produced a series of six-reelers about them. During the early forties they appeared successfully in comic-book form.

Just Kids was something else again. Carter drew more economically, and the atmosphere of his strip was more small-town than suburban. There was less motion, less action, and often a four-panel strip consisted almost entirely of a brief dialogue, with only slight variations in the spotting of his characters. Calmer, much more homey than other kids, Mush Stebbins and Fatso Dolan faced life with good nature. Carter's lack of violence and gentle flow of incident may reflect his own wistfulness; he was orphaned at eleven, and missed most of the pleasures of youth. He picked up jobs as an office boy until Clare Briggs, who was caricaturing for the Brooklyn *Times*, had him taken on as a reporter. Carter shifted to the *Eagle* and originated *Just Kids* in 1921. It was syndicated immediately by King Features, and Carter drew it until his death in 1958.

"Kid strips" are notably long-lived. *Reg'lar Fellers* ran for over thirty years, *Just Kids* for thirty-seven; *Freckles*, still going strong, was begun in 1915, *Little Mary Mixup* in 1918. *Freckles* was a schoolboy strip from the beginning, and its cast has aged perhaps four years in over forty; its

AD CARTER'S *Just Kids*, in 1931. Mush Stebbins and Ignatius Conway were often at sword's point. © 1931 King Features Syndicate, Inc.

adolescents are more sophisticated, better-looking (the girls much more curvaceous) and in general sleeker than they were. Mary Mixup has aged even more— from about five to almost twenty, in forty years— and the drawing is sharper than it was. Once upon a time it was, as Waugh described it, of "a fluttering, crinkling quality that reminds one of a crimped-edged, deep-dish apple pie." There is still an old-fashioned air about her; she is constantly engaged in "good works," and her adventures are not of the gritty or breezy kind that befall many young comic-strip heroines.

Skippy was probably king of them all. No one who ever saw him will forget the scratchily drawn figure, voluminous cap at a rakish angle, the boy almost always in motion, almost always headed for youthful defeat by a force too great for him. His ambition was both formless and boundless; there seems to have been no challenge offered by the world which he could bring himself to refuse. The result was several years of constant warfare between him and his society. The adult reader, even while laughing, found it hard to sympathize completely with Skippy. He was— no question about it— a mischievous young man. How many hundreds of thousands of mildly evil ideas he planted in the receptive brains of his juvenile readers we will never know. There may be greenhouses all over the United States which lost one or more panes of glass because of him; and the number of silk hats dashed to earth by a well-directed snowball would undoubtedly be much larger if Americans ever bothered to wear the silly things.

Skippy's creator, Percy Lee Crosby, is remembered chiefly for his comic strip. But he deserves better; an enormously talented man, he has lived an enormously full life. He was born in Brooklyn, on December 8, 1891. After attending public schools in Queens and New York City, he enrolled in the Pratt Institute and the Art Students League. He developed *Skippy* during his thirties and forties, but meanwhile he had been holding exhibitions of his serious work wherever and whenever possible (the National Academy of Design; the Anderson Galleries; the Seligman Galleries; the Pennsylvania Academy of Fine Arts; the Corcoran Gallery of Art). One aspect of his serious work had begun during the First World War, in which he served overseas. He found himself sketching on board ship both ways and while at the front. (He rose, incidentally, from second lieutenant to captain during the war, and was awarded the Purple Heart.)

One of PERCY CROSBY's war sketches. © 1918 the McClure Newspaper Syndicate, Inc.

By the mid-1930s he had been exhibited in Paris, Rome and London, and had achieved a place in permanent collections at the Musée du Jeu de Paume in Paris and in the British Museum. He was awarded an Olympic Silver Medal for drawing at an International Art Competition in Los Angeles in 1932. If he had concentrated on his serious work, he might be in college textbooks today. If he had concentrated on *Skippy*, he might have lived to a richer and more comfortable old age. If he had concentrated on his writing, he might have ended his days as a dignified and recognized author. Crosby evokes respect and admiration almost automatically. He spread his vast talents over a vast range of self-expression. Between 1919 and 1938 he wrote fourteen books and countless pamphlets. This was a large output for a man who was painting furiously at the same time and keeping up with a commercial comic strip. (Among the books were, of course, several Skippys; *Dear Sooky; Sports Drawings;* and, in the political area, where Crosby's opinions were vehement, *Three Cheers for the Red, Red and Red,* 1936, an essay on Roosevelt's second inaugural address, 1937, and *Would Communism Work Out in America?* 1938.)

He now lives quietly, in poor health, writing occasional poetry, as obvious an example of burning one's self out as we have in the whole of cartooning. He is thought of with affection and laughter; if he had been less intense, less fiery, he might still be working actively.

An early and great *Skippy* by PERCY CROSBY in 1925. Copyrighted by Percy Crosby.

A superb *Skippy* by PERCY CROSBY from 1934. Copyrighted by Percy Crosby.

Pessimists had predicted that once women got the vote, they would take everything else. During the war women had fearlessly manned coffee-and-doughnut centers; after the war, skirts were shorter, language was looser and now and then a woman was seen to be smoking in the street. Amid so general a collapse of all civilized values, it was inevitable that young ladies should go out to seek jobs, particularly in the big cities. A new layer of society was forming: the American working girl had come into existence. She was not a factory hand or a sweatshop laborer; she was a secretary, a reporter, a fashion designer. Whatever she was, she had a life of her own, and it was inevitable that she would appear in comic strips.

The first of these white-collar heroines was Martin Michael Branner's *Winnie Winkle*, who has been with us since the early months of 1920. Winnie's family must be described as lower-middle-class, and barely that. Her struggle, from the very beginning, was to achieve some sort of genteel security for herself, her warmhearted mother and her shiftless, though harmless, father. Winnie was, as Martin Sheridan points out, not only the first career girl in comics, but the first to use contemporary fashions to attract female readers.

Winnie had a brother named Perry, and for some time during the forties Perry and his pals stole the strip— particularly the Sunday page— from Winnie. The most memorable of Branner's creations was Denny Dim-

Another great *Skippy* by PERCY CROSBY, from 1935. Copyrighted by Percy Crosby.

Winnie Winkle by MARTIN BRANNER, 1928. Winnie has changed much since then, but is still highly attractive to enterprising men. © the Chicago *Tribune*– New York *News* Syndicate, Inc.

A Sunday *Winnie Winkle* of 1948, featuring Denny Dimwit. Homely and simple, Denny nevertheless managed to win through most of the time. © 1948 the Chicago *Tribune*– New York *News* Syndicate, Inc.

wit, one of Perry's friends, who became a celebrity in the comics world during the forties. Denny was not bright, to say the least, and he was miserably poor, but he had a heart of gold. He wore a coat at least twelve sizes too large, and a pointed green hat, much like a dunce cap; the reader was quite sure that it was a perfect fit for his head. For a long time Denny was the butt of his friends' minor Machiavellian sadisms; but the tables were turned shortly. Denny's basic goodness was indestructible and incorruptible; he was a kind of terrified, stammering, stubborn hero. Here Branner had run across one of the paradoxes of the comic strip. The strip itself must be built around a recognizable type, to give the reader instant orientation in this world of fantasy. Winnie Winkle is such a type. But a type can be confining, and it is often in a subsidiary character that the cartoonist finds scope for his originality. We saw it with Guggenheim in *The Nebbs,* with some of the fairy-tale figures in *Little Orphan Annie,* with the Plushbottoms in *Moon Mullins,* even with the cat in *Polly and Her Pals.*

Branner's private life sounds closer to romantic fiction than does his comic strip. Back in 1905 he was an assistant to two men who booked vaudeville acts. Branner himself was a hoofer, and when he was eighteen he teamed up with Edith Fabrini, who was fifteen, in a dance act. They fell in love in a matter of minutes. He called upon her a few days later, proposed rather awkwardly and was accepted. The couple gave a loitering youngster a quarter to watch Edith's younger sister, went downtown, and were married. (No certificates or consents were required in those days.)

Their troubles began immediately. Neither had a job; both families tried to have the marriage annulled. But the Branners were in love, and stayed married. They worked up an act and found bookings. After years of devastating poverty, they clicked, and by 1914 they were drawing four hundred dollars a week. Branner joined the army when we entered the war; after the Armistice the two picked up where they had left off.

But Branner had been sketching and cartooning for years, in his spare time, and in 1919 he sold the Bell Syndicate a Sunday feature called *Looie the Lawyer,* and then he did a Sunday page for the New York *Sun* and *Herald* called *Pete and Pinto.* The Chicago *Tribune*–New York *News* Syndicate spotted him, liked his work and offered him a contract in the spring of 1920. (McCormick and Patterson again!) Branner signed.

Winnie Winkle was the result. At first a gag strip, it rapidly became a continuing story. Its following is large and devoted; Branner's "protest mail" comes seldom, because he makes few errors, but it comes in large batches. (Now and then he pulls a boner purposely, to see how readership is standing up.) In later years Winnie's husband, Will, has been missing; she is a pseudo-widow, still the focal character in the strip, and Will's disappearance has set up any number of plot possibilities. Periodically he is reported alive, and Winnie drops everything to find him— and fails.

Career girl plus paw 'n' maw plus kids plus soap opera equal close to forty years of continuing success.

Russ Westover's *Tillie the Toiler* was the second to appear; Westover conceived the strip in 1920, and it first appeared in January 1921. Tillie was in her early twenties, a slim, wide-eyed, curly-haired beauty; she has changed, in almost forty years, only as fashions changed in clothes and hair styling. Like her living counterparts, she had a boss (Mr. Simpkins, proprietor of a fashion salon) and a boy friend (Clarence MacDougall, or Mac). Mac is in many ways more interesting than Tillie. Possibly four feet six inches tall, he has a bank of hair much like wheat in the wind, a nose like a potato dumpling and irisless eyes. He is the perennial loser, the sum of all frustrations. For four decades he has sought Tillie's hand in marriage, brought gifts, extricated her from situations created by her own whimsical foolishness. But Mac is the persistent, romantic optimist; when he has a lonely dinner in his bachelor quarters, he sets two places at table.

Tillie did much to reassure an essentially post-Victorian world. Her boss was not an unreliable lecher; her boy friend was a gentleman of rare gallantry; her scrapes and difficulties were hardly harrowing. It was all good clean fun, and perhaps young ladies could, after all, go to work in the big city without fearing damnation. (Later strips, in the forties and fifties, might take the same girl and examine her life realistically; but by that time we were living in another world, and traumata were commonplace.)

Westover was born in Los Angeles, and managed to lose several jobs by sketching during work hours before he finally landed on the San Francisco *Bulletin*, about a year after Tad Dorgan had left for New York. He shifted to the *Chronicle*, then to the *Post*. He did political cartoons, caricatures and a sports strip called *Daffy Dan*. In 1913 the *Post* folded, and he headed for New York, where he drew *Betty* and *Fat Chance*. When the *Herald* merged with the *Tribune* in 1919, Westover was lopped away; a year later he had a contract with King Features for *Tillie*.

Tillie the Toiler, by RUSS WESTOVER in 1932. © King Features Syndicate, Inc.

The finale for Tillie and Mac: after decades of courtship, the inevitable plans. Drawn by BOB GUSTAFSON; © 1959 King Features Syndicate, Inc.

Tillie's impact on the world was considerable. She was, in almost a literal sense, a fashion plate, and Westover was kept busy by annual changes in skirt length and "line." Tillie's fans demanded patterns, and a service was established for them. Her only defection from the world of *haute couture* was during the late war, when she served in the WAC for over two years. Like several other comic-strip heroines (and heroes), she was tapped by Hollywood, this in 1927, and a feature film was produced about her innocent adventures. In 1959, after thirty-eight years, the strip came to an end. (Its style had changed, becoming prettier but less distinctive.) Fittingly enough, its last few panels showed Mac proposing to Tillie once more, and this time being accepted. We may never see them again; good luck to the happy couple!

Ella Cinders, who came along in 1925, was, naturally, a twist on the old fairy tale. Ma Cinders, her stepmother, is the villain of the piece; only Pa and brother Blackie offer comfort and human kindness. Ella is married (to a man named Patches), but the three men are rarely present at one time, and Ella's battles against Ma— and of course against the brutality and hypocrisy which Ma represents— are usually compounded of two

A properly sentimental *Ella Cinders* of 1930, with a touch of the poet added by Blackie. © United Feature Syndicate, Inc.

parts heartache, one part sweetness and one part disappointment, with here and there a pinch of hope. Artist Charlie Plumb has a sharp, somewhat detailed style, and his faces are conventionalized: Ella, for example, has exactly five lashes on each eye. Bill Conselman, later a scenarist and play-wright, did the continuity for years; when he died, his assistant (and Plumb's), Fred Fox, took over the story line.

For many, *Betty*, which ran for years in the New York *Herald Tribune*, remains the most glamorous of the "girl" strips. Russ Westover drew *Betty* back during the First World War, but Westover's great achievements lay ahead of him, with *Tillie the Toiler*. The man who gave Betty her glamour was Charles A. Voight, a native New Yorker. He had begun his career with the New York *Evening World* in 1901, and eventually became

Cʜᴀʀʟᴇs A. Vᴏɪɢʜᴛ's famous *Betty*, with swain Lester de Pester. These are the first three panels of a Sunday page. © 1938 New York Herald Tribune, Inc., reproduced with permission.

sports cartoonist there; he went on to the Boston *Traveler*, where he created *Petey Dink*, a comic strip, in 1908. After periods on the New York *Evening Mail* and the Chicago *Post*, he signed a long-term contract with the New York *Herald Tribune* Syndicate and settled down with *Betty*.

Voight was primarily an illustrator; he had successful flings in advertising art and in magazine illustration. His men and women— with the important exception of Lester DePester, Betty's faithful, frustrated suitor— are tall, vigorous and beautiful. It was their beauty and Voight's feeling for composition that made the strip a pleasure to read. The gags were undistinguished, but sufficient justification for the illustrations. And, as might be expected, it was Lester DePester who shone forth as the one touch of humor and pathos. Like *Tillie's* Mac, Lester was short, funny-looking and inept. He had a parrot's nose, an infinitesimal chin and eyes that looked like spectacles, or vice versa. But without him there was no gag.

VOIGHT's earlier creation, *Petey*, this one dated June 27, 1921. © 1921, 1949
New York Herald Tribune, Inc., reproduced with permission.

The setting was contemporary, and so were the clothes and the language.
The drawing was distinguished.

Also beautiful, but drawn very differently, was Edgar Martin's *Boots*.
Here was a rounded, plumpish wench, totally sweet and innocent, but with
an interesting figure and a perfect baby-doll face. She was launched in
1924, and has undergone several transformations. Originally a naïve
mandolin strummer of roughly college age, she became successively a
modest flapper, an independent woman of the modern world, a wife and a
mother. (The transitions, during which she aged perhaps five years, took
place over two decades.) Boots was probably the most frankly feminine of
the girls of the twenties, compounded entirely of graceful curves, with an
occasional sly assist from Martin in the form of quiet highlights on the
rump. Not blatantly sexy, she was nevertheless more a glamour girl than
her contemporaries. She lived with a gently humorous, slightly crotchety
professor, Stephen Tutt, and his wife Cora, who were also attractive in

A recent *Boots* by EDGAR MARTIN. All grown up and settled down now, Boots and
husband Rod have time to supervise the love life of others. © 1959 NEA Service,
Inc., reprinted by permission of NEA Service, Inc.

another way, and who were the perfect background for her: steady, calm, reliable, where she was giddy. Martin's use of dialogue, as Waugh noted, was highly colloquial, and he reproduced the slurs and elisions of American speech carefully. A couple of subsidiary characters, Babe and Horace, were eventually successful enough to deserve a strip of their own. Horace has a button nose, round eyes and a baby mouth; he is the perennial sophomore. Babe is that rarity among comic-strip heroines, a stout girl with a voracious appetite. The two counterpoint each other perfectly, and the reader feels justified in laughing at them. They are healthy and unglamorous, true low-comedy characters.

Paul Robinson, who created *Etta Kett* in 1925, had been an animator with the Bray Studios after the First World War, and helped turn out the

A daily *Etta Kett* from 1950. Detail is absent from the faces, very much present in the clothes. © King Features Syndicate, Inc.

first animated cartoon in color, in 1920. He stayed in animation until 1925, when he originated a strip designed to pass along helpful hints in etiquette. As such, it had limited appeal and a limited future, but Robinson, an excellent draftsman, soon found that readers were calling for more of his pretty girls. He uses a fine, meticulous line with carefully spotted patches of black, and there is generally at least one area of fine detail: a man's jacket with the herringbone clearly drawn, or a print dress complete to the last whorl. Robinson has never believed in "flaming youth," and his rather blandly good-looking young people cavort in total innocence.

The only species so far missing from this gallery of girls is the poor little rich girl, and it was in the New York *World*, in 1922, that she made her debut. Her name was Fritzi Ritz, and money was no problem, though practically everything else was. Fritzi was a tall, doll-faced, gracefully formed creature. She had been named by Meyer Marcus, comics editor of the *World*, and a man named Larry Whittington drew her. *Fritzi Ritz* was a gag strip, with continuity of setting only, and the gags were higher-bracket gags than those we associate with *Tillie the Toiler* or *Winnie*

81

Fritzi Ritz, the heroine of ERNIE BUSHMILLER's earlier comics, who has now yielded the spotlight to her niece, Nancy. © 1958 United Feature Syndicate, Inc.

Fritzi's ever-devoted beau, Phil, a constant suitor, eternally frustrated. © 1958 United Feature Syndicate, Inc.

Winkle. Fritzi was soon seen in a Hollywood setting, for example, among putteed, bespectacled studio executives. The gags, against this background, could range from the purchase of roadsters to the niceties of Klieg-light courtship.

But Fritzi's true fame was yet to come. The agent of that fame was a kid from New York named Ernie Bushmiller, who was doing odd jobs at the drawing board when Whittington created Fritzi. Bushmiller, whose father had done funny chalk-talks at Tony Pastor's in the 1890s, had always felt the attraction of cartooning, or at least of drawing. When he was fourteen he answered two advertisements in the *World*, one seeking an office boy for the newspaper itself and the other seeking same for the Cunard Lines. He was accepted by both employers, and chose the *World*.

Likable and extroverted, Bushmiller soon promoted himself into the position of sweeper for the art department, at that time the traditional first step on the ladder. What his employers did not know was that he was not counting on an ill-defined professional osmosis, but was out taking art lessons at the National Academy of Design several nights a week. He was also prepared for free-lance work of all sorts, and recalls that one of his early assignments was laying out the squares for Simon and Schuster's first books of crossword puzzles. ("It did nothing for my sense of perspective," he recalls with solemn dignity, "but it gave me a lasting familiarity with the T-square.") When he was sixteen he did the art work for a Sunday-supplement feature on Houdini, entitled "Red Magic," and he performed that educational chore for two years.

In 1925, by which time he was a thoroughgoing professional, Bushmiller moved to the newly established New York *Graphic*. (A close friend of his since has been Gus Edson, who took over *The Gumps* from Sidney Smith; Edson was the second man hired by the *Graphic*.) He stayed with the *Graphic* for only three months, during which time he drew a strip called *Mac the Manager* (and during which time two columnists broke in with the *Graphic*— Walter Winchell and Ed Sullivan). Bushmiller was learning his way around, and meeting people. He had run copy, on the *World*, for Alexander Woollcott, Deems Taylor and F.P.A.; had swapped pen points with a young artist named Carl Rose; had lorded it over an office boy in short pants named Norman Krasna.

Bushmiller went back to the *World* and was given a panel to do in the Sunday sections, consisting of sophisticated comment on current events.

His next step was the decisive one. Whittington dropped *Fritzi Ritz*, and Bushmiller picked her up. (Whittington went over to Hearst, to draw the now defunct *Maisie the Model*.) Fritzi has been Ernie's girl ever since, but Bushmiller's greatest fame was still to come. We meet him again in the thirties, and after that in 1947. He is not only a true career cartoonist— having begun at the age of fourteen, in a sense— but also one of the most enduringly successful.

What F. Scott Fitzgerald was to the literature of the 1920s, a man named Russell Patterson (with John Held, Jr.) was to its fashion and décors. As an artist Patterson is not easy to place: he never drew an editorial or a sports cartoon, and his one venture into the comic strip was not conspicuously successful; yet he has been variously cartoonist, architect, landscape painter, set and costume designer (on Broadway and for Twentieth Century-Fox in Hollywood), clothes designer, and the decorator of many hotels and restaurants. The Patterson Girl was to the twenties what the Gibson Girl was to the nineties and what the Petty Girl was later to the forties; but the Patterson Girl was drawn with more verve and wit. Patterson himself has run through a couple of fortunes and is still happily at work. His living room (in an apartment building designed by Stanford White) is an atelier, and visitors are immediately aware that they are in the home of an artist at work.

Patterson was born in Omaha, but his father was a railroad lawyer and before long the family had moved to Newfoundland, then to Toronto, and then to Montreal with the Canadian Pacific. Patterson *père*, a man of solid instincts, would not pay for art courses, but would support his son in the study of architecture. The result was one year at McGill University; Patterson had to leave and go out on his own when a hotel owned by his father burned to the ground. He got a job promptly, taking ads over the counter for the Montreal *Star*. A staff artist tipped him off to an opening in the sports department with a new weekly, *The Standard*. Patterson got the job, and was fired almost immediately for turning in too much material and managing to get it printed under the noses of the editors. Patterson took his work to one of the city's French newspapers, *La Patrie*. They liked it and offered him seventeen dollars a week. As a staffer he did a strip in French called *Pierre et Pierrette*. He also did extensive sketching, because photography was still in a rudimentary stage, and the photographers themselves, being lazy and conniving, were only too happy to let Patterson do the work.

After an abortive attempt to join the Canadian Army in 1914— his father and brother went overseas with the first Canadian troops— Patterson went to Chicago, arriving with eight dollars. After months of work as a sweeper, dishwasher, and what have you, he got a job as a lettering man. He had believed that art students must be wealthy; but he found them working in cafeterias, and was happy to join them. He attended the Chicago Art Institute and at night the Fine Arts Academy. Soon he was designing houseware ads for Carson, Pirie Scott and Company and then interiors for Marshall Field; he became known as the best man in Chicago for such work. But he tired of domestic American interiors. In 1920 he packed up and went off to France, where his annual rent for a house was sixty-five dollars. He did chateâu interiors, and sold them back in Chicago, but most of his efforts went into landscape painting. Back in Chicago after a year or so, he sold a few paintings, did some strictly commercial work, and finally left for California. He was briefly marooned in the desert and was reading *This Side of Paradise* when the flapper came to him complete in all her details.

He promptly returned to Chicago and began to draw for the flappers. He was given more advertising work than he could handle. *College Humor* approached him and accepted all the drawings he could contribute, for three issues, at twenty dollars an illustration. He was off to New York then, and the serious promotion of the Jazz Age began. It would be an exaggeration to say that Patterson designed most of the clothes of that era, but it is true that he imported the raccoon coat and galoshes from Canada, where there had been a gay collegiate era from 1908 to 1912. He had sketched fashion shows in France, experience which now became very valuable. By the mid-twenties he had done at least one design which became the most popular dress in the United States; hardly a major store window was without it. By now he was appearing regularly in *Cosmopolitan*, *College Humor*, *Redbook*, *Harper's Bazaar*, the old *Life* and the *American Magazine*. His effect on styles everywhere was great. Through those magazines he reached every corner of the country, and well-dressed girls in small towns owed much of their elegance to him.

Inevitably he was called in to the theater. He did the sets and costumes for the *Ziegfeld Follies* of 1922, for the last George White's *Scandals*, and for another dozen or so Broadway shows.

The illustrator's style *par excellence:* an illustration by Russell Patterson for an article by O. O. McIntyre in 1928. Copyright 1928, The Hearst Corporation.

This was all fine during the twenties, but work was harder to find after 1929, and Patterson had almost fallen into a bad professional trap— that of identification with one style and one subject alone. But his talents had not been overlooked on the West Coast, and his second trip to California was far more successful than the first. He spend most of the thirties acclimating himself to the Hollywood atmosphere and doing set and costume design for films. (Most of the films he worked on were lavish musicals, reminiscent of his major projects on Broadway.) Soon enough Patterson was bored; he remembers thinking at the time, "I haven't any money, so I'll retire." He had made a good deal of money, of course, in the twenties and thirties, but he had never saved. Fortunately he had never invested either; he was pinked but not run through by the depression. In the late thirties he returned to New York, cut expenses to the bone, found an apartment which also served as a studio, and did only what work he wished. But the demand for him was still great, and with the return of prosperity it became greater. In 1940 I. J. Fox asked him to design that season's coats; later Macy's called, and he did Christmas-toy windows for five years. Again, he had all the advertising work he could handle. Even the war was no deterrent to him: he designed the WAC uniforms. He did the interior work on fifteen trains for the Western Pacific; he designed hotel lobbies, decorated restaurants, and in his spare time did a few Sunday pages for metropolitan newspapers, a chore he dropped in 1956.

Patterson has been sketching, drawing and painting almost incessantly since 1914. But he finds his eagerness waning now. In the twenties it was he who created styles, but he is a bit out of touch with style now and is frankly disappointed in today's trends. These days style (in all areas) is created, he feels, more by broadsides of propagandistic advertising in national magazines and large newspapers; he enjoyed his work more when styles came out of life and were created by small groups of people who set the pace.

Patterson is another man who defies classification. He is an extremely handsome, personable and intelligent man, none of which did him any harm in his various careers. He is probably the only artist in this history who drew comic strips in two languages— *Pierre et Pierrette*, and then, much later, *Mamie*, for United Features Syndicate— and yet he is certainly not primarily a comic-strip artist. He is not primarily a comic artist at all; but he is a great illustrator, and his style has been imitated by more currently successful comic artists than would like to admit it. And he has the one indispensable quality for real creativity: no one knows what he will come up with next.

One strip of the period which became a favorite with the comic-strip artists themselves— and still is, in memory— was Harry Tuthill's *The Bungle Family*. George Bungle was its hero, a good fellow a bit sour on

"Don't you simply loathe the thought of being just another housewife again?"

PATTERSON's beauties facing demobilization. © 1945 King Features Syndicate, Inc.

life who had constant difficulty with women of all kinds. Whatever his intentions, his actions embroiled him with female members of the family who simply refused to understand him. In a way he was an advance guard in what later became James Thurber's war between men and women, and Tuthill invested the strip with a wry, almost bitter mood. Tuthill himself was a strange one, a St. Louis boy who did editorial cartoons locally, and who sent his strip idea to Virgil McNitt (of McNaught, naturally) in 1918. His original title was *Home Sweet Home*, but it was quickly changed to *The Bungle Family*. ("Bungle" was of course appropriate. George, the hero, was a thorough bungler.) The strip ran for twenty years; a cult grew up around it; and Tuthill himself became fairly well-known. He represented himself as a backward western boy, with a constant air of bewilderment (he invariably wore white socks with a dinner jacket), but he was actually quick of mind and drily satirical. When he had a disagreement with his syndicate, in 1939, he simply quit, and returned to Ferguson, Missouri, where he lived quietly until his death a few years ago.

So much for the families; so much for the girls; so much for the kids. There was little in the way of "true adventure" in the twenties— the thirties would see much more— but there was another area of comic-strip work, directly descended from the free-and-easy early days, which audiences found hilarious and newspapers found indispensable. It was the area of fantasy, satire and parody, and the twenties produced three classic examples: *Popeye, Barney Google* and *Krazy Kat*. It has been suggested— often, and possibly with some truth— that these three strips appealed to readers in an ascending order of intelligence. There is room for doubt. True, *Popeye* was always the most simply drawn, *Krazy Kat* the most complex, with *Barney Google* somewhere in between. But to establish hierarchies is to assume an order of excellence that may not correspond to human reactions. *Popeye* is fantasy and action, *Barney Google* is fantasy and satire, *Krazy Kat* is fantasy and poetry. Readers needed all three.

Oddly enough, *Popeye* was not *Popeye* until almost the end of the decade; the character himself properly belongs in the 1930s. But the background against which he came to life— *Thimble Theatre*— had been running since 1919. Elzie Crisler Segar, the creator of *Thimble Theatre*, had come out of Illinois via the traditional series of vocational flings— he was an accredited motion-picture projectionist, a house painter, a wallpaperer, a window dresser, a snare-drummer, a photographer. The story goes that he took careful note of the salaries earned by successful cartoonists and decided to be exactly that. He drew a cartoon immediately and sent it to the St. Louis *Post-Dispatch*, reminding the management that he had an uncle who worked in their pressroom. The cartoon was nevertheless returned, and Segar sent off twenty dollars for a correspondence course in cartooning. In eighteen months he was granted a diploma; he went directly to Chicago, where Richard F. Outcault, who had dropped

THE THIMBLE THEATRE
Now Showing— "The Obliging Angler."
To-morrow— "Some Baby."

A good sample of the pre-Popeye *Thimble Theatre*, this one starring Castor Oyl. Drawn, of course, by ELZIE SEGAR, in 1920. © King Features Syndicate, Inc.

The Yellow Kid and was doing even better with *Buster Brown*, got him a job on the *Herald*, doing *Charlie Chaplin's Comic Capers* daily and Sunday. (A good many artists, budding or established, worked on this strip over the years. It was good practice, and not difficult; the character was

87

ready-made, established, instantly recognizable. Ed Carey and Gus Mager were two others who did it at one time or another.) But by 1917 the *Herald* folded; Segar was lucky enough to find a job with the Chicago *American.* After two years of staff work he went to New York, presented his proposed *Thimble Theatre* to King Features and was given a contract.

Thimble Theatre was a maverick among comic strips. There was little action (unlike, for example, Ed Wheeler's *Minute Movies,* of which derring-do was the basis), and the gags were only dubiously original. Every day its cast acted out a one-scene play. It was funny because the drawing was funny. Its characters were ludicrous, and perhaps it was the well-worn gag issuing from such original caricatures that made the strip viable.

It was not an instant success. As Waugh noted, it did not appear on Fridays (in Hearst's *Evening Journal)* and when there was heavy department-store advertising *Thimble Theatre* was lopped off.

The Oyl family supplied the strip with most of its heroes and heroines. Olive Oyl and Ham Gravy provided love interest, and occupied the center of the stage for the first few years. Olive consisted of a loop (her head), a dot (her nose) and a squiggle of hair. Ham was a banana-nosed scribble. (Segar played variations on the schnozzola for years: "Is that your nose or are you eating a cucumber?") Castor Oyl, Olive's brother, was the first addition; he was nasty and stupid—but in his stupidity lay all the resources of the direct, primitive mind. Olive's father was Cole Oyl; her mother, simply Ma for many years, proved to be Nana Oyl.

A first step toward continuity, rather than the daily gag, was Blizzard's arrival. He was a gamecock, and his adventures carried the story for eighteen months or so; he was then fricasseed. By now we were in the late twenties, and when Bernice, the whiffle hen, arrived, the stage was set for Popeye. (The theatrical metaphors are not misplaced. In the early twenties an experimental theater opened in New York's Greenwich Village. It was called the Thimble Theatre. Segar was having his first effects on American culture.) Bernice contained a reservoir of good luck, but only a gambler named Fadewell knew how to tap it. (Fadewell was running a casino on Dice Island.) Castor solved the problem, finally, discovering that if he

A fighting Popeye by ELZIE SEGAR. No spinach in evidence, but none may be needed. © King Features Syndicate, Inc.

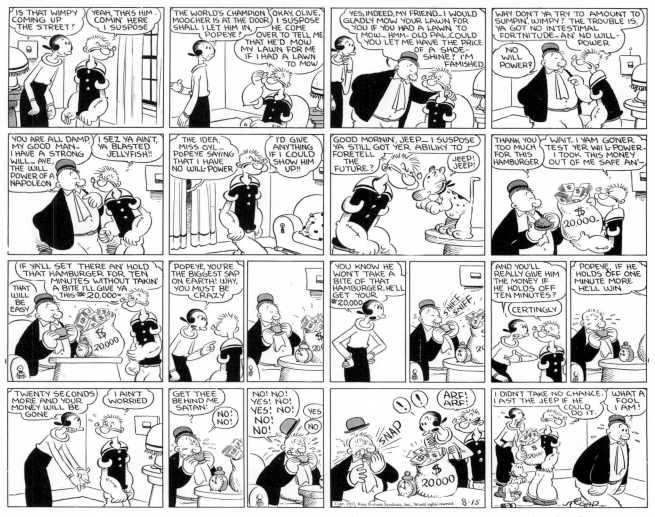

A *Popeye* Sunday page. J. Wellington Wimpy's passion for hamburgers was almost as well known as Popeye's for spinach. © 1937 King Features Syndicate, Inc.

rubbed the three hairs on Bernice's head, she would bring him luck. He did so, wishing for $10,000; shortly he had it, and had escaped with Bernice. His object: to buy a ship, sail to Dice Island and clean up at the tables. He bought his ship ("with not a hole in her," her owner said, "except in the bottom, where they don't show") and alerted Olive and Ham, who prepared for the trip. At the last moment— they were already aboard— it occurred to them that they knew nothing about sailing. Castor strode out on the dock, saw a bell-bottomed, one-eyed sailor smoking a corncob pipe and asked, "Hey there! Are you a sailor?" It was January of 1929; Popeye's first words were his answer: " 'Ja think I'm a cowboy?"

From then on, two themes shaped the strip. One was the affection, at first dubious, between Popeye and Olive Oyl. The other was Popeye as gladiator— the first serious fighting man in the comics, although "serious" is surely the wrong word. Popeye was a vastly distorted personification of

A backwoodsy *Barney Google* of 1937, by BILLY DeBECK. The city slicker outslicks himself. The last long panel is fine for both depth-of-field and humorous pathos. © King Features Syndicate, Inc.

an eternal popular hero— himself good, generous and affectionate, he was devastation incarnate when challenged by evil. He owed his unlimited strength to spinach— a popular touch, almost a household hint. His English was atrocious (he once tried to use the word atrocious, later on, and failed utterly to pronounce it), his face ugly, his forearms like watermelons attached to his shoulders by pipe cleaners. But he was the defender of the weak, a nautical Lancelot, and whether or not he restored manhood to the comics pages, he supplied justifiable mayhem in large quantities.

Popeye figures are, to the thoughtful, symbols of a nostalgia for the free, conscienceless exercise of force. *Superman*, a later phenomenon, has been much criticized for this, and we have already discussed *Orphan Annie's* Daddy Warbucks. But Popeye was saved from all such pessimistic exegesis by his total unreality. Where Superman is made semi-real by pseudo-scientific hokum about the planet Krypton, Popeye is just plain impossible. Riddled with bullets (like Al Capp's later Fearless Fosdick), he rises, merely annoyed; attacked by dozens of snarling felons, he dispatches them in a whirlwind of fists. If he appeals to a love of violence, he does it with innocence, and he appeals just as much to the love of burlesque, exaggeration and slapstick.

He has starred in any number of Max Fleischer animated cartoons; his song is nationally famous and constantly parodied; his penchant for spinach has eradicated leguminous prejudice from the breasts of millions of laughing children. Dolls, cutouts, cakes of soap have reproduced him for the home; thanks to him, and possibly to General MacArthur, the corncob pipe has been sporadically fashionable. At one time he appeared in over six hundred newspapers, which is spectacular. And his popularity has brought to life any number of minor characters, like Wimpy— J. Wellington Wimpy, devourer of hamburgers, shiftless coward and confirmed con man— or Rough-House, the short-order cook, or that horrendous creation Alice the Goon, about whom mothers wrote that she was very funny but that their children were having nightmares.

Segar died in 1938. He was mourned as Popeye's creator, and his professional success naturally obscured the fact that he was a kindhearted, generous, much-loved man whose colleagues accorded him great affection and total respect. He had lived to see a monument erected to Popeye, in Crystal City, Texas, heart of the spinach region; and he must have been pleased that when Mussolini banned all comic strips in Italy, public opinion forced the exception of Popeye. Later the old swab was a central figure in U.S. Navy recruiting posters (this time drawn by Joe Musial, who is now King Features' educational director, and who draws *The Captain and the Kids*). Beginning in 1939 *Popeye* was written by Tom Sims and drawn by Bela Zaboly. Since then Zaboly, Ralph Stein and Bud Sagendorf have continued the work. The strip has lost none of its fantasy or vitality in their hands, and one more generation will grow up around Popeye, one of the funniest, ugliest and least grammatical of all American heroes.

Barney Google was something else again: realer— at least in the beginning when he was of more normal height than later— and the occupant of much more plausible predicaments. Whether or not he was easier to identify with than Popeye is moot; but the jams he found himself in were of this world, and bore at least a vaguely generic relationship to the troubles that any of us might find ourselves in at any moment. Barney Google was a man who had great difficulty paying his rent, keeping a job, accumulating prestige or establishing himself as any kind of serious, responsible citizen. His adventures were those of the fool, the dupe, the pawn of society.

A *Barney Google* of 1931, with Sparky semi-nude. Barney is worried because an International Derby is coming up. © King Features Syndicate, Inc.

He looked the part, and more so as his height diminished. He had huge saucer eyes, capable of a wide range of emotion in themselves; a potato-dumpling nose, the coloration of which could express anything from flat calm to absolute fury; and his speech, which was profuse, emerged invariably from one or the other side of his mouth, which was no more nor less than a black hole peeping out from behind a mustache. His reactions — chiefly irritation— were what ours would have been in the same situation; he had a great talent for evoking sympathetic indignation.

But all the sympathy he evoked during the three years after the strip's start in 1919 was as nothing compared to the delighted waves of laughter he called forth beginning in 1922 when a horse named Sparkplug came upon the scene. Sparky was to horses what Barney was to people; even the manner of his acquisition was fortuitous and grotesque. Barney, standing outside a saloon, found himself perfectly positioned to break the fall of a person who had been violently ejected. In an access of generosity, the lucky ejectee presented Barney with the finest two-year-old in his stable— Sparky. Sparky too had large eyes; he had a head like an oversized baloney; his body was usually draped in a checked blanket, every bit large enough and flamboyant enough to justify the contemptuous remarks which have been made for decades about horse blankets. (Now and then Sparky was momentarily divested of the blanket. His embarrassment at those times was unbearably acute; the moments were few. Friendly critics will be forgiven for observing that a horse in an ankle-length checked blanket, buttoning down the front, is a good deal easier to draw than a naked steed, and is a far more effective trade-mark.)

Well, who created these two sterling Americans? His name was Billy DeBeck; he was a small man, and he liked to wear a beret. He was born in 1890, and before he was eighteen he had enrolled at the Chicago Institute of Fine Arts. He lasted less than a year; his proclivities were more comic than classic. In 1908 he took a job as a staff artist with the Chicago *Daily News*, but soon afterward his traveling began. From 1912 to 1916 he did editorial cartoons for the Pittsburgh *Gazette Times* and *Chronicle Telegraph*; during 1916–17 he did comic art for the Chicago *Herald*; and in 1918 he made the most momentous decision he had yet faced, and joined Hearst's organization. He did not begin immediately producing *Barney Google*. He had been hired on the basis of a panel called *Married Life*, which had nothing to do with bulbous little men or sentimental race horses. But in that same year, 1918, he brought in his first samples of *Barney Google*. The strip was accepted immediately and began appearing before the year was out.

Sparky enabled DeBeck to achieve a transformation in *Barney Google*. Oddly enough— almost incredibly— Sparky won a horse race, the first in which he had ever run. One consequence of Barney's resultant affluence was the appearance of a silk hat which was for years afterward his trademark. Another consequence was one of the classic love stories in American comics: Barney Google's pursuit of "Sweet Mamma." Sweet Mamma was DeBeck's third great popular creation, and there were more to come. Trying to explain the origin of her name, he once confessed that it had simply come to him, and that he had had many doubts about continuing to use it, particularly when a large segment of the public seemed to be protesting. He persisted, however, and she, like Barney, like Sparky, like half a dozen of DeBeck's phrases, became a part of the English language. Incidentally, DeBeck was a considerable phrase-maker. Among the most memorable of his additions to the language are "the heebie-jeebies," "so he took the fifty thousand dollars" and "Osky-wow-wow." Much later (probably with Fred Lasswell's help) he outdid himself with, for example, "taitched in the haid," "shifless skonk," "jughaid" and, during the Second World War, "yard bird," which received the widest currency of all.

But these last phrases arrived only with the advent of Snuffy Smith and company, in 1934. Before that time, DeBeck had added to the strip an ostrich named Rudy, who kept Barney in perpetual trouble, but who loved him so deeply that no revenge was ever possible. There was also Sully, the world's champion wrestler. Sully was a strong man, unbelievably strong, but his intelligence was in inverse proportion to his strength. Barney was much more than his manager. Barney was father, banker, big brother, con-

Barney Google two days later. DeBeck could let his imagination run wild. This is a fine parody of countless sports panels. © 1931 King Features Syndicate, Inc.

fidant. When a crisis rose and both Barney and Sully had to leave town for a short period of time, they chose to go south; there they met Snuffy Smith, and a new epoch began in comic-strip history.

Snuffy, his wife Lowizie, and their enormously popular nephew, Jughaid, were hillbillies of the purer variety. They were no realer than Al Capp's Yokums, but their dedication to illicit moonshine whisky and their general belligerence brought them much closer to the archetypical idea of the American hillbilly. Physically, Snuffy was not too different from Barney. He was short; his eyes were flexible dots, rather than saucers; but he had the same huge nose, with the same capacities for variety in the discoloration. He wore a huge, flopping, wide-brimmed black hat. His nephew, Jughaid, on the other hand, while diminutive, had a fairly normal comic-strip boy's face, and was chiefly distinguished by the fact that he wore a coonskin hat. To Snuffy and family, the great enemy was the "Revenooer," and their war against the United States is a comic-strip epic. Where Barney had defeated the world's nefarious plots through solidarity with Sparky or Rudy or Sully, the Smiths held their own through an intense family solidarity, one which extended to certain cousins, though it was denied others.

DeBeck, meanwhile, had been having troubles with life. For some time during his career with King Features the comics editor was a man named Rudolph Block. Block was not too well liked by cartoonists, chiefly because he had a rather authoritarian personality and treated cartoonists in a condescending, superior manner. DeBeck was afraid of him— not physically, of course, but professionally. Yet DeBeck needed discipline; his work habits were entirely anarchic. Block used to take DeBeck on trips and lock him up to get his work done. This persecution decreased as Block slowly lost his influence, and ceased when DeBeck moved to Belle Isle, Florida. DeBeck was an inveterate golfer, and it is probably more accurate to say that he moved south for the golfing opportunities than to say that he was escaping Block. (At least once his golf betrayed him. He shot in the low 80s and high 70s, and one day he ran across a gambler in a Florida locker room, the quiet, nerveless type. A match for $500 was proposed. DeBeck, who had seen the gambler play, knew that he himself was much better. An innocent bystander named Rube Goldberg was so confident of the outcome that he took half the bet. The gambler turned out to be so gentlemanly, so gracious, so urbane, so unbearably polite, that DeBeck became totally unnerved and blew the match sky high.)

DeBeck loved drawing and spent a good deal of his time outdoors sketching whatever was available. Now and then he turned out a watercolor. With his love of golf and leisure, it was inevitable that he would have a trusted assistant. This assistant was named Fred Lasswell. Lasswell began with DeBeck in Florida at an early age indeed. A very talented man in his own right, he may, for the purposes of *Barney Google* and *Snuffy*

Smith, be said to have been brought up artistically by DeBeck. The two men together were responsible for one of the more hilarious periods in the lives of their two truncated heroes, that of World War II. The desperate efforts of Barney and Snuffy to enter the armed forces of the United States and their ultimate success (Barney in the Navy, Snuffy in the Army) are one of the most mirthful chapters in the entire story.

DeBeck was an erratic man who never had been able to handle money properly and often had difficulty getting his work out on time. But he married a rather wonderful woman, Mary, who was the stabilizing influence in his life. Toward the end of his life he was quite sick and required several operations. There is no question of Mary DeBeck's helpful devotion to him; no doubt that he lived longer and was able to work longer because of her love and ministrations. He died in 1942. In 1947, when the National Cartoonists Society established an award for cartoonist of the year, it was known as the Billy DeBeck Award and was presented every year under the aegis of Mary DeBeck: it was a silver cigarette box, with DeBeck's characters etched on the cover. At Mrs. DeBeck's death in 1952 the award was retitled and became simply the National Cartoonists Society Award, nicknamed the "Reuben"; it was a statuette designed by Rube Goldberg and wrought by William Crawford of the Newark *News.*

Barney Google and Snuffy Smith were left in good hands. Fred Lasswell had been with them for most of his life, was an accomplished artist and had absorbed DeBeck's particular attitude toward his creations. The strip has lost none of its popularity or vitality; it remains original, slightly grotesque, unashamedly fantastic in spots and invariably funny. From the time when Billy Rose wrote a song called "Barney Google with the Goo-Goo-Googly Eyes" to the present, the antics of these characters have brought explosive guffaws from a large, faithful, grateful following. It will probably be with us for decades to come, which is all to the good.

George Herriman's *Krazy Kat,* the third corner of this fantastic triangle, will come up for discussion later; at the moment the ubiquitous shadow of Rube Goldberg looms once more upon the horizon.

After his initial successes in New York, Goldberg, essentially a conservative man, could never have been called financially insecure. Yet the man's one worry, throughout his life, seems to have been that a day would pass when no work was required of him. In casting about for reserves of labor into which he might dig on a possible unemployed afternoon, he hit upon the literary field. He had already had some experience of books: *Foolish Questions* came out in book form in 1909, and since then there had been *Chasing the Blues* and *Books Abroad.* In 1929 he produced *Is There a Doctor in the House?* which is still famous.

He seemed to like this kind of work. Even as Boob McNutt toiled against a malign fate, Goldberg was discovering the popular magazine, and was discovering too that there was a demand for his work there— literary as well as graphic. Between 1928 and 1935 we are treated to a rather ostentatious display of talent, including: *Saturday Evening Post,* December 15, 1928, an article called "Comics, New Style and Old"; *Photoplay,* December 1930, an article called "Rube Goldberg's First Picture," which was about Hollywood; in the *Post* again, 1932 this time, "What Do I Know after Forty"(!); and in 1935, in rapid succession, a short story in *American Magazine* called "Read 'em and Weep" and an article in *Good Housekeeping* called "Buffet Supper" (many of these were illustrated by the author, of course). This is hardly a complete list; for a time it seemed impossible to buy a popular magazine without running into this bewildering output. During this period he rather neglected comics, doing very little work in the field; on the other hand, he did the scenario for a Marx Brothers movie called *Soup to Nuts* which is an acknowledged comic classic.

Goldberg's way of life was by now very close to ideal. In 1916 he had married Irma Seeman, and even his marriage produced an anecdote. Miss Seeman's father controlled the White Rose grocery empire; upon being introduced to Goldberg, he stated flatly that he had never heard of the man's cartoons. Goldberg replied quite innocently that he had never heard of Mr. Seeman's groceries.

By the time the twenties rolled around, the Goldbergs had two sons, Thomas and George, who were certainly brought up to be blasé about celebrities. The Goldbergs had a large house on west Seventy-fifth Street in New York when the children were small; they had servants, and they threw huge parties. They went so far as to buy the house next door, and when the parties were big enough they simply moved the furniture to the other house. Visiting around was a very free process in those days; a really good New Year's Eve party might boast the presence, at one time or another during the evening, of two or three hundred public figures. Charlie Chaplin once came up, found the children in their cribs and acted a brief scene for them. The boys had laid out a miniature golf course in the house and they hawked games at ten cents apiece to Goldberg's guests, among whom might be counted Fannie Brice, William Gaxton, Buddy DeSilva or Jimmy Walker. This being a creative household, there was naturally a house newspaper, which consisted largely of servants' gossip. It started out as one simple sheet, but somehow kept growing. Al Jolson, arriving for a bit of festivity one day, bought an advertisement for one dollar, notifying the world that there existed a singer who needed work.

This way of life ended rather abruptly in 1929, not because Goldberg had been "wiped out" or even hurt badly by the Depression, but because the general tone of life lost a good deal of its gaiety and carefree friendliness. Goldberg was still writing, and there were many who wondered if he was not lost to cartooning forever. They were in for some very pleasant surprises.

CHAPTER IV

Added Attractions

ONCE UPON A TIME there was a machine called the Phenakistoscope, invented by a Frenchman named Plateau. There was also the Daedelum, invented by an Englishman named Horner. They were, roughly, cylinders mounted on shafts, with peepholes in the cylinders, and drawings, in sequence, pasted inside; when the cylinder was rotated, the drawings simulated motion. As curiosities, these machines drew chuckles in the early nineteenth century. But in 1867 William Lincoln, an American, patented a "Wheel of Life," an improvement over the earlier versions, and in France in 1877 Emil Reynaud produced ten meters of animated drawings on a strip of transparent material. A technical advance at least as important as the invention of color presses was under way.

As usual, it was not a single invention, but a number of steps, which led to the new technique. Riffling a series of pictures to achieve continuous motion was hardly a new idea; in the sixteenth and seventeenth centuries it had been applied, naturally among the upper classes, to pornography. At the turn of the twentieth century in America flip-books were a common diversion, and the Zoetrope— which was based on the same process— was in fairly common use. To an American named J. Stuart Blackton goes the honor of having first used motion-picture film as a medium for animated drawings. One of his earliest products, created for Vitagraph in 1905, was *Humorous Phases of Funny Faces*, in which, among other action, a man rolled his eyes and blew smoke rings.

For the first successful commercial animation, we return to one of the early greats: Winsor McCay, the creator of *Little Nemo*. As was usual among cartoonists (it is still common), the decisive gathering, at which the idea jelled and a whole group of creative men was inspired, took place at a restaurant— in this case Reisenweber's, one of those venerable outposts of *Gemütlichkeit*, now gone from the scene, where sermons in steins were dispensed to eager young artists. It was in 1913; McCay was the speaker of the evening, and he demonstrated his first animated cartoon, *Gertie the Dinosaur*. Gertie was a good-natured brontosaurus; in the course of the cartoon she drank from a good-sized lake, drying it up. McCay then

Three drawings by Winsor McCay which were used as frames in his *Gertie the Dinosaur*, the first commercially successful animated cartoon. Courtesy of Paul Terry. Reprinted by permission of Winsor McCay's family.

reversed his reel, and Gertie regurgitated thousands of gallons of water, restoring the balance of nature.

Among the celebrants that evening were Robert Ripley, Rube Goldberg and a very alert young man out of San Francisco named Paul Terry. Terry had, in 1905 and 1906, shared offices with Bud Fisher on the San Francisco *Chronicle* and with Goldberg on the San Francisco *Bulletin*. All in all, he had served a ten-year apprenticeship in the newspaper business, as an artist, a cartoonist and a photographer, with occasional excursions into caricature for the drama page. He had worked all over the Far West, touching at the Portland *Oregonian* and the Anaconda *Standard*. (While at Polytech High in San Francisco he had been an usher in a vaudeville theater, which may have helped develop his fine later instinct for popular entertainment. It is one of those now banal coincidences that three of his classmates were Dorgan, Hype Igoe and Herb Roth.)

In the atmosphere of *début-de-siècle* between 1900 and 1915, anything seemed possible. There were jobs, there was industrial excitement in the air, we were relatively well insulated from the troubles of the rest of the world (either primitive or decadent) and— perhaps most important— a young, single man could support himself without yielding all his time, energy and personality to his employer or corporation. He had plenty of all three left over, and if he were blessed with intellectual or professional curiosity, he could satisfy it. Roaming about in that atmosphere, Terry reached New York, where for a few years he did car cards for the trolleys, worked on the New York *Press* and did a comic strip for Hearst. The turning point, for him, was the meeting at Reisenweber's; before it was over he knew that he had found his field.

There was freedom, and consequently satisfaction, in this unexplored area. Terry experimented at home, in a loft, wherever he could find room. From the beginning the general range of subject matter was settled: he would humanize animals, stay in the area of fantasy. He would concentrate his capacities for development and innovation in the area of technical resources and artistic techniques. His choice of animals was based on a few very simple observations: that they would not compete with live actors, who performed before cameras and were bound by a relative realism; that they offered a wide range of appearance and personality; and that people, by nature superior to them, therefore liked them.

While Terry planned and experimented, McCay had been touring with *Gertie* and added two others to his repertory, one on a mosquito and one on the sinking of the *Lusitania*. John R. Bray leaped into the field in 1913 with *Colonel Heeza Liar in Africa*. Earl Hurd, another pioneer, was successful in using a double-strip technique: a permanent background, with the action run off on a strip of celluloid that passed before it. Terry improved on that technique with his second cartoon, but his first, *Little Herman*, was put together laboriously in the old-fashioned way, with a single drawing for each slightest change in position. The celluloid (early nitrate celluloid) was highly— almost eagerly— inflammable. There were periodic fires, and Terry saw much of his early work destroyed. (Acetate celluloid later reduced this hazard.)

Terry sold *Little Herman* outright to a New York distributor, Tannhauser Films. (A good deal of the film industry was centered in New York in those days; Luben and S&A were New York firms, and Long Island City was the early Hollywood.) Tannhauser, among whose products was *The Perils of Pauline* and who had studios in New Rochelle, favored Terry with a munificent $1.35 per foot for his cartoon. Little Herman ran three hundred feet (at sixty feet per minute); Terry's first tedious months of labor had grossed him $405.

At that, it made him a tycoon. There were others in the field who earned less, but they were all contributing to what would become a major industry. (It is still expanding.) Pat Sullivan was working independently; Bud Fisher and Terry talked about doing *Mutt and Jeff*; Raoul Barry and Terry argued about the best way to register— i.e., to line up the drawings and backgrounds accurately. (Barry used pegs; Terry used overlaid crosses.) These were the first, feverish, underpaid days, and every pioneer insists that they were happy days.

The First World War, far from interrupting Terry's labors, took him into new fields. The Army had been producing instructional films, but in one area it found cameras impossible: medicine and surgery. Quick training in battlefield surgery was an imperative for a nation of peaceful general practitioners, but operations could not easily be filmed. The presence of blood, clamps, drains, assisting personnel, etc., obscured many of the important surgical steps. Terry was called in, and produced a series of animated cartoons on surgical technique (including one on obstetrics, the need for which in the trenches was never fully explained). While in Washington he met Frank Gilbreth, the pioneer in visual time-motion studies; Gilbreth's diagrams were already a kind of animation.

When the war ended, Terry was ready, a master in his field. He spent the year 1919 with Paramount, presumably learning to streamline his operation and to get along with executives. From 1920 to 1929 he did the first world-famous series of American animated cartoons: *Aesop's Fables.* Terry's primary interest was independent production and distribution, and in 1928 he took his first steps toward freedom: a firm called Audiocinema was ready to join forces with him and to give him a free hand. But in the next year American business was devastated by the crash, and Audiocinema, among many others, went out of business.

PAUL TERRY's Farmer Alfalfa, now known as Farmer Gray. © 1959 CBS Films Inc.

Terry went ahead on his own. He was not wiped out; he had capital; he had a staff; he had talent; he knew the public. Cartoons were not, as other entertainments were, a drug on the market when America became poor. Admission to the movies was still only a nickel or a dime or a quarter, and exhibitors found that children, who loved animated cartoons, would drag their parents to the theater for an evening of relatively cheap entertainment. (The exhibitors were working on the right principle, but their methods were hardly scientific. Some years they would buy fifty-two cartoons from Terry and find that they had used only twenty-six. Terry was both benevolent and shrewd: in return for signing on for another year, the exhibitor was excused from paying for the surplus.)

Throughout the thirties and forties Terrytoons were big business. In the early forties Terrytoon characters began to appear in comic books: *Mighty*

Mighty Mouse, the super-rodent, in a series of characteristic poses. Defender of the weak and oppressed, he is a favorite with kiddies. © 1959 CBS Films, Inc.

Tom Terrific and Mighty Manfred in characteristic attitudes. © 1959 CBS Films Inc.

Mouse, Heckle and Jeckle, Dinky. (Mighty Mouse is still being published.) Terry's foreign operation was extensive; his cartoons were shown all over the world, regularly. An intelligent businessman, Terry proved a boon to many foreign distributors: he was scrupulously fair, helped them often when business slumped and never called for advance guarantees. He was therefore personally liked and admired.

All in all, he made about 1,400 cartoons between 1919 and 1955, of which some 650 were Terrytoons. In 1955 he retired, having sold 600 Terrytoons to television for a price considerably above anything Tannhauser had ever offered. Mighty Mouse and Farmer Gray (or Farmer Alfalfa, as he was originally known) continue to enthrall the youngsters. In *Heckle and Jeckle* the flights of fantasy and imagination are more extreme— beautifully mangled classical references have been known to creep into the dialogue, and the resources of the drawing board have been stretched almost to the point of satire; adults, pausing to watch for a moment, have been brought up short by chases in direct parody of the Keystone Cops.

Terry never made long feature cartoons. He believes that it is difficult to sustain adult attention over a long span of time; his aim was to let the adults relax for five minutes or so, secure in the knowledge that they had not really come here to see this kid stuff, but enjoying themselves mightily all the time. Terrytoons never tried to reflect the outside world; there were no political or social morals drawn, except perhaps the occasional implication— by means of wooden mallets, explosions, knock-down-and-drag-out fights and fiendish trickery, all followed by a reconciliation— that enemies may become friends. Terry has always felt that the basis of comedy, and particularly of visual comedy, was the establishment of smugness and superiority in the audience: the cartoons have their pratfalls, their scapegoats, their eternal victims, and the adult spectator knows very well that nothing of that sort will ever happen to *him*. (Terry's respect for Walt Disney, who came along later, is extreme. Competition for audiences, which expressed itself as competition in techniques and creativity, was the soul of the industry for thirty years, and, as Terry has said, "Disney made us all hump.")

Television has broadened the market for cartoons, and Terry believes that we would be foolish to fear either saturation of the airwaves or the death of the cinema. If anything, cartoons on television will ultimately help the cinema by pointing up the vast difference in size and scope between the two media.

All this time there were others at work, of course. Thousands of drawings are required for each cartoon, and among two generations of staff artists, script writers and technicians there have been many with ideas of their own.

Heckle and Jeckle reviewing the pitchman's art in a series of poses against one background. © 1959 CBS Films Inc.

Among the many independent producers was Walter Lantz, whose *Woody Woodpecker*, inspired, so the story goes, by a raucous specimen who kept the Lantzes awake in their mountain lodge, became an enormous success with both children and adults and proved viable as a comic-strip and comic-book character. Max Fleischer was another great name in the pioneering days; certainly *Betty Boop* was as unforgettable to one generation as *Snow White* was to the next. (Miss Boop appears to have lost none of her vitality over the years, and now attracts millions of children as a television star.) In more recent times there have been many interesting productions, some of which will be discussed shortly. *Crusader Rabbit*, produced in California by Alexander Anderson, should be mentioned here for two reasons. It was the first series produced for television exclusively; and in tone, craftsmanship and imaginative surprises it is extremely reminiscent of the best of Paul Terry's experimental work, such as *Heckle and Jeckle*. *Crusader Rabbit* is now a confirmed success on television, and is probably watched by more adults than any other animated cartoon series.

We think of Walt Disney as a product of the late thirties and the forties; we forget, perhaps, that his first Mickey Mouse cartoon, *Steamboat Willie*, was released in New York in September of 1928. And it is not generally known that Disney's first animations were advertising films, which he turned out in Kansas City in 1920, when he was only nineteen. We associate him now with *Snow White*, *Dumbo*, *Fantasia*, *Davey Crockett*, and

103

the general belief is that he came along and capitalized on the work of the pioneers.

To some extent, of course, that is true; Disney's first experiments took place eleven or twelve years after McCay's, and Paul Terry was producing *Aesop's Fables* when Disney was in Kansas City. But Disney too suffered and sweated through the lean years. He sketched in his youth, and even studied at night at the Chicago Academy of Fine Arts (he is Chicago-born); but during his middle teens he was variously a "news butcher" (the boy who sold candy, peanuts, magazines on trains between Chicago and Kansas City), a letter carrier and an ambulance driver (this last in France in 1918). It was at the war's end that he took his first job in art; six months later he quit and opened his own commercial-art studio. The studio struggled along briefly, and died when Disney answered a want ad for a cartoonist's job with a slide manufacturer in Kansas City. It was then, in his spare time, that he turned out his first reels of animation. The legend goes that he worked far into the night at his own drawing board, and that a courageous mouse became his friend and confidant; Disney talked freely to him, named him Mortimer and changed the name to Mickey when their relations progressed to a less formal plane.

At any rate, Disney had an idea. He wanted to animate fairy tales. He persuaded a few young cartoonists to help him, for a share in the possible profits; the first of their efforts was *Little Red Riding Hood*. This and six others were sold to a New York distributor, who promptly went bankrupt.

After three discouraging and hectic years in the Midwest, Disney went to Hollywood. He had $40, they say, and his brother Roy had $250, and an uncle lent them $500 more. They also had a print of the last fairy tale he had animated; Disney sent it to New York, prepared for a long wait. He was surprised: a distributor wrote back shortly, asking for a series.

Working feverishly in improvised studios, Disney and his "staff" turned out their first *Alice in Cartoonland*. It made use of a technique for which Disney later became famous: the combination of cartoon and live action in the same frame. For financial and technical reasons, the technique was not used; but Alice was, and six more Alices followed. They gave Disney breathing space, time to consider his next projects. Like Paul Terry before him, Disney saw the advantages of humanizing animals, and his next series was *Oswald the Rabbit*.

Oswald was successful, and Disney might have confined himself to a new series every few years, but he was impatient and experimental. He needed money, and in his efforts to get it he broke with his New York distributors. Now he needed a new series— and a new backer, and a new chain of distribution. And now (to revert to the story) Disney remembered Mickey Mouse.

The first Mickey Mouse cartoon was silent and disappointing. Exhibitors were scarcely interested; Al Jolson had, after all, opened in *The Jazz*

Three frames from DISNEY's *Steamboat Willie,* starring Mickey Mouse. This was the first animated cartoon to use sound— it was made in 1928. © Walt Disney Productions.

The stars of *Who Killed Cock Robin;* Jenny Wren was patterned after Mae West. The cartoon appeared in 1934. © Walt Disney Productions.

Singer, and a revolution was under way in films, and no one had time for Disney. The latter nevertheless went ahead with a second Mickey Mouse; halfway through it he felt that he had solved the problem of synchronizing sound to image. He completed the second, but reserved his heaviest efforts for a third, to be called *Steamboat Willie.*

Steamboat Willie went over. Distributors were enthusiastic, but Disney found that they wanted to buy the idea, or even the company, and not the finished product. He resisted the temptation. "I wanted to retain my individuality," he once said. "I was afraid of being hampered by studio policies. I knew if someone else got in control I would be restrained, held down to their ideas of low cartoon cost and value."

Mickey was good enough, however, to keep the small Disney outfit afloat, and Disney had meanwhile given serious thought to the possibilities in sound. The product of that thought was a series of Silly Symphonies, the first of which was based on the rather ghoulish but quite melodic *Danse Macabre.* It was the germ of what later became *Fantasia;* it was released in 1929. Three years later, in a Silly Symphony called *Flowers and Trees,* Disney used color for the first time. Audiences were enthralled, and the cartoon won for Disney his first Academy Award.

The man's successes from then on make a vertiginous account. From 1933 to 1943 he won nine Academy Awards for the best cartoon of the year, with special awards for the creation of Mickey Mouse, for scientific achievement and for *Snow White*. From magazines, critics' circles, governments, civic groups, technical societies and women's clubs he garnered a trunkful of plaques, ribbons, certificates, medals, cups, scrolls and citations, for shorts and full-length features including *The Tortoise and the Hare, Who Killed Cock Robin, The Three Orphan Kittens, Ferdinand the Bull, Pinocchio, The Ugly Duckling, Fantasia* and *Victory Through Air Power*.

After World War II he entered a new phase— two new phases, really. One was a reversion to his early desire to combine animation and live action. The other was his serious entry into straight documentary work. The former technique is exemplified by *Song of the South* or *Fun and Fancy Free;* but the documentary work is of more permanent significance. (It is difficult to keep Disney within categories. He also entered two other phases, cutting across both those mentioned: except for 1938 and 1944, he has produced at least one full-length feature a year; and he is represented by several hours of television every week in most areas.) His documentaries are not rooted in human activities and passions, as Flaherty's were. They are in color, as Flaherty's were not, and there is more concern for the "artistic" value of the scene— although again, because he loved and dealt with human beings, Flaherty's "art" is incomparably higher. But Disney's are education on a more popular level, aimed roughly at the early adolescent, and as such they do their job beautifully. Disney has received awards for *Beaver Valley, Seal Island, Nature's Half Acre, The Living Desert* and half a dozen others. In 1954 he received four Academy Awards for four separate films: *The Living Desert, Bear Country, The Alaskan Eskimo* (one of his few serious treatments of human beings, and a very good one) and a short cartoon called *Toot, Whistle, Plunk and Boom*.

Note that by 1958 he had come a long way from simple comedy. His short subjects were ranging from admonitory (and funny) cartoons on traffic safety, to man in space; his awards ranged from television "Emmys" to honorary high-school diplomas, by way of scrolls for his contributions in the field of fire prevention. He makes feature documentaries, short documentaries, feature adventures, feature cartoons, short cartoons, television serials; he uses color and black-and-white. His production is enormous, and his hand is sure. His early training and work were sound, and he learned much in the early forties when he devoted over ninety per cent of his studio's activities to the war effort, in one way or another. His is a wide-ranging, free-swinging, creative mind, and he has never been afraid to take chances or to experiment with innovations. Mickey Mouse may be ancient history; his most recent incarnation is as the inspirational central figure in a daily television variety show composed of talented song-and-dance youngsters, a cliff-hanger serial, an occasional continued documentary, a cartoon and a barrel of good clean American camaraderie. But Disney is big business now— which, let us remember, he would not be if

A homey scene from DISNEY's first full-length feature, *Snow White and the Seven Dwarfs*. © Walt Disney Productions.

Mickey Mouse conducting a scene from *Fantasia*. Mickey is dressed as the Sorcerer's Apprentice. © Walt Disney Productions.

he were not a great entertainer. And yet those of his creations which have remained alive in the comics pages of the daily newspaper are the old reliables, the original greats: Mickey Mouse and Donald Duck.

In Paul Terry's cartoons the drawing was simple and vital, almost stark; only as many lines or patches of black were used as were needed for the outrageously effective action. With Disney the lines became more sophisticated, the forms more detailed, the faces and bodies somewhat less conventionalized. Yet there are flashes in the work of both men— particularly Terry— which suggest a brief movement in the direction of free form, implication, stylization. A long dash in that direction was taken in the early 1950s by UPA's producer Stephen Bosustow; a phenomenon named Gerald McBoing-Boing burst upon the land, was acclaimed by many, was misunderstood by some, and was followed by another phenomenon named Mister Magoo. The UPA studios had meanwhile been busy, and soon the public was dazzled by a display of highly stylized, occasionally almost abstract, animated cartooning.

The idea was not new, but to act on it was daring. Where Paul Terry's primary inspirations were comic-strip figures and economically drawn caricatures, and where Disney's seemed to be in the tradition of nineteenth-century book illustration, UPA's came out of the whole dizzying world of art. There were bits of formal classical portraiture; there was a flash of the Blue Riders; here a haze of impressionism, there a cubistic distortion; now the imitation of an English tapestry, now what seemed to be pure Saul

Gerald McBoing-Boing banished; his sound-effect vociferation was too much for a father who shaved with a straight razor. From *Gerald McBoing-Boing*, which won the Academy Award for Best Short Subject in 1950. © UPA Pictures, Inc.

Steinberg. These styles whirled about, succeeded one another, broke apart, synthesized into something nameless. Motion followed motion, and the narrative was highly literate— but out of all this came a story, and the audiences loved it.

It began with McBoing-Boing, the young man whose vocal chords are unable to form words, and who must, instead, communicate in a series of sound effects: the squeak of a door, the barking of a dog, the blast of an automobile horn. Gerald is a cute little fellow, of the kind that produce bright sayings, and what makes him hilarious is the incongruity— the elephant's bellow rising out of that frail larynx. (Incongruity, by the way, is what pedants call the basis of all humor. A man is walking; walking is a regular succession of steps; when he slips on a banana peel we laugh not because he has bruised himself painfully but because the expected did not transpire.) Gerald's companion in success, Mister Magoo, is woefully nearsighted, and here the incongruities are even more obvious. He also has an incredible, whinnying, dogmatic, hearty, boor-in-the-club-car voice (excellently created by Jim Backus), and when he finds himself in an alley, for example, having missed his way at a Rutgers dance, and peers blindly into the murky gloom, muttering to himself, "By George, they've redecorated the ballroom without consulting the members!" audiences collapse helplessly. Magoo is a dogmatist; his judgments are incontrovertible; and we laugh as much to see the enormity of his error as we do to watch him committing it.

There are critics who like Magoo and Gerald, but who object to the style of drawing. Almost certainly neither hero would be effective without

Mr. Magoo taking a typical drive through the city, in *Magoo's Puddle Jumper,* which won the Academy Award for Best Short Subject in 1956. © UPA Pictures, Inc.

precisely the appearance and background he is given. UPA has married two kinds of inventiveness, the auditory and the visual, and the result is a new and stimulating technique, where color, design and subject matter seem to merge perfectly into one effect— where, in other words, style and content are no longer quite distinct one from the other. This merging is a mysterious process; perhaps another example will help. One of UPA's early productions was a cartoon short of Ludwig Bemelmans' *Madeleine,* a popular children's story. The animation was in Bemelmans' own style, a

Bert and Harry Piel. Bert is an aggressive pitchman, Harry a mild-mannered, ingratiating sort of fellow. Together on television, they sell a lot of beer. © 1959 by Piel Bros. Courtesy of UPA Pictures, Inc.

combination of vigorous, ungeometrical line with equally ungeometrical backgrounds and asymmetrically baroque ornaments. Madeleine herself was simply drawn, with a minimum of detail and a maximum of expression. To say that she was "perfect for the context" might be meaningless; but to say that Little Lulu or Orphan Annie would have been grotesquely out of place is to approach an explanation. (Perhaps it is only a question of what we are used to, of our habits and preconceptions: we can almost visualize Major Hoople in Magoo's part. Almost, but not quite.)

At any rate, UPA has opened a new door, and others will follow through it. (They did the cartoon commercials for Piels Beer, animating the characters Bert and Harry, which the Young and Rubicam advertising agency had conceived; they were so successful that Tip-Top Bread, via the J. Walter Thompson advertising agency, was unafraid to follow suit with Miss Emily Tipp, who is in the same vein.) "Wit" is a word often applied to UPA's creations. The incongruities are no longer so simple (e.g., mouse hits cat on head with hammer). They have become sufficiently complex to give audiences the odd feeling that somewhere behind it all— behind Gerald's deficiency, behind Magoo's perilous inability to see even himself correctly— there lurks a good-natured dig at themselves.

UPA has indicated a direction; there are many others. Animation is not restricted by human limits or the bounds of trick photography, as live films are; and its subject matter may be anything. It need pay no regard to what is or is not available in the way of actors or sets or technical experts. Disney has explored outer space in animation; Terry has created a zany world where the laws of nature are arbitrarily suspended; UPA has shown us history and art with a minimum of fuss and budget, and a maximum of admiration and laughter. Animation has instructed college students in the sciences, has reconstructed classics of literature, has persuaded housewives to choose their brands carefully and urbanites to keep their streets clean. We may tire, and quickly, of watching cans and bottles grow arms and legs on television and sing inane songs; our only consolation is the knowledge that any art can be, and usually is, perverted sooner or later. In compensation there is the sly twinge of nostalgia we feel when we see Betty Boop again. We have not all aged so gracefully.

Betty Boop, a MAX FLEISCHER creation who was once everybody's sweetheart. Courtesy of Max Fleischer.

111

CHAPTER V

A Century of Magazines: From Corny Almanacks to The New Yorker

IN AN AGE OF COMPLEXITIES, the virtues of simplicity are often exaggerated. There are many who look back at the work of colonial American cartoonists with a reverent nostalgia, and who are ready to say that nothing as significant, as "artistic," has been done since. Ben Franklin's vivisected serpent is one of their examples, and the superiority of the woodcut is an article of faith. Not many realize that the snake was only one of dozens that Franklin turned out, and that many of the others were rather unremarkable. His first, or the first attributed to him, was a stale anachronism: a wagoner praying for assistance while his horses founder in the mire, with Hercules to one side reminding him that "Heaven helps only those who help themselves." (The reference was to Pennsylvania's lackadaisical approach to defense.) This is generally considered the first American political cartoon. It is not particularly imaginative, and Franklin's point of view was (as always) homey and virtuous, which is to say, banal. The cartoon is properly saved from oblivion by its venerable origins— but not by its thought or its artistic technique.

All of which is a way to begin saying that most early American cartooning has little impact, in our day, except upon students of Americana who recognize the situation— often a minor political eddy, now forgotten— behind the drawing. This may be an inherent characteristic of political cartooning; perhaps our own Pulitzer Prize winners will be forgotten in fifty years. While that reflection may diminish our awe of the antique, it should not weaken our respect for the journalist-cartoonist. His function is not to produce masterpieces for all eternity (although an occasional classic is inevitable), but to make a brief, effective impression on public opinion, and then to pass on to the next day's work.

This meandering is prompted by a superficial view of the pre-Civil-War cartoon in America. Practically all those cartoons were political, and most of them were in the crowded eighteenth-nineteenth-century style; what humor remains lies largely in what has become, for the modern observer, a quaintness closely related to the rugged simplicity, the natural virtue of the early American. No longer do we feel the cynicism of past ages; we have plenty of our own, and it is vented upon the eccentricities of a world more different from colonial America than colonial America was from the Roman Republic.

For all of that, the modern gag cartoon, as perhaps best exemplified by those in *The New Yorker*, had its beginnings in the relatively naïve political cartoons and caricatures of our earliest years. If these were all political, it is because graphic reproduction was difficult; newspaper circulation was low (and magazine circulation almost nonexistent); the United States was young, and nothing was of greater moment than the politics of the time; and our economy, our medicine, our morals, our economics, our recreation were all fairly simple. There was no place for gadfly cartooning outside of politics, and there was no audience more sophisticated than the political audience. Paul Revere was an engraver (natural for a silversmith) and turned out several cartoons; they did not bear upon the vicissitudes of the artisan or the domestic infelicities of the well-to-do, but upon American resistance to British tyranny.

If any one man pointed out a possible new direction to American cartoonists of the early nineteenth century, it was probably James Akin, a Carolinian who settled in Massachusetts. Akin liked figures, people, portraits, and his work shows, here and there, a little of the detailed ferocity of Goya's etchings. His first non-political success was earthy enough. Having argued with a publisher named Blunt, he reproduced his antagonist in the process of flinging a skillet in a fury which reflected badly upon Blunt's reputation and dignity. Not content with his artist's revenge, Akin shipped a print to England and ordered it reproduced on chamberpots, which he then imported in great numbers and sold around Newburyport.

Akin went on from personal revenges to social comment, widening his field to include European political figures. Meanwhile Elkanah Tisdale of Connecticut was making a reputation for himself, largely in book illustration, and an engraver named Amos Doolittle carried on a personal war against England. The War of 1812 saw the emergence of Alexander Anderson, whose famous legacy is the "Ograbme" cartoon, exulting over the effects of the Embargo Act of 1813.

Until 1814 these cartoons were reproduced either as flyers— on a single sheet, for sale to art dealers and bookstores— or, occasionally, in collec-

"Dicky Folwell," a drawing by JAMES AKIN in 1808, when it was still practicable to quote Othello. Courtesy of the Historical Society of Pennsylvania.

ALEXANDER ANDERSON's most famous cartoon, "Ograbme," a sharp comment on the Embargo of 1813. Courtesy of the Historical Society of Pennsylvania.

tions of humorous art. In 1814 a prominent portraitist named John Wesley Jarvis designed a cartoon specifically for newspaper reproduction. It was the first, aside from masthead decorations and Franklin's hortatory slogans, to appear in a newspaper (the Washington *Federal Republican*).

It remained for another engraver, William Charles, to demonstrate that versatility was possible. Charles did political cartoons, social satire, book illustration. He disliked hypocrisy, bankers, clergymen, England and opportunistic public servants. He was free-swinging and fearless, as most cartoonists were and are; he was also very popular. Some of his work appeared in a small book, *The American Magazine of Wit*; some of it as prints; some of it in newspapers; some of it in small books and pamphlets of his own design and publication. Charles seems to have been the American equivalent of the eighteenth-century European *littérateur*; within his field he could do anything, and he was constantly at work, issuing a prodigious amount of comment, most of it rather bitter, over a period of fifteen years.

By 1820 a lull had set in. Charles was dead, and the others retired. No new generation rose to replace them. But society itself was changing, and during this artistic interregnum the preoccupations of America changed.

"Johnny Bull and the Alexandrians" by the great WILLIAM CHARLES, drawn in 1818. Courtesy of the Historical Society of Pennsylvania.

After the War of 1812 we were not so crabby, not so fearful; we had more confidence in ourselves as a nation, and felt less need to claw at our enemies. The cartoonists' target broadened somewhat, to include bluenoses, the curse of liquor, the pomposity of the professional soldier. By Jackson's time, while political cartooning was as vituperative as ever, a mellowing had begun in other areas. We were beginning to relax. We were taking each other less seriously.

In the early 1820s commercial lithography became feasible in America. Before then all illustrating had been from engraved steel plates, etched copper plates, or woodcuts. Now reproduction of drawings was simpler and less expensive; and (so go the accidents that make progress) in 1828 Andrew Jackson became President. He was a violent man, and no one was indifferent to him. He was also eminently fit for caricature. Physically, he had the bearing of a soldier, with flashing eyes and a cockatoo's head. His career was studded with both glory and shame. His policies were controversial. He and lithography probably raised American cartooning to an unforeseen level of national importance. By 1840 the profession was healthy again, and a series of "Almanacks" had appeared, forerunners of the later *Judge* and *Puck*. Many of these were imitative of Cruikshank's almanacs in England; the *Old American Comic Almanac* of 1841 bore on its cover the legend "Designs and Matter Entirely Original." Murrell lists several of these publications: *The Comic Token, Broad Grins, The American Comic Annual, Elton's Comic All-my-Neck, Finn's Comic Almanac, Davy Crockett's Almanac of Wild Sports of the West*, and *Life in the Backwoods, The Rip Snorter, Whim Whams, The Merry Elephant, The Devil's Comical Texas Oldmanick*. It is worth noting that these almanacs contained brutal caricatures and low (but funny) scatology; they were not, however, obscene, as many of their modern successors are. They were not even sophisticatedly salacious. If a breast or leg were exposed, it generally belonged to a disastrously homely woman; the aim was not individual titillation, but social fun.

By 1850 cartooning had benefited by the free lunch, the California Gold Rush, the arrival of Jenny Lind and a steady rise in literacy and in efficiency of printing. We were ready for the deluge of Civil War cartoons that would raise the art to a new popular height. Understandably, there was less humor during the war, which was a major cataclysm; its importance to America's future has been underestimated for almost a century, and so has the intensity of feeling on both sides. For ten years America breathed war and politics, and cartooning was as grim as in 1812. The breakthrough to civilized humor came in the 1870s.

We shall look at *Puck* and *Judge* in a later chapter, and see Jump, Beard, the Gillams, and Nast at work; with them, or after them, were

"One way to raise a pup."

An old CHIP BELLEW gag, which is practically a strip. BELLEW loved to draw dogs.

Grant Hamilton, Homer Davenport, Frederick Burr Opper, George Luks, Horace Taylor and Eugene Zimmerman, among others. A New York weekly called *Wild Oats* played host to many of these, and gave James Wales his start. With Wales was Chip Bellew.

The work of these men was impressive enough to launch an illustrated daily, the New York *Daily Graphic*, which became the first newspaper to carry humorous panels as a matter of policy. That New York City was able to support such a newspaper hints at a change in public response to graphic humor. Looking back, it seems to us that the world was more complex— almost bewildering, surely, to a man who had lived through the nineteenth century. It may be wrong to see simplicity in every age before our own, but on a journalistic level, at least, the nineteenth century had not been terribly involved before the 1870s. Issues were generally clear-cut, if emotional: you were or were not a Copperhead, you did or did not believe in the permanence of social classes, you preferred the hegemony of the wealthy urbanites or that of the landed gentry. But with Grant, with industrialization, with immigrants by the million, with panics and foreign involvements and the cigarette replacing the cigar, a man hardly knew where to turn.

Cartoonists had no need to turn. They simply had more to observe, and therefore more to poke fun at. More and more, types rather than individuals were caricatured; more and more, foibles rather than policies were ridiculed. A new generation of cartoonists was rising, most of whom would live well into the twentieth century, and all of whom would have a share in shaping the journalism of a later age. Out of the illustrated periodicals of the late 1800s came A. B. Frost, Edward Windsor Kemble, C. J. Taylor, F. M. Haworth (who later did Sunday comic strips), W. A. Rogers, Peter Newell, Palmer Cox, Hy Mayer, Charles Dana Gibson.

There were hundreds of others. It was as though a regiment of talented madmen had broken loose and were laying waste the society that had sheltered them. No group, no class, no human activity was safe. Even women became pretty, in cartoons, the better to make idiots of men. C. J. Taylor's Taylor Made Girl was followed, and displaced, by the Gibson Girl, still one of the best-known symbols of the nineties. Kemble's Negroes and Sullivant's Irishmen were hilarious to those not Negro or Irish and both men also did superb work requiring no scapegoats.

Whether Hy Mayer can properly be called an American artist is open to question, but the question is silly. He was a man of the world and a citizen of the world. He was born in Worms on the Rhine in 1868, and came to the

One of EDWARD WINDSOR KEMBLE's Negro children. In a period when broad, savage caricature was the rule, Kemble never sneered.

118

One of C. J. TAYLOR's he-she cartoons, done about 1907. From *Judge*.

A Compensating Blessing

BOB— *"Yes; since the Smiths lost their money I have stopped calling there."*
ETHEL— *"How good of you! That ought to cheer them up a whole lot."*

United States in 1886. Over the next twenty years he drew, wrote, illustrated books and entertained his fellow man generally, becoming editor-in-chief of *Puck* in 1914. Still, during this time he also appeared regularly in *Fliegende Blätter* (Munich), *Figaro Illustré* and *Le Rire* (Paris), *Black and White, Pick-Me-Up, Pall Mall Magazine* and *Punch* (London), not to mention every major American humorous magazine. He was a jovial man and energetic. Some of his book titles— there were too many to reproduce them all— were *The Autobiography of a Monkey* (1896), *The Adventures of a Japanese Doll* (1901), *Alphabet of Little People* (1901). All his books were of course illustrated by himself. His part in early animation is greater than is generally assumed; all in all, he released some fifty animated cartoons called "Travelaughs," caricaturing his own travels. His style was always clean and sharp. The drawings reflect his personality to a great extent; he was meticulous, cheerful and a bit patrician, and so is his line. Few American cartoonists who were working early in the twentieth century failed to acknowledge an admiration for Mayer and very often a deep debt to him. He died in 1954, having enjoyed life for eighty-six years.

Charles Dana Gibson, an excellent draftsman, must bear most of the responsibility for the six decades of pin-up girls that followed him. Like Russell Patterson and John Held, Jr., later, Gibson set the style for a whole era: clothes, manners, coiffure, and most of all a queenly disdain for the importunate American male. From the early nineties to the First World War, the Gibson Girl was the American ideal: women imitated her,

WHEN THE SHIP ROLLS AND YOUR BERTH BECOMES
UNCOMFORTABLE TAKE YOUR PILLOW AND SLEEP ON THE WALL.

A fine HY MAYER from *Puck,*
in about 1910.

men desired her. She is now all that rests of Gibson's fame; but the man
was an imaginative and versatile cartoonist. As early as 1888 he had
satirized the Irish demand for Home Rule in a savage but funny cartoon.
And all through the nineties he sketched brilliant scenes of life among the
middle and lower classes. He was observant. From a slouch, or from the
tilt of a silk hat, he could evoke a whole philosophical attitude or imply a
deficiency in social standing. He was not at all a chronicler of high society.
He drew sports fans— and an occasional tout. He drew middle-class banquets— and an occasional drunk. And he was funny in his social comment,
which he rarely was with the Gibson Girl. His Gibson Girl, though, was
peerless. Other cartoonists might be funnier (Sullivant was, for one), but
none was prettier.

Sullivant has been mentioned several times here. In this whole burgeoning tribe of funnymen, he was probably the funniest. He was not the most
popular, except among his colleagues, and his output was relatively small,
but there is nothing like him in the whole history of art. He was a periodical man, and not a journalist. He had tried his hand— an intelligent

Two (CHARLES DANA) GIBSON Girls. The man in the middle is not only confused; he is drawn (about 1900) in an early version of a technique very controversial later on, when it was transmuted by the cubist Duchamp and the futurist Giacomo Balla. From *Language of Vision* by Gyorgy Kepes, Paul Theobald & Co., 1951.

editor had tempted him with a high salary— at editorial cartooning, but the day-to-day grind was not to his taste. He liked to take his time. He liked to cross-hatch carefully, to throw shadows, to illuminate his figures with almost theatrical lighting techniques. What it is, precisely, that makes him unique is hard to say. John Bray and A. S. Daggy and even Ed Carey drew figures like Sullivant's— the enlarged heads, the exaggerated features, the bland expressions; often they used the same careful shading, avoiding black entirely; yet Sullivant's work is different from, and superior to, any other's. His animals are the most inert of all beasts. His Irishmen, in an age when dozens of cartoonists picked on them, were far and

Following are four by T. S. SULLIVANT, done between 1900 and 1910. Comment would be superfluous. From *Judge*.

"Everything Going Down Hill"

No Time to Waste
MRS. FARMER— *"If I offered you a job would you refuse it?"*
WEARY WILLIE— *"No, lady; I couldn't spare de time. I'm simply
rushed ter death refusin' offers uv jobs."*

All Right

CASEY— *"Riley, ye owe me an apology— ye called me a liar."*
RILEY— *"Ye're a liar— Oi didn't!"*
CASEY— *"Well, it's all roight, then, an' ye don't owe me an apology."*

away the most Irish. Schoolteachers, laborers, social climbers are unmistakably identifiable. Somewhere Sullivant had learned to extract essences from his subjects, and then to draw those essences. Any beast or human that looked at all like his drawings would be cast out by society; yet he drew the most thoroughly real beings of his period. His name and reputation have been forgotten, except among comic artists, but his work is hilarious even today. He caused no revolutions in art, no upheavals in politics, no shifts in the course of civilization. He was a gentle observer, a slow, careful worker and something of a genius.

Collections of wit and humor prior to the First World War show clearly that draftsmanship had outstripped wit. In any hundred cartoons of the time, eighty will be no more than excellent illustrations of a bad (or at best middling) joke. Ten will be simple puns ("Iced Tee"). And perhaps ten will combine the visual with the verbal to make a cartoon that we can still laugh at. The drawing was good, though. "Zim" was still producing. So were C. J. Taylor, Conacher, Albert Levering, Peter Newell and Hy Mayer. The list of younger contributors is impressive: James Montgomery Flagg, Outcault, Frank Nankivel, Cornell Greening, Carl Anderson (so famous later for *Henry*), George Herriman, Art Young. Each of those men reached fame in some other area of cartooning; but each of them learned part of his trade doing gag panels.

"Iced Tee."

The primitive pun, by A. S. Daggy, who was a popular cartoonist of the turn of the century. From *Judge*.

Held in Reserve

Philanthropist— *"And have you anything laid by for a rainy day?"*
Pat Ducy— *"A whole quart, sor; an' it's a glorious drunk Oi'll hov th' foorst day it's too wet to worruk."*

The great Zim (Eugene Zimmerman) drew this in 1908. After the First World War the Irishman ceased to be a victim of cartoonists, possibly because he was better assimilated. From *Judge*.

It's still a little hard to say what happened after the war. There was a new disillusionment, certainly— a distrust of authority, once we realized that the authorities had not done too well by us during the war and had no intention of seeing to it that there would never be another one. Jingoistic platitudes, broken promises and official hypocrisy had made the old naïve moralities look like so much balderdash, at least to intellectuals. The grass-roots population was less affected, but among writers, painters, journalists and most cartoonists disenchantment was the prevailing mood. Mencken was a little Messiah, and *The Smart Set* and the *American Mercury* on an end-table marked a home as cynically progressive. Satire and irony were no longer simply useful critical tools; they were a way of intellectual life. Only the world of the arts seemed to have any integrity; *The New Yorker* and *Vanity Fair* supplied Americans with the only fearless, illusionless graphical periodical journalism they could find. *Time* was a new wrinkle— a magazine devoted solely to news of the week. If *Time* stood for the old virtues, it was nevertheless informative and did much to penetrate an almost invincible American parochialism.

But it was *The New Yorker*, and to a lesser degree *Vanity Fair*, which led the parade toward sophistication. And panel cartoonists, always a little more observant, a little more sensitive to stupidity and irony and lunacy than most, found that nothing was sacred. Within ten years all the ikons were broken. Fortunately, one of the glories of America is that it produces new ikons with astonishing rapidity. The panel cartoonist is now in the fourth decade of a boisterous heyday.

Between 1925 and the present the abundance of talent has been fearsome. Literally hundreds of men and women have turned out, week after week, genuinely funny and well-drawn cartoons. By now even the "home magazines" and the "women's magazines" run cartoons more daring and more pointed than any before the First World War; even the *Reader's Digest*, a bastion of respectability and faith, publishes anecdotes which thirty years ago would have been too racy for the mails.

The New Yorker declared itself "not for the old lady from Dubuque." If the old lady is now often less sedate than the magazine, the fact remains that for thirty years *The New Yorker* has edified without pedantry and amused without titillation. Its outlook has always been forward and liberal, which contributes to its success; conservative organs tend naturally to be worried and humorless.

The magazine has published almost a thousand cartoons a year since its origin in 1925. A list of its contributors is almost a Who's Who of panel cartooning, and, for that matter, of caricature. Covarrubias, John Held, Jr., Helen Hokinson, Ralph Barton, Rea Irvin, Gluyas Williams, Otto Soglow, Carl Rose, Al Frueh, Bruce Bairnsfather, James Thurber, Gilbert Bundy are only a beginning.

The function of the *New Yorker* cartoon was not to shock but to punc-

JAMES THURBER.

"Well, if I called the wrong number, why did you answer the phone?"

Copr. © 1937 The New Yorker Magazine, Inc.

JAMES THURBER.

"It's a naïve domestic Burgundy without any breeding, but I think you'll be amused by its presumption."

Copr. © 1937 The New Yorker Magazine, Inc.

HELEN HOKINSON.

Copr. © 1926 The New Yorker Magazine, Inc.

ture. Civic pride, industrial pomposity, social pretension and man's eternally o'erweening ego were the targets. Once safe and smug amid its assumed superiorities, the American myth was reduced, piecemeal, to rubble. Had Nature labored lo these many centuries toward its final perfection, the American male? Rea Irvin took evolution in hand, and the American male was Mencken's *homo boobus*. Had we cast off the fetters of darkness and ignorance? Alan Dunn knew better. Were our upper classes the ultimate

"Aunt Claire asked you a question, dear.
Are you the pitcher or the catcher?"
PERCY BARLOW.
   Copr. © 1954 The New Yorker Magazine, Inc.

in dignity and taste? Not after Peter Arno's dissection. The sacred cows of Traditional Emotion and Lachrymose History were elegantly butchered by John Held, Jr. Helen Hokinson had not yet perfected her clubwomen, but had made a devastating start on high suburbia.

Looking back in 1930, some of the pre-crash cartoons must have seemed coldly prophetic. *The New Yorker* was no raging Isaiah, and its editors were no more aware than the rest of us that Armageddon was on the way. Yet its cartoons, jabbing away constantly at our shams and illusions, touched upon social truth. Mary Petty's stockbroker was a figure of fun in 1928; by 1930 we were beginning to realize what Miss Petty had been saying. Reginald Marsh had known even better.

Marsh, like George Luks and many others, did his best, most permanent work in the traditional area of non-humorous painting, engraving and etching. Born in Paris in 1898, he was graduated from Yale in 1920, studied with many private teachers, and became an instructor at the Art Students League in New York City. He is in the permanent collection at the Metropolitan and the Whitney in New York, and is represented in Chicago, Boston, Philadelphia and innumerable other large cities. Many critics consider his frescoes in the customs house in New York City and the Post Office in Washington, D.C., his best work. Marsh's subjects have always been contemporary, his attitude progressive; there exists in his work an irony, a bite which is missing from that of most panel cartoonists.

(There were many other bitter men in the thirties: for example, Alexander King, whose work appeared in *Americana*, a magazine of high quality which was a sounding board for mordancy— it published cartoons rejected elsewhere— and which was turned out by King and Gilbert Seldes.) But Marsh stuck to his first loves and showed no desire to go off into allied arts. Among the honors he accumulated were the first W. G. Clark Prize ($2,000), the Corcoran Gold Medal at the Corcoran Biennial in 1945, the Salamagundi Purchase Prize in 1945, and membership as a Fellow in the Royal Society of Arts, London, and the American National Academy.

He died in 1954. His home base had always been New York; he was one of the authentic American talents.

After the crash, *The New Yorker* kept its sense of humor. If the depression was no joke, there was still the whole range of humanity's eccentricities. Barlow spoofed culture, Carl Rose noted Hitler's rise, George Price's angular idiosyncratics parodied us all. James Thurber's graphic communiqués reported the first skirmishes in the war between men and women, and Peter Arno's rabbity Eternal Husband foretold its conclusion. Syd Hoff's Bronx was a stronghold of individualism, and William Steig was sorting and classifying the individualists. Charles Addams was breaking in, not yet macabre but already pessimistic. They were all there: Barbara Shermund, Garrett Price, Whitney Darrow, Jr., Robert Day, Richard Decker, Alain, Richard Taylor, Gluyas Williams. Many of them had done book illustration previously; many were graduates of the older humor magazines; some broke in with *The New Yorker* and there made their reputations. The lineup was dazzling. Seen as a whole, it was the most remarkable collection of cartoonists any periodical had ever assembled. Their work was consistently of the highest quality, and with them the new kind of cartoon (the one-line cartoon), in which the words and drawing were inextricable and neither was witty without the other, came to full flower. Critics were impressed; if they had reservations about *The New Yorker*, it was still in many respects the best magazine in America. And if they had a reservation about the cartoons, it was only that such excellence could not last forever.

Perhaps not forever, but it has certainly shown no signs of disappearing up to now, almost thirty-five years after the first issue. On the contrary, the cartoons have kept pace with a progressively madder world. James Thurber's genius shone even brighter in the forties. Charles Addams found his *métier* in a somehow familiar world of horror. Chon Day stepped up his pace to become a regular contributor. And one of *The New Yorker's* greats slowly perfected his art: Sam Cobean.

Cobean was prolific. He could afford to be; he had one of the quickest minds in the trade, never lacking ideas, and he was the undisputed master of the variation-on-a-theme. If for nothing else, he will be remembered for his man-visualizing-woman-as-nude. The changes he rang on that theme

MARY PETTY.

"Which one is the love potion?"

Richard Decker.

Otto Soglow.

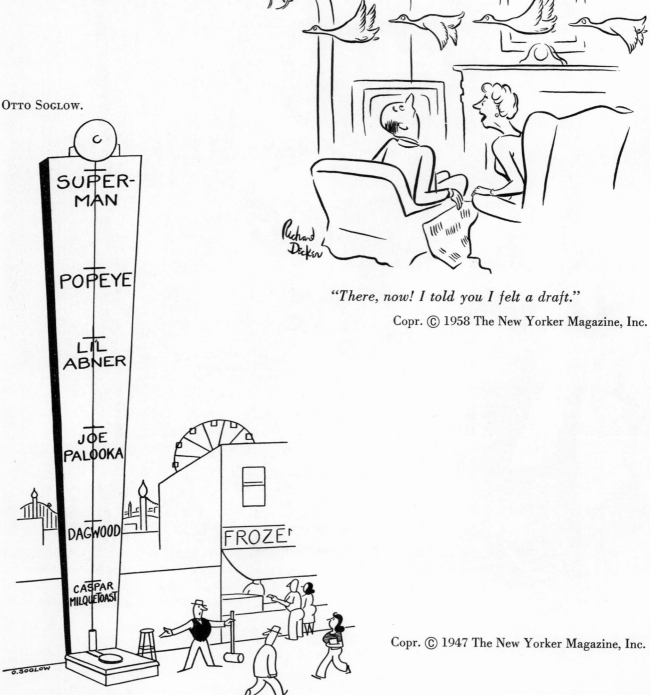

"*There, now! I told you I felt a draft.*"

Copr. © 1958 The New Yorker Magazine, Inc.

SUPER-MAN

POPEYE

L'IL ABNER

JOE PALOOKA

DAGWOOD

CASPAR MILQUETOAST

FROZE

O. SOGLOW

Copr. © 1947 The New Yorker Magazine, Inc.

Carl Rose.

"I'm afraid I haven't been much help to you, Miss. I'm awfully sorry."

were abundant, various and always funny. They included the setting (lamp post becoming palm tree) and the clothing (knight in armor stripped to union suit , Moslem woman stripped only of veil) ; the threat-to-morals (minister visualizing man visualizing nude woman) ; and the athletic (male umpire visualizing female softball player in shower). Once the visualization had become a trade-mark, nudity was no longer necessary (bored party-goer visualizing talkative woman with her mouth shut) ; and Cobean reached the ultimate with his portrait of a dizzy blonde incapable of visualizing *anything*.

His range was almost unlimited. He could spoof animals, spiritualist mediums, unwed mothers, Boy Scouts, athletes, drunkards. And one idea seems often to have led to another, as with the visualization theme. In a collection of his work published in 1952, after his death, there are five unwed-mother cartoons, and each seems to spring naturally from the others. One hat cartoon leads to another; one life-in-a-trailer cartoon gives birth to several more; one sandwich-man gag is followed by two others.

The public loved him, and his colleagues admired him. This is part of the introduction Charles Addams wrote to *Cobean:*

His drawings were beautiful— he drew more easily than anyone I ever knew. Oddly erect before the drawing board, he worked quickly, the pictures moving from his head to his hand to the paper— and they came out finished— the helpless but non-committal men, the predatory chippies, and the world's funniest dogs, bums, and

STRICTLY RICHTER

11-26

"No, I will not increase your allowance, Edna. Does anybody have any other questions?"

© 1958 King Features Syndicate, Inc.

132

peacocks. I own about a hundred Cobeans, many of them done when we were in the Army together. There was something about me, namely my nose, that amused, even amazed, Cobean, and he drew it endlessly. He was carried to great heights by my nose. I wish you could see these drawings, besides the remarkable collection in these pages.

On the evening of July 2, 1951, I received at Westhampton Beach a telephone call from Watkins Glen. It was Anne Cobean and she said: "Did you hear about Sam? He was killed this afternoon in the Jaguar." As fast as that. I didn't believe it, nor will I ever, quite. I hope he knew or at least suspected that he will be long remembered as one of the great comic artists of all time.

CHARLES ADDAMS

New York
April 23, 1952

The early forties are synonymous with "the war," and *The New Yorker*, like most magazines, found humor not in combat, which is never funny, but in the by-products of combat: rank, communications, pomp and ceremony, servicemen on the prowl, the enemy's deficiencies, and— given the scope of the war— international understanding or misunderstanding. There were no great anti-war cartoons, partly because this was more a war of survival than a war of self-interest. America was totally involved; pacifism and conscientious objection were at their lowest ebb in our history. Surely *The New Yorker*, like most private citizens, disapproved of war in

CHARLES ADDAMS.

133

Comic Art in America

WILLIAM STEIG.

general, but there were few who disapproved of this particular war. Our emotional pitch was so high (though we could still be disenchanted about generals, wasted matériel and strategic blunders) that we tended to be somewhat childishly flippant about the enemy; we drew back in horror at the concept of genocide (a product of the Nazis), while we shouted our determination to "wipe the Jap right off the map." Hiroshima, and the ten years since, have altered our adolescent view of war; a few of *The New Yorker's* anti-enemy cartoons, funny at the time, now seem superficial and overenthusiastic. Yet who can take more credit for educating us about war than that magazine, which devoted an entire issue to John Hersey's *Hiroshima*, a landmark in the literature of war and peace?

Where *The New Yorker* did its finest war work is in the international area. Here was a perfect target for its educated urbanity: the crude, easygoing American among the refinements of older civilizations. The GI drawing mustaches on a totem pole, the puzzled Russians leafing through a dictionary in search of "Spam" and "Mazola," the baffled sergeant coping with local superstition— here was the sophisticated irony subscribers had come to expect and admire.

Among the best in this area were Saul Steinberg's graphic reports from overseas. Steinberg had contributed previously, and was to become, ten years later, the magazine's most imaginative artist. His first real triumphs in *The New Yorker* were the drawings— pages of them— he sent in from

BARNEY TOBEY.

"This one is dated May 10, 1934. You can no longer go on without me."

Copr. © 1954 The New Yorker Magazine, Inc.

REA IRVIN.

GARRETT PRICE.

Copr. © 1942 The New Yorker Magazine, Inc.

Copr. © 1925 The New Yorker Magazine, Inc.

ALAIN.

"Do you mind?"

Copr. © 1945 The New Yorker Magazine, Inc.

GEORGE PRICE.

". . . and what's more, you probably never will find an ad requesting intelligent companionship for an elderly millionaire."

Copr. © 1952 The New Yorker Magazine, Inc.

SAM COBEAN.

China and India. His use of line, simple, distorted but "right," and set off by irregularly ornate decoration, was individual and original. To say of another artist, "He draws like Steinberg," is a complimentary exaggeration, but it identifies a man's style. Steinberg, as unlike Gibson or Sullivant or Billy Ireland as possible, was like them in one respect: he was seminal. He owed nothing to any American predecessors, and is closer to the French political cartoonists than to any other group. He is an architect who lives in New York City, but his background, tastes and training are cosmopolitan, to say the least. Nothing in the history of art is quite alien to him, and no axiom of contour or perspective has gone unchallenged by him. Among his sketches are figures which resemble comic-strip drawing of the early 1900s, American primitives, Lautrec lithographs. Some of his lines begin conventionally, continue erratically and end in a logical insanity. Buildings look like cars, cars like people, people like buildings. And of course there is nothing slapstick about the man; he is a serious artist working in the cartoonist's medium.

Comic Art in America

Sam Cobean.

1

2

3

4

5

138

6

7

8

SAM COBEAN.

"Save your breath, Betty-Lou."

SAM COBEAN. From *The Cartoons of Cobean*, Selected and Arranged by Saul Steinberg, Harper & Brothers. Copyright 1952 by Anne M. Cobean.

SAM COBEAN. From *The Cartoons of Cobean*, Selected and Arranged by Saul Steinberg, Harper & Brothers. Copyright 1952 by Anne M. Cobean.

The breadline as seen by REGINALD MARSH in 1930. This was hardly comic art;
it was an extension of the magazine cartoon into the area of serious social comment.
Copr. © 1930 The New Yorker Magazine, Inc.

By 1950 more first-rate men had come to appear regularly in the magazine: Modell, Barney Tobey, CEM (Charles Edward Martin), Claude, Anatole Kovarsky. Into the fifties the cartoons lost none of their bite. As America became richer, zanier, automationized and more colorful, cartoonists found more to satirize. Dana Fredon, Mischa Richter, David Langdon appeared more frequently; Ton Smits, who had been famous in Europe, added his gloomy nonsense; and Eldon Dedini's full-bodied drawings poked fun at practically everybody. By now Charles Addams was famous as an intimate of ghouls and a guide to the sinister. And the old-timers— Arno, Decker, Darrow, Barlow and their cohorts— were better than ever. The gag cartoon, with a strong assist from caricaturists, newspaper cartoonists and a few good men who appeared regularly in other magazines, had come of age in *The New Yorker*. The one-line gag (and the *"sans légende"*) had permanently replaced the old He-She illustration. The cartoonist is now a contemporary critic, and no longer an illuminator of Joe Miller. And happily the end is not in sight.

142

BREAD LINE   REGINALD MARSH

"They also serve who only stand and wait."

Another breadline, seen a bit differently but no less effectively by ALEXANDER KING
in *Americana*, December 1932. Courtesy of Alexander King.

Eldon Dedini.

Copr. © 1959 The New Yorker Magazine, Inc.

Chon Day.

CEM.

Copr. © 1951 The New Yorker Magazine, Inc.

"Martha, I can't find a damned thing!"
Copr. © 1953 The New Yorker Magazine, Inc.

RICHARD TAYLOR.

Copr. © 1941 The New Yorker Magazine, Inc.

CLAUDE.

Copr. © 1953 The New Yorker Magazine, Inc.

FRANK MODELL.

Copr. © 1954 The New Yorker Magazine, Inc.

145

ROBERT DAY.

*"And now for the weather forecast
for New York City and vicinity."*

Copr. © 1947 The New Yorker Magazine, Inc.

ALAN DUNN.

*"When did you first discover you were the
salt of the earth?"*

Copr. © 1954 The New Yorker Magazine, Inc.

WHITNEY DARROW, JR.

"Oh, he's my fiancé."

H. L. Mencken by COVARRU-
BIAS. Reprinted from *The
Prince of Wales* by Miguel
Covarrubias by permission of
Alfred A. Knopf, Inc. © 1925
by Alfred A. Knopf, Inc.

Between them, *Vanity Fair* and *The New Yorker* set most of the fires of
sophistication in the 1920s (though *Vanity Fair* had come out a few years
before, and *The New Yorker* in 1925). The name *Vanity Fair* as a magazine title was by no means new; the first version of it had been founded
in 1859, was published through 1863, and featured the work of Hoppin
and Bellew. But this later version was something new. To the modern eye
its early issues seem strange. There was excellent artwork by people like
Edmund Duffy, Djuna Barnes, Sidney Joseph, a first-rate book designer,
John Held, Jr. (who also did covers); there were reproductions of paintings by George Bellows (fighters) and George Luks (ashcans); Edward
Windsor Kemble, Ralph Barton, and Norman Bel Geddes. An English girl
named Fish introduced a crowded, caricaturish style in cartoons of social
comment. There was much good photography, some of it almost revolutionary and all of it certainly noted by those more commercial journalists
who later established the news magazines. But there was also page after
interminable page of automobile advertisements: the Templar, the Pierce
Arrow, the Standard 8, the Apperson, the Locomobile, The Jordan, the
Daniels-Light and the Paige. Fittingly, because this was a magazine directed

John Barrymore by COVARRU-
BIAS. Reprinted from *The
Prince of Wales* by permis-
sion of Alfred A. Knopf, Inc.
© 1925 by Alfred A. Knopf,
Inc.

The movie star Marie Dressler
as seen by AL FRUEH. Copr.
© 1930 The New Yorker
Magazine, Inc.

primarily at the upper classes, or at worst the upper middle classes, there was a good deal of haberdashery on display in other advertisements.

In the whole period, though, the most significant artistic development seems to have been the emergence of American caricature, in both *Vanity Fair* and *The New Yorker*. One of the first caricaturists to attract the public eye was Alfred Frueh, who published a collection called *Stage Folk* as early as 1922. He attracted serious notice while working for the New York *World*, and in the late twenties he began caricaturing for *The New Yorker*, chiefly theater people. He is still with them, and his work has lost none of its sharpness or vigor; he has, on the contrary, improved steadily over the years with an ever more economical line and an ever keener knack for spacing figures within a panel.

Ralph Barton, who died much too early, in 1931 (he was 40), had appeared for many years in *Vanity Fair* and in various humor magazines. He was in demand as a book illustrator, one of his most famous contributions being the work he did for *Gentlemen Prefer Blondes*, in 1925.

Two ladies did noteworthy work during this period, and each published a brilliant collection. Eva Herrmann's *On Parade*, a book of caricatures, was published in 1929. This woman's style was not like any other of her contemporaries; it is almost playful, in appearance occasionally almost juvenile, and always telling. Peggy Bacon's volume was called *Off with Their Heads!* (1934) and in it she focused on a parade of prominent

EVA HERRMANN's Sinclair Lewis, drawn in 1929. From *On Parade* by Eva Herrmann, edited by Erick Posselt, Coward-McCann, Inc., 1929.

Franklin P. Adams by PEGGY BACON, 1934. Obviously the man was irresistible to caricaturists. From *Off With Their Heads*, by Peggy Bacon, Robert M. McBride Co., 1934.

Franklin P. Adams by WILLIAM AUERBACH-LEVY. Courtesy of *American Artist* Magazine.

149

Rudolph Valentino by Covar-
rubias. Reprinted from *The
Prince of Wales* by Miguel
Covarrubias by permission of
Alfred A. Knopf, Inc. © 1925
by Alfred A. Knopf, Inc.

New Yorkers, being often unkind and even vitriolic, but always first-class artistically. She was a careful, hard worker, and often took copious notes before beginning a drawing: her finished product, not at all economical in line or brush stroke, was much like what we might expect from an accomplished editorial cartoonist who had mastered the art of caricature.

There were several other excellent caricaturists during these years. Many of them seem now to have derived from some of Oliver Herford's better work at the turn of the century; others are absolutely distinctive, and seem to derive from no one. William Auerbach-Levy, for example, can produce brilliant likenesses in less than a dozen lines with one touch of black for the hair. Auerbach-Levy is as much a painter as a caricaturist and is also an etcher. His oil portraits are considered among the best done in our time. He is also a writer of considerable charm: in his *Is That Me?*, containing instructions for beginners in caricature, he raises pedagogy to the level of mature wit. Fortunately his work is still on display regularly in the drama pages of the New York *Post*.

Probably the best known of all the caricaturists of the twenties was Miguel Covarrubias, a Mexican artist of great distinction. During the period of reform under President Obregon, between 1920 and 1924, the Ministry of Education had established a department of drawing and handicrafts, which included a number of outdoor schools where the public might take beginners courses in art. Covarrubias had been one of the staff of young artists who taught. (This was when the mural became a common art form in Mexico. During a period of social reform the mural was

Covarrubias by Covarrubias.
This was the last caricature in
his book, titled "The Mur-
derer." Reprinted from *The
Prince of Wales* by Miguel
Covarrubias by permission of
Alfred A. Knopf, Inc. © 1925
by Alfred A. Knopf, Inc.

Duke Ellington by Irma Selz.
Copr. © 1943 The New Yorker
Magazine, Inc.

The unforgettable Bobby Clark, made even more unforgettable in this caricature by
AL HIRSCHFELD. Courtesy of Al Hirschfeld and the New York *Times*.

naturally popular, as a kind of art which could be enjoyed by all the people and not simply by private collectors.)

In the mid-twenties Covarrubias came to New York and turned temporarily to caricature. He did not work always in this same style. There are those who profess to see reflections of a rather monolithic primitive Mexican art in his work (the caricature of Captain Patterson, for example); yet his caricature of Ralph Barton, done in 1925, is Puckish, fluid, and relatively detailed. It is true, as Murrell pointed out, that there is a sculptural quality to all of his drawings, but within his basic technique he achieved a great variation in mood and texture.

Covarrubias could not long remain exclusively a caricaturist. In one of the later issues of *Vanity Fair* (1933) is his mocking, satirical version of Roosevelt's first inauguration; it is an ornate, complex and crowded piece of work, with some thirty human figures visible and with highly fanciful architectural backgrounds. Covarrubias went on to canvas painting and lithography, and then his interests widened considerably: he immersed himself in anthropology and archaeology. *Island of Bali* (1937) was the first of many books in those disciplines written and illustrated by him. More recently he has done a great deal of panel decorating, chiefly for public buildings in Mexico City. He remains a thorough master of line and composition, as well as a man of wide and sympathetic cultural interests.

By now we were in the thirties and a secondary line of caricaturists— a new generation, so to speak, not in the least inferior to the early artists— had begun to appear. One of these was Abe Birnbaum, whose work still adorns the pages of *The New Yorker* and who does occasional covers for that magazine. Birnbaum has one of the surest lines in the business — firm, strong, unmistakably emphatic. His caricatures are so forceful that they seem always to have been done quickly, in the heat of a moment's inspiration, with no need for later alteration. Al Hirschfeld had also begun to publish extensively. He had a keen eye for the world's weaknesses— particularly institutional weaknesses, as beautifully expressed in his caricature of the Supreme Court, done in 1937. In the beginning his lithographs attracted as much·attention as his caricatures, but as the years went by he became more and more specialized and is now known chiefly for the superb weekly drawings he does for page one of the New York *Times's* theater section. These are of a lightness and an accuracy unmatched in the field, and his distortions always seem perfect. He can draw little-known but rising young actors and actresses and make them as distinctive and unforgettable as any of the old standby subjects of caricature, like Katharine Hepburn or Clark Gable. And he probably composes his panels— large panels, by the way— better than any caricaturist in our history. His book illustrations are equally entertaining and equally skillful, and signing him up to illustrate S. J. Perelman's prose was pure inspiration. Perelman, incidentally, rejoices as much in describing Hirschfeld verbally as Hirschfeld does in adding his verbal thrusts to Perelman's literature. Hirschfeld is a rather stocky, intense-looking man, with a full beard and a distinctive taste in haberdashery. With a cigar in his mouth he looks quite fierce, as fine a subject for caricature as any of those he has drawn.

The New Yorker remains the stronghold of caricature, and one of the talents it brought to light was that of Irma Selz; her portrait of Martha Graham, for a profile of that lady, was an excellent job in the best *New Yorker* tradition. Miss Selz works fast; she is known for her economy of line; and even more, she is able to do things with lines of varying widths which add infinitely to the mood and depth of her caricatures.

The New Yorker may have led the way for urban sophisticates, but its effect on the general public was indirect, and there were newspaper artists who reached millions where *The New Yorker* reached thousands. There were also many other weekly and monthly magazines with circulations in the millions which carried panels perhaps less intellectual than *The New Yorker's*, but with more immediate meaning to a public more devoted to the homely virtues. Many contributors to *The Saturday Evening Post, The Ladies' Home Journal, Collier's, Esquire,* and other magazines never appeared in *The New Yorker*. E. Simms Campbell's flossy beauties and Jefferson Machamer's busty Amazons shared honors (in magazines) with Jay Alan's and Don Flowers' leggy charmers (in newspapers). Dave Breger's *G.I. Joe* and *Mister Breger* appeared in both media, as both panel and comic strip in newspapers. Breger's work today is largely in panels, and he thinks of himself as more a panel cartoonist than a comic-strip artist. Greg d'Alessio, who did appear in *The New Yorker*, is published in many magazines, but considers his daily newspaper panel his primary work.

The popular national magazines are difficult to deal with because they publish thousands of cartoons each year by literally hundreds of talented cartoonists. Some of the contributors have become known for one kind of cartoon, or one set of characters, like Larry Reynolds for his lovable burglar Butch. But most of these men, with or without a series, are capable of commenting on practically any human (or animal) activity. Some combine their magazine work with regular newspaper panels. One such is Reamer Keller, who has been entertaining us for years with wild, slapdash sarcasms. Known to his colleagues as one of the best gag men in the business, he is one of our less inhibited draftsmen, with a style and an outlook that lie somewhere in the neighborhood of George Lichty's and Bill Holman's. His newspaper contributions usually appear on Sundays, several of them on a full page, and the reader may be forgiven for lingering over them. They have an untamed quality and are invariably funny.

Another instantly recognizable panel cartoonist is Virgil Partch, who signs his work VIP. He is another proponent of logical insanity; his subjects defy all known laws of physics, chemistry and physiology, always

One of DON FLOWERS' curvy creations in a moment of fierce intellectual effort. Flowers' general title for these panels is *Modest Maidens.* © 1949 King Features Syndicate, Inc.

"Now, let's see— did you tell me to keep my eyes shut and my mouth open, or my eyes open and my mouth shut?"

stretching the particular situation far beyond its natural boundaries. Partch has a highly individual style, with sharp, heavy lines; his people are, among other impossibilities, impossibly angular. Partch's drawings were, incidentally, among the first to be reproduced on cocktail napkins and were enormously successful with the bibbers.

The list could go on for pages— Tom Henderson, George Wolfe, John Norment, the Roth brothers. These last are intriguing: there are four Roth brothers, and they are all panel cartoonists. There is Ben, who has pre-empted the family name by signing himself Roth. And there are Irving, who signs himself Roir; Salo, who uses his first name; and Al, who has altered the family name to Ross. They were all born in Seletyn, in the Carpathian Mountains, which no other practicing cartoonist can claim.

The hundreds who supply cartoons every week to mass-circulation magazines are the bread-and-butter men of magazine cartooning. Their work appears every year in dozens of anthologies, and they deserve a history to themselves; but it would be obsolescent as soon as published. Every year a crop of new talents rises. The public's appetite for their work is apparently insatiable— as it should be. Their cartoons have become an indispensable staple of our periodical journalism.

And many of them have gone on to success with strips, from their beginnings in the *Saturday Evening Post*, the now defunct *Collier's*, or a hundred other magazines, popular and obscure. (The *American Legion Magazine*, for example, is not everywhere well known, but its circulation is over four million.) Buford Tune was a ranking panel cartoonist before his success with *Dotty Dripple*; so was Johnny Hart before he created *B.C.*; so was Frank O'Neal before he came up with *Short Ribs*; so was Mel Lazarus before he began to draw *Miss Peach*. Some, indeed, have gone on to spectacular heights, like Mort Walker, whose *Beetle Bailey* is discussed elsewhere, or Hank Ketcham, whose *Dennis the Menace* has brought him fame and fortune.

Once in a while a single character will make its creator's reputation. Marge Henderson's *Little Lulu* was originally a feature in the *Saturday*

"Are you sure he'll make a good salesman, boss? I just said 'no' to a date with him, and he gave up so EASILY!"

A *Miss Jones* by GREG D'ALESSIO, a versatile cartoonist who here specializes in the thought processes of stenographers. © Publishers Syndicate.

155

"TELL ME WHICH IS THE TYPEWRITER
AND THE JOB IS YOURS."

The irrepressible REAMER KELLER. This is from one of his Sunday pages. © 1959 the Chicago *Tribune*–New York *News* Syndicate, Inc.

VIRGIL PARTCH ignoring time and space again. Courtesy of Virgil Partch.

"Ooooh! Your feet are like ice!"

Evening Post, and went on to even greater commercial success as an integral figure in a long advertising campaign for a facial tissue. Carl Anderson's *Henry* also began in the *Post.* Ted Key's *Hazel* is an exclusive feature in the same magazine.

On the other hand there are men who make a living solely from an enormous, varied output of panels. Bo Brown is one; for over thirty years he has been selling to dozens of magazines. Trade journals, incidentally, are a

AL Ross plumbs the mysteries of creation. Courtesy of *Look* and Al Ross.

good source of income. There are over two hundred major trade journals in this country, and there are cartoonists who avoid the intensely competitive world of national magazines by confining their efforts to those journals.

"Intensely competitive" is perhaps an understatement. It is rumored that the *Saturday Evening Post*, which publishes some thirty cartoons a week, selects those thirty from four thousand submitted. The competition keeps quality high, which helps to account for the fact that in Europe, Australia, and South America it is the popular-magazine cartoon which is most often reprinted and not *The New Yorker's* more urbane products. These cartoons abroad are more often pirated than purchased, and one cartoonist, Ben Roth, has taken it upon himself to remedy the situation. By trips abroad and a heavy correspondence, he has induced many foreign editors to abide by the rules of international copyright. (Foreign commercial artists and advertising agencies who steal American cartoons and build publicity campaigns around them for a local product are largely insensitive to Roth's rebukes and cajolery.) In the process Roth has established an agency for the legitimate sale of American cartoons abroad. Some four hundred and fifty cartoonists have contracted for his services. He also brings to American publications the work of a few top-flight European cartoonists.

Considering the huge number of cartoon submissions, it is no wonder that magazines value their cartoon editors. A good one can add immeasurably to a publication's sparkle and variety. Even more, he can spot a coming talent. More than one nationally known gag cartoonist— or comic-strip artist— owe their present eminence to sharp-eyed men of excellent taste, a fine example of the latter being Gurney Williams, who was cartoon editor on the old *Life,* moved to *Collier's,* and is now with *Look.* (Gaar Williams, Gluyas Williams and Gurney Williams are a confusing trio.)

In books and magazine pieces *The New Yorker* tends to overshadow the less racy, less suave wit of the national magazines, partly because it is a convenient publication for research, and partly because writers like to show their sophistication. But if *The New Yorker's* cartoons are a distillation, the popular magazines are the vineyard, and the laborers in that vineyard are the great majority of panel cartoonists.

In newspapers the panel is older than the political cartoon; in the early days one was much like the other. In the loosest sense, any illustration with point was a panel cartoon, but by 1870 the point was so often political that a distinction had to be made between the gag (tactical; small-arms fire, sniping away at manners and morals) and the editorial cartoon (strategic; the Big Bertha, blasting at leaders and policies). Most newspaper panels since have stressed the spot gag, like magazine cartoons. But some have maintained a tighter or looser continuity, and a few of them have acquired a cumulative effect, as though a small universe were being revealed inch by inch.

Among the daily-gag panels, Ed Reed's *Off the Record* and Fred Neher's *Life's Like That* are very similar. Neither artist confines himself to any

A sample of ED REED's *Off the Record.* © 1955 The Register and Tribune Syndicate.

"Pardon my still laughing, sir, but outside I just saw a man wearing some of those silly shorts."

FRANK O'NEAL's *Short Ribs*. O'Neal was a top-ranking panel cartoonist before he created this strip, which is one of the best of the simple, stylized, daily-gag strips. ⓒ 1959 NEA Service, Inc. Reprinted by permission of NEA Service, Inc.

one topic; all their panels are one-line gags; and each has done a series of "baby" gags. Neher is a graduate of the Chicago Academy of Fine Arts, which Reed also attended. Both panels began in 1934. Neher is with the Bell Syndicate, Reed with the *Register* and *Tribune* Syndicate.

George Clark and William Galbraith Crawford (not to be confused with the William Crawford who does editorial cartooning for the Newark *News*) also have a good deal in common. For one thing, Clark, who once did animation drawings of *The Gumps* and now does *The Neighbors* daily, originated a panel called *Side Glances* in 1929, which Crawford (who has always signed himself Galbraith) took over in 1939. For another, the two men have similar drawing styles. Clark originated *Side Glances* for NEA Service, and created *The Neighbors* in 1939 for the Chicago *Tribune*–New York *Daily News* Syndicate. He has never attempted to induce the belly laugh; he feels that a gently humorous reminder of something that has probably happened to his reader will suffice. Galbraith's approach is not much different, and his panels are in rather startling contrast to those he ran in *The New Yorker* in the late twenties and early thirties, which generally featured lush, reclining beauties and the millionaires who kept them. (One had a classic caption: "I never told her about the depression. She would have worried.")

Some of the daily panels are specialized, like Robert Ripley's *Believe It or Not*, imitated by Elsie Hix's *Strange as It Seems*. Dudley Fisher's *Right Around Home* is specialized only to the extent that home and family are. Fisher likes crowded, active, full-page drawings in which a typical family activity— a barbecue or the weekly car-wash— is annotated by a swarm of friends and relatives, while dogs, cats, passing postmen and total strangers offer advice, congratulations and sympathy. The mood of his pages is small-town mid-America, and it scored its first success with readers of the Columbus *Dispatch*, where Fisher had been doing weekly features. In January of 1938 King Features syndicated Fisher, and *Right Around Home* became a national success.

Life's Like That, a FRED NEHER panel of
1959. © Consolidated News Features.

GEORGE CLARK's panel *The Neighbors.* Only barely
an exaggeration, and the basic problem is every parent's. © 1948 the Chicago *Tribune*–New York *News*
Syndicate, Inc.

*"Be sure he's all dressed and his hair combed
before he goes into school."*

ADD TO THE LIST OF A WAITER'S DELIGHT ... THE PARTY WHO RUSHES IN FOR A QUICK BITE

QUICK, WAITER! HAMBURGER WELL AND PIE! HURRY!

GOTTA CATCH A PLANE! GIMME THE VEAL PARMEGAN!

GOULASH FOR ME! SNAP IT UP!

YES SIR! YES SIR! YES SIR!

1959, McCLURE NEWSPAPER SYNDICATE

AND TWO HOURS AFTER THEY'VE FINISHED THEIR SUPPERS ... THEY'RE STILL SITTIN' ROUND AND PICKIN' THEIR UPPERS

Thanks to 8. FRANK SMIGGEN, SMIGGEN'S, YPSILANTI, MICH.

FAGALY & SHORTEN

5-20

AL FAGALY's and HARRY SHORTEN's *There Oughta Be a Law.* More happy cynicism. © 1959 McClure Newspaper Syndicate.

A *Side Glances* by GALBRAITH (WILLIAM GALBRAITH CRAWFORD), who once directed his shafts at the moneyed and their mistresses, but in his newspaper panel pokes fun at the happy middle classes. © 1959 NEA Service, Inc. Reprinted by permission of NEA Service, Inc.

"Can you folks come over for dinner right away? I'd have invited you sooner, but I waited to see how the meal turned out!"

161

DUDLEY FISHER'S *Right Around Home*. Confusion, if not chaos, is Fisher's specialty. © 1945 King Features Syndicate, Inc.

Jimmy Hatlo's *They'll Do It Every Time* is something else again. Hatlo, as Martin Sheridan commented, "deflates the ego of chiselers, pests, fakers, office loafers and bombastic bosses." Behind every assertion of the human ego, Hatlo might say, there lurks a blatant hypocrisy. Behind every accident of bad timing, there lurks a malignant fate. If Hatlo, in originating these panels, had ever been worried about his ability to come up with material seven days a week, he soon relaxed. For almost thirty years Hatlo has received a couple of hundred suggestions a week from his happy readers. He gives public credit for those he uses, which adds to his popularity. Hatlo is another graduate of the sports cartoonist's desk. He had worked on the Los Angeles *Times*, the San Francisco *Call* and the San Francisco *Bulletin*, and when Tad died in 1929 the San Francisco *Examiner* asked Hatlo to take over his space. Somehow, *They'll Do It Every Time* evolved, and when King Features signed him, Hatlo was in business for good.

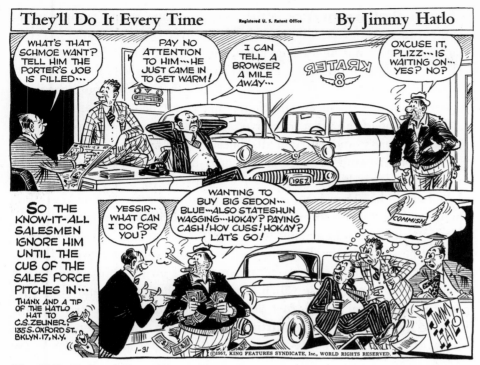

They'll Do It Every Time, JIMMY HATLO's popular creation. The stuffed shirt punctured. © 1957 King Features Syndicate, Inc.

[BELOW LEFT] *Our Boarding House*, 1959, in BILL FREYSE's version, which differs hardly at all from Gene Ahern's. Major Hoople is— unfortunately— a vanishing type. © 1959 NEA Service, Inc. Reprinted by permission of NEA Service, Inc.

[BELOW RIGHT] *Room and Board*, created by GENE AHERN after he relinquished *Our Boarding House.* © 1957 King Features Syndicate.

They'll Do It Every Time is the second-ranking comic feature in the country, in terms of circulation: Hatlo has over 800 newspapers. Yet he has time to turn out another creation, his popular *Little Iodine*, starring one of the most contrary little girls ever invented. Little Iodine's gleefully malicious triumphs won so large an audience that she was published in a paperback-book version, in addition to her comic-book appearances.

Hatlo is one of the great inventive minds in the trade. His eye for pomposity, hypocrisy and outright dishonesty is as keen as Tad's was. But Hatlo is better-natured; there is less acid in his work, and more of the milk of human kindness.

And Hatlo has been fortunate in one important respect. For years Bob Dunn has been his hard-working assistant, and Dunn is a talented veteran. He was Milt Gross's lieutenant for a long time, and considers those years as spent beside a genius. Dunn himself is a quick-witted extrovert, famous as a toastmaster and as an inveterate smoker of large cigars. And he is a master of the frenetic style which characterizes both Gross and Hatlo. He runs his own panel called *Just the Type* (he did a sports strip for the *Evening Journal* back in the thirties, *Moe and Joe*), and has published a couple of very funny books— *I'm Gonna Be a Father* and *One Day in the Army*.

[BELOW LEFT] An *Out Our Way* by J. R. WILLIAMS, reprinted by NEA in 1959. Machine shops were one of his first loves. © 1959 NEA Service, Inc. Reprinted by permission of NEA Service, Inc.

[BELOW RIGHT] A GLUYAS WILLIAMS panel from the thirties. His dissections of Suburbia were delicate and accurate. Courtesy of the Bell Syndicate, Inc.

Among the panels which attempt some continuity, four stand out: *Everyday Movies, Out Our Way, Room and Board,* and *Our Boarding House.* These last two were created by Gene Ahern, who originated *Our Boarding House* for NEA, and more than ten years later left it to do *Room and Board* for King Features. (Bill Freyse now does *Our Boarding House* for NEA.) The panels were essentially the same, revolving around a pretentious and usually penniless householder, full of ceremonious self-importance and get-rich-quick schemes, most of which came to nothing. Grim reality was supplied by a cynical, domineering wife; and general comment was provided by the boarders, a crew of quick-witted, ordinary-looking citizens who might have been traveling salesmen, white-collar clerks or city employees. These panels have great charm and good humor, not because they puncture hypocrisy but because they display a peculiar American genius at work. Major Hoople and Judge Puffle have an eye for the main chance, and they stubbornly refuse to believe that hard work is better than quick wits. Moreover, they have the courage of their convictions, and will stand any amount of criticism and chaffing sooner than abandon their principles.

Of a different order entirely was *Out Our Way,* drawn for thirty-five years by the late J. R. Williams. Signed up by NEA in 1922 after an early career which included work as a railroad fireman, a cowboy, a U.S. Cavalryman and a machinist, Williams became a chronicler of the small-town, lower-middle-class American home. His recurrent titles indicate the sources of his humor of frustration: *Why Mothers Get Gray, Heroes Are Made— Not Born, Born Thirty Years Too Soon, The Worry Wart.* His machine-shop scenes are as real as anything in comics, and the unlimited nature of his appeal was proved by his circulation; at one time he ran in over seven hundred newspapers, near the record for a panel. On Sundays, Williams ran his humor in normal strip form, and restricted it to the mundane adventures of the Willett family, surely the most ordinary family in comics— but of all-consuming interest for that very reason. The Willetts were neither grotesque nor glamorous; they were plain, uninspired people who made trouble out of life's most banal ingredients. Williams himself did not live in a small town, much less the suburbs; he was a rancher in Arizona and California. After his death his panels kept running; most of them are timeless, and if his syndicate were to start them again from the beginning a new generation might never know that they were four decades old.

Gluyas Williams drew a panel for the Bell Syndicate until the 1940s. Now known for his book illustration and his work in *The New Yorker,* he ran his first efforts in the Harvard *Lampoon* almost fifty years ago. After a year of art study in Paris he became art editor of *The Youth's Companion,* remaining with that magazine until 1929, when a period of intense and frustrating free-lance activity began. This Williams, unlike

J. R., was interested in the upper-middle class. His suburbia is, if not well-to-do, at least genteel, and he experimented for some time with comic strips, panels and daily gags before he found the perfect setting. There is a literary quality to his work, as we might expect from an educated man of innate good taste; his captions and legends are uncompromisingly grammatical and written with style. (Among those who encouraged him during the dark days were Henry Seidel Canby, Stephen Vincent Benét and Christopher Morley.) Williams' pen technique is his own; his work has never been successfully imitated. He uses occasional blacks, with a minimum of lines (all of them fine), and produces motion, attitude and elegance in a triumph of economy. His satirical eye is sharp; there is no American type of the upper-middle or upper class which he has not reduced to devastating caricature. Many of the best of them populate his series "America's Playgrounds," which runs all too seldom in *The New Yorker*.

There remain the urbanites, lower or lower-middle class, dispossessed or muddling through. Their spokesman was Denys Wortman, and in his work is a mixture of irony and sympathy unmatched in daily cartooning. Wortman had a painter's education, and his panels are carefully composed and toned. But what he enjoyed in life was not a scene, not a particular graphic beauty; what he loved was the "moment," the illumination of a small, dark corner of the urban soul. His *Everyday Movies* are an endlessly various panorama of the modern nickel-and-dime metropolis. Here are the secretaries, not glamorized and not flibbertigibbets but baffled and

"*We gotta get busy. Summer's nearly over and we ain't put in our supply of boy friends for all winter.*"

DENYS WORTMAN's view of urban humanity— unvarnished but compassionate. © 1935 United Feature Syndicate, Inc.

The Toonerville Trolley That Meets All Trains— sooner or later. © 1949 by FONTAINE FOX.

Mr. Bang explodes again. Note the delighted caddie. © 1954 by FONTAINE FOX.

aspiring in their $5.95 mass-produced dresses; here are the park-bench bums ("Mopey Dick and the Duke"), more at peace with the world than most of us; here is Sam ("In and Out of the Red with Sam"), making an honest living in a clothes store but beset by bill collectors and discount-hungry friends; here are sailors, shoppers, workmen, clerks, salesmen and always the girls— almost pretty, almost intelligent, doomed by the mechanics of megalopolis to a brassy, defensive, wise-cracking existence.

Wortman used a soft pencil always; he said no other tool could catch the shadings and subtleties necessary to real character studies. His work was thoroughly professional. His drawings are finished; there are no scribbled backgrounds, no inexplicable strokes, no rococo distractions. He was not urbane, but urban: direct, busy, crowded, a little sooty and honestly compassionate. His death in 1958 was the loss of a fine artist.

The third oldest daily comic creation in America was a panel called *Toonerville Folks,* which fact entitles its creator, Fontaine Fox, to the adjective "venerable." Only *Mutt and Jeff* and *The Katzenjammer Kids* have also been running for more than fifty years, and neither of those is now done by its originator. And while dozens of other strips have introduced thoroughly memorable characters, probably no one in the business created quite the variety that Fox did. The Terrible Tempered Mr. Bang and the Powerful Katrinka are unforgettable; Mickey (himself) McGuire is the original juvenile scourge; Tomboy Tailor, Aunt Eppy Hogg, and Handlebar Hank were three more; Cy Wortle, owner of a laughing cow, was another; and Suitcase Simpson, who appeared frequently in the panel, attained such national renown that when Kansas City received, almost simultaneously, a major-league baseball franchise and an outfielder named Simpson, he was immediately dubbed Suitcase.

Fox was born in Louisville, in 1884, and has reported that the prototype

Katrinka in action. Even the cat is distinctive, and the little boy in the foreground is obviously ecstatic. © 1954 by FONTAINE FOX.

of his bully, Mickey McGuire, was in his class in public school. Fox was a leader of a youthful gang— way back in the days when youthful gangs were relatively innocent and confined their mayhem to weaponless if enthusiastic assaults— and when McGuire plays the tough in Fox's panel, the authenticity of his manner is indisputable. By 1908, when he was twenty-four, Fox had moved north to Chicago, with the now defunct Chicago *Post*. In those days, remember, the daily comic strip was practically unknown. The Sunday supplement was well established; and Bud Fisher had begun to do *Mutt and Jeff* dailies, but otherwise the weekday newspapers relied upon spot sketches and panel cartoons for graphic spice. Fox's editor was astonished at the artist's proposal that he run humorous drawings of children; Chicago was John T. McCutcheon's town, and McCutcheon had already established himself as the great kid cartoonist of the time. But Fox was stubborn, and his editor asked to see samples. The samples were forthcoming; the editor liked them and ran one of them on the front page; Fox then worked up to a daily panel slowly, beginning with a sketch a week. Inevitably, this work caught the eye of syndicates, and in 1913 Fox signed with the Wheeler Syndicate, now the Bell Syndicate.

The Toonerville Trolley itself, a landmark in American transportation, was drawn, with some exaggeration, from real life. Before the turn of the century trolley service in Louisville was picturesque, irregular, and possibly more a hindrance than a help to travelers. Fox's first published drawings of trolley cars accompanied a series of editorials in a Louisville newspaper. But the true prototype of the Toonerville Trolley was a trolley car in Pelham, New York, which Fox and his wife boarded one day in paying a visit to Charles Voight. The car itself was so distinctive and its bearded conductor so independent— when they arrived near the Voights' house he left the car, led the Foxes to a nearby hill, and pointed it out— that the combination proved irresistible. In no time at all Fox had worked out a series of Toonerville Trolley panels all of which fit in quite well with his original suburban small-fry idea. Now the small fry receded somewhat in importance, and the major adult characters came to the foreground. They wore well for decades.

Fox's style is deceptively simple. At first glance his work seems cheerfully but regularly laid out; but at second and third glance odd bits of technique become noticeable. Vehicles which should be erect are oddly tilted; so are telephone poles, and so, more often than not, is the horizon. And Fox handles perspective brilliantly. Mickey McGuire and his sheepish companions are often shown on a baseball diamond— broken windows are a stock misdemeanor among characters of that age, and no projectile can improve upon the baseball. These baseball drawings seem properly laid out; the boys are in roughly the positions that boys occupy; yet closer examination reveals the fact that the distance between bases is no more than twice the length of a child, and that some ten or a dozen figures, plus a clearly defined background, have been compressed without distortion into the space of Fox's panel. But in the end it was not so much his technique as the figures which made the panel universally popular. Each of them is distinctive— Mr. Bang had his fierce temper, Katrinka was capable of prodigies of physical exertion (and had a boy friend who was a cigar-smoking dwarf); Mickey McGuire, with his floppy hat and the eternal blade of grass in his mouth, was unmistakably a small-sized villain. Only a very short exposure to Fox's work is sufficient to turn a casual reader into an addict— a sure indication of the man's originality. He created a world and peopled it with mirthful parodies who never bore us. Not many cartoonists can say the same. And when the artist retired recently, he refused to let *The Toonerville Trolley That Meets All Trains* pass into another man's hands— a gesture of artistic pride, and no one was more entitled to it than Fontaine Fox.

One of the daily panelists brings us back to that region of partial insanity from which the best fantasy arises. His name is Lichty (George Maurice Lichtenstein); and his quality is total irreverence. He was born

Two by LICHTY. Seemingly slapdash, the style suits the attitude perfectly. © Field Enterprises, Inc. Courtesy of Chicago *Sun-Times* Syndicate.

". . . and it's gratifying to note that public cooperation in the test evacuation of this city was 100%. . . . They had traffic hopelessly snarled within minutes!"

"I'm sure you remember what a dreadful experience it was being out of debt . . . how we lost our feeling of 'belongingness'! . . ."

Comic Art in America

The Franciscan virtues in action. A *Brother Juniper* by FATHER JUSTIN MCCARTHY, from *More Brother Juniper*, 1958, Hanover House, New York. Courtesy Publishers Syndicate.

in Chicago in 1906, and Martin Sheridan reports that he was expelled from the Chicago Art Institute at the age of eighteen for placing gag lines under the Rembrandts and El Grecos. Apocryphal or not, the story rings true. Lichty respects laughter and little else. His vast, slightly sympathetic disdain for the downtrodden American husband is matched only by his tooth-and-claw resistance to the overbearing American wife. Regularly he makes mincemeat of the American politician; his senators and congressmen are the most blatantly bombastic and hypocritical of the species. He has carried Soviet logic to a lunatic extreme in his satires of commissars and bureaucrats. He spoofs birthday parties, patriotic holidays, clubwomen, Sunday drivers, doctors, lawyers and Indian chiefs, and he does all this with a diabolical gusto instantly communicated to the reader.

He broke in with the newly established Chicago *Times* in 1929; in 1932 appeared his first *Grin and Bear It* page. United Feature Syndicate carried him from 1934 to 1940, at which point the Chicago *Times* Syndicate was organized, and reclaimed its prodigy. Lichty works fast. His style is apparently slapdash; he pencils in outlines and features, and then brushes on tones or color. (He once said that he could finish a week's work in two days.) But the antic drawing— the fiendish expressions, the fierce glares of disapproval, the bland arrogance of the governmental face— is the perfect medium for his antic humor. He maintains a large file of jokes, and will accept gags from any source, but they never come to full flower until he has drawn or painted them. His jokes are not sophisticated, but his drawing is. He has made as much of slapstick and burlesque as any cartoonist of the day.

In one way, at least, the most unusual of the panels is *Brother Juniper*, a product of the 1950s. Over the decades occasional cartoons have featured ecclesiasts (Chon Day's *Brother Sebastian* appears in magazines), but *Brother Juniper* is the first series to offer a man of the cloth as its daily hero. "Hero" is perhaps not the word. The panel is drawn by Father Justin McCarthy, a Franciscan, and Brother Juniper, in the true Franciscan spirit,

A poignant sequence from DORGAN's satirical serial, *Silk Hat Harry's Divorce Suit.* © King Features Syndicate, Inc.

170

[ABOVE LEFT] TAD DORGAN's sidelight on crapshooters, in an *Indoor Sports* of 1929. © King Features Syndicate, Inc.

[ABOVE RIGHT] An *Indoor Sports* by DORGAN. © King Features Syndicate, Inc.

is simple, mild-mannered and affable. Equally Franciscan is his love for children and animals, an emotion which often lies at the heart of the joke. (Juniper is his monastery's cook, and his preoccupation with food, while not Lucullan, is perhaps more Benedictine than Franciscan.) This series is heart-warming and funny. There is an air of frivolity about it simply because we are not accustomed to newspaper panels poking fun at the clergy. But Father McCarthy is a man of excellent taste, and his work is highly approved by his superiors. Even in an age of television it is rare for religion in any form to reach fifteen or twenty million people daily.

There were two men whose panels remain, very simply, classic. They were Clare Briggs and H. T. Webster. They sprang not from the world of magazine panels, not from *Judge* and *Puck* and *Life*, but from the ranks of newspaper artists. Their predecessors were not Zimmerman and Sullivant, but T. E. Powers and "Tad" Dorgan. They did not create humor; they re-created life.

Of the two earlier men, Dorgan was certainly the more famous and better loved, but even he owed a great deal to Powers (that same Powers who had done editorial cartoons for Hearst). Powers' humor was bluff and uncomplicated, his drawing was simplicity itself. His subject was the American businessman— Napoleon in the office, a slave at home— and the inevitable domineering wife. Here was the war between men and women in its bluntest, most exaggerated form. The wife was not only boss, she looked the part, being huge, unattractive and forceful. Worse still, she thrived on her dominance, becoming steadily more impressive, more self-assured, more arrogant, as her pipsqueak husband diminished almost before her eyes. There has been much foofaraw in our time about the diminution of the American male, but labor-saving devices have softened at least

171

When a Feller Needs a Friend, a BRIGGS panel from 1922. Courtesy of Ruth Owen Briggs.

the physical serfdom; when Powers' henpecked hero rose at six to trim the lawn, he was without benefit of power mower. His tribulations generally involved more physical discomfort, which added an element of real brutality to Powers' work.

Between 1910 and 1920, when Powers' work was at its best, Dorgan was also on the New York *Journal* and the New York *American*. Like Sullivant and later Billy Ireland, Dorgan has always been held in a kind of reverence by his colleagues and successors.

He reached his widest audience and his greatest fame in the 1910s and early 1920s with Hearst's New York newspapers, but his work before then had been equally great. Before 1905 he had been the country's best sports cartoonist, in San Francisco, of course, and it was his excellence there that prompted Hearst to lure him east, where circulations were higher. Dorgan had a fine sense of the zany, and many of his pages and half-pages defied all the rules of unity, coherence and emphasis. He was alert and imaginative, and thought nothing of embroidering a basic theme with extraneous figures or two-line jokes. Often he wrote essays to accompany his drawings; they were usually printed. With the keen nose of a man who had seen fights dumped and horse races fixed, he sniffed out the phony; and when he came later to do *Indoor Sports* he was merciless on the subterfuges of the weak poker-player— of the weak in general. He was a toughie, Dorgan was, and enriched popular slang (in a daily panel of riddles, poems and fables called *Daffydils* and illustrated by stick figures) with

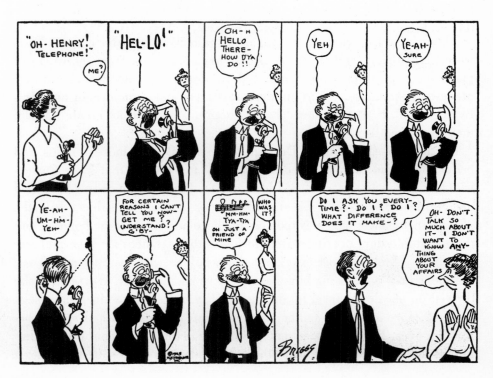

Movie of a Woman Trying to Get a Line on a Phone Conversation, a CLARE BRIGGS panel from 1925. An obvious variant of Briggs's later *Mr. and Mrs.* Courtesy of Ruth Owen Briggs.

THE THROW-DOWN

The Days of Real Sport, a BRIGGS panel from 1922. Courtesy of Ruth Owen Briggs.

expressions like "You'll find Sympathy in the Dictionary," or "Half the World are Squirrels, and the other half are Nuts." Probably his finest single creation was *Silk Hat Harry's Divorce Suit*, a panel which generally ran beside *Indoor Sports* or *Outdoor Sports*. All its characters were dogs in human dress, but here was no sentimentality; these were cynical, egotistical dogs, looking out for Number One, with no sympathy for the fool or the weakling. (Milt Gross, incidentally, was an office boy in Dorgan's department, and was obviously affected by Tad's sense of the goofy.)

Dorgan died on May 2, 1929, and by then Clare Briggs (who died the same year) was at his peak. Briggs had known a small prominence back in 1904, when he created *A. Piker Clerk* for the Chicago *American* (the first

The last three panels of a Sunday *Mr. and Mrs.* by CLARE BRIGGS. © 1921, 1949, New York *Herald Tribune*, Inc., reproduced with permission.

strip, technically; it used the strip form, had a regular cast, and dealt with horse playing. *Mutt and Jeff* was the first of this kind to last). The strip folded shortly, and Briggs, who was born in Wisconsin and had lived in Nebraska and St. Louis, and had sketched in New York for Hearst, moved to the Chicago *Tribune*. He had been influenced by McCutcheon, as were many cartoonists of the day, but he was developing his own slant on the inner recesses of the small-town secret heart, and when he went to the New York *Herald Tribune* in 1917 he was ready for greatness. He drew emotions. His titles give the key: *That Guiltiest Feeling, When a Feller Needs a Friend, Ain't It a Grand and Glorious Feeling?* "It's the idea that gets you," Waugh wrote: "the hominess, the truth of it, the insight, the looking into so many tiny dramas, hopes, and frustrations, which no one else ever bothered with and which are utterly real."

He did a strip, too, carried on by Arthur Folwell and later Kin Platt, called *Mr. and Mrs.*, in which Joe and Vi carried on one long marital

[BELOW LEFT] H. T. WEBSTER's Caspar Milquetoast in a panel. Courtesy of the New York *Herald Tribune*, Inc., reproduced with permission.

[BELOW RIGHT] Another WEBSTER panel, this one entitled *Bridge*. Courtesy of the New York *Herald Tribune*, Inc., reproduced with permission.

squabble, with only occasional flashes of affection. But his enduring fame was as a panel cartoonist, and his effect on his admirers was so strong that many of them refuse to believe that he has been dead for thirty years; they "seem to remember" him in the thirties and even the early forties. Greatness lingers.

Harold Tucker Webster was ten years younger than Briggs, and is still confused with him by occasional readers. One obvious reason is his titles, which were something like Briggs's: *The Thrill That Comes Once in a Lifetime, Life's Darkest Moment, The Boy Who Made Good.* Webster too revealed the inner heart of the average man (or woman or boy), but he was a touch more suburban, a touch less cruel, a touch more witty than Briggs. His comic-strip creation, Caspar Milquetoast, was funnier, if not longer-lived, than *Mr. and Mrs.* Milquetoast was the hero of *The Timid Soul,* and he was in many ways the opposite of Dorgan's dogs: impossibly timid and impossibly resigned to a hostile universe. Milquetoast is a direct, though enfeebled, descendant of the hero of Webster's first strip, *The Man in the Brown Derby,* which he created for the New York *World* in 1923. The Man was Egbert Smear, and he was, as Waugh put it, neither gorilla nor mouse. If he never knew the joys of the thrill that comes once in a lifetime, neither did he know the gloom of life's darkest moment. He was not dominated by his wife; neither did he dominate her. Here was a normal couple, deriving honest low-key pleasures from unexceptional activities, motivated from within by a sense of democracy in its purest form. Egbert's occasional attempts at grandeur were inevitably failures.

Neither Egbert nor Caspar was Webster's triumph; his daily panel was. Bridge players screamed in delight at his perfect understanding of them; fishermen rejoiced in his sympathy; middle-aged men recalled their years of barefoot adolescence. In many ways his "bridge" panels were his best, but they were too specialized for the general public. The small-boy or adolescent panels, again showing a debt to McCutcheon, were his most popular. His death in 1952 was difficult to accept. He had become a habit, quietly and unassertively, and most of us never realized how good he was until he was gone.

CHAPTER VI

Comics: No American Home Complete Without Them

THE TWENTIES, like most decades born in fire, died in ashes, which made a sad beginning for the thirties. But the comics were indestructible. Just as animated cartoons lost none of their appeal or commercial value during the depression, so the comic strips continued to attract a daily audience of tens of millions. Newspaper circulation dipped when three cents became a large sum of money; but often one newspaper served three or four families, and if prosperity wasn't just around the corner, a newsstand was.

The comics section, in fact, began another period of expansion. We were a long way from the day when one newspaper (the Washington *Post and Times Herald*) would carry thirty-two strips daily, plus panels, but that day was already predictable. For one thing, the comics were surviving the worst economic tragedy in our history; for another, they were expanding; and for a third, their expansion was not limited to more strips of the already familiar type— the subject matter of comic strips now seemed unlimited. If life was real and earnest, we would have real and earnest comics. If Capone was a national figure, Dick Tracy would shortly be even better known. If the China Clipper could connect America and Asia, so could Milton Caniff.

The adventure strip was the significant development of the 1930s. The adventures and adventurers might seem pleasantly farfetched to armchair readers, but we all had a pretty good idea that somewhere in the world there *was* a fearless, square-jawed plain-clothes cop; somewhere in the world there *was* a free-lance pilot running guns; somewhere in the universe there might even be a handsome space-man with a paralysis ray. True, of the five great strips originated in the thirties, only one is strictly an adventure strip; but that one, Milton Caniff's *Terry and the Pirates*, spawned more variations and imitations than any other strip in history. The other four also set styles: *Blondie*, followed over the next twenty years by half a dozen lighthearted family strips; *Dick Tracy*, the first of many police strips; *Li'l Abner*, from which came a few regional satires; and *Joe Palooka*, father of the straight sports strip.

Strictly speaking, *Palooka* itself had antecedents. Sam Leff had been doing a strip called *Joe's Car*, and then *Joe Jinks*, since before 1920, and had used day-to-day continuity when it was not yet the rule. Joe was a small, unhealthy, beleaguered man, tolerated by his wife only because he struggled manfully to make a living in a world that cared little whether he succeeded or not. Starting out (like *Gasoline Alley)* as a strip devoted to exploration of the mysterious ways of internal combustion, *Joe's Car* lost its point when the automobile became reliable; Joe promptly moved into the world of aviation. His motive all along had been to succeed in an avocation, to find some little patch of nervous glory outside the complexities of business. In this he is only slightly like Ham Fisher's Knobby Walsh, who was a fight manager from *Joe Palooka's* inception; Joe Jinks himself became a fight manager in 1944, and the title of his strip was changed to *Curly Kayoe* at the end of 1945. As a fight strip, *Curly Kayoe* was late on the scene, and derived from *Joe Palooka*, but for years Joe Jinks had lived for sports. As a character, he comes out of the cigar-chewing, fast-talking fight fans of the early 1900s, and because his travail was real (while Palooka is a little too good, a little too liberal, a little too sweet to be true), Leff's creation ought to be remembered: Joe Jinks, all cigar smoke and frustration, was, with the exception of Augustus Mutt, the first sports fan in the comics.

Joe Palooka may have started out as a fight strip, but it rapidly became something else. Ham Fisher, its creator, had become almost a one-man art staff for the Wilkes-Barre *Herald* in the 1920s. From childhood he had wanted to be a cartoonist, but the idea of doing a strip came to him late, around 1926. He had been interviewing a peaceful, childlike fighter, and

Joe Jinks in 1931, when VIC FORSYTHE had taken over the the strip. Cars and boxing were Joe's first loves; then came fishing. © United Feature Syndicate, Inc.

the contrast between the man's nature and trade struck home. What better device than an unbeatable heavyweight with a heart of gold? It was the old, wistful portrait of power that did not corrupt. Here were all the human virtues embodied in a man who could, if he were not so pure, have become a menace to society, but who, being so pure, was the kind of idol America invariably bowed to. Even the name, Joe Palooka, was perfect: Joe, one of the most common names in the world, and Palooka, with its implications of middle-European immigrant background, and its obvious prize-ring significance.

Fisher's strip was turned down time and again. His persistence is one of the legends of cartooning. He came to New York almost penniless in 1927, with all the work he had thus far done on the strip, got a two-bit job in the advertising department of the *Daily News*, and started *Palooka* around the syndicates once more, piling up further rejections. The turning point was the day he found a job as a salesman with the McNaught Syndicate. After a period of daily contact with Charles McAdam, then general manager, Fisher extracted a promise from him that *Palooka* would be tried out later.

To prove his sales ability, Fisher took to the road with *Dixie Dugan*, a snappy, modern career-girl strip by J. P. McEvoy and John H. Strieble,

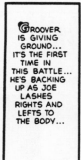

Joe Palooka in 1955, with virtue, as always, triumphant. Courtesy the McNaught Syndicate, Inc.

"True Love": Joe Palooka and Ann Howe in a tender postwar scene. They were married later. Courtesy the McNaught Syndicate, Inc.

which had begun as a show-girl strip. *Dixie Dugan* was in the general category of girl strips, with *Betty* and *Boots* and *Tillie* and *Winnie,* but after a good start it had gone quietly downhill. By the middle of 1930 it had only a few newspapers. Fisher took it on a forty-day road trip. When he came back *Dixie Dugan* was in over forty papers, and the strip has flourished ever since.

McAdam was pleased; Fisher was a born salesman. He could stay on the road for a while, not with *Palooka,* of course, but with some strip that might have a chance. Fisher's gloom deepened. He hung on, though, until McAdam went on vacation. Then Fisher took a long chance and went out with *Joe Palooka.* In three weeks he had sold twenty newspapers, and a star was born.

Considering the setting, *Palooka* is the most sentimental strip in America. Here are all the paraphernalia and appurtenances of the fight racket: fighters, managers, seconds, gamblers, horse-playing hangers-on. Yet look at its hero: tall, good-looking in a snub-nosed way, mild-mannered, even affectionate, totally virtuous (though capable of anger at real injustice) and a Juggernaut in the ring. His girl friend (now his wife) is also a paragon. Her name is Ann Howe (simple and possibly patrician); she is rich, beautiful and unflaggingly sweet. Many of the secondary characters, particularly in the last fifteen years, are homey and kind; certainly Ma Palooka seems out of character when not baking an apple pie, and little Max, the mute, is the all-time number-one tyke. Manager Knobby Walsh and friend Jerry Leemy provided the Palookas with intrigue, necessary to melodramatic conflict; they were in a sense contact men between Joe and the world of ordinary sin and crime. But nothing that they brought into the strip could prevail against Joe's insuperable good will.

As Coulton Waugh made clear, Joe never goes out of his way to be good. He *is* good. He is incorruptible because he bears humanity a great love. If at first that love was the love of the simple, grateful, physical being, it has become a touch more sophisticated lately; Joe is now fully capable of recognizing evil, and is rarely taken in by the con men of the heart. And Joe's goodness is not spoiled by either evangelism or intelligence; he was for long almost naïvely stupid, and his preaching was pitched very low. His mild manglings of the English language only made him more of a hero to those who had trouble with who, whom and words of three syllables. His inability to meet the demands of high society is no drawback; he simply forces the rich and mannered to accept him on his own terms, establishing at one stroke his own and the readers' superiority.

Fisher has been criticized occasionally for glorifying the physical and denigrating the intellectual, but it makes much more sense to say that Palooka glorifies the virtuous and moral, as distinguished from the complex and clever. (Fisher himself was complex and clever, by the way.) Joe respects brains; his excuse for enlisting as a private in 1940, and not going after a commission, was that he did not know enough to be an officer. (As an enlisted man he naturally maintained a lively sense of identification on the part of millions of readers.)

The key to Palooka as a comics hero is not that he is simple, or naïve, or anti-intellectual, or basically rural, but that he is the personification of the ideals of an American majority. Each of his attributes has two sides; he may be called a boob, which is bad, or unsophisticated, which is good; a sucker (bad) or an idealist (good); a sentimentalist or a saint. But in every panel of the strip there is such an effusion of traditional virtue, of bonhomie, of democracy, that Palooka has come to personify the glories of the simple life. He is what, until very recently at any rate, the American morality was supposed to produce: a man trustworthy, loyal, helpful, friendly, courteous, kind, obedient, cheerful, thrifty, brave, clean and reverent. A world full of Palookas might be dull; in so much goodness man, an imperfect being, might drown; but Palooka is the hero of millions precisely because we do not live in such a world. Joe Palooka is Galahad in boxing trunks, or, out of the ring, in a tweed jacket and bow tie.

Or, during the war, in uniform. Palooka represented the majority there also. He was an enlisted man; he had been against involvement in the war, but once it came he would give it all he had; our side was good, the other side was bad; there was evil on the home front too, wherever greed and selfishness existed; labor and management would have to work together; and a man was a man whether he was black or white, and whatever his religion.

None of these conclusions was revolutionary; in principle none of them was even controversial. A man with a bullet in him is generally too hurt and angry to worry about political philosophy, much less to talk about it; but when Joe told a friend's girl that the man "said to tell you— he was proud to die for the right of other men t' justice and democracy," it sounded good. If American soldiers had to die, that was what they were supposed to die for.

Fisher himself died a suicide in 1956, and the strip has been carried on

Joe Palooka after a double victory— he had recovered from a wound and defeated a challenger in the ring. This is the last page of a comic pamphlet distributed by the government to stress the importance of courage and persistence in physical rehabilitation. Courtesy the McNaught Syndicate, Inc.

with little change in style or matter by Moe Leff. Fisher was a complicated man, difficult to fathom, yet he created a character of monumentally simple innocence.

In the end Joe Palooka is the great democratic hero. When Little Orphan Annie's "good" friends are in trouble, someone rich and powerful will often help them out of it; when Palooka's "good" friends are in trouble, their very goodness gets them out of it. The compassionate, generous, moral man *must* win, because that's the way it's supposed to be. If it were not so, America itself would make no sense. Joe Palooka is the free man, strong, good, invincible. If he is also entertaining, so much the better.

The only American hero with whom readers identify even better is one whom we have already met: the Husband and Father. It is understood that the American husband and father is at least bumbling and more often downright incompetent, but that his instincts are good. Bounded by the legend that our H&F is woefully undeserving of his wife and children, our family strips have flourished. And in this garden of domestic exaggeration and fantasy, no weed has sprung as tall as Dagwood Bumstead.

The creator of this futility symbol is a man named Murat Young, known to his friends, including an international public, as Chic Young. He was born in 1901, into a family much given to sketching, drawing and painting. Early on there was little to hint at his future fame; for a time he was a stenographer in a railroad office. The first signal from an unfathomable Destiny was a wire from Edgar Martin (creator of *Boots*) that NEA Service could use a girl strip. Young rushed to Cleveland, where the syndicate found a place for him in its art department. Here he plodded for several months, in a lunatic atmosphere consisting of short spurts of labor followed by days of interoffice joking, practical and impractical. The jokes were so frequent and so farfetched that when Young picked up the phone one day and heard a man from King Features offering him $10,000 a year to come to New York, he barely smiled before hanging up. Months later, fired when he asked for a raise, Young went to New York and scouted for work. King Features seemed interested, and Young was asked to see J. D. Gortatowski, who was then in charge of comic art at KFS. Why, Gortatowski wanted to know, had Young been so cavalier about that phone call?

Young's horrified explanations were accepted, and he was set to work doing a strip called *Beautiful Babs*, about a society girl; it lasted four months. For almost a year afterward Young did apprentice work in the art department. His next strip, which ran for five years, was *Dumb Dora*.

One of America's most famous couples before their marriage— Blondie and Dagwood, here shown with Bumstead *père*. © 1930 King Features Syndicate, Inc.

The Bumsteads five years later. CHIC YOUNG's expose of the American husband. © 1935 King Features Syndicate, Inc.

(It was taken over later by Paul Fung, the first Chinese-American to reach the top in comics.) It was funny enough, but Dora was a flapper, and when the Flapper Age ended, her humor rang hollow. Women were becoming women again, releasing their curves from ten years of durance vile and turning their attention once more to feminine pursuits.

On September 8, 1930, the New Woman appeared. In several respects she was like her predecessors: she was flippant and independent, and carried in tow a pusillanimous, adoring male. Her name was Blondie; she was penniless and irreverent. His name was Dagwood; he was the heir to millions. She was not a gold-digger, and cared not a whit for the millions, but the strip's first suspense was built around the Bumsteads' dislike of their prospective daughter-in-law. Young then accomplished several purposes with one well-timed stroke. By having the two marry, and having Dagwood consequently disinherited, Young first solved the immediate plot problem, then avoided the "when-will-they-marry?" trap which has plagued so many comic-strip artists, and finally established the basis for a milieu that would be strictly middle-class American.

Young's success with *Blondie* is incredible. The strip runs in more than twelve hundred newspapers all over the world. Young must feed his readers a new gag every day of the week; the continuity is one of environment and not one of plot. And for almost thirty years Young has been at the top of the heap— by means of infinite variation on one simple principle. There was a popular series of Blondie movies; there has been a Blondie television series; the Bumsteads were on radio for years. The Dagwood sandwich— our H&F's one uninhibited burst of creative genius— is a national institution; if it is not international it can only be because they don't sell sliced bread in those other countries.

The bumbling Bumstead is not the sole reason for this popularity. Blondie is much prettier, and better constructed, than the casual reader thinks. Young's drawing is excellent, simple and full of punch; if he was ever tempted to fill in the wallpapers, chintzes and five-and-dime knickknackery that go with middle-class life, he resisted successfully. He is closer to George McManus as an artist than to anyone else, using the same bold

183

blacks to focus his panels and a minimum of decoration elsewhere. All the realistic details are implied; only the characters are explicit.

And they are explicit! When Young draws a traveling salesman there is never the slightest doubt of either the man's profession or his temperament. Dagwood's boss is probably the grumpiest and most harassed boss in the country. Even the Bumsteads' dogs overact. Dagwood's occasional poker sessions are models of grim greed and cigar smoke (though Dagwood has been observed to hold six cards, a practice frowned upon in the fraternity). Dagwood's children are brighter than their father, but no brighter than other children; they are simply more expressive.

It is hard to specify what makes Dagwood so lovable. (He is far more lovable, incidentally, in the comic strip than in any of its adaptations to other media.) In family strips all fathers are objects of ridicule and sympathy; why does Dagwood stand out? All wives are goddesses come to life; why does Blondie stand out?

There is one statistical hint: Dagwood's defeats run about six-to-one over his small victories; but he does have small victories. He has the potential, and has even been known to triumph over his boss, Mr. Dithers. Over three decades this has added a tenuous strain of suspense to the strip: there must be many readers who stick with the Bumsteads for the sake of that one day a week when man, as a gender, is vindicated. And then even his defeats spring from his good nature, and not from real deficiencies. What he lacks is not a sense of discipline, but the capacity for cruelty; not a good head for shopping, but sales resistance; not a sense of his own existence, but a sense of his own importance.

Not to put too fine a point on it, even his defeats are triumphs— for somebody else. That somebody else may be Blondie, or the children, or Herb Woodley next door, or Mr. Dithers, but more often than not it is the reader, who has been through just what Dagwood undergoes, but who has acquitted himself better. Who is, in other words, proud of himself when he has Dagwood as a standard of comparison.

Maybe all this is too deep. Maybe it is simply that Dagwood goes through what we all go through, but that Dagwood's triumphs and defeats are simple and unambiguous, while our own are confused by the exigencies of reality. Our own debates with door-to-door salesmen are to some degree determined by our moods, the state of our bile, our successes and failures at the office this week; Dagwood's are more melodramatic, the stark conflict between seller and buyer, intruder and householder, expressed in its most direct terms.

Dagwood's experiences with his children are to the point. Baby Dumpling was born on April 15, 1934, and Dagwood's ignorance of the techniques of fatherhood was practically total. The rest of us know a little something about formulas and diapers; we cope with infants and hope for the best. But Dagwood's dilemma was unalloyed by any random shred of knowledge or experience; here was desperation in its purest form. Seven years later, in 1941, Cookie was born. Was Dagwood, by now an old hand, any more use than the first time? Of course not. His troubles were simply doubled.

Listing those troubles, in order of frequency or importance, would be futile. Whether the basement is flooded or Dagwood is late to work or a delegation arrives from a women's club while he is in the bath, the intensity of emotion is the same. *Blondie* is no detailed analysis of the difficulties of the home-owning H&F. The strip is a flat statement of an ancient dogma: that once man has padded the cave with evergreen boughs, brought home skins and meat, and perpetuated his kind, he becomes a useless supernumerary, tolerated for his weaknesses and barely permitted to delude himself with the ludicrous notion that he is of value to society.

A beautifully composed Sunday page of *Blondie,* as the mantle of fatherhood fell heavily upon Dagwood. © 1941 King Features Syndicate, Inc.

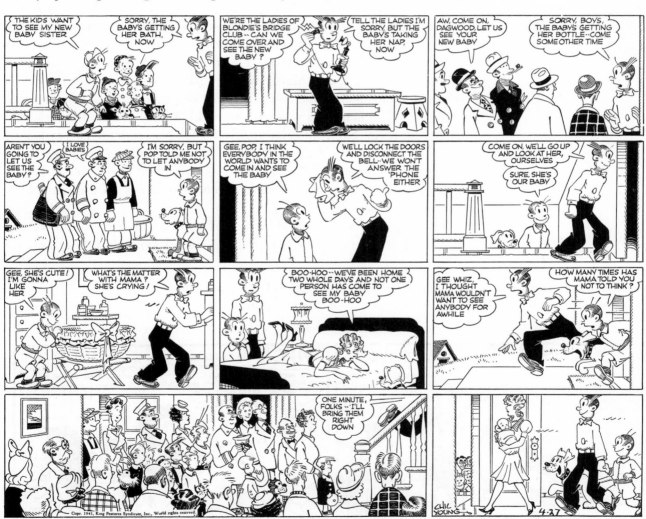

A daily *Blondie* of 1957. Dagwood and Dithers, though usually at war, are obviously bound by a strong personal tie. © King Features Syndicate, Inc.

The next most famous marriage in the history of comics occurred during the last week of March 1952, when a tall, powerful, idealistic young American as unlike Joe Palooka as possible was trapped by an impatient, angry Fate and forced to submit to the hoomiliation of matrimony with his faithful inamorata. The groom, Abner Yokum, was resplendent in polka-dotted shorts; his bride, Daisy Mae, wore her habitual tattered black skirt, a minimal, dotted bodice and an abbreviated veil hanging back from a crown of flowers. The marriage was performed by a duly constituted authority named Marryin' Sam, who charged $1.35 for his services. The ceremony climaxed a courtship dating back to 1935; during those seventeen years the groom had successfully evaded bliss some half-dozen times, always with the aid of some logic-defying mental gymnastics on the part of his creator, Al Capp.

The strip is of course *Li'l Abner*, and Capp is, with Rube Goldberg and a handful of others, in a select group of mental gymnasts: those who are

The long-delayed, oft-postponed wedding of Daisy Mae and Li'l Abner Yokum. A social note of the first magnitude. © 1952 United Feature Syndicate, Inc.

186

taken seriously by the intellectuals of the time. Capp has been taken so seriously that he has become in many ways as fascinating as his strip— particularly when the reader discovers that accounts of his prodigious creative powers are not at all exaggerated. The man is an intellectual Gargantua— nothing human, subhuman or superhuman is alien to him— and through the panels of his strip has paraded, for twenty-five years, the most outlandish collection of caricatures since Daumier.

There was no guarantee in 1934 that any such talent was about to begin showering the world with hot potatoes. Born in New Haven, Capp had struggled through a poor-boy-in-the-big-town childhood. He flunked plane geometry for nine consecutive terms, a feat made possible only by the fact that he remained in high school for five years without graduating. He lost no perspective on the way, but became tough enough to survive the early

AL CAPP's hillbillies in trouble. The villain is named "Soft-Hearted John." © 1947 United Feature Syndicate, Inc.

years of a career in art. He studied at the Pennsylvania Academy of Fine Arts and at the Boston Museum School, working up to a career as a serious landscape artist. With no money, he used his wits, paying a small deposit on each course and staying in it until the authorities expelled him. ("That way I got three or four years more in, at nine different art schools," he said later.) Perhaps the difficulty of staying alive altered his view of oil painting; perhaps, as Coulton Waugh suggests, it was the chance remark of an unimpressed hillbilly ("That don't make sense"). At any rate, he turned to cartooning.

His first months in New York were almost enough to make him turn back to oils. As a staff artist with the AP, he was assigned to do *Mr. Gilfeather*, a comic strip syndicated nationally. He labored long and faithfully, and his labors were rewarded: an editor wrote in to say that the new *Mr. Gilfeather* was "by far the worst cartoon in the country." He quit after six months, with a minimum of polite protest from the AP. His job was taken over by a retoucher named Milton Caniff, whose work, Capp later complained, was "so superior to mine that I shudder just to think of it."

Capp retreated to Boston and went back to the Museum School. He sold a few cartoons—not even enough to encourage him. He married. He sketched. He conceived, mulled over and discarded idea after idea. Finally he returned to New York. New York was big; there were people; there was activity, creation, production, movement. New York was where things happened.

The first thing that happened was that a fresh batch of cartoons was rejected by every editor in the city. The second thing was a little more helpful. Capp was plodding up the street with his portfolio under his arm when a burly, flashy stranger, sitting next to a good-looking girl in an equally good-looking car, pulled up and called out to him. Capp was intrigued by the presence of obvious wealth (even then there was something larcenous in his imagination, something that delighted in the unexpected, the sudden switch, the masterly swindle), but he had been through a trying day and was inclined to be surly toward the well-to-do. The man identified him correctly as a cartoonist, and then introduced himself: he was Ham Fisher, and he drew *Joe Palooka*, and he needed a Sunday page finished. Would Capp do it for ten dollars?

Capp did, and became Fisher's full-time assistant. This was in 1933. It was Capp's first real break, and he took full advantage of it by devoting his spare time to his own work. Without ever phrasing the thought to himself, he had begun to realize that he was not the kind of man who works well as a subordinate, on any level. Trimming his own exuberance and imagination to the demands of another man's ideas was stultifying. By 1934 he felt cramped and impatient, almost ferocious in his desire to be independent. And in that year his idea finally arrived. One story has it that *Li'l Abner* was triggered by reminiscences of a walking trip through Kentucky; another that hillbilly music on the radio brought him to life. There is truth in both versions.

AL CAPP's view of one aspect of higher education. Vanity, vanity, all is vanity. © 1947 United Feature Syndicate, Inc.

A Sunday page of *Li'l Abner*, when our hero and heroine had been married for five years. © 1957 United Feature Syndicate, Inc.

But Capp was not only independent, imaginative and poor; he was also thoughtful. He saw what was happening to comics in the thirties, and he drew conclusions. The family strip was solid; the adventure strip was the coming thing, and cops-and-robbers or blood-and-thunder would soon crowd comics pages. What was missing? Humor. What was Capp's basic cast of mind? Skeptical, exuberant, satirical.

Li'l Abner was the result. The strip took a year or so to settle down; Pappy and Mammy Yokum (from "yokel" and "hokum") were originally of a more normal size, and the humor was relatively restrained, much less broad. But Capp was on the way. With Raeburn Van Buren, Walt Kelly later, and a few others, he would restore the traditions of the early days, bringing back broad humor, a zany gusto and flair for social caricature.

Capp resembles Li'l Abner physically, and in a sense the two are complementary. Abner is stubborn, shy, indestructibly naïve; Capp is a thinker, gregarious and sophisticated. The strip itself can be read on at least two levels: as the adventures of a queer lot of bumpkins, or as a considered, Hogarthian attack on American shibboleths and pretensions. (If "Hogarthian" sounds extreme, remember that Capp has been likened to Swift and Dante, among others.) From time to time *Li'l Abner* may reveal a stroke

189

of delicate irony; but Capp's primary technique is Falstaffian— the broad stroke, the mocking burlesque, the devastating parody. Indignity is heaped upon indignity: Capp's southern Senator not only makes speeches that sound suspiciously like direct quotes from such luminaries as the late Senators Vardaman and Bilbo; he not only wears a broad hat, a black frock coat and a string tie; but he is also some three feet high— which makes his effrontery, certitude and pugnacity all the funnier— and his name is Jack S. Phogbound, abbreviated affectionately to "Good Old Jack S." Capp's proper names alone are a clue to his comic genius. Does he need a Bostonian socialite? He creates Henry Cabbage Cod— much more than a simple pun. Does he need a jejune Englishman? Presto: Sir Cecil Cesspool. Was America driven daft by the conga, back in the early forties? Capp created a modern Casanova, Adam Lazonga (one of the most repulsively fascinating creatures in his repertory), from a song called "Six Lessons from Madam Lazonga." His dialect wit is unlimited, and not restricted to hillbillies; when he created the mythical kingdom of Lower Slobbovia his inspiration was almost entirely Yiddish, and resulted in such unlikely names as the Gulf of Pincus, twin cities called Tsk-Tsk and Tch-Tch, and a good king named Nogoodnik, who lived in a capital called Caesar Siddy; not to mention leading citizens who were called Harry S. Rasputintruman and Clark Bagle.

The point is not that he makes puns, but that his puns have some consistency and meaning. They either expose a basic fraudulence in their objects, or illuminate some swindling charade long accepted as legitimate by the public. This is particularly true of his symbols— Kickapoo Joy Juice, with its almost magical powers; the Shmoo; the Kigmy. Of these the Shmoo was the most interesting, and the most controversial. It was a winsome, bulbous, friendly little creature, totally boneless, "which, when broiled, came out steak and, when fried, tasted like chicken. It also laid neatly packaged and bottled eggs and milk, all carefully labeled 'Grade A.'" Milton Caniff, one of Capp's fans, once commented in a national magazine:

The Shmoo kept large portions of the public in a state of dithering excitement for many months, and it seduced some of our sharpest academic minds into helpless blather. It was, for example, a womb symbol, because it supplied all man's needs. Or it stood for an economy of plenty rather than an economy of scarcity and was, therefore, anti-capital. Or maybe anti-labor. Or maybe anti-both-of-them, because it made them both unnecessary. Anyway, letters poured in; congressmen became agitated; magazines veered off on Shmoovian tangents.

On one point, all critics agreed: Capp's creations— animal, vegetable, or mineral — were symbols. And with the Shmoo, Capp had fallen into a trap of his own making. His symbol was too good; it had hit the reader too close to home. It had one of the basic ingredients of the fairy tale, like the purse that never empties, and it struck people way down inside where all those primitive greeds and fears live.

And now the effect of mass circulation was evident. Capp had become a storm-center, not because his art was "higher" (or, let me add immediately, "lower") than that of the novelist or the etcher, but because he reached at least fifty million people every day. Intellectuals hesitated to take him seriously because he created for the many and not for the few. They gave him their attention only when they believed he had crossed the border into their own territory. In that, I think, they were wrong. He had been reaching his readers for a long time on a very deep level, through symbols which have moved men's hearts for thousands of years.

Capp, enjoying the ruckus but too intelligent to belabor a good device, dropped the Shmoo after a few months. But he came right back with the Kigmy, epitome of masochism— an animal that adored being kicked around and, in Capp's words, "made it unnecessary for people to kick each other around." The reaction? More mail, more heated charges, more journalistic psychoanalysis. Was Capp agitating for pacifism? Did the Kigmy stand for labor and its tormentors for capital, or vice versa? What kind of brutes did Capp think Americans were, that they would need anything like the Kigmy?

The poor Kigmy was all scapegoats in one, and then some; when all of man's frustrations had been taken out on the beast, and the insatiable Kigmy asked for more, man would find inevitably that he had exhausted his capacity for hate. (One commentator approached blasphemy by comparing the Kigmy to Christ.) And seen in this light, as a particular character from which general ideas may be drawn, even Jack S. Phogbound becomes something more than just a windbag, something more than the political fool in its purest form; he has a touch of Nestor and Polonius and William Jennings Bryan; he is the ubiquitous Dogmatic Uncle.

The Schmoo, one of AL CAPP's contributions to the national mythology. © 1948 United Feature Syndicate, Inc.

Li'l Abner himself never impressed the intelligentsia until he married. Then he was suddenly seen as a representative of male freedom, and Daisy Mae was the eternally pursuing female. Capp had struck a nerve again. A comic strip had roused the multitudes once more, and *Life* covered the wedding.

It is hard to say where Capp will go from here. A low rumble of discontent was heard a couple of years after Abner's wedding, and certainly (as Capp knew it would be) an element of suspense and satire had to be abandoned when he married. Capp's circulation— he is carried by United Feature Syndicate— remains enormous, and he has other strings to his bow. He is a good writer, and has appeared in national magazines, both egghead and meathead; for years he did the continuity for Raeburn Van Buren's *Abbie 'n' Slats*, and he now does it for Bob Lubbers' *Long Sam*. He is a good public speaker, and a public critic of public affairs. Somewhere in that cluttered, explosive mind more surprises are germinating. Somewhere in the darkness, an outrage lies in wait for some cherished American idiocy. Capp is bitterly resentful of the fact that Americans have become afraid to laugh at each other, and at their leaders, and at their own pretensions, and at their national ikons. When that resentment comes to a head, he will strike back. Watch out.

Dick Tracy is the daddy of all cops-and-robbers strips, and Chester Gould, born in Pawnee, Oklahoma, in 1900, has been announcing to the world since 1931 that crime does not pay. Crime and punishment taken together, on the other hand, pay very well; *Dick Tracy* runs in over five hundred newspapers with a combined circulation of somewhere around fifty million, so that his readership probably exceeds a hundred million.

Gould's first audiences were considerably smaller. One of his uncles owned a small motion-picture theater in Pawnee, and Gould acquired his first commercial experience at the age of twelve (after having completed one art course) when Universal Pictures ran a contest for exhibitors. The theme of the contest was the pulling power of films, and Gould promptly submitted a drawing of a magnet, neatly labeled "movies," pulling a vast audience willy-nilly in its wake. For this effort he won five dollars, and, like many other cartoonists, he was astonished that so much fun could also be profitable. His father, publisher of a weekly newspaper, knew very well that "artists die poor," and wanted Gould to become a lawyer. Gould compromised; he would go through high school and college, but would not pretend that he wanted to be anything but an artist. His father accepted, probably in the hope that Gould would change his mind later on, and the young cartoonist put in two years at Oklahoma A&M and two years at Northwestern.

He did not change his mind. He went to art school at night and sketched in his spare time. He made his first submission to Captain Patterson in 1921, and continued to harass the man for ten years. Meanwhile he was with Hearst's Chicago *American*, beginning in 1923, where he worked on his first strip, a Hollywood satire called *Fillum Fables* which was only moderately successful. After six years of relative drudgery (during which time his submissions to Patterson continued), he shifted to the Chicago *Daily News*, where he did advertising art.

Up to that point he was just another competent artist, working anonymously in large organizations. His break came in August of 1931; he was drawing a far too complicated Oriental rug for an advertisement when his wife called from their home to read him a wire which had just come from Patterson, indicating high interest in Gould's most recent brainstorm. The Oriental rug was never finished. Patterson wanted six weeks' worth of the strip, and he wanted it done in two weeks. Gould averaged two hours' sleep a night, and on September 1, 1931, *Dick Tracy* was born.

Gould, like many of his neighbors, had been angered by ten years of rampant gangsterism. The anger was not the general righteousness of those

CHESTER GOULD's *Dick Tracy* in his first years. The original cops-and-robbers strip. © 1931 the Chicago *Tribune*– New York *News* Syndicate, Inc.

Dick Tracy in mid-1932, with Pat Patton and Chief Brandon to the rescue. © the Chicago *Tribune*– New York *News* Syndicate, Inc.

who oppose crime; it was directed specifically at the laxity of the local police, and the seeming impunity with which hoodlums operated. Prohibition, as many observers have pointed out, was so brutal an outrage to the dignity of the average free, democratic, mature social drinker that the bootlegger rapidly became a kind of national hero; if he was breaking the law, he was also restoring to great numbers of people that freedom of choice ("I'll go to hell in my own way, thank you") which has always been man's essential guarantee against despotism. That the bootleggers were controlled by mobs, which were in turn controlled by a few major racketeers, was a sad but probably necessary concomitant of foolish legislation.

At any rate, local comment was directed largely against the authorities, who were not only powerless to defeat the mobs, but were often colluding with the racketeers. The most frequent comment seemed to be on the order of "Too much red tape. Too many legalisms. I'd clap 'em in jail and let 'em rot." Direct action, in other words, was worth more than knavish conniving. The basis of Gould's new strip was eminently satisfactory: a plainclothes policeman brought racketeers and hoodlums to book, and made the charges stick.

Gould had titled the strip *Plainclothes Tracy*; it was Patterson, with his

Dick Tracy in 1940, when Gould and Tracy had risen to the top of the heap. © the Chicago *Tribune*– New York *News* Syndicate, Inc.

194

customary acumen, who changed it to *Dick Tracy*. (Gould's admiration for Patterson is undiminished to this day.) Patterson outlined a few sequences, seeing to it that Tracy became a full-time bona-fide policeman in the first; he named Tracy's girl friend (Tess Trueheart); he conferred with Gould once a month, suggesting transitions and sequels, keeping a careful eye on proofs, teaching Gould the fine points of continuity and passing along his always accurate views on reader interest. This had always been Patterson's habit. He considered cartoonists important, and felt that they would be even more important with the benefit of his own judgments.

Dick Tracy was the debut of violence in the newspaper comic strip. Previously, guns had been more or less taboo, and so had blood, and so had the techniques of crime. Gould and Patterson were careful to make Tracy a policeman; if the gangsters were taking the law into their own hands,

PRUNEFACE
1943   MRS. PRUNEFACE
1943   FLATTOP SR.
1944   MUMBLES
1947, 1955   "NOTHING" YONSON
1955   FLATTOP JR.
1956

A gallery of grotesques from *Dick Tracy*. Any resemblance to actual persons, living or dead . . . © the Chicago *Tribune*– New York *News* Syndicate, Inc.

honest citizens would lick them without imitating them. Tracy has never been a vigilante; he is the law.

There was immediate public reaction, of course, and there still is. In 1931, with the First World War a patriotic memory and the second an impossibility, we were not yet callous about blood and guts. Gould felt, quite rightly, that the truth was far more gory than his comic strip, and he refused to change his techniques. There were a few rare cancellations in the early days, but never for more than a week; *Dick Tracy* was invariably restored as soon as the blood was mopped up.

Gould's slightly terrifying caricatures began to appear almost at once. Tracy himself is a caricature: the square jaw and the hook nose are famous all over the world. And Gould's drawing technique is obviously better suited to caricature than to subtle shadings of character. The elements in each panel are reduced to their essential minimum, and are then blocked in flatly, squarely and powerfully. Backgrounds are generally stark, with no decoration and practically no curved lines. Light and shadow are usually ignored, and each panel is drawn as though under a battery of floodlights. Where rare shadings are required, Gould uses a series of fine lines. The faces and figures are equally simple.

Under those circumstances, the simple process of distinguishing one character from another led Gould into caricature. And what grotesques he has created! Tracy's friends are normal enough— Pat Patton, Junior, Tess, Chief Brandon. But his crooks and incidental characters (Flattop and B. O. Plenty, for example) are unmistakably outside the pale, and, taken as a group, they produce an eerie, chilling effect— which is, of course, Gould's intent.

Gould is after reality, or an impression of reality, but he is not after realism in his characters. He can be realistic when he wants to, as with police techniques. From proper fingerprinting procedure to police radio codes, from a bench in the police laboratory to a .38 police special, Gould is absolutely accurate in detail. The need for accuracy, for maintaining the illusion he had taken pains to create, was borne in on him as early as 1936, when, for the first and last time in his career, he tried to deviate from reality. Tracy had been thrown into a mine shaft, and a boulder of several tons had been rolled over the entrance, settling firmly into the clay walls of the shaft. Here was the ultimate cul-de-sac, and Tracy knew it; turning to the reader, he said, "Gould, you have gone too far." Whereupon Gould's hand was shown erasing the rock. The strip came back from Patterson's office with the flat comment that it was no good. Gould redid the two panels, found a way out for Tracy and never again shattered the illusion.

Gould's activities as a citizen are of interest. He has an office in the Tribune Tower in Chicago, to which he repairs twice a week; the rest of his time is spent on his farm in Woodstock, Illinois, or at his avocations, all of which have some connection with police work. His "Crime Stoppers," small graphic comments near the title of his Sunday pages, testify to his patient and fond research, and he considers his two-way wrist radio, which has been in the strip for over a decade, a minor triumph, because an adaptation of it is now being tested by several municipal police forces. He has the Chicago *Tribune* files at his disposal; he has subscribed for years to the *Journal of Criminal Law, Criminology, and Police Science,* published by the School of Law at Northwestern University; one of his automobiles is officially registered as a sheriff's car, Number 41 of the McHenry County police. Some of the widespread legends about him are simply not true— for example, that he has a large collection of Tracyana at his farm, or a cemetery in which are the mock gravestones of his criminals, or that he is officially connected with the F.B.I. Gould is a sober citizen who enjoys his work and his life, and he is not given to any such egotistical fantasies. He toured the F.B.I. establishment once, as any private citizen may. On a trip to England recently he made friends in Scotland Yard, and was cheerfully given demonstrations of their methods and techniques, some of which he has used in his strip. He has received occasional awards for his work, one from the Police Athletic League in

1949, a plaque of the Associated Police Communication Officers in 1953 and— of all things— a plaque from the American Institute of Men's and Boy's Wear in 1957, because of Tracy's general good grooming and because of his efforts to divest young America of its thuggish silver-riveted leather jackets.

He considers himself a teller of tales, and not a policeman. If he became a policeman, he would lose his sense of audience, and possibly begin to show off the esoterica of police procedure— much of which would bore his readership. He needs accurate knowledge, of course, but feels no need to be any more of a policeman than the rest of us are. Occasionally he fulfills speaking engagements, but he is careful about his public commitments; his major public commitment is *Dick Tracy*, which must come first.

His attitude toward the strip, and toward journalism, is thoroughly businesslike. He refuses to engage in artificial feuds with his colleagues, or in parody; yet, when asked about Al Capp's famous *Fearless Fosdick* series, he broke into a huge grin, assured all within hearing that he was greatly fond of Capp, that he had approved the parody from the beginning, and that he was immensely pleased to be the only cartoonist in the world who had a great comic artist for a press agent, absolutely free. He is cheerful and gregarious in private life, married, and with a married daughter whose son is named Tracy Richard O'Connell. Among his friends have been many cartoonists: Capp, Milton Caniff, Carey Orr (editorial cartoonist for the Chicago *Tribune*), Harold Gray, Frank King and the late Frank Willard, whom Gould considered an inspired clown, as funny as anyone in the business.

Gould's impact on that business has been impressive. All police and detective strips must be considered descendants of *Tracy*, if only because Gould broke through the wall of public resistance to them. Even strips which are only marginally crime strips— like *Don Winslow of the Navy*, originated in 1934 by Frank Martinek, himself a former newspaperman, fingerprint expert, G-man and author— owe a good deal to Gould's patient exegesis of police methods, and to his insistence that justice be sought within the law. Lank Leonard's *Mickey Finn*, begun in 1936, is very different from *Dick Tracy*, being more concerned with the family life of its policeman hero, more gentle, more humorous and barely violent at all; yet, without Gould's pioneering, police strips of any kind might still be dubious. Even Jay Irving's comic cops owe something to Gould; they are funny because we respect them— otherwise they would be fools— and we'll never know how many of us are just a little happier about policemen in general because we were brought up on daily doses of *Dick Tracy*.

To the public and to his colleagues, Milton Caniff is one of the giants of the craft. The most common judgment offered by his fellow artists is

JAY IRVING's amiable Pottsy, gentle and often poetic, and the mildest policeman in the business. © the Chicago *Tribune*– New York *News* Syndicate, Inc.

that "Caniff would have been great in any line." The line he chose, fortunately, was cartooning, and through his two major creations, *Terry and the Pirates* and *Steve Canyon*, he has raised realism and draftsmanship to levels of respectability and effectiveness unmatched in the history of his profession.

Milton Caniff was first published when he was thirteen or fourteen. The Dayton *Journal* accepted contributions from its readers, and one of Caniff's cartoons, a panel, appeared while its artist was in the eighth grade. Caniff's youth in general was almost suspiciously successful. He was a good student, an Eagle Scout, cartoonist for the local Scout newspaper (it was a daily, and he did illustrations, a daily strip, and a full-page strip for the Sunday edition), an admirer of John T. McCutcheon. His proficiency in self-expression flourished when he reached high school: he worked for the school newspaper as cartoonist and caricaturist, writing his own captions and gags, which were forceful and literate; he was a member of the debating society, the yearbook staff and the student council; and in his spare time he trod the boards as a spear carrier with the road companies that passed through Dayton.

He had worked as an office boy with the Dayton *Journal*; and during the summer of 1925, after his graduation from high school, he worked on the Miami, Florida, *Daily News*, owned by James M. Cox of Dayton. Back in Ohio, he entered Ohio State University in the fall, got a job with the Columbus *Dispatch*, drew reams of art work for the university publications, joined half a dozen clubs and rose to campus prominence as a member of the University Players (in 1928 he played the lead in the year's biggest production, *Beau Kay*; artist for the show was Jon Whitcomb, now one of the country's most successful illustrators). Graduating in 1930, Caniff continued full-time at the *Dispatch*; with the security of a degree and a job, he married Esther Parsons, his childhood sweetheart. A year later, when the depression devasted the Midwest, he was fired.

But during that year he had benefited by the advice of a great cartoonist, Billy Ireland, who had criticized his work and, at one crucial moment, kept him within the fold. Caniff had tried to "pull a sure-fire set of Pop and Pow characters out of the inkwell," but everything he sent to the syndicates came back immediately. Discouraged, he had considered acting as a career, and it was then that Ireland made a remark Caniff has never forgotten: "Stick to your inkpots, kid; actors don't eat regularly."

Jobless (and there were no jobs to be had), Caniff teamed up with a friend, Noel Sickles, to open a commercial-art studio in Columbus. Sickles later drew *Scorchy Smith* for a while, after John Terry (Paul Terry's brother) had created it, and eventually became an illustrator who is the despair and envy of his fellows. Caniff and many others describe him as the best draftsman in the country, with the strongest influence on comic-strip technique.

An early *Dickie Dare*, as drawn by MILTON CANIFF. © 1933 AP Newsfeatures.

A couple of months later a break came: the Associated Press in New York, which kept its eye on the out-of-town papers, had noticed his work in the *Dispatch*, and now offered him a job. (The AP had begun as a news-service, but the success of other syndicates with features had induced the AP to branch out.) Caniff arrived in New York in the spring of 1932, and was set to work doing pen portraits of all thirty-five potential nominees for the Republican and Democratic candidacies for President and Vice-President. (His sketch of Roosevelt was reproduced nationally after the Democratic convention.) Assignments came his way: a one-column panel called *Puffy the Pig*; a human-interest panel called *The Gay Thirties*; and, finally, an adventure strip of his own, the original *Dickie Dare*. Now Caniff's experience on the *Dispatch* was of value to him, and he remembered two things particularly: "One was that drawing a newspaper feature is not a matter of fashioning paper dolls for the kiddies. If the feature doesn't sell papers, it is useless. The second thing came from a remark by the late Heinie Reiker, managing editor of the *Dispatch*. He said, 'Always draw your stuff for the guy who pays for the paper. Kids will never see it if the old man doesn't buy the paper and bring it home.'"

Much of Caniff's early work is still instantly recognizable as his own. His line is consistently fine, careful and accurate; his highlights and shadows are rendered delicately; his facial expressions are thoroughly readable; and his panels are never finished sloppily— even the least important corner of the background is given full attention. A combination of influences — McCutcheon, Ireland, Sickles and a new comic-strip artist named Roy Crane, who had originated *Captain Easy* in 1932— was working on Caniff. Crane used heavier contours and was a master of screening (the reproduction of lighter or darker grays mechanically, in the printing process); Caniff avoided screening and used a much finer pen point, but displayed the same visual imagination— for example, in using silhouette, or in placing figures within the panel— as Crane.

Four or five exotic adventure strips had come into being— Alex Raymond's *Flash Gordon*, Lyman Young's *Tim Tyler's Luck* (Lyman is Chic Young's brother), Frank Miller's *Barney Baxter*, Harold Foster's *Tarzan*, Crane's *Captain Easy*. Captain Patterson, of the New York *Daily News*,

199

was momentarily behind the others: he had no such strip, and he wanted one badly.

As usual, Patterson was after universal appeal, which meant a handsome hero, a boy as his companion, a farcical factotum and a bushel of lovelies in distress. (*Dickie Dare* had used many of those with success.) What, the two men asked themselves, was the last outpost of old-fashioned adventure? The Orient, obviously; there was the setting. The hero would be Pat Ryan; the boy, Tommy Tucker. Probably the crucial inspiration came to Caniff when he considered his villains. He had seen reports of a female pirate along the China coast, one Lai Choi San ("Mountain of Wealth"). Why not combine two ingredients in one character: a beautiful villainess, desirable, cold and cruel, smart enough to outwit our hero but not smart enough to keep from falling for him in a careful way. She would be called The Dragon Lady.

Patterson did not approve of the name "Tommy Tucker." Caniff submitted a list of boys' names; Patterson circled "Terry," and added the words, "and the Pirates." Moreover, Patterson insisted on comic relief, which turned out to be a weird amalgam of the traditional Chinese houseboy, the semi-Americanized Oriental, Sancho Panza and Joe Penner. This paragon's name was George Washington Confucius, shortened to "Connie."

The strip appeared first on October 19, 1934. Its first episode was not startlingly original— a trip upriver in search of an inherited gold mine. But even in the earliest days the strip had a quality hard to define, an added dimension. The women were beautiful and flippant, the men fearless, the heroes heroic and villains villainous— all as it should be. But intimations of intelligence and literacy kept creeping into the dialogue, and Caniff's realistic accuracy of detail was there from the beginning. The combination— plus Caniff's superb drawing— raised the strip to an unexpected level of sophistication.

A *Terry and the Pirates* of 1942, when its hero was pretty well grown up. So was Rouge. © 1942 the Chicago *Tribune*– New York *News* Syndicate, Inc.

CANIFF's Thanksgiving celebration: a covey of quail from *Terry*, served up on November 25, 1945. © 1945 the Chicago *Tribune*– New York *News* Syndicate, Inc.

Terry grew up in the strip, and the strip itself matured in the late thirties. Caniff might have continued to produce a series of exotic tales, perhaps a cut above the Rover Boys but essentially the same. But Caniff himself was a man of intelligence, experience and warmth. In 1934 it might be all right to portray Connie as a slapstick caricature of "John Chinaman," but by 1937 Connie and his people were engaged in a fierce, horrible struggle for survival against an enemy as brutal as any in history; how could anyone go on making fun of the Chinese, even innocent, friendly fun?

To mention the war at all, which Caniff did in late 1937 and early 1938, was a bold step. From then on, disguise and pretense disappeared bit by bit. Officially, America was neutral, and the Japanese were referred to in the strip as "invaders," but by late 1938 Caniff's readers knew that the artist (1) knew a good deal about China, (2) admired the Chinese people and (3) was backing the Chinese against the Japanese.

But the basis of the strip was adventure, and so it continued to be,

201

through 1939 and 1940. When the Japanese attacked Pearl Harbor in December of 1941, Caniff was in the midst of a totally unrelated episode, which had to be finished before he could move Terry and Pat into action. When the action began, it was as real as an Army manual. Caniff had been drawing planes, tanks, uniforms, weapons for over four years; he was an encyclopedia of Far Eastern warfare, and no other cartoonist ever overcame Caniff's head start. He not only knew the physical details of the terrain and the war matériel; he understood the issues of the war, and he knew how men and women would react to those issues. Significantly, Pat Ryan began to fade from the strip in 1942, and his place was taken by Flip Corkin (who, as many remember, was based roughly on an old friend of Caniff's, Colonel Philip G. Cochran of the Army Air Corps). Corkin contrasted with Ryan in several ways. He was older and had a touch of mortal gray to his hair; he was a career flier, and not a barnstormer; he represented command, organization, specific training for a specific and important job. When Terry went into flight training, Corkin became his avuncular idol.

All this while, circulation had continued to grow. Once in the war, Americans concentrated on it, and the reality that leaped out of Caniff's pages was every bit as dramatic as official communiqués. Terry's adventures were toned down, quite properly; there was less mad derring-do, there were fewer gorgeous jades, there was more thought, more purpose and more war. Terry's reality and the world's reality were now one; nowhere is that point better demonstrated than in Caniff's famous Sunday strip of October 17, 1942, in which Corkin attempts to convey to Terry some of the meaning of his newly won wings. That strip was reprinted over and over for months; the Hon. Carl Hinshaw of California inserted it into the *Congressional Record*, a unique accolade indeed for a comic strip.

Caniff drew another strip during the war, which millions of men will remember with unbounded affection: *Male Call*. Originally he had done a special version of *Terry* for service newspapers, but his syndicate objected to the duplication. (Burma, one of his warmest and most gorgeous creations, was the heroine of that one.) Caniff then produced *Male Call*, an original strip with nothing of Terry in it at all; its heroine was Miss Lace, and she was, for over two years, America's best-loved vivandière.

Caniff never owned the copyright on any of his characters or on the name of his strip; as well as he did professionally, he was still in the position of a hired hand, and he felt a desire for more independence. In the summer of 1945 a provocative news report appeared: when Caniff's contract with the *News-Tribune* Syndicate ran out in 1947, he intended to

Possibly the most famous single Sunday page: Colonel Corkin and Lieutenant Lee. © 1942 the Chicago *Tribune*– New York *News* Syndicate, Inc.

The girl we didn't leave behind us: Miss Lace, one of the very few pleasant memories of World War II. © Milton Caniff.

switch to Field Enterprises, publishers of the Chicago *Sun-Times,* and to create a new strip.

The circumstances were unique. No other cartoonist had ever abandoned a top-rank strip to create another; no other cartoonist had ever been signed two years ahead of time to create a strip from scratch, with no strings attached, and with perfect freedom from editorial control.

Meanwhile *Terry* was still running, and there was no relaxation of Caniff's high standards for *Terry* during that last year and a half while he worked on the new strip. A few conclusions were taken for granted: it would be an adventure strip, with an exotic background; there would be pretty girls in it. What else it would be, no one could say.

The answer, first appearing on January 13, 1947, was *Steve Canyon,* and its first sequences were typical of Caniff— in thought, approach and drawing. Here was Caniff approaching his full power. His use of "camera

Enter *Steve Canyon.* Suspense was created in the very first Sunday page, on January 19, 1947. © Field Enterprises, Inc. Courtesy of Chicago *Sun-Times* Syndicate.

204

STEVE CANYON
by MILTON CANIFF

WHY, IT'S STEVIE CANYON! ME SISTER IN SHANNON WRITES THAT YE PAID HER A PERSONAL CALL!

THAT I DID! SHE LOOKS FINE!

GLAD TO SEE YOU BACK, MR. CANYON! MY BOY GOT THE SOUVENIR YOU SENT FROM EGYPT!

GOOD!

CHECKING IN, SARGE!

CAPTAIN CANYON! I REALLY SWEAT YOU OUT THIS LAST TRIP! HEY! I HAVE A FINANCIAL STATEMENT FOR YOU...YOU'LL NEVER REGRET HAVING BACKED ME ON THIS DEAL!...

WANT A FLOWER FOR YOUR BUTTONHOLE, MR. CANYON?

NOT TODAY, POSIE — BUT YOU AND YOUR MOM ARE ABOUT DUE TO SEE A MOVIE ON ME...

GOING UP?

THIS CAR, MR. CANYON! —AND FOR YOU WE DON'T WAIT TILL IT'S FULL! RIGHT, IRMA?

R-R-RAJAH!

OH... HERE IS MR. CANYON, NOW...

HORIZONS Unlimited

Steve CANYON

IT'S A MR. DAYZEE, SECRETARY TO COPPER CALHOON, THE BIG SHE-WOLF OF THE STOCK MARKET...

HMM—THEY CALL HER "THE COPPERHEAD" I WONDER IF SHE HOWLS OR HISSES?

MR. CANYON?... MISS COPPER CALHOON WISHES TO ENGAGE YOUR PROFESSIONAL SERVICES! PLEASE COME TO MISS CALHOON'S APARTMENT AT ONCE...

...BUT WHAT IF I DON'T WANT TO PLACE MY SERVICES AT THE COMMAND OF MISS COPPER CALHOON?

MIS-TER CANYON! PEOPLE DO NOT REFUSE WHEN SUMMONED BY COPPER CALHOON!

AND ALL THIS TIME I THOUGHT I WAS A PEOPLE! GOOD MORROW, MR. DOOZIE!

WHY, MR. DIZZY, WHAT YOU SAID!..AND ME SO YOUNG AND IMPRESSIONABLE! ...THE CLICK YOU HEAR WILL MEAN YOU'RE SOLOING!

WELL, IT WOULD HAVE BEEN NICE TO HAVE MONEY TO PAY THIS OFFICE RENT BUT I GUESS IT'S BAD FORM TO GET INTO REGULAR HABITS LIKE THAT...

COPPER! YOU HEARD ON THE EXTENSION WHAT STEVE CANYON SAID!.. I HAVE NEVER BEEN SO---

I WANT THAT MAN!! ...GET HIM!

1-19

205

SUMMER SMITH OLSON

DOE REDWOOD

angles," his alternation of close-up, long shot, middle distance, his creation of suspense in two or three panels— all were superb.

Essentially, Caniff explained, his new strip was a picaresque novel. Canyon had been a captain in the Air Transport Command during the war, and had previously had a couple of years of college. Courageous and intelligent, he was also handsome. All of which opened up the following possibilities:

Canyon would know intimately the world's major airports, and would have private knowledge of many smaller strips, used for emergency landings during the war. As an intelligent man, he could be counted on to grasp the ins and outs of a complicated intrigue. As a courageous flier, he would be available for risky jobs. As an experienced warrior, he would be a man's man; as a handsome, urbane type, he would be a ladies' man.

The strip was an immediate success, but Caniff did not escape trouble entirely. For one thing, he was not quite satisfied with Canyon's physical appearance for some time; it was over a year before he had finished broadening Canyon's face slightly and relaxing some of the signs of tension in the features. By then Caniff was in a different kind of trouble: his heroines had become a bit too gaudy for certain areas of the public taste.

Mild controversy now and then has done Caniff no harm. The most severe public protest he has experienced was a result not of leaving Steve in the clutches of a gorgeous harpy, but of failing to marry Steve to a beautiful "good" girl. Caniff's fan mail has always been impassioned, which is his own fault: having taken such pains over the years to create a world of "reality," he must accept the bellows of outrage when readers, no longer aware that "this is just a comic strip," react with disappointment and frustration.

Caniff has tried to explain his readers' involvement with the strip. (It has become a successful television series, with the approval of the United States Air Force.) Caniff's circulation is between forty and fifty million. He feels that possibly the American outlook has been shaped, in part, by a belief in a special magic, the magic by which ordinary, imperfect beings are made to feel that they are, after all, perfectible. The American hero lives within all of us, and it is an article of faith that any native-born boy may grow up to be President. We are not heroes ourselves, but we are all hero-ridden. We are the descendants, and not the makers, of a legend; yet we persist in identifying with it. Caniff's strips reflect that legend in modern terms; they are built around the hero. There lies the strength of public reaction— which is also the measure of Caniff's success.

In what seemed like no time at all Canyon had involved himself with a double handful of lovely heroines and slinky villainesses. ©️ Field Enterprises, Inc.

POTEET CANYON

HOLLY HALL

HERSELF
MULDOON

MISS MIZZOU

PRINCESS
SNOWFLOWER

FEETA-FEETA

MADAME LYNX

J55/JS/2375

HEADQUARTERS
CONTINENTAL AIR DEFENSE COMMAND
EMF AIR FORCE BASE
COLORADO SPRINGS, COLORADO

EMFP 50.2

SUBJECT: Newspaper Report of Fight Involving
Air Force Personnel   14 November 1956
TO:
    Commanding Officer
    Big Thunder Air Force Base

    1. Reference is made to photostat of newspaper clipping
attached hereto.

    2. The incident described therein as a "clash between
civilian patrons and Air Force Personnel from Big Thunder AFB"
has not been mentioned in reports received at this Headquarters.

    3. You will reply by indorsement, giving fullest details.

                    BY ORDER OF THE COMMANDING GENERAL

1 Incl
1. Photostat from   Charles E. Brennan
   Big Thunder ARROW   CHARLES E. BRENNAN
                               Colonel, USAF
                               Air

DOOLIN, TAKE A LETTER IN REPLY TO THIS! FIRST INDORSEMENT, AND SO ON.

PARAGRAPH ONE... ON AN EVENING FOLLOWING THE RECENT ELECTION TWO OFF DUTY AIRMEN ATTACHED TO THIS BASE ENTERED A LOCAL PUBLIC TAVERN SEEKING REST AND RECREATION

2. In the discussion of the recent election, reference was made to the support given local candidates by Air Force personnel at Big Thunder AFS

3. The Airmen pointed out good-naturedly that no Big Thunder AFB personnel had been eligible to vote at local polls, but had cast ballots by lawful absentee arrangement.

4. Expressions of amazement led to further discussion. While one Airman pursued the subject, the other telephoned for additional interested Air Force people to come and take part in the exchange of ideas.

5. A general round robin discussion followed.

6. In the course of this stimulating seminar, some fixtures of the public house were disarranged.

7. It was suggested that the results of the assembly had been so exhilarating to Air Force personnel present that a modest sum be volunteered for the depreciation to the premises.

8. Members of the local constabulary who chanced to drop in following the incidents here described were heard to comment that such a spirited and open forum should have been held in this particular arena long ago; since the proprietor and his regular patrons had certainly been requesting it.

...chanced
...been requesting it... in this spirited and open forum were
...proprietor and his regular patrons had long ago
    9. No charges having been filed and no arrests
made, it would appear that the writer of the attached news story had been misinformed.

Incl
n/c
                    Stevenson B. Cany
                    STEVENSON B. CANY
                    Lt. Col. USAFR
                    Officer-in-

Copyright 1956, Field Enterprises, Inc.   11-18

The profession of comic-strip artist has supplied nothing closer to a baggy-pants burlesque comedian than Bill Holman, formerly guardian of a popcorn machine in Crawfordsville, Indiana. Holman wears neither baggy pants nor floppy shoes, and his work has none of the bluish quality of real burlesque; but his inventiveness, his verbal juxtapositions and misunderstandings, and his irrepressible manglings of the English language are the marks of a man to whom reality is subordinate to art. The word "foo," for example, was originally the name of an automobile in a panel he sold to *Collier's*. Perhaps the best explanation of Holman's genius is that he has made that one monosyllable stand up for thirty years, has used it, so to speak, as every imaginable part of speech, and has come instantly to be identified by it. If he had achieved the same results with "holy mackerel" or "by gum," his would have been a pale success indeed.

His early days provided no clue to his future triumph, anything but pale. He was born in Crawfordsville, in 1903, and fittingly enough his childhood ambition was to be a fireman. In his teens he came no closer to industrial success, or indeed to the realization of any ambition, than keeping his job as watchdog at the popcorn vending machine in a Crawfordsville five-and-ten; but when he was sixteen a creative urge took hold, and he was off to Chicago. He enrolled at the Academy of Fine Arts and was fortunate enough to be able to study under Carl Ed. His early associations were all fortunate. Within a year he had talked himself into a job as copy boy for the Chicago *Tribune* (at six dollars a week), where two of his new acquaintances were Garrett Price and Harold Gray.

From then on the pattern was similar to that of many Midwestern cartoonists. He edged a bit closer to the Eastern seaboard by moving on to Cleveland, where he drew his first strip, *Billville Birds*. Again, he found himself in good company; he soon made enduring friendships with J. R. Williams and Chic Young.

The next step, of course, was New York, where Holman arrived when he was twenty-one. Incurably gregarious, he found himself in the company of Charles Voight, Clare Briggs and Frank Fogarty (Fogarty, with Weare Holbrook, turned out for years a strip called *Clarence*, the demise of which has evoked a great deal of nostalgia). These men were all with the *Herald Tribune* Syndicate, and the leader of the gallant band was the immortal Winsor McCay. The office was apparently an occasional madhouse, as any haven for comic artists should be: W. C. Fields dropped in and taught Holman to juggle, and Will Rogers was a frequent visitor. This was 1929, and Holman was drawing a strip called *G. Whizz Jr.*, a kid strip, as the name implies.

"That's an old stunt with Joe— he always pulls that pipe out when you loan him tobacco!"

BILL HOLMAN's panel *Nuts and Jolts*. Notary Sojac creeps in even here. © 1949 the Chicago *Tribune*– New York *News* Syndicate, Inc.

The Sunday *Steve Canyon* of November 18, 1956, a high point in verbal and visual wit. The strip of tape in the last panel is a superb touch. © Field Enterprises, Inc. Courtesy of Chicago *Sun-Times* Syndicate.

A Sunday *Smokey Stover*, by BILL HOLMAN, 1952. The puns are as outlandish as ever, and so are the characters. © 1952 the Chicago *Tribune*– New York *News* Syndicate, Inc.

A kid strip was not enough. Holman's instincts and sympathies lie rather with baggy pants than with baggy diapers. Holman began to free-lance for national magazines, and has described the five years he spent on the loose as "happy and profitable." He recalled those years to Martin Sheridan: "Hundreds of my drawings infested the pages of *Collier's, The Saturday Evening Post, Life, Judge,* and *Everybody's Weekly* of London. The outcome was a syndicate contract to draw *Smokey Stover, Spooky the Cat,* seven daily cartoons, and *Foo.*"

The syndicate was the Chicago *Tribune*–New York *Daily News* Syndicate, but there is no record that Holman ever experienced any poignant passages at arms with either Captain Patterson or Colonel McCormick. Instead, he threw himself into his work with unmitigated glee, and from 1935 on created so many memorable departures from rationality that his work must be ranked with that of uninhibited geniuses like Rube Goldberg and Milt Gross.

Some of his devices are outrageous, while others are outrageously simple. "Foo" is a perfect example of the latter. Among the former are picture frames which fail to contain their subjects entirely, so that cats' tails, human noses and occasionally a string of sausages or an ear trumpet constantly protrude, occupying space to which they are not entitled. Holman took the traditional expression of surprise— hat popping off head— and extended it beyond even fantasy: when Smokey is astonished his hat pops up in several sections, his ears fly away from his head, and his cigar, if any, lies suspended some inches from his mouth. Smokey's constant companion in the strip (Smokey is, of course, a fireman) is the Fire Chief, greedily baptized Cash U. Nutt. The chief's expressions of surprise are as outlandish as Smokey's.

What Holman seems to like best, and what his readers go mad over, and what makes it necessary to classify *Smokey Stover* as an intellectual strip, is the pun. The puns are most often captions for his badly framed pictures. They are not of the kind made immortal by English wits, in which a public figure is transfixed; they are rather of the basic single-twist variety, a variety which gave rise to the opinion that a pun is the lowest form of humor. In Holman's hands they are not at all low. They are chronic, for one thing; nothing can be done about them, and the reader who can't lick them joins them. A *Smokey Stover* without puns would be like a meal without wine or a day without sunshine. Holman addicts open the Sunday comics supplements nervously, reaching out with their minds for his latest bit of grammatical mayhem.

Two other phrases are headed for immortality, thanks to Holman's sponsorship. One is "Notary Sojac," and the other is "1506 nix nix." Their origins are obscure. Theories have been advanced by interested parties, one to the effect that the latter phrase was a warning to a friend about a certain hotel room. No speculation about these phrases is supported by fact. Both of them seem to have sprung full blown from Holman's noble brow. Probably the most famous anecdote about either of them, contributed by Gus Edson, is this: "We were flying 7,000 feet over the stormy North Atlantic when the pilot turned to Bill and said, 'There's a Norwegian weather ship right below us,' and with that the pilot radioed the ship and told them, 'I have Bill Holman aboard, famous American cartoonist who

Another *Smokey Stover*. HOLMAN's invention never flags. The man has been perpetrating these outrages for a quarter-century. © 1952 the Chicago *Tribune*– New York *News* Syndicate, Inc.

draws *Smokey Stover*.' The ship radioed back, 'Ask that crazy guy what Notary Sojac means!' "

There are many anecdotes about Holman. His personality seems to be a cross between that of the four Marx brothers and that of Phineas T. Barnum. He is reputed to be fond of money; and when John Pierotti (sports cartoonist for the New York *Post* and twice president of the National Cartoonists Society) once saw him stuck with a dinner check, he felt that the incident was worth reporting in print. He is famous also for large stogies, which he smokes with almost avuncular fondness; the legend drawn from this innocuous habit is that he has never offered one to anyone else and has been known to smoke butts if they seemed to him unreasonably long. The truth about the man— much like the truth about Jack Benny— is that he is quite generous, particularly to artists who need help. He is short, effervescent, dynamic and happy. He is also uninhibitedly outspoken, a quality which he combines with a fine stage presence in entertaining troops or invalids, of which he has done a great deal. He has been known to stride vigorously on to a platform, a lit cigar in his mouth and a fireman's hat on his head, glare uncompromisingly at his silent audience for a few seconds, and open his performance with the phrase "Shut up, you crazy screwballs!" Invariably, his audience howls. Al Posen, creator of *Sweeney and Son* and the chairman or leader of many cartoonist forays into the world of domestic and overseas entertainment, reports that Holman once performed before an audience of GIs who were all psychiatric patients. He had been warned by the doctor in charge to make no reference to mental aberration or to the condition of the patients, but he began immediately referring to his audience as nuts and screwballs, and apparently they loved it. Posen feels, and he is probably right, that no one else in the profession could have gotten away with it.

It may take a special talent to like *Smokey Stover*, because *Smokey Stover* is the product of a special talent. Yet the strip has been a perennial favorite in two major metropolitan newspapers whose proudest boast is that they are in touch with the masses. The conclusion is inevitable: Holman has the true touch of genius. He has wedded idiocy to real wit, and the result is a constantly surprising, never disappointing comic strip. Stover and Holman are another of those perfect combinations. The strip derives from nothing but the creator's mind. Holman himself might sum up his genius in one word: Foo.

Much more happened in the thirties. A successful magazine illustrator named Raeburn Van Buren signed on with United Feature Syndicate and drew a strip called *Abbie 'n' Slats*, which was unlike anything that had been done before. Van Buren had illustrated regularly for America's mass-circulation magazines, but the limited context of a short story was apparently not enough for him. On the surface, *Abbie 'n' Slats* revolved around the adventures of a good-looking young roughneck— no giant physically, capable of good manners, and with a heart of gold. This was Slats. Aunt Abbie was the homely spinster, also with a heart of gold, who was there to help when Slats needed her. Slats had a girl, Becky Groggins, and Becky had a father, Bathless Groggins, who was the distillation of fifty years of bums: a confidence man, a blandly righteous sinner and Van Buren's contact with the world of fantasy. For years the Sunday strip has been given over to the unlikely adventures of this unwashed swindler; its setting has ranged from Main Street in Crabtree Corners to remote islands populated by lovely heteiras, and its cast has included everything from villainous bankers to amiable dinosaurs. Van Buren's style is clean and melodramatic; his vernacular is accurate and funny; and his sense of pure fantasy is the best since Winsor McCay's.

Two strips written by the same man appeared in the mid-thirties: *Mandrake the Magician* in 1934 and *The Phantom* in 1936. The writer was and still is Lee Falk; *Mandrake* was and is drawn by Phil Davis, while Ray Moore, the original artist of *The Phantom*, has been succeeded by Wilson McCoy. Oddly enough, the drawing styles are not dissimilar, but the stories are. Mandrake's adventures occur in all settings, but chiefly the urban, where he is quite at home in his formal attire, including cape. But *The Phantom* is set in the depths of Africa, and is a jungle strip. Both strips remain popular a quarter of a century later; *The Phantom* runs in over four hundred and fifty newspapers.

Within the existing categories, new strips sprang up. Eddie Sullivan and Charlie Schmidt created *Pinkerton, Jr.* for the Boston *Daily Record* in 1933; a year and a half later King Features took it over, changed its title to *Radio Patrol* and syndicated it nationally. *Don Winslow of the Navy*, as much a police strip as a Navy strip, appeared in 1934. (*Navy Bob Steele*, a Sunday page, began to appear after the outbreak of war in Europe. It was much more a war-action strip than *Winslow*.)

Aviation strips flourished. *Scorchy Smith* had first appeared in 1930; when Noel Sickles took it over in 1935, Milton Caniff had already begun

Slats Scrapple in action, by Raeburn Van Buren. © 1946 United Feature Syndicate, Inc.

Action and fine draughtsmanship in this NOEL SICKLES strip of *Scorchy Smith*. Sickles' influence on his contemporaries— e.g. on his close friend Milton Caniff— is obvious. © 1935 AP Newsfeatures.

Terry, and between them the two men inaugurated a new kind of comic-strip art. By 1938 Sickles had left *Scorchy;* its next artist was Bert Christman. Christman was a young and capable artist, but his involvement in the strip, and in the world of the thirties, was too strong for him: he got up from his drawing board one fine morning and applied for Naval air training. He was accepted. Impatient, he left the States when his training was over and joined the Flying Tigers in Burma. He came through battle after battle, with only one slight wound, until January 1942, when he was shot down. He had time to bail out, but the enemy came after him even then and killed him as he drifted down. Among his personal effects was a scrapbook of sketches— the Burmese landscape, friends of his, designs for insignia.

Howell Dodd had replaced Christman on *Scorchy;* Frank Robbins was the next artist, and Robbins changed the style of the strip from the delicacy and detail of the Sickles school to the heavier, blacker, more punchy technique that has marked his work since. Robbins remains one of the most popular of the "aviation artists"; in 1946 he signed with King Features to do a strip of his own, *Johnny Hazard,* essentially similar to *Scorchy.* The latter was taken over by Rodlow Willard.

There were other air strips— *Barney Baxter* and *Tailspin Tommy,* for two; and during the war aviation flourished. Zack Mosley's *Smilin' Jack,* begun as a Sunday page in 1933 and a daily strip in 1936, was an example. Mosley's drawing comes in for a lot of criticism, but his technical accuracy about planes saves the day for him, and even if his characters are considered grotesque, they are original and melodramatic. And his readers are faithful enthusiasts, all over the world.

There was adventure on land in the thirties, too, and a good deal of it glorified the American West. *The Lone Ranger, King of the Royal Mounted, Way Out West, Red Ryder* were the modern successors to James Swinnerton's *Little Jimmy* and *Rocky Mason.* Leffingwell's *Little Joe,* which began

Little Joe and Utah in the wild Wild West. © 1937 the Chicago *Tribune*– New York *News* Syndicate, Inc.

in the early thirties, had enormous, simple appeal; here was a kid in a wide black hat, under the wing of a sheriff named Utah, and between them they whupped all kinds of varmints. Since the war *Little Joe* has moved steadily toward humor, rather than derring-do. (There had been a very funny Western strip in the New York *Herald Tribune* on Sundays, from 1929 to 1938, called *Brutus*. Brutus was a little fellow, but a powerful man; he ran a place called the Hot Dog Ranch, assisted by a hired hand named Sampson and Sampson's sweetheart, named Sooky. The basis of this strip was fantasy, and some of the flights of fancy of its originator, John Gruelle, were worthy of the Marx Brothers.)

One of the Western strips, *Chief Wahoo*, has had a long and curious history. Originally published in 1937 under the title *The Great Gusto*, this strip centered around a medicine show and was an attempt to reduce to manageable proportions the words and deeds of the world's outstanding windbags; as CoultonWaugh noticed, Gusto himself bore a fair resemblance to W. C. Fields. Chief Wahoo was Gusto's Indian, indispensable to a self-respecting medicine show, and it was Wahoo, primitive but perspicacious, outsmarting Gusto too often, who soon became the strip's star.

A daily *Chief Wahoo* of January 1941 showing Wahoo with Steve Roper as he looked in those days. © Publishers Syndicate.

Steve Roper, 1959. Long shot; close-up; medium close-up; slick chick and handsome hero. Drawn by WILLIAM OVERGARD, who succeeded Woggon.

Ultimately, though, Wahoo was himself displaced by Steve Roper, the handsome combination of brains and brawn formerly called upon when some need for a normal human being arose. As the thirties became the forties the public turned more and more to Roper, apparently preferring straight adventure to the winsome weirdness of the Chief; and by the fifties the Chief was rarely seen.

From the beginning, the strip was drawn by Elmer Woggon to continuities by Allen Saunders. As an example of organization, planned effort and co-operation between syndicate and artists, the strip is fascinating. Publishers Syndicate distributes it, and every change in character, continuity or emphasis has been the result of amiable discussion among the artist, the writer, the syndicate editor and the head of the syndicate. This co-operative effort— aided by fairly accurate surveys of public opinion— was the beginning of a new approach to comics, of which more later. Its immediate effect was to keep *Steve Roper* alive and popular through its first two incarnations, by offering its creators room for a certain flexibility and help in finding new directions. All good strips must grow and change with time, and *Steve Roper* is the first good example of one whose growth and direction were carefully guided by a pooling of talents.

This development was no accident. The science of sampling— of public-opinion polls, for example— had been crude indeed before the thirties. It took a resounding failure— the *Literary Digest* poll of 1936, which forecast a sweeping victory for Landon over Roosevelt— to bring such techniques into the public awareness. But newspapermen, and particularly the higher echelon of editors, had been concerned with them for some time; journalism was becoming a quiet science rather than a flamboyant art, and the public would no longer be damned— the public would get what it wanted. Slowly, traditional notions of what a newspaper should be were changing. Slowly, editors and syndicates were coming to exchange views as colleagues, rather than to compete as buyer and seller. Comics sections were vastly different by the late thirties; they were no longer an after-thought, thrown in to give the reader a three-minute pause for laughter. The contemporary adventure strip had altered the function of comics. People were now seeking "life" in them, as much as fun; the comics page carried overtones of news-of-the-day and editorials.

Publishers Syndicate was one of the first to use public-opinion samplings extensively. They were able not only to keep existing strips on the right track, but to shape new strips with a fair chance of success. *Steve Roper* is an example of the former kind; in the fifties *Judge Parker* and *Rex Morgan, M.D.* would illustrate the latter. And perhaps the most spectacular example of combining the two techniques took place in and after 1938, when Publishers Syndicate refurbished an old sentimental melodrama originally called *Apple Mary*.

Apple Mary was created in 1932 by Martha Orr (niece of the Chicago *Tribune's* editorial cartoonist, Carey Orr). Apple Mary was a homely, dowdy, friendly, generous, self-sacrificing woman of sixty or so, who specialized in the role of *deus ex machina*— intervening whenever possible to solve other people's problems, because she rarely had any of her own. She was a classic figure— the aged, wandering sage, righting wrongs, averting tragedy and dispensing folk wisdom despite the indifference of those she helped. She was a good old girl; but she was a busybody and she lacked glamour. She belonged to another age, perhaps the gentler world of the 1900s.

Miss Orr was successful with the strip until 1938, when she requested a release from her contract. Her assistant, Miss Dale Connor, joined forces with Allen Saunders to continue the strip. They used a single byline: Dale Allen.

Saunders revolutionized the strip immediately. He took Apple Mary out of the lower-middle-class neighborhoods in which she had purveyed her naïve simplicities. He slimmed her down and dressed her up. He bought

Apple Mary, Bill Biff, and Little Kenny, stars of MARTHA ORR's original *Apple Mary*. Courtesy Publishers Syndicate.

her tickets for far places. Most significantly, he brought her into contact with young, modern men and women, so that she developed a certain sophistication.

The next steps in the metamorphosis were the arrival of Ken Ernst, originally a Chicago artist, and a change in the title to *Mary Worth*. Ernst is an illustrator of the new school. His women are glamorous, his details are accurate and he uses illustrational techniques— white space, position, long-shot and close-up— freely and imaginatively. Thanks to his drawing and Saunders' continuity, Mary Worth has ceased to be a meddling good fairy. She still represents traditional virtues, to be sure; but she carries on her subtle work in a real— if ultra-sophisticated— world of troubled adolescents, marital spats, show-business egos and even alcoholics. (The sequence touching on alcoholism appeared during 1958, when presumably even comics audiences were ready for it; it was handled with perception and honesty, and the public approved.)

Mary Worth represents better than most strips the transition in public

A Sunday *Mary Worth*. Apple Mary has risen from the slums to the height of modernity and fashion. ALLEN SAUNDERS' continuity is sophisticated and KEN ERNST'S drawing is in the best illustrator's syle. © 1959 Publishers Syndicate.

attitudes that took place from 1935 to 1950. Life became not only more earnest, but much faster-paced. The old thirty-day serials disappeared from almost all our newspapers because they were replaced by strips like *Mary Worth,* which were more entertaining, more gripping, more stylish and far more real, in their concern with contemporaneous problems, than the saccharine pseudo-literary efforts they succeeded. And graphic techniques were becoming the order of the day. By the mid-thirties cigarette and beverage manufacturers were running comic strips in color, in the Sunday comics sections, to advertise their products; "visual aids" were being used in educational experiments; and picture magazines were solidly established as a new journalistic species. With our preparations for war came a flood of illustrated manuals (on which many of the better-known comic artists worked). By 1955 we would be treated to the enjoyable spectacle of a major American bank advertising its facilities by means of a pamphlet in comic-book form; and long before that our politicians would be issuing comic-strip biographies of themselves.

And still the new strips came. Alfred Andriola, who had once been Milton Caniff's assistant, won prominence of his own with *Charlie Chan,* done in the best illustrator's manner: sleek, delicately contoured figures positioned with imaginative care and variety. Loy Byrnes came along in 1940 with *Spunkie,* the story of a refugee child, which bore out the thesis that Americans wanted more reality on the funny pages. Monte Barrett introduced *Jane Arden,* girl reporter, adding another pretty, independent, competent career woman to the list. By 1940 the activities of a Washington correspondent were of sufficient general interest to induce United Feature Syndicate to run *Hap Hopper,* drawn by Jack Sparling with continuities ostensibly by Drew Pearson and Robert S. Allen; from time to time real political figures appeared in the strip.

Inevitably there were strips which appeared, lasted a year or so and then disappeared. The funnies were expanding; the old favorites remained, and many of the newer strips found it impossible to survive. The old standbys were in the traditional categories— kids, families, animals. Doc Winner's *Elmer,* one of the most popular little-boy strips since 1926 ("Crim-a-nentlies!" was Elmer's cry of despair), was not to be rudely displaced by a newcomer. Neither, of course, was Carl Anderson's *Henry,* which remains, with Ernie Bushmiller's *Nancy,* among the most basic and most widely read of all strips.

Anderson was an old-timer, born while the Civil War was still in progress. He spent his boyhood in Madison, Wisconsin, but began his newspaper career as a pen-and-ink artist with the Philadelphia *Times* and the Pittsburgh *Comet* (both defunct now). Newspapers kept folding under him, and he made a virtue of necessity by deciding to become a free-lance. Inevitably he reached New York— in time to become a pawn in the great battle between Hearst and Pulitzer, shuttling back and forth between the *World* and the *Journal* so many times that he lost count.

His first notable effort at a comic strip was one of the earliest. He drew it for the McClure Syndicate, and it was called *Herr Spiegelberger, the Amateur Cracksman.* It began in the *World* in 1903, and was a Sunday page for many years, poking fun at a loud-mouthed slapstick German who resembled the notorious Munchausen.

For the next thirty years, roughly, Anderson appeared in all sorts of newspapers and periodicals, including *Judge, Puck,* the old *Life* and the old *Daily News,* which was not at all like Patterson's *Daily News. Henry* first appeared in *The Saturday Evening Post,* as a series of occasional cartoons. Hearst saw them first in a European reprint, and wired Anderson immediately; *Henry* has had a home, daily and Sunday, with King Features ever since.

Henry is not only mute, but also expressionless. The gag is everything; there is no opportunity for mugging or funny chit-chat. Yet Henry himself adds humor to the gag. He has a round head, perfectly hairless, and round feet; he wears shorts and a T-shirt in all weather. He is one of those basic, unvarying characters whom we are tempted to call symbolic; but what could he be symbolic of? Defenselessness, perhaps; he has no protection against wind and weather or hostile humans; nor can he complain, being speechless. But he always wins. His ingenuity, rarely corrupted by greedy motives, triumphs over the forces of darkness and illogic.

And people love him; some, because they enjoy not having to read a text; some, because they like to laugh a little with the kiddies. His public is international, problems of communication being largely solved by the absence of speech.

Ernie Bushmiller's *Nancy* is another subsidiary character who ultimately stole the limelight from a principal. Originally Fritzi Ritz's niece, in-

CARL ANDERSON'S *Henry.* This was drawn three years after Anderson's death, though signed with his name. Henry hasn't changed a bit. © 1951 King Features Syndicate, Inc.

Nancy once more. ERNIE BUSHMILLER'S strip is one of the half-dozen most popular in the world. © 1958 United Feature Syndicate, Inc.

troduced from time to time for a specific juvenile comic effect, Nancy slowly became almost the whole strip. (It was Milt Gross who advised Bushmiller, in 1938, to let Fritzi fade away, and to concentrate on Nancy.) She and her tough little boy friend Sluggo are now featured, and Aunt Fritzi appears only when an adult is needed for balance or contrast— or as the butt of a joke. For a time during the early forties the strip was called *Fritzi Ritz and Nancy;* now it is simply *Nancy.* Its gags are absolutely unsophisticated and unembroidered; they are humor on an almost primitive, childlike level— and Nancy runs in almost six hundred newspapers, being one of the best-loved strips in existence. (She runs in ten newspapers in Sweden alone.) The dialogue is so short, snappy and simple that translation is no problem. Why, during a period when the general drift of comics was from the simple to the sophisticated, Bushmiller should buck the trend successfully is a mysterious question. *Fritzi Ritz* might very easily have become more serious, more detailed, more like the typical career-girl strip. Instead it became a classic kid strip, and its circulation soared. (It almost disappeared altogether: Bushmiller spent most of 1930 in Hollywood working out gag situations for Harold Lloyd, and might have stayed on for years. But cartooning won out.)

There was one important change in an old strip during the thirties. Sidney Smith, you recall, had signed his million-dollar contract and died tragically on the same day, back in 1935. But *The Gumps* could not be permitted to die with him; it was much too valuable a property to neglect. The *News-Tribune* Syndicate ran a competition among its personnel, and a cheerful young sports cartoonist, who had drawn a feature of his own called *Streaky*, inherited *The Gumps*.

His name is Gus Edson. Like many good cartoonists, he first made efforts toward classical painting. Informed by Pratt Institute that he had no talent, he left to study under George Bellows, and went on from there to the Art Students League in New York City. There he met the present Mrs. Edson; they were married after a four-day courtship, and responsibilities began to accumulate. The New York *Graphic* was started up about then; it was a sensational newspaper with heavy accent on artwork. Edson applied for work and was the second man hired. The high point of his career with the *Graphic* was attained when he became the only man ever to be hit by a car on the third floor of a New York City office building— a display model got loose, singled him out, and struck.

He survived. He spent three years performing assorted chores for the *Graphic*, and then quit to free-lance. He turned out some sample sports cartoons which the Brooklyn *Standard-Union* liked; they gave him a pair of binoculars and a ticket to the Tunney-Heeney fight. Edson's sketches got him a job— $100 a week for a year.

After that year he was relatively well known. Joe Connolly, the late president of KFS, friend and benefactor of many cartoonists, brought him into the King Features Syndicate, where Edson did *Here's How* for a year and a half, in fifty-eight newspapers. By 1931 he had come to the attention of one of the shrewdest comics editors in the business— Captain Patterson again.

The Edson-Patterson interview remains a classic. Ushered into the imposing sanctum, aware that he was at the nerve center of a huge news-

The Gumps again— Gus Edson's Christmas strip, 1939. Andy, Bim, and Tilda are as homely as ever, but Min has become a bit prettier. © the Chicago *Tribune*– New York *News* Syndicate, Inc.

A daily *Dondi*, created by GUS EDSON and IRWIN HASEN in the aftermath of the war. Its circulation has risen steadily. © 1959 the Chicago *Tribune*– New York *News* Syndicate, Inc.

paper and a thriving syndicate, Edson was properly deferent but a mite suspicious. After the requisite amenities, he asked Patterson, "What about a contract?"

"Contract?" Patterson raised an eyebrow. "We don't use contracts here. I don't even have one."

Edson nodded. "You don't need one. You own the place. I don't own the place."

Patterson expostulated gently, calling in his managing editor to witness that contracts were not his policy. Edson suspected by now that Patterson was serious about hiring him, and with the tenacity of the ex-free-lance he refused to give in. He got his contract.

He did sports cartoons for a couple of years, and tried half a dozen strip ideas in 1933 and 1934. One of them, *Streaky,* won Patterson's approval, and succeeded. Edson was doing the strip regularly when Sidney Smith died.

In tribute to Smith, Edson did a cartoon the next day of the Gumps, *en masse,* in mourning. Miss Mollie Slott, the syndicate's comics editor, liked it; so did Patterson. Once more there was a discussion; Patterson wanted Edson to run off two weeks' worth of *The Gumps* in his "spare time," and Edson was shrewd enough never to admit that he had any spare time. He wangled a two-week leave of absence, did the strips and was assigned to the Gumps permanently.

At first his style was a respectful imitation of Smith's, and he has never tampered with the basic features of his characters. But over the years a refinement crept into the strip, particularly where the women were concerned. It was inevitable. The country was changing, the times were new; there wasn't a housewife in America more that a hundred miles from a beauty parlor, and there wasn't a husband in America who didn't once in a while cast a musing glance at another woman. Min Gump eventually blossomed and took her place in the modern world (she is, after all, sister-in-law to a billionaire).

Edson had been doing *The Gumps* for almost twenty years when he developed a second strip; but that story belongs to a later decade.

There was even one old-fashioned rough-and-tumble strip which came to life in the thirties: C. D. Russell's *Pete the Tramp*. *Pete* is another strip of international popularity, relying as it does on the sight gag and only occasionally on dialogue; and probably there is some universal appeal in the footloose, finagling, unwashed cigar-smoker whose basic concern is survival. The story goes that Russell used to watch the tramps in Manhattan's Bryant Park— men who would share a liberal crust of bread with the pigeons, and five minutes later put the arm on a well-dressed stroller.

Russell's own life has nothing in common with Pete's. He was born in Buffalo, studied at the Chicago Art Institute, and came to New York just before we entered the First World War. He joined the Marines, served overseas and became sports editor of the old Marine Corps *Leatherneck*, sketching for them regularly. During the twenties he worked on the New York *Evening Mail* and the old *Evening Post*, meanwhile contributing regularly to *Judge*. (*Judge* had contracted for exclusive rights to his cartoons, to keep him out of the old *Life*.) *Judge* boasted a great roster in those days: George Jean Nathan and S. J. Perelman wrote for it, and it ran cartoons and drawings by Jefferson Machamer, Bill Holman, Bruce Bairnsfather and James Montgomery Flagg.

Pete appeared first in *Judge* as a spot gag, and Russell found himself doing variations on the tramp theme with some regularity. Now and then he ran off a full page of drawings for the magazine; it was invariably printed. By 1931 King Features was after Russell, and he signed with them in December of that year. A month later *Pete the Tramp* began as a full-color Sunday page (periodically on page one of the comics section) in the New York *Mirror*. He began as a daily feature in 1934. In 1936 he was moved to the *Journal*, where he found a permanent home.

Russell's style is forthright and confident. Pete is thoroughly conventionalized, with only the eyebrows showing expression, and with a fan of mustache-beard as his trade-mark. More often than not he is in the company of a dog and a small boy— a key to his appeal. A tramp, yes, but if he loves children and dogs, we can only approve of him, and wish him luck in his struggle to survive with honor. Pete is much loved in Europe, perhaps because many Europeans are, happily, as preoccupied with food and warmth as we Americans are with bathtubs and cufflinks. All during the Second World War the mats of *Pete the Tramp* were dropped into Oslo by parachute, and Russell is understandably proud of the fact that *Pete* ran every day in that city.

Russell's life abounds with anecdotes; he has known most of the best cartoonists for years, and has found occasional adventure with them. The classic story is of the time he and Percy Crosby took part (as allies) in an uninhibited brawl in New York City. They emerged battered but with the scutcheon untarnished, only to find a policeman glowering at them. "What's your name?" he asked Crosby. "Percy," Crosby said. The officer nodded; he

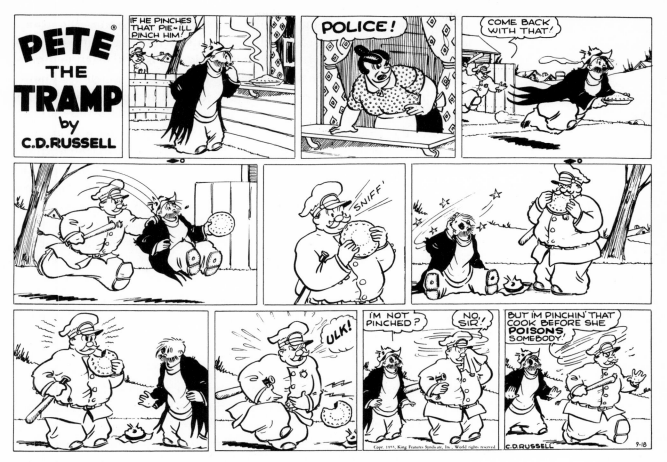

A Sunday *Pete the Tramp* by C. D. Russell. Pete is as popular abroad as he is in this country. © 1955 King Features Syndicate, Inc.

had met wise guys before. "What's yours?" he asked Russell. "Clarence," Russell said. The officer nodded again, and ran them in immediately.

Another new area opened up in the thirties, both in popular magazines and in the comics: science fiction. Much of it seems old-hat now, because we have invented horrors to equal most of the early fantasies, and because science fiction has acquired overtones of actuality and morality since the war, relying more and more on sophistication and psychological comment, and not so much on melodrama.

But in 1929 *Buck Rogers* was the last word in science fiction, and all through the thirties it ran daily and Sunday in the newspapers and enthralled children by the millions as a daily radio serial. It was created by John Dille, president of the National Newspaper Service in Chicago, and was for many years drawn by Lieutenant Richard W. Calkins, who had been commissioned an Army pilot in 1918. The two men met in the late twenties, and were associates thereafter at the syndicate. A running argument preceded the creation of *Buck Rogers*: Calkins had always loved to draw prehistoric animals, and wanted to do a strip set in dinosaurian or Neanderthal times; Dille had always felt that the future, which was unknown, was more fascinating than the past, which was known. Ultimately Dille succeeded in plotting a strip set in the twenty-fifth century and prevailed upon Calkins to draw it.

It was the straight, raw stuff: men and women in space suits, with paralysis-ray guns and anti-gravity belts; oddly shaped space ships and oddly shaped villains; a hero and his girl, and a villain and his girl, and a young boy to keep juvenile interest fresh. Some of the science was simple: Rogers might be seen frisking about the surface of a planetoid, taking thirty feet at a stride because gravity was low. Some of it verged on the complex, with talk of orbits and airlocks and asteroids. But all of it was fascinating. The strip itself is a study in "pioneering"— as the first of the science-fiction strips, it now seems overmelodramatic, drawn plainly and simply, and even— strangely enough— slightly unimaginative. But its impact during the thirties was powerful, and it led the way for many imitations and variations. If history has caught up with it— or almost— *Buck Rogers* is not to blame.

It was five years before a worthy competitor challenged Buck Rogers, and the creator of the new strip was, during his lifetime, matched only by Caniff and Sickles as a draftsman. He has another distinction, however, which is his alone: he was the only modern cartoonist to have created four entirely different— and entirely successful— comic strips. His name was Alex Raymond.

Raymond had been destined for a life in Wall Street; the crash was, paradoxically, what saved him from ennui and routine. He was not yet twenty when the financial world fell apart. In one last burst of rationality he wangled a job soliciting for a mortgage broker, but at the same time he enrolled in the Grand Central School of Art. He had been drawing and

Buck Rogers in 1934, when PHIL NOWLAN had taken over the continuity. Reprinted with permission of National Newspaper Syndicate.

Secret Agent X-9, by DASHIELL HAMMETT and ALEX RAYMOND, in the early days. Note the straw hats. © 1934 King Features Syndicate, Inc.

sketching since early boyhood, with the encouragement and co-operation of his father (who would come home from a day's work and say to the youngster, "Draw me"). And he was a flop as a salesman: "I always believed prospects when they said 'No.' "

One of Raymond's neighbors in New Rochelle was Russ Westover, who needed an assistant on *Tillie the Toiler.* Raymond took the job with pleasure, began to learn the trade and soon found himself a staff artist with King Features. Very shortly his break came: KFS had decided to go ahead with an adventure strip called *Secret Agent X-9,* and Raymond walked off with the strip after a turbulent competition.

It was only the beginning. Following brief speculation, a couple of years later, on the possibility of an interplanetary adventure strip, Raymond drew up a Sunday page. It was rejected. He redrew it. His editors liked it. Within weeks he was working full-time at two strips: *X-9* and *Flash Gordon.* By 1939 the load was too great; Raymond also produced and drew *Jungle Jim,* and there was a limit to one man's capacity. He gave up *X-9.* (Mel Graff took it over. Graff had created *Patsy* back in 1934, a whimsical little-girl strip which soon became less whimsical and more frantic when Patsy arrived in Hollywood. *Patsy* lived on, done by a succession of artists and writers. The continuity for *X-9,* incidentally, had originally been done by mystery writer Dashiell Hammett, but by the time Graff took over Hammett had bowed out.) Raymond concentrated on *Flash Gordon* for several years. His career was interrupted in 1944 and 1945, when he became a captain in the Marine Corps Reserve as a public-information officer and combat artist; other artists carried on his strips.

What made *Flash Gordon* outstanding was not the story; along the unmarked trails of interstellar space practically any continuity was original. Nor were Flash and his lady friend, Dale, radical departures from the traditional hero and heroine. But *Flash Gordon* was beautifully drawn; and its narrative and dialogue were literate. Raymond did not use balloons here; like Harold Foster with *Tarzan,* he ran a narrative in the present tense in one corner of the panel, with the dialogue set off by quotation marks. The

227

A *Jungle Jim* by ALEX RAYMOND, 1940. Superb drawing— note the light and shadow, and the change of pace in "camera angles." © King Features Syndicate, Inc.

total effect— slick, imaginative drawing with literate narrative— was one of melodrama on a high level, which should not obscure the fact that Raymond's villains were thoroughly wicked, or that his female characters were generally sexy.

Flash Gordon rapidly became the premier space strip. It was wittier, and moved faster, than *Buck Rogers;* it was prettier and less boyish than William Ritt's and Clarence Gray's *Brick Bradford.* Yet even *Flash Gordon* was not enough for Raymond; when he came back from the war he approached his editors with an idea for a new strip, something modern and almost too intellectual.

This was Rip Kirby, a former Marine Corps officer turned detective— and yet much more than a detective. Kirby's was the world of the intelligent man, and his fight against crime was not that of the two-fisted man of violence. For one thing, Kirby wore glasses— a shocking violation of the pattern. For another, he read books, preferred classical music, enjoyed golf, took a drink now and then, and understood both chess and women.

It was a long gamble for KFS to take. There have always been strips with a superior intellectual content— from Feininger's early fantasies through Rube Goldberg's satires to *Krazy Kat,* to much of Caniff's work, to Al Capp, to (in the fifties) Walt Kelly's *Pogo* and Charles Schulz's *Peanuts.* But most of those strips were deliberately intellectual. *Rip Kirby* was an invasion of melodrama by sophisticated intelligence, and editors were dubious.

But the strip succeeded. Whatever Kirby's character, Raymond was a master of illustration and story line. In *Rip Kirby* he displayed all his talents to the fullest. Facial expressions were subtle, backgrounds were full of fine but unobtrusive detail, the dialogue (this time in balloons) was racy and unstilted. (The girls were also racy, which did not hurt.) Raymond had done it again.

From then until his tragic death in September of 1956, Raymond stayed with *Rip Kirby*, refining his techniques, boldly defending the thinker as hero, adding to the world of comics one more character who refused to conform to prevailing patterns of violence and anti-intellectualism. Then, like Sidney Smith and Sam Cobean, Raymond died in an automobile accident. Among his colleagues were many who loved him and none who had ever been jealous of him; the shock of his death was felt throughout the profession.

One of the early *Flash Gordon* pages, 1936, by ALEX RAYMOND. Less light and shadow here, but more action. The combination of narrative and dialogue is characteristic. © King Features Syndicate, Inc.

A *Rip Kirby* of 1953, by RAYMOND, with Desmond, Kirby's Man Friday. The lighting effects add eerily to the obvious mood of suspense. © King Features Syndicate, Inc.

Another *Rip Kirby*, by RAYMOND, this one of 1954. The man is an unashamed intellectual— pipe, typewriter in use, spectacles. © King Features Syndicate, Inc.

A *Rip Kirby* of 1958, drawn by JOHN PRENTICE. The illustrator's style is still brilliant, the facial expression excellent. © King Features Syndicate, Inc.

As fantastic as either *Buck Rogers* or *Flash Gordon*, and a lot funnier, is V. T. Hamlin's *Alley Oop*, which began as the strip about prehistoric man which Calkins would have liked so much, and rapidly burlesqued its way into a kind of Cro-Magnon science fiction. Oop himself is courageous, only moderately bright and immensely powerful. His arms and legs are drawn in the *Popeye* tradition: skinny upper arms and thighs, but huge forearms and calves. He generally wears what looks like a mammoth-skin bathing suit, his only article of clothing; occasionally, for plot purposes, he dons the garments of the time and place he temporarily inhabits.

Time and place vary; the beginning of Oop's journey into fantasy took place five years after the strip's inception. Hamlin was tired of prehistoric wars in the kingdom of Moo, of feuds between Alley and his sovereign, King Guz, even of frustrated romance between Alley and his curvy inamorata, Ooola. In April of 1939 Ooola and Alley, fugitives from Guz's wrath, disappeared before the eyes of their pursuers— and of their readers; a note from Hamlin advised the public that they must "say goodbye to Moo" if they were to follow Alley "in this strangest of many strange adventures."

Strange it was. Enter Dr. Wonmug, twentieth-century scientist, who has perfected— almost— a time machine, and who has inadvertently brought Alley and Ooola into the modern era. Enter also Dr. Boom (J. Oscar Boom), a clever villain, himself a scientist. With the manipulation of the time machine, good (in the person of Alley) battles evil (Boom) on many fronts in many centuries— Egypt, the Roman Empire, the Middle Ages. Hamlin's history is by and large accurate; he came to the strip originally through an interest in geology and paleontology. And the device of the time machine gives him unlimited scope. *Alley Oop* remains a consistently funny strip, almost in the old tradition: plenty of Pop and Pow, occasional satire and a fine continuing process of *non sequitur*.

V. T. HAMLIN's *Alley Oop*. A recent strip, but happily the same old prehistoria, complete with caveman carrying off sweetheart. © 1959 NEA Service, Inc. Reprinted by permission of NEA Service, Inc.

A REX MAXON *Tarzan*. Danger, action, and the ever-present jungle. The strip is now done by JOHN CELARDO and DICK VAN BUREN. © 1939 by Edgar Rice Burroughs. Courtesy of United Feature Syndicate, Inc.

One adventure strip of the thirties takes us into the jungles: *Tarzan,* naturally based on the series of books by Edgar Rice Burroughs. The original *Tarzan of the Apes* was written in 1914; the first comics page appeared in 1929, the result of a calculated decision by the Metropolitan Newspaper Service, which ran the first series as a complete ten-week story. Newspapers carrying the feature were not obliged to continue it beyond the ten-week mark.

Of course, they *were* obliged to; reader reaction was violently favorable. Metropolitan was sold to United Feature Syndicate the next year, as *Tarzan's* circulation soared; the first Sunday page appeared in 1931. The drawing was in the solid vein of realistic adventure from the beginning. Harold Foster drew it, and whether the strip owed more to the artist, or the artist to the strip, is immaterial. The combination was unbeatable. Foster withdrew after a time, however, and Rex Maxon took over; Maxon soon found that six-a-week-plus-Sunday was a devastating schedule for a strip which required a high standard of illustration. Foster came back then to do the Sunday pages. When Foster went to King Features to do *Prince Valiant,* Burne Hogarth took over the Sunday *Tarzan.*

That Foster was a rare illustrator became apparent when he began *Prince Valiant.* Here again was an artist not in the comics tradition at all, but rather in the book illustrator's. There have been single panels in *Prince Valiant* which must have taken longer to draw than entire Sunday strips of other comics. Aside from the draftsman's accuracy of line and perspective, Foster enjoys sweep, crowded detail, delicate shading; yet his panels never seem too "busy." Like *Tarzan* and *Flash Gordon, Prince Valiant* uses no balloons, but a printed narrative with quoted dialogue. That enables Foster to use his whole panel— to compose carefully and to create stunning effects. His technique is perfect for the subject. Val is a Norseman, a Viking prince, and inevitably Foster uses vast seascapes, long reaches of shoreline, distant views of assembled fleets. Many of his panels are superior illustrations of medieval life; from a long shot of soldiers struggling up a hillside he may return to a close-up of his terrified— but accurately

A full page of HAROLD FOSTER'S *Prince Valiant.* Note the variety of scene, the litera narrative, the accuracy of medieval detail. © 1958 King Features Syndicate, Inc.

Prince Valiant IN THE DAYS OF KING ARTHUR
WRITTEN AND ILLUSTRATED BY HAROLD R FOSTER

Our Story: IN AN ANCIENT BURIAL CHAMBER HIGH ON A MISTY MOUNTAINSIDE, PRINCE VALIANT TUNES A LUTE AND SINGS. ALL DAY HE PLAYS AND SINGS UNTIL THE RUSTINESS LEAVES HIS VOICE, ONCE AGAIN HIS FINGERS ARE NIMBLE ON THE STRINGS, AND ALL THE OLD SONGS COME BACK TO HIM.

AND FAR INTO THE NIGHT HE PRACTICES THE SLY DECEPTIONS HE LEARNED LONG AGO FROM SLITH, THE GAY MASTER OF DECEIT.

WHEN AT LAST VAL FEELS HIMSELF READY FOR HIS ADVENTURE, HE ARRANGES A SET OF SIGNALS BY WHICH SIR WALDOC AND RUY CAN TELL HOW THEIR PLANS ARE GOING.

THEN HE RIDES TOWARD GRIM OSWICK SINGING. AND THE SONG HE SINGS IS ONE THAT HE AND GAWAIN HAVE OFTEN SUNG TOGETHER. IF GAWAIN IS BEING HELD BEHIND THOSE WALLS, HE WILL HEAR AND PERHAPS BE ABLE TO SIGNAL HIS WHEREABOUTS.

"STAND ASIDE, HOMELY ONES, AND MAKE WAY FOR CID, GREATEST OF TROUBADOURS! I BRING SONGS, MAGIC AND WIT. AND, I MIGHT ADD, AN EMPTY BELLY!"

TROUBADOURS ARE ALWAYS WELCOME, SO VAL ENTERS THE CASTLE EASILY TO TAKE THE PLACE MADE VACANT WHEN RUY LEFT TO ESCAPE THE HEADMAN'S AXE.

HAL FOSTER

KING OSWICK HEARS OF THE NEW ARRIVAL. "BRING HIM IN AND LET US TEST HIS SKILLS," HE ORDERS.

NEXT WEEK- **Discovery?**

1142.

12-28-F

IN EVERY HALL AND CORRIDOR IN CAMELOT THERE HAPPENS THAT BREATH-LESS MOMENT WHEN GALLANT PEOPLE BID FAREWELL, SOME FOR THE LAST TIME.

A touching moment from *Prince Valiant*, July 6, 1958. In one panel HAROLD FOSTER has had to be accurate about architecture, interior decoration, heraldry, clothing and weapons. © 1958 King Features Syndicate, Inc.

garbed— heroine, lips parted in fear as she watches her knight go forth.

Accuracy is important to Foster because he is a conscientious artist. Few readers would have the knowledge needed to point out errors, but part of *Valiant's* appeal lies in the realistic representation of life as it was, presumably, in about 500 A.D., when Good King Arthur ruled Britain, and the Norsemen were alternately enemy and ally. In one sense Foster's realism is the most faithful in comics. The knight in armor is a fine hero, a great inspiration to the young— but medieval battlefields were strewn with disemboweled victims, with stray arms and legs, and Foster has been careful to point out (always within the strictest bounds of good taste) that the battle is not always to the brave; that even the victors lose a hero now and then; that the aftermath of war is not usually celebration, whoever wins, but rather weariness and grief. Nor is his strip devoted exclusively to derring-do. His heroes have wives and children, eat lavish meals, take baths, discuss news of the day— all much as men must have done in those times.

All in all, *Prince Valiant* is a tour de force. Day after day, week after week, Harold Foster has created living characters who reflect their epoch faithfully. He has drawn those characters and their world with great fidelity, spending more hours at the drawing board than anyone else in the profession. He has told their story in excellent English, with a high sense of drama and an abhorrence of the cliché. His taste has never faltered. *Prince Valiant* is a superb example of comic-strip art at its best: beautiful to look at, exciting to read and educational in its ultimate effect.

A broad panorama by HAL FOSTER. The succession of long shots, close-ups, and interiors in *Prince Valiant* is very effective in maintaining pace and authenticity. © 1956 King Features Syndicate, Inc.

AT SUMMER'S END VAL AND THE KING RIDE ABROAD TO ESTIMATE THE YEAR'S HARVEST. *"LOOK,"* SAYS THE KING, *"ALREADY OUR MARINERS OVERTURN THEIR SHIPS FOR WINTER SHELTERS."*

"BEFORE SPRING COMES, THERE WILL BE HUNGER AMONG THEM, YET THEY WILL NOT LEAVE THE SEACOAST AND THEIR BOATS TO SEEK FARMLAND IN THE INTERIOR."

"SIR VALIANT, YOU MUST EXPLORE THE INNER VALLEYS TO FIND IF THERE BE LAND WE CAN CULTIVATE TO FEED OUR INCREASING POPULATION!"

NEXT WEEK:-Into the Wilderness.

234

CLIFFORD McBRIDE's *Napoleon*, making trouble for himself and Uncle Elby, 1935. Reprinted with permission of Margot McBride and *Times-Mirror* Syndicate, Los Angeles.

There was much more in the thirties. New strips were launched every few months; some lived and some died. The old favorites plugged right along. Advertising through comic strips became a major industry. More and more schools turned to film strips, animations, visual techniques. Strips changed hands, as when Coulton Waugh continued *Dickie Dare* after Caniff turned to *Terry;* or cartoonists died and their work was taken up by others. Homey strips like Cliff McBride's *Napoleon and Uncle Elby* and Edwina Dumm's *Cap Stubbs and Tippie* ran on the same page with Ken Kling's highly successful comic-strip racing form, *Joe and Asbestos*. From England came J. Millar Watt's *Pop*, one of the rare strips of foreign origin to be syndicated in this country. Otto Soglow ran a series of cartoons in *The New Yorker* which were syndicated for the newspapers as *The Little King;* he added to it *Sentinel Louie*, and two more symbols were born. In the early years of the decade Garrett Price did a strip about a pioneer boy and an Indian girl and their animal friends; it was called *White Boy*, and brought some of the quiet beauty of the West onto the comics page, without benefit of shoot-'em-up.

The trends were obvious, though. More and more, the public wanted

The British import, *Pop*, by J. MILLAR WATT. The artist liked to run his scene across more than one panel. The drawing is not as simple as it looks. © 1935 the Bell Syndicate, Inc.

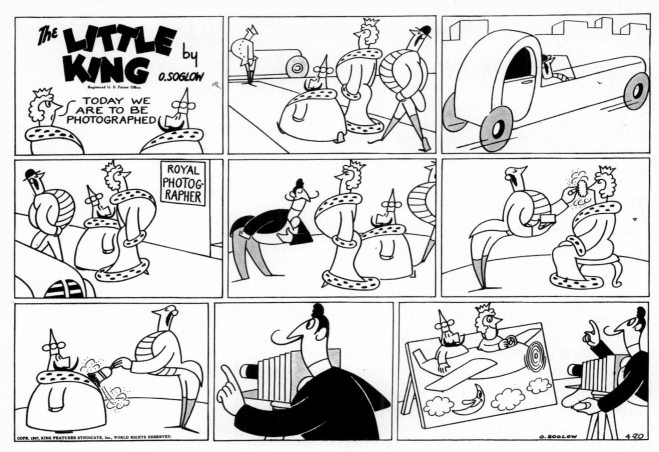

OTTO SOGLOW's famous *Little King*, probably the most put-upon monarch extant. © 1947 King Features Syndicate, Inc.

reflections of the contemporary world. The comics were becoming illustrated fiction, and even the new fantasy strips relied on realism and detail. Yet kid strips like *Nancy* and family strips like *The Gumps* rolled on; so did *Popeye* and *Barney Google* and *Krazy Kat* and *Dave's Delicatessen* and *That's My Pop*.

CHAPTER VII

More Big Business

Underneath all the activity of the thirties, a new kind of strip was coming to life, and with it a new kind of periodical. The prototype of the new strip was *Superman*, and it was largely thanks to him that comic books rose to startling heights of popularity. He was not the first character to be put between paper covers; he never appeared in print until June 1938, and comic books had been published as early as 1933. But *Superman's* appearance triggered an explosion in the comic-book world.

There had been collections of comic strips, printed from the newspaper plates, even before the First World War. One of them, of *Mutt and Jeff*, issued by the Chicago *American* as a circulation stunt, was phenomenally successful, with readers writing in for almost fifty thousand copies, but the idea was dropped right there. Popular fiction, as represented by pulp magazines and newspaper serials, still provided the bulk of our mass-circula-

Some *Big Little Books*, widely popular precursors of the comic book. Courtesy of Larry Ivie.

tion entertainment, and few publishers were willing to risk untried methods. Late in the twenties George Delacorte, now publisher of Dell Comics, experimented with a tabloid-sized book, containing original comics drawn for publication in that form, rather than reprints of newspaper strips. The collection was not a "book," strictly speaking, but rather a small newspaper full of comics. Which, as Coulton Waugh pointed out, probably accounted for the failure of the experiment: they looked like detached sections of newspaper, and not sufficiently like independent publications.

An oblique approach was made during the thirties, with the Whitman Publishing Company's "Big Little Books," in which the left-hand pages were set in type, offering a continuous narrative, while each right-hand page was one panel of a continuing strip-illustration. These books were about three inches square and two inches deep; most popular strips of the early and middle thirties appeared in Big Little form. Big Little Books achieved wide circulation; their demise was not natural, but a consequence of the boom in comic books.

The boom came late, and with an assist from the advertising industry. In the middle thirties many manufacturers used comic books— made up of reprints— as premiums; that is, free copies of them were given away to customers, on the theory that if mothers shopped with their children, or liked the funnies themselves, they would select the brand which offered them something extra. M. C. Gaines, one of the pioneers in comic-book sales, took several copies of one of these premiums, entitled *Famous Funnies*, adorned them with stickers reading "10¢" and persuaded a few news dealers to carry them for a few days. They sold out almost immediately.

The next step was a larger experiment. George Delacorte agreed to publish thirty-five thousand of these books and to release them through chain stores (still with the lingering notion that they would not be bought for themselves, but only as part of a general shopping tour). The printing sold out quickly; but these were not yet comic books in their final form. They were reprints still; they were not distributed through ordinary magazine channels; and the experts continued pessimistic about any larger-scale operation.

In early 1934 the New York *Daily News* revitalized the issue of comics in general by running a thoughtful advertisement which pointed up the value of comic strips to a newspaper. The flurry of reappraisal induced the Eastern Color Printing Company, which had printed most of the early efforts, to publish the first comics magazine specifically for newsstand sales. It was called *Famous Funnies*. It sold for ten cents. It contained reprints of *Mutt and Jeff, Toonerville Folks, Hairbreadth Harry, Tailspin Tommy, The Nebbs* and other strips, plus a generous sprinkling of puzzles, magic tricks and "oddity panels" patterned on Ripley's *Believe It or Not*. The first issue lost money; the second was profitable. Gaines took heart and published a reprint magazine consisting entirely of old strips of *Skippy*.

238

[ABOVE LEFT] The cover of one of the first commercially distributed comic books. Unlike most of today's, the early comic books contained many different strips in one issue. Courtesy Dell Publishing Co., Inc.

[ABOVE RIGHT] One of the early *Popular Comics*, again with a varied cast. Courtesy Dell Publishing Co., Inc.

The idea was taking hold. In 1935 Gaines produced, and Delacorte published, a comics magazine called *Popular Comics*. The next year United Feature Syndicate brought out *Tip Top Comics;* King Features leased the right to reprint its strips, and the McKay Company issued *King Comics*.

In 1937 there appeared *Detective Comics*, the first time a comic book had offered one specific kind of strip. (The theory may have been that this would combine comics appeal with the sure-fire appeal of the detective-fiction magazines of the time.) In 1938 its publishers added another category, with the publication of *Action Comics;* Gaines, who had been interested in *Superman,* saw a spot for it in this publication. Within a few months the circulation of *Action Comics* had doubled; by the spring of 1939 *Superman Quarterly Magazine* was inevitable. Comic books were here to stay. There were sixty titles in 1939–40; by the end of 1941, one hundred sixty-eight.

Superman was created by two stubborn young men (both in their mid-twenties at the time) named Jerry Siegel (who wrote the continuity) and Joe Shuster (who drew the strips). They were from Cleveland, and Siegel evolved the idea of *Superman* while he was still in high school. Their efforts to sell the strip were strenuous and unremitting; for five years they sent it to editor after editor, and suffered refusal after refusal, usually on the grounds that their character was too fantastic and had no relation to life.

In 1939, after its first comic-book successes, the strip was syndicated by McClure. In 1940 *Superman* was a radio program; by 1942 contracts had been signed to produce him in animated cartoons. A dozen imitations had sprung to life: a fairly good one was *Captain Marvel*. And the critics were in action, pro and con. Superman was the ideal outlet for youth's unruly instincts; Superman was in the tradition of the American hero; Superman was a force for good in a world of evil. Or: Superman expressed an irresponsible social philosophy in which the average citizen abjured his own duties and let the marvel fulfill them; Superman was a glorification of the physical; Superman represented absolute power, which is ultimately corrupting. While the battle raged, kids bought the comic books, listened to the radio program, heeded Superman's preferences in literature, clothing, bubble gum and toys.

A recent cover of *Superman Comics*. © 1959 by Superman, Inc.

One of the first *Superman* strips, by JERRY SIEGEL and JOE SHUSTER in 1939. The baby survives, arrives on earth, and becomes Superman. © 1939 McClure Newspaper Syndicate.

He seems a little easier to explain now, twenty years later. The thirties were a period of trial, and many of us had lost our old faith in the traditional virtues. The gangster was an American institution, a salient figure in fact and fiction. War was imminent in Europe; Hitler seemed the personification of absolute evil with unlimited power. Superman may have been partly a wish fulfillment: hesitant to accept battle with the evil loose in the world, parents quietly approved the presence of this fictional strong man who would have been such a comfort had he existed. And then there were legitimate elements of suspense and melodrama. Superman's origins (he was a native of the planet Krypton) were mysterious and otherworldly. Set down on earth, he had become an American, which was properly patriotic. When war broke out, the country went through the necessary psychological preparations for battle, which included the process of persuading men that they were heroes. Irresponsible social philosophy or not, Superman was the sensation of the early forties (during which time many of the staid, conventional children's magazines were quietly laid to rest). He has persisted successfully into the fifties, as both a comics hero and a

Superman in his earthly guise, as Clark Kent, reporter on the *Daily Planet*. This strip is from 1959. © 1959 Superman, Inc.

The cover, slightly truncated, to one of PAUL TERRY's comic books. Mayhem was the order of the day—but innocent mayhem.

television hero. With trick photography now a fine art, his deeds are potentially as spectacular as they ever were, and his popularity seems as high.

He was not, however, the whole story. Among the hundreds of titles of the early forties were many of the old humorous stand-bys, including Paul Terry's and Walt Disney's more famous, and wholly innocuous, animal characters. M. C. Gaines, who had produced many of the more flamboyant early comic books, later turned out several of quieter and more permanent interest. George Heckt's *True Comics* gave children (including teen-agers and many members of the armed forces) educational stories, historically accurate, which were no less exciting than the wildest fantasies on the market. Exercising a responsible social philosophy, *True Comics* produced *They Got the Blame*, the story of scapegoats of history, and *There Are No Master Races*, a considered view of anthropology.

It was soon apparent that comic books could serve many purposes. Many of them had only one purpose: to make money for their originators. Others were used to plead for religious tolerance, to present Bible stories, to promote justice and international understanding. War comics induced more than one young man to enlist (as did war films, which were often much sillier and more vulgar than the comic books).

After the war a distinction became obvious. The newspaper comic strip was part of a daily publication essential to almost all American families. As such, it had to maintain the standards of propriety and taste raised by the newspaper itself. The comic book, on the other hand, was an independent publication, available to anyone for (usually) a dime, and responsible to no one for the quality of its contents. And during the war there had been a subtle but perceptible change in human attitudes. The species had been subjected to the most severe attack yet on its morals, its principles, its sense of proportion, even its existence. Whole races had been liquidated; prisoners had been tortured, innocent women and children murdered; Hiroshima and Nagasaki had practically ceased to exist. Brutality— our

Two panels from "The Story of Amelia Earhart" in *True Comics*. Courtesy the Bell Syndicate, Inc.

awareness of it, and ultimately our habituation to it— had been necessary when survival was at stake, but the constant representation of it in newspapers, movies, magazines and comic books had debased our capacity for horror. What was considered straight news-reporting in 1945 would have been called neurotically sadistic in 1940.

None of this was too dangerous yet; if comic books became gory, they could hardly compete with the war for honors in sadism, and they could point out with some justice that other media were no less sensationalized. But by the early fifties two difficulties had set in: one was that the other media were all responsible to someone— advertisers, or stockholders, or directly to the public, like newspapers. Comic books just appeared. Most of them appeared once, sold out and gave way to a new issue. The publisher was not a public figure, with direct responsibility for his product; half the time no one was sure who the real publisher was. Which was fair enough until a very few comic books began to go a little too far, and to portray violence for its own sake, devoid of any pretense at a justifying context.

And at that point, the second difficulty arose: a new generation, which had no direct knowledge of the war and had not experienced, even indirectly, the debasement of morality brought on by the war, came of age. That generation was out buying comic books. And when these youngsters ran across the occasional comic book which specialized in gore and grue, they were unable to relate the blood, the sadism, the sexual overtones, to any universal human experience. The kids, lured on by a fairly natural juvenile love of sensation, and growing up in a world where there seemed to be no meaningful morality, accepted that sensation as normal— as "fun."

There were only a handful of such comic books, but they were enough to arouse alarmed citizens— including a few who specialized in righteousness and responded to many crises with shouts of "Doomsday!"— and to bring into the world of comics, for the first time in its modern history, a clear threat of censorship.

The threat was met, and defeated, by the comics profession itself. No one denied the existence of a few dangerous comic books. No one denied the drift toward apathy and casual acceptance of the horrible which the whole country had undergone. (Those who disapproved of comics tried to lay the blame for that drift on the funnies alone, an obvious confusion of cause with effect.) Publishers, artists, syndicates and continuity writers reacted vigorously. Codes were drawn up; pending censorship legislation was opposed and defeated; self-appointed censors were resisted.

The critics— even the most vociferous of them— had a point, and once the situation was made clear no responsible cartoonist denied that point. The point was that comics are generally available to the very young, and that a very small percentage of comic books was unhealthy reading. (Subsidiary, problematical points were strenuously contested by the cartoonists

One of the gorier comic-book covers. These have been fewer and farther between since the industry cleaned its own house in response to public criticism. Published by Comic House, Inc.

Tip Top Comics, put out by the Dell Publishing Co., and containing a variety of harmless and entertaining juvenile strips. Courtesy Dell Publishing Co., Inc.

— for example, that all funnies were in themselves bad for intellectual development, or that they retarded a child's progress in reading.) When the problem was identified, cartoonists and their publishers solved it. Many comic-book publishers joined the Comics Code Authority, committed to maintaining high standards; only Dell, now one of the major producers of comics, plus Gilbertson and Educational Comics, refused to join, on the justifiable grounds that they had never published a comic book which violated the standards under discussion.

Unanimously, comic artists came to the defense of their medium. Men whose work had never appeared in comic-book form were just as vociferous as those who appeared primarily in comic books. By now the cartoonists had their own professional society— its establishment is part of Chapter IX— and the National Cartoonists Society saw the threat of censorship not as a limited, temporary pressure, but as the first step in what might well become a loss of freedom for the whole medium. One restriction often leads to another; the Society was determined to hold the line against legislative oppression, and to eliminate excesses through action by its own committees.

The Society's position was established in a statement drawn up by Walt Kelly, then president of the Society, Milton Caniff, chairman of the Society's Ethics Committee, and Joseph Musial, chairman of the Society's Education Committee.

The National Cartoonists Society views as unwarranted any additional legislative action that is intended to censor printed material. The Society believes in local option. We believe that offensive material of any nature can be weeded from the mass of worthwhile publications by the exercise of existing city, state and federal laws.

Further, we believe that the National Cartoonists Society constitutes a leadership in the cartoon field which has previously established popular trends. We therefore will restrict any action we take to continually improving our own material and thus influencing the coat-tail riders who follow any successful idea.

We believe good material outsells bad. We believe people, even juveniles, are fundamentally decent. We believe, as parents and as one-time children ourselves, that most young people are instinctively attracted to that which is wholesome.

Our belief in this sound commercial theory is only in addition to our belief in free expression and the noble traditions of our profession. Our history abounds in stalwarts of pen and pencil who have fought for freedom for others. For ourselves as artists and free Americans we too cherish freedom and the resultant growth of ideas. We cannot submit to the curb, the fence or the intimidating word. The United States of America must remain a land where the Government follows the man.

The statement was effective. It reminded a few producers of comic books that they had a responsibility to the public, to their profession and to themselves. It reminded the public, and the legislators, that the funnies had survived a long history, and survived it with honor; that cartoon techniques were a part of American life; that the actions of two or three disreputable publishers could not negate the enormous contribution to entertainment, advertising, education, the war effort, made by cartoonists as a whole.

The Ford Motor Company had made effective use of comic books; so had the C.I.O. So had the U.S. Steel Institute; so had the National Labor Service. There were hundreds of others: the National Lutheran Council, the Voice of America, the National Mental Health Foundation, the United Nations Association, General Electric, the National Tuberculosis Association— the list could go on for pages. Steve Canyon had starred in Milton Caniff's *Strictly for the Smart Birds*, which described opportunities for men in the Air Force; *Dagwood Splits the Atom* and BLONDIE! were two of Chic Young's contributions, respectively familiarizing laymen with atomic power and its uses, and interpreting mental hygiene. The Cartoonists and Illustrators School in New York City, the only classroom school to give a three-year certificate course in cartooning, taught the most reputable kind of commercial comic-strip technique; now known as the School of Visual Arts, it aims primarily at advertising art, but still gives a five-day-a-week course in aspects of cartooning.

The furor died down. There are still faint echoes of it, and there always will be, just as there are constant whispers of protests against books, films and the theater. The comic-book industry is now respectable and thriving. Without some public outcry, the excesses might have gone further and lasted longer; the point is not that there must be no criticism, but that any intelligent profession can clean house without the dangerous aid of restrictive legislation.

The industry employs thousands of men, and has proved a good starting point for aspiring cartoonists. Many of the more popular strips are prepared for comic books by "ghosts"— a writer and an artist reproducing the continuity and characters as their originator would, and always with the approval of the originator. Doing another man's work, and doing it at high speed under pressure of deadlines, develops an extraordinary discipline (both artistic and commercial); with that discipline many ghosts have gone on to their own new strips, and not a few have been nationally syndicated, achieving a fame of their own.

The industry lacks only one distinction: Rube Goldberg's work has never appeared in comic-book form.

The cover of an educational public-service comic book issued by the City of New York. © William R. Hutton Associates, Inc.

The cover of an educational, and incidentally promotional, comic book. Courtesy of General Electric Co. and Pictorial Media, Inc.

CHAPTER VIII

Sports: Indoor and Outdoor

Sports cartooning, via the hunt scenes in cave painting, has an unsurpassed claim to venerability among the arts. That it has reached its greatest heights in this country may be due to two assumptions: first, that Americans are a highly competitive people; second, that Americans are a very peaceful people. Logically the competitive spirit would exhaust itself in two areas, business and recreation, and competitive recreation is simply another phase for sports. But we fatten up and settle down; we have children and join lodges; eventually— and not too long after the end of education, for most of us— we cease to be participants and become spectators, more or less rabid as our early experience taught us the capacity for enthusiasm. And then, we were always very good at inventing games. Baseball and basketball are native American sports. Both rugby and soccer proved unsatisfactory; American football was the result. And any achievement, in however minor a sport— badminton, riflery, even the indoor table sports like billiards— is counted a personal triumph for the man who brings it off. It would take a sporting sociologist to analyze the American athletic spirit with any success; it is enough for us to say that spirit pervades the smallest towns of the Republic, and that the batting average of a twelve-year-old first baseman may be of as much moment to his family and immediate circle of friends as the situation in the Middle East or the fallout rate.

Another mystery which we are not required to solve is this: why did the first great American burgeoning of sporting art take place in San Francisco, during the years immediately after the turn of the century? There were two men working in the east who were as good as any: Bob Edgren of the old *Evening World*, who was, ironically enough, originally a native of Los Angeles, and Edward Windsor Kemble, whose baseball drawings, which appeared in *Harper's Weekly* at just about the turn of the century, were as good as anything done since. But most early practitioners of this free-and-easy art were San Franciscans. Tad Dorgan is the first name to come to any mind. Rube Goldberg stepped in when Dorgan left for the East Coast. One of Goldberg's cronies was Hype Igoe, who slowly relinquished

Floyd Johnson never reached the top, but HYPE IGOE did. The cross-hatching was almost an IGOE trademark. Courtesy of King Features Syndicate, Inc.

Sketches of Tim Hegarty and Kid Lavigne, by the great DORGAN, from the New York *Evening Journal* in December 1904. Courtesy King Features Syndicate, Inc.

TAD DORGAN once more. This *Outdoor Sports* was drawn shortly before he died. © King·Features Syndicate, Inc.

his fine hold on drawing and became an excellent boxing writer as time went by. A fourth who contributed to the sports scene in those days was Robert Ripley, later so famous for another creation.

Dorgan, they will tell you, is the granddaddy of them all. Those who knew him, or who remember, will add the startling fact that as a child in San Francisco he lost all but the index finger and thumb on his drawing hand. But with Dorgan drawing technique was not the major factor. Dorgan had ideas. He was, not to put too fine a point on it, a cynic— a card player, a mild gambler, a nonconforming, independent worker whose editors were invariably buffaloed and invariably satisfied. As befits a cynic, Dorgan saw the seamy side of practically everything. His indoor and outdoor sports are indistinguishable in point of attitude. Always it was the hypocrisy, the lie, the brag that he spotted. His sporting figures, far from being the idols that most sports-page subjects are today, were cheap, self-centered and worse. Yet his cartoons, savage, unmerciful, unrelieved by a moment of kindness or sympathy, were always a joy to behold. When we laugh at Tad there is a fierce undertone to the laughter. He influenced a whole generation of sports cartoonists away from hero worship, and, while the reasons may have lain deep in his psyche, his effectiveness as a cynic is obvious in any one of his cartoons.

Dorgan's departure from San Francisco and his replacement by Goldberg have already been described. Tad was at the top of the heap on the West Coast and it took him only months to arrive at the same eminence in the East, with the *Journal*. His imagination ran wilder with every year in New York, and each of his innovations seemed another attempt to convince the world that something— if not everything— was rotten in Denmark. This is not to say that he was himself a disagreeable man. Rube Goldberg

RUBE GOLDBERG'S preview of the Dempsey-Carpentier fight. This was done fifteen years after he left San Francisco, and the figures at the right give some idea of the kind of thing he had been doing all along. Courtesy of Rube Goldberg.

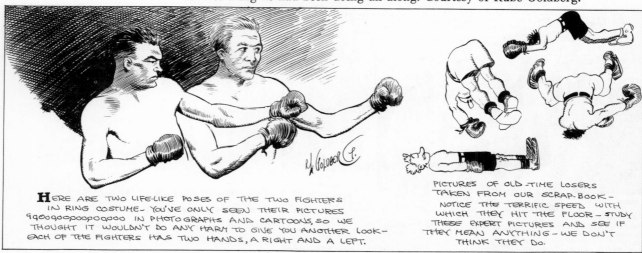

HERE ARE TWO LIFE-LIKE POSES OF THE TWO FIGHTERS IN RING COSTUME— YOU'VE ONLY SEEN THEIR PICTURES 9900900900900900 IN PHOTOGRAPHS AND CARTOONS, SO WE THOUGHT IT WOULDN'T DO ANY HARM TO GIVE YOU ANOTHER LOOK— EACH OF THE FIGHTERS HAS TWO HANDS, A RIGHT AND A LEFT.

PICTURES OF OLD-TIME LOSERS TAKEN FROM OUR SCRAP-BOOK— NOTICE THE TERRIFIC SPEED WITH WHICH THEY HIT THE FLOOR— STUDY THESE EXPERT PICTURES AND SEE IF THEY MEAN ANYTHING— WE DON'T THINK THEY DO.

Four immortals drawn by BOB EDGREN for the New York *World* in 1927. He used many techniques; this was soft pencil. Courtesy the Press Publishing Co.

admired him from the beginning, and those who knew him well liked him enormously, practically without reservation. He had, when the occasion demanded, a far more charitable sense of humor than he ever displayed in his work. But his business was not to make friends; it was to dissect a world whose spoils, dishonesties and phony attitudes he had discovered for himself, retaining the right to sneer at them. There were and are better caricaturists and better draftsmen, but Tad remains The Dean. He nipped in the bud what might very well have become an extended period of romantic veneration, and turned it into a period of realism. In doing so, he saved his art— the art of sports cartooning— from degenerating into a technique of wistful portraiture. We were still a sporting nation; but Tad's fans knew a little more. They knew that the fight might be in the tank; that the horse race might be a boat race; that the national hero, lugging three bats and chewing tobacco, probably owed his wife half a year's alimony or had abandoned her altogether. Perhaps, rather than saying that Tad nipped romanticism, we ought to say that he opened the way to realism. At any rate, since his time the sports cartoon has rarely falsified, and most of the credit for that must go to him. He was rough, tough and intelligent, and he brought the best of himself to his art.

Edgren, back in New York, had a very different attitude. He did glorify the athlete. His heroes looked like heroes, with magnificent torsos and imposing muscles; and a cartoon derived from any specific triumph was intended to memorialize that triumph, and to apotheosize, in a journalistic way, the man who had achieved it. Edgren wrote too, and very well; he was often given whatever space he wanted by his editors, and rarely abused the privilege, probably because he was working hard enough as it was.

Meanwhile another Easterner was doing sketches which fell halfway between Dorgan's and Edgren's. E. W. Kemble was a great draftsman. His sketches were more like the studies made by master artists preparatory to serious work on canvas. He showed no affiliations and no bias; he was simply interested in the sporting figure— like the baseball player at work. He was, of course, famous in another field; his drawings of Negro children, already referred to, remain classics of amiable folk sketching.

Back in San Francisco, Robert Ripley was doing a thoroughly competent job for the *Bulletin*. The turning point of his career occurred there. Lacking a focus, a current event on which to concentrate, he drew what the trade calls a "cheater": a series of small spot drawings of odd happenings in sports. He lacked a title, and it was his sports editor who penciled in the words *Believe It or Not*. The instant success of the innovation is history, and its effect on Robert Ripley's life is known to practically everyone. He became, over the years, a universal authority on oddities, the paradoxical, the unbelievable. He collected Chinese junks, bizarre statuary, and specimens of oddity from all over the world, most of them sent to him by enthusiastic well-wishers. *Believe It or Not* achieved huge newspaper syndication, was imitated several times— none of the imitations achieved Ripley's special flair— and led him to spend the rest of his life buried in the incredible. In a way Ripley's success as a curio-monger was a disservice to him. The public was so impressed with his ability to dig out the unbelievable that it lost sight of the fact that he was, and had been throughout his career, an excellent cartoonist, with a fine sense of position, emphasis and lighting. Certainly the day he did the "cheater" in San Francisco made him the enormous success he was and deserved to be, but in gaining an explorer of the bizarre, the United States certainly lost a sports cartoonist *par excellence*. (Ripley was not the only loss. Walter Hoban left sports cartooning to do *Jerry on the Job*, and Jimmy Hatlo, who was one of the best in this area too, left to create "They'll Do It Every Time." One of the most popular sports cartoonists, incidentally, was Tom Webster, an Englishman who had fathomed the mysteries of American Sport.)

Ripley and Goldberg were by no means the only cartoonists to start in sports and switch to major careers in some other department. Burris Jenkins, Jr., for decades editorial cartoonist for the New York *Journal-*

Suggestion for an inexpensive but effective battery.

"Pulling down" a high fly.

Rooting for the home team.

The Catcher's signals are not always considered in good form.

This is called a dead ball.

No, this is not Macmonnies' Bacchante. It is the average pitcher showing the proper curves for a curved ball.

Stealing the bases.

A very Short stop.

The walking delegate: "Say, pard, shake hands; we both make our livin' callin' strikes."

A slide to first.

Kemble

SOME FINE POINTS OF THE NATIONAL GAME.

Some of EDWARD WINDSOR KEMBLE's baseball figures, from *Harper's Weekly* of July 28, 1900.

Comic Art in America

A typical *Believe It or Not,* this one from 1935. Two of the items are on sports, ROBERT RIPLEY's first love. © King Features Syndicate, Inc.

QUADRUPLETS

FOUR TREES GREW TOGETHER 15 FT. ABOVE THE GROUND
Owned by J.A.GUEST
Pittsburg
Texas

TWO GOLF BALLS WERE FOUND TOGETHER 10 MILES FROM THE TEE

THEY WERE DRIVEN INTO THE *YAKIMA RIVER* AND FLOATED MANY MILES BEFORE COMING TO REST SIDE BY SIDE

ELY CULBERTSON
PLAYING ON THE DETROIT ATHLETIC CLUB *BRIDGE* TEAM–WON 3 NATIONAL CHAMPIONSHIPS– YET *HE HAS NEVER SEEN THE DETROIT ATHLETIC CLUB*

PITCHER TOMMY BRIDGES Detroit Tigers

ALLOWED A *HOME RUN–TRIPLE–DOUBLE* AND A *SINGLE* IN ONE INNING AND ALSO *STRUCK OUT* THE SIDE
APRIL 22, 1935

© 1935, King Features Syndicate, Inc., Great Britain rights reserved.

EXPLANATION OF YESTERDAY'S CARTOON: THE DOG EXPRESS—In 1844, two Englishmen established what they called a "caniposta" between Blankenberghe and Bruges, Belgium. Four whippets, harnessed to a small railroad car, regularly carried fish over the distance of 10 miles in record time. A dead rabbit was fastened in front of them, and they were not allowed to feast upon it until after their run was completed. For the rapid transportation of mail over the same route, two whippets were harnessed to a lighter car, with a stuffed rabbit dangling before them.

A RECORD IN "BOOKKEEPING"—In 1883 Victor H. Middleton, pharmacist of Grand Rapids, Mich., loaned a book, "Wyeth's Pocket Dose Book," to one of his apprentices. It was not returned until 1933, when the apprentice's son gave it back to Mr. Middleton's son, Louis V., who still operates the drug store in Grand Rapids.

American (a chore which he shared, after 1950, with Rube Goldberg), started in the middle 1920s as a sports cartoonist with that same newspaper. Another editorial cartoonist with a national reputation, William Crawford, of the Newark *News,* was for years a sports cartoonist with that newspaper, and his superior technique with editorial cartoons can probably be attributed to the fact that he learned his craft while in sports.

A Mexican, Pete Llanuza, hooked up with the *Telegram* in the mid-twenties and many modern sports cartoonists acknowledge a serious debt to him. He was more of a caricaturist than a straight cartoonist, and he knew practically nothing about sports. He made horrendous mistakes; one of them on record is his interpretation of the letters ND in a football cartoon as North Dakota. This was during Knute Rockne's heyday at Notre Dame, when he was probably better known than the Secretary of State. But then Llanuza had style, and he had great drawing ability, and he was original. To a great many young cartoonists, trying to break into journalism, he was a good model to follow.

The nature of sports cartooning changed in the 1920s. Before the First World War a sports department generally employed two or three men who could be counted on to pick up an assignment anywhere from a block to five hundred miles away, get there on time and return with a bulging sheaf of publishable sketches of whatever event had called them out. One of Rube Goldberg's early triumphs, remember, was his coverage of the Hart-Root fight in Reno for a San Francisco newspaper. There was no such thing as wireless photography, and Goldberg's fine drawings were the first visual impression that the citizens of San Francisco would have of the fighters and the fight.

As late as 1930 Gus Edson, trying out for a permanent berth with the Brooklyn *Standard-Union*, was given a ticket to the Tunney-Heeney fight and told to bring back sketches. He did, and got the job, and later went on to national fame as the artist and author of *The Gumps*. But during the 1920s photography began to edge the artist out of the sports department. Very few men could draw cartoons to compete in dramatic intensity with a well-timed, sharply defined photograph of a throw reaching the first baseman as the batter's foot touched the bag. Sports cartooning became less a matter of news and more a matter of feature: the caricature, the manager's foible exposed, the tribute to an ailing hero. Now imagination and the

Drawing to a Finish!   -:-   -:-   -:-   **By Burris Jenkins, Jr.**

The lost days of fistic glory: comment by BURRIS JENKINS, JR., on the Ross-McLarnin fight, September 1934. Courtesy of Burris Jenkins, Jr. and the New York *Journal American*.

BILL CRAWFORD helps the Dodgers toward victory. Courtesy of Bill Crawford and the Newark (N.J.) *News*.

Golfing luminaries as drawn by PETE LLANUZA in 1931. Courtesy of the New York *World-Telegram*.

254

knowledge of personalities were as useful as the presence of the artist at an event.

One of the first of the modern cartoonists, and still one of the best— many swear by him and will have no other— is Willard Mullin, who followed Pete Llanuza on the *Telegram*. By then it was 1935 and the newspaper was the *World-Telegram*. Mullin took a year or two to get started, but when he hit his stride he brought to the sports pages of the *Telegram* a magnificently individual feature, artistically exciting and certainly, in the opinion of any editor, a circulation builder. Mullin recalls the day that he made the medium his own. It was in the summer of 1937, when a defenseless Boston Red Sox club had only Jimmy Foxx and his powerful bat to keep the opposition at bay. Joe Cronin, shuffling his line-up as Casey Stengel would in a later era, put Foxx behind the plate one day. As Murray Olderman tells it, "I showed Foxx in catching regalia," recalled Wil-

[BELOW LEFT] WILLARD MULLIN's comment on the desertion of the Dodgers and the Giants. Courtesy of Willard Mullin and the New York *World-Telegram & Sun*.

[BELOW RIGHT] Another MULLIN. His bums— originally Brooklyn Dodger fans— are now classic. Courtesy of Willard Mullin and the New York *World-Telegram & Sun*.

lard, "getting ready for the pitch. It starts coming to the plate. A real nothing ball. Foxx is waiting. He turns to the umpire to gab in one panel. He retires to the water cooler in the next. And still the pitch is coming. Finally, in desperation and exasperation he grabs a bat, strides to the plate, and wallops hell out of the ball himself." With that kind of inventive mind and with powers of observation that enabled him to comprehend the affection behind the word "bum" as used by natives of Brooklyn for the onetime Brooklyn Dodgers, Mullin was soon at the top of his profession. His drawing seems casual and almost ragged at first glance; but a closer look shows no line out of place, no unnecessary stroke of the pen, and an expressiveness, a rakishness, an unbeatable, angular aggressiveness to the figures which make them models of emotion in action.

Mullin was the beginning of a new generation of sports cartoonists. There are not too many of them; the camera has slowly replaced them. But many persist in entertaining the public, pitting themselves against the forward march of automation. There is, for example, Karl Hubenthal, who does both sports and editorial cartoons for the Los Angeles *Examiner*. There is Lou Darvas, who holds forth in the Cleveland *Press*. There is Bob

Lou Darvas, in the Cleveland *Press*, comments on the infrequency of Floyd Patterson's heavyweight title defenses. 1958. Courtesy of Lou Darvas and the Cleveland *Press*.

MURRAY OLDERMAN's comment on Bill Veeck, a startlingly individualistic baseball executive. © NEA Service, Inc. Reprinted by permission of NEA Service, Inc.

Bowie of the Denver *Post*, whose happily distorted figures catch the essence of any sport. And, thank heaven, there are the syndicate cartoonists, whose work reaches hundreds of newspapers which could not afford the services of a full-time sports cartoonist. Tom Paprocki of Associated Press News Features, who signs his work Pap, is one of the best of these. One of the most versatile stylists is Murray Olderman, who since 1952 has held down the sports-cartoonist berth with NEA. Olderman can work in a variety of styles; he can do busts or face portraits which look as though they had been copied from bronze statuary; or he can cover a large panel with many small sprawling figures each drawn differently and each in fine relationship to the others. (For a time NEA did without a sports cartoonist, after Al Vermeer successfully created a comic strip— *Priscilla's Pop.* It was not long, however, before they found themselves reaching for Olderman's services.) Allen Maver's work reaches all corners of the country through Central Press. (Howard Brodie, who did fine sports cartoons for *Yank,* now does a syndicated religious panel.)

The syndicate men face a different problem. A man whose work must be

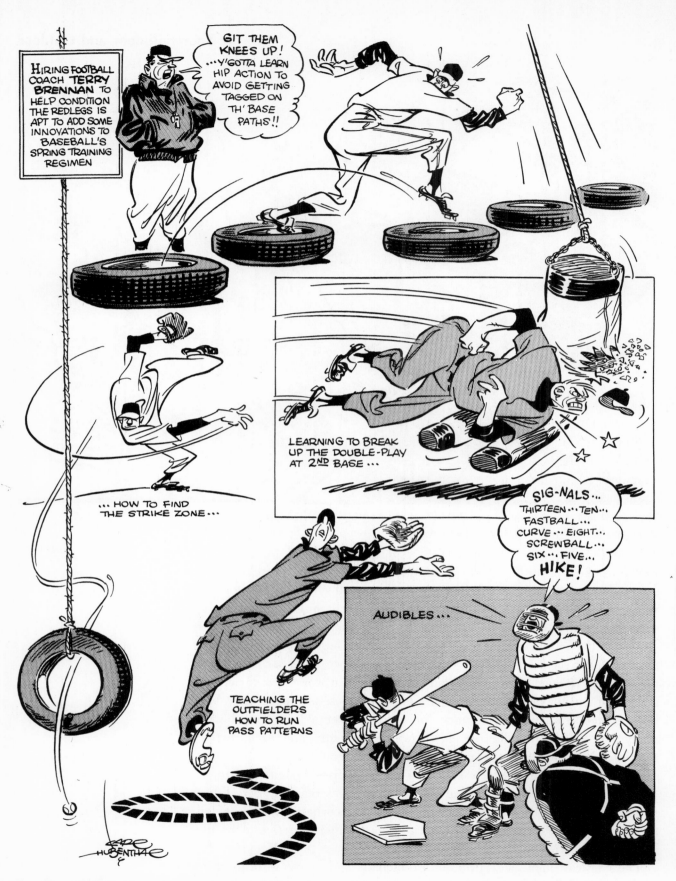

A group of sketches by KARL HUBENTHAL for the Los Angeles *Examiner*. Hubenthal does editorial cartoons for the same newspaper. Courtesy of Karl Hubenthal and the Los Angeles *Examiner*.

SIGNS OF SWING.　　By Pap.

LOU GEHRIG, TAKING HIS STANCE IN THE BATTERS BOX, IS A SIGHT TO BEHOLD

AL SIMMONS DID ALL RIGHT DESPITE HIS "ONE FOOT IN A BUCKET" POSITION AT BAT

Mel -OTT- of the GIANTS, COCKS HIS RIGHT LEG AS HE IS ABOUT TO TAKE HIS CUT AT A PITCH

-BABE- SWUNG HIS BIG BAT WITH THE SPEED OF LIGHTNING !!

All Rights Reserved by the Associated Press.

One of TOM PAPROCKI's great cartoons for the AP. Pace, variety, and good drawing. Drawn in April, 1937. Courtesy of AP Newsfeatures.

in the mails a week ahead of time can hardly afford to attempt any kind of interpretation of spot news. An athletic event more than a day or two old is a dead issue. The only hope for immediacy in syndicate cartooning would be prophecy; a man with an accurate crystal ball could look ahead seven days and give the readers spot drawings. This being impossible, syndicate men generally keep their material in the feature area. As Murray Olderman put it, "You will never go wrong pointing out that Mickey Mantle is good to his mother." On the other hand, the syndicate artist has certain advantages. He is not required to keep up with current events, or at least need give them no more than nominal attention. He may wander afield into fantasy, prognostication, profiles of personal favorites and creating suspense about the season to come.

A few of the remaining sports cartoonists do more than the cartoon itself. One of the most ambitious— or possibly the most harassed— is John Pierotti of the New York *Post*, a man famous in the field because he rarely uses pen and ink and works almost exclusively with the brush and the grease crayon. Pierotti rarely runs a cartoon which can be properly identified as such. His spot drawings, however, are liable to pop up on any page of the newspaper. The brush-and-grease-crayon technique enables him to achieve wonderfully weird effects, particularly in the area of human grotesquerie. Recently he has produced several dozen caricatures of Jerry Mitchell, a *Post* sports writer who travels a good deal; Pierotti, catching him in various environments, and giving him clothes and expression to match the milieu, has come up with the funniest sustained effort in sports cartooning for several years. (He is not syndicated, and the *Post* is very much a local New York newspaper; yet his colleagues thought highly enough of the man

LEO's version of the old Brooklyn Dodger fan. Courtesy the Chicago *Tribune* – New York *News* Syndicate, Inc.

and of his work to elect him president of the National Cartoonists Society for two successive terms.) Pierotti, Mullin and Leo O'Mealia and Gallo of the New York *Daily News* are, for practical purposes, the only four regular practitioners of the art in New York City, which has an effective population of ten million and boasts seven major newspapers. This is as good an indication of the plight of the sports cartoonist as any. Only the best survive.

The future of sports cartooning is precarious. It depends partly on the future of sports, which seems secure; but it also depends upon newspapers with sufficient imagination and/or sufficient money to keep alive an art which has proved one of the most entertaining in the whole graphic world, and has spawned any number of expert practitioners who shifted to other fields. Maybe it depends a little bit on the future of individuality itself; the absolute accuracy of the camera and the speedy transmission of its images will do for many readers, but perhaps there will always be a hard core who demand the personal view, the sharper vision— in other words, the independent artist at work.

JOHN PIEROTTI looks askance at the complicated struggle for the middleweight championship. Courtesy of John Pierotti; reprinted by permission of the New York *Post*. © 1957 New York Post Corporation.

CHAPTER IX

Comics: The War and After

Mᴏʀᴇ ᴋɪɴᴅs ᴏꜰ ɪꜱᴏʟᴀᴛɪᴏɴ than one ended in 1941. When the United States was drawn into the war, and into the world, and ultimately into a position of leadership and responsibility, its citizens could no longer delude themselves that there existed a life unrelated to the terrors and triumphs of far-flung nations. And when our armed forces went overseas, place names previously unknown became part of our national vocabulary. Our treaties committed us not only to joint action with our allies, but to some attempt at understanding them. The nature of the world, the attitudes of foreign leaders, the aspirations of peasants thousands of miles away were no longer matters of indifference to families with sons whose lives were at stake.

The national consciousness became richer through our added responsibilities; the national vocabulary, through our heightened awareness; and inevitably the mass media, through our need to publicize and explain the hazardous, complex world in which we found ourselves. Magazines, newspapers, films, advertisements all drew on this "new material," and responded to the public cry for news, information, reflections of reality. A good many of the established comic strips sent their heroes off to war, like *Terry* and *Joe Palooka*, but that was hardly enough. New strips were born, similar to the adventure strips of the thirties but with a direct bearing, now, on the lives of millions of readers. China might once have been the last outpost of exoticism; by 1942 or 1943 it was home to thousands of Americans. Graustarkian intrigue had once been the province of imaginative writers like E. Phillips Oppenheim; during the war it was all about us, and there was a fresh tale every week of some American intelligence officer whose adventures put fiction to shame.

Small wonder that new strips flourished. Two of them first appeared in a new newspaper, New York's famous *PM*. That newspaper's policies were extremely liberal, forthright and vigorous (it was known as a "radical" newspaper); *PM* had fought the Nazis from its first issue. In late 1941, just a week before Pearl Harbor, *PM* began a strip called *Vic Jordan*, which ran all through the war; its hero was an American working with the underground in occupied Europe, and the ramifications of resistance movements provided the mechanics of the plot. In May of 1943 *PM* began another strip, this by Jack Sparling, who had done *Hap Hopper* for years. His new one was *Claire Voyant*, a beautiful amnesiac whose comic-strip life began the day she was rescued at sea. She had no discernible past, and her future was at best hazardous; she was a creation of the war, and her adventures were wartime adventures.

Even established artists turned to new strips. In 1943 Roy Crane, who had done *Captain Easy*— a natural for wartime complications— switched over to King Features to originate *Buz Sawyer*, with a Navy pilot in the title role. Crane is an illustrator of the first rank, and there was never any

A daily *Vic Jordan*, by PAINE and WEXLER, 1942. Action and politics mixed. © Field Enterprises, Inc.

Claire Voyant awaits a gentleman friend, in this strip by JACK SPARLING. Courtesy the *Sun-Times* Syndicate.

The Cisco Kid, by JOSE LUIS SALINAS, admired by many artists for its draughtsmanship. © 1951 King Features Syndicate, Inc.

doubt that Buz would succeed. Perhaps inspired by the memory of Wash Tubbs, and persuaded that an adventurous hero needed a comical sidekick, Crane created Rosco Sweeney, a bumptious, warmhearted, loyal, middling-bright sailor, who went over so well that in time he took over the Sunday page himself. Crane's switch to *Buz Sawyer* left *Captain Easy* open, and the comics world profited doubly when Leslie Turner took it over. Turner is, like Crane, an illustrator in the modern manner, and *Captain Easy* has lost none of its pace, impact or glamour in his hands.

Crane has always had the complete respect of his colleagues. In the thirties he was a primary influence; *Wash Tubbs* (the original title of *Captain Easy)* was one of the best early adventure strips, and Caniff, among many others, makes no secret of Crane's effect on him. Crane's style— basically the illustrator's— might have evolved toward the fine line and the brilliant highlight, like Alex Raymond's; but Crane chose instead to retain the powerful stroke and to exploit a technique for which he is justly famous— delicately differentiated shading. His strips have always

A LESLIE TURNER *Captain Easy.* Action, guns, and a girl. © 1953 by NEA Service, Inc. Reprinted by permission of NEA Service, Inc.

Roy Crane's *Buz Sawyer* sees action in the Pacific. © 1943 King Features Syndicate, Inc.

demonstrated a perfect command of tone and texture. His subject matter, with *Buz Sawyer,* is the world of naval aviation, but when Buz travels Crane displays a fine eye for exotic scenery, and in Rosco Sweeney, the artist has created a truly funny character. When the National Cartoonists Society awarded Crane its Reuben in 1950, it occasioned great pleasure throughout the profession, and no surprise at all.

The armed forces had their own journals, of course, and in one of them, *Yank,* there appeared two features that rose to enduring fame. One was by an established cartoonist, Dave Breger, and was called *G.I. Joe;* the other was by an ex-Disney man, Sergeant George Baker, and was called *The Sad Sack.*

"G.I. Joe," as a term for the American enlisted man, was Dave Breger's invention. It is one more instance— and probably the most immediately successful of all— of a contribution to the language by a practicing cartoonist. Breger's hero, a reduced and sharpened version of Breger himself, was neither warrior nor stumblebum, but somewhere in between, like

A quick travelogue by Roy Crane, in a *Buz Sawyer* of early 1958. Note the degrees of shading. © King Features Syndicate, Inc.

265

most American soldiers. He tried hard; followed orders; was capable of ferocious grimaces indicative of savage determination; and made all the mistakes that betray the civilian-at-heart. (He wore spectacles, which were the tip-off.) Readers, particularly selectees and their families, could identify with him immediately; he was too real to be satirical. Satire was not Breger's intent; sympathy was.

The panel had already been widely syndicated by King Features under the title of *Private Breger*; it was in the first issue of *Yank* that he appeared under his new name. (For the forgetful, "G.I." stands for "Government Issue"; it bears connotations of "by the book," "disciplined," "in good military order.") No salient incident had inspired the term; it had come to Breger when he was shaving one morning in New York, on leave from maneuvers in Louisiana. Breger himself is a mild-mannered, humorous, articulate, conscientious man. No one, to look at him, would suspect that he had been held up five times, shot at point-blank by a gangster and graduated from Northwestern in psychology. He has traveled all over the world, and was once "a kingpin in the sausage business" in Chicago; in 1937 he sold his first cartoons, and *G.I. Joe* shot him to the top of the industry.

Private Breger was mustered out eventually and became *Mr. Breger* again, still beset by the universe, still struggling with a world he never made. Breger has contributed panels to all the major magazines. Ironic, perhaps, that after a full life he will be best remembered as the author of one phrase; but it was a phrase heard 'round the world.

DAVE BREGER'S *GI Joe* in two manifestations. © 1945 King Features Syndicate, Inc.

"*Some people might try figuring out the MORE important enemy!*"

"*Gee, Pete, these glasses sure bring the Germans up close!*"

REST

GEORGE BAKER'S *Sad Sack* wins out in the end. The sergeant embodies ferocity. Courtesy the Bell Syndicate, Inc.

The Sad Sack was something else again. George Baker's creation fared worse than *G.I. Joe;* he was driven back almost from the beginning on a resignation that bordered upon fatalism. Whatever indignities, whatever abuse, whatever inhumanity the Army could heap upon a benighted civilian, the Sad Sack suffered. To begin with, Baker drew him as a caricature, immediately recognizable as The Goat, with a nose like a knackwurst and a few blades of untamable hair. Baker's training in animation had given him a sense of spotting and depth, so that his strip is composed almost entirely of thin lines, whites and blacks, with the emphasis on contour, position and facial expression. The exaggeration extends to bodies and to movement; the Sack does not walk so much as shamble, and the subsidiary characters emote in the strained attitudes of the old melodrama.

The Sack is doomed: he is a figure of total frustration. What he does, he usually does with laudable motives; the result is always a boomerang. But none of this is his fault. He is the little fellow, essentially good-natured, often generous, who becomes the natural prey of the world's evil forces. He is equally helpless against the Army, the enemy, women, forceful civilians. Discharged from the army, he resumes his natural vocation — victim— as a private citizen; but nothing has changed at all. Where

"Hubert, will you see what Mother's yelling about?"

DICK WINGERT's *Hubert* wages man's eternal war on his mother-in-law. © 1958 King Features Syndicate, Inc.

some possibility of comfort, success, pride exists for the Sack, Nemesis (usually in the form of someone bigger, shrewder and more selfish) intervenes, and tragedy results.

There is something of *Happy Hooligan* in George Baker's work. The drawing techniques are not dissimilar: the exaggerated head and feet, the simple line, the use of solid black. And the Sack receives from life no more than Happy ever did. Baker's success in creating a durable symbol was confirmed when *The Sad Sack* appeared in book form in 1944 (it was the comic counterpart of Bill Mauldin's *Up Front*, which appeared at the beginning of 1945) and swept the market. The Bell Syndicate ran the book strip by strip for a time; then the war ended, and fans were afraid that the Sack was gone. Not so: in 1946 he came back as a civilian, and went right on absorbing punishment for us.

There were other developments during the war years, not all of them related to battle. Bert Whitman created *Debbie Dean*, a young-career-girl strip in the traditional vein but with slicker, more modern drawing; Ray Bailey came on with *Bruce Gentry*, the hero of which was an airline detective; Walt Disney added new characters; Chic Young ran a shorter Sunday strip along with *Blondie*, called *Colonel Potterby and the Duchess*. Alfred Andriola, who had been doing *Charlie Chan* for years, decided, as many had before him, to create a strip of his own, and was given a chance by Publishers Syndicate: if he would finish out a year of *Dan Dunn* still to run, he could go on with a strip of his own. The result was *Kerry Drake*, one of the best of the police strips, in which accuracy of police techniques (and dialogue) is made dramatic by the presence of exaggerated, sometimes grotesque villains— the principle behind *Dick Tracy*, although Andriola's drawing is entirely different, being in the modern illustrators' style.

Meanwhile the new *Mary Worth* was flourishing, and a few strips from the 1930s had proved their worth, surviving the first uncertain years and

ALFRED ANDRIOLA's *Kerry Drake* is a rarity— a married hero in an adventure strip. Obviously, trouble lies ahead for his wife, Mindy. Courtesy Publishers Syndicate.

A good specimen of DICK CAVALLI's *Morty Meekle*, almost always a three-panel strip, ending in a healthy laugh. © 1959 NEA Service, Inc. Reprinted with permission of NEA Service, Inc.

achieving popularity in the forties. Mal Eaton's *Peter Piltdown* was one of these, an amiable juvenile prehistoric strip, combining a dinosaurian background with the eternal pranks of children. Another was Ralph Fuller's *Oaky Doaks*, a kind of mid-American Don Quixote cavorting through the Age of Chivalry. There was a hilariously anachronistic side to Oaky, with *pow* and *bop* and modern slang studding the medieval landscape. Fuller's women were pretty and occasionally a bit earthy, which set off Oaky's incorruptible naïveté.

An interesting import, and one of the best-drawn contemporary strips, was *The Cisco Kid*, done in South America by José Luis Salinas and sent to New York for distribution by King Features. The original drawings of this western strip are photographed for reproduction and then destroyed, to preserve their duty-free status as works of art.

With the end of the war and the return of eleven million men to civilian life, more and more new strips appeared. The rate of submissions in syndicate offices must have been at its highest ever. A new generation of men had been through war and was settling into its civilian patterns; in that generation were hundreds of budding cartoonists. Eric Ericson drew *Herkimer Fuddle*; also for King Features, Dick Wingert introduced *Hubert*, which had been a huge success in *Stars and Stripes*, even edging out Bill Mauldin's work in occasional polls. Ray Gotto's *Ozark Ike* started out as a sports strip; its hero was a healthy baseball player only a little more sophisticated than Li'l Abner. (Bill Lignante and Ed Strops have also worked on that strip.) Dale Messick created another career girl, *Brenda Starr*, a reporter. Michael O'Malley and Dean Miller introduced *Vic Flint*, an adventurer, and Bob Montana created *Archie*, a pleasant goof of high-school age. Later on Dick Cavalli, a fine gag cartoonist, created *Morty Meekle*, the saga of an unassuming young man whose life consists largely of contretemps. Cavalli uses a daily gag with a continuing cast of characters, rather than a continuity, and the drawing itself is funny and simple.

COULTON WAUGH's experimental *Hank*. The date is May 16, 1945, just eight days after the end of the war in Europe. Courtesy of Coulton Waugh.

There was one strip, unfortunately short-lived, which promised a new attitude and new techniques. Coulton Waugh, who had taken *Dickie Dare* from Milton Caniff, had relinquished it in 1944 to Odin Burvik (Mrs. Waugh), and had begun work on a new strip of his own. This strip, called *Hank*, first appeared in April of 1945, in the newspaper *PM*, and its basic plot structure was a departure from the traditional. Its hero had lost a leg overseas, and the implications of that loss, in a comic strip, are obvious: he would not be a dashing and active hero; he might have a strong tendency to introspection; his impulse would not be to conquer the world, but to come to some understanding of it. His mission, in other words, was knowledge; he was determined to discover why his loss "had been necessary and to prevent his son from having to make such a sacrifice." Waugh commented later, "This was to be a deliberate attempt to work in the field of social usefulness." Unfortunately, Waugh's eyes, strained by years of work at the drawing board (among other things, he had done editorial cartoons in the twenties for the New York *Herald Tribune)*, gave him serious trouble toward the end of the year, and *Hank* was discontinued on the last day of 1945.

The ideas behind *Hank*, and some of the techniques (like using black balloons with white lettering), were heady stuff. Waugh's attempt was to draw modern history in the making, not writing down to the reader, and

JACOBSEN's old *Silent Sam*, one of the early pantomime strips. © 1935 Consolidated News Features.

not evading the serious issues of the time, which might be expressed as political or economic issues but were essentially moral problems: the function of the responsible man in a living society.

No such strip has since been published, but there was ferment, and several of the more popular strips of the late forties and the fifties reflect that ferment. Not all of them, of course. There were good strips in the old categories. Buford Tune's *Dotty Dripple* was a descendant of both *Blondie* and Fred Locher's *Homer Hoopee*. Mik's *Ferd'nand* was a charming pantomime strip, using the hallowed conventions of the art (hat rising from head to denote astonishment), the heir to Jacobson's *Silent Sam*. So was Harry Hanan's *Louie*. Frank Robbins had given up *Scorchy Smith* and was a success with *Johnny Hazard*. Kreigh Collins had created *Kevin the Bold*, a rival to Harold Foster's *Prince Valiant*. Ed Dodd ran the popular outdoor strip, *Mark Trail*. Kid strips and family strips went on, seemingly immortal, like Darrell McClure's *Little Annie Rooney* or Al Posen's *Sweeney and Son*. Where Harry Haenigsen's *Penny* and *Our Bill* might have been supposed to pre-empt the adolescent strip, Al Vermeer created *Priscilla's Pop*.

MIK's *Ferd'nand* in a happy moment. © 1959 United Feature Syndicate, Inc.

Posen, particularly, found a new field for his talents. Properly he belongs in the thirties, when he created *Sweeney and Son* and its companion strip, *Jinglets*. *Sweeney* is drawn simply and effectively, and its jokes are warm and funny. The style might be called "basic," and is reminiscent of the unadorned style of a few very early strips. The characters are friendly and winning— Sweeney, his wife, young Pushface and his girl friend Beverly, and an adopted younger son called "Me-Too," from his habit of responding to practically anything with those words. *Jinglets* is one of the most successful second-strips in the field. Often the rhyme consists simply of four words, each illustrated; sometimes it runs to four full lines.

Posen is a popular man with his fellow artists, because he is a consistently funny and hard-working veteran. (He is usually ten or twelve weeks ahead on his work.) During and after the war Posen's contributions to the public— and to the profession— reached a new significance. No one did

Harry Haenigsen's *Penny*. Like all teen-age girls, she is surrounded by hopeless incompetents. © 1959 New York *Herald Tribune*, Inc., reproduced with permission.

more in the way of entertaining troops, active or hospitalized, and since the war Posen has headed up tour after tour of our installations overseas. (His habit of working far ahead frees him for these voluntary and of course unremunerated efforts.) Not only the armed forces benefit by his performances; orphans and sick youngsters see him regularly. A cartoonist's life need not be all deadlines and wrangles with the syndicate; and Posen more than any other (he confesses to being a bit of a ham, and to enjoying his personal appearances immensely) has gone out of his way to spread cheer where it is needed.

One of the more reassuring developments of the forties was George Wunder's success with *Terry and the Pirates* after he took it over from Caniff in 1947. Wunder's career had been varied. A native New Yorker now in his forties, he had moved upstate to Kingston in his teens, and when his education was completed he had gone to work in the Kingston branch of a New York City brokerage house. He studied art in all of his spare time, and in the mid-thirties went back to New York, where he worked for several years as a staff artist with a news feature service. He spent the war in the Army Air Corps intelligence service— a perfect background for *Terry*— assigned to various posts in Europe, North Africa, the Middle East and India.

After the war he returned to art and won *Terry* in a fairly fierce competition. There was speculation— what would the strip become in Wunder's hands?

Well, the line became a little thicker and the solid blacks a little more prominent, but the story moved as rapidly as ever, and— very important — *Terry* remained in the top ten in popularity polls (where, logically enough, it was very shortly joined by *Steve Canyon*. Caniff, by the way, is full of unfeigned admiration for Wunder's draftsmanship, and considers today's *Terry* as formidable competition). Wunder researches heavily, is careful about accuracy, and has a fine knack for suspense. He may begin a sequence with an episode apparently far removed in space and context from Major Terence Lee; but shortly the plot thickens, Terry finds himself hip-deep in intrigue, and the apparently loose ends begin to tie themselves together. Wunder has done a beautiful job with the strip, using a style not far removed from the original but altering it somewhat by the individual touches in his own drawing. *Terry* is in good hands.

Something new was happening. Where formerly realism had been a primary technique only in the exotic or glamorous strip, and where the "homey" strip had relied on stylization or caricature, the two techniques were drawing closer. The public seemed to want straight strips, about conventional people, drawn with realism. To be a professional man, an intellectual of sorts, was no longer embarrassing, it seemed. Why not portray doctors, lawyers, judges as they really were? Why not take a tip from *Mary Worth* and re-create the drama of life (a touch glamorized, of course)?

AL POSEN's *Sweeney and Son*, with its companion strip, *Jinglets*. © 1957 the Chicago *Tribune*–New York *News* Syndicate, Inc.

A *Terry and the Pirates* by GEORGE WUNDER, 1955. The strip has lost none of its vigor or popularity. © the Chicago *Tribune*–New York *News* Syndicate, Inc.

It was a step forward for the comic strips. Where the adventure strip had, in the thirties, all but replaced the thirty-day newspaper serial, the real-life strip would, in the late forties and fifties, replace the radio soap opera (a replacement facilitated by the temporary demise of radio as television came into the home).

Publishers Syndicate, the backers of the refurbished *Mary Worth*, took the lead in this area. Harold Anderson, head of the syndicate, had always felt that sophistication was a sign of maturity in any popular art. In the beginning, anything goes; but over the years audiences become more demanding. (A strip like *Steve Canyon*, in its present form, might well have been incomprehensible to comics readers of the 1920s.) It was obvious in the first days of television, for example, that audiences lacked discrimination; programs have improved since, a prevalent critical contempt notwithstanding, and even if they hadn't, the critical outcry would have increased. But as a popular medium becomes more complex, Anderson felt, it becomes less possible for any but a man of supreme talent to keep up with it— to do, for example, both the continuity and the drawing of a modern, real-life strip.

Anderson had the benefit of public-opinion surveys; where Patterson and Hearst had an instinct in the early days, Anderson had science in the modern period. He knew fairly well what kind of characters the public wanted, and even what names to assign to his heroes and villains.

The result was a pair of comic strips developed on an entirely new basis, with audience preferences all but predetermined, and with two or more men working on each strip to ensure the best in story and the best in art. The strips are *Rex Morgan, M.D.* and *Judge Parker*.

After Anderson, the man primarily responsible for these strips is Dr. Nicholas Dallis, now of Toledo, Ohio. Dallis received his M.D. in 1938, but even before that he had worked with Dr. Victor Robinson, a historian of medicine, and had proposed historical lectures in strip form. The idea lay neglected. Years later, in 1945, Dallis came to Toledo to head the Mental Hygiene Center there. He met Allen Saunders, a long-time resident of Toledo, and the two discussed a strip based on the activities of a doctor. With Frank Edgington, Dallis drew up a project, and through Saunders' intervention took it to Anderson. Marvin Bradley was called in to draw the characters; Edgington did backgrounds; Dallis did the continuity. Within months the strip, *Rex Morgan, M.D.*, was set for a long run.

Here the efficiency of the new technique was obvious. Dallis has an inventive, imaginative mind and years of practice on which to draw for material; as a physician and a psychiatrist, he is responsible to the medical profession for ethics and good taste. But Dallis is no cartoonist; therefore Bradley and Edgington. And even before the strip was tried out, Anderson had a fair idea that it would go.

Not like the old days, when one man transferred his own genius to paper. But the purpose of *Rex Morgan* and of its companion strip, *Judge Parker*, is different: it is to reflect life much as it is lived, adding dramatic emphasis and a dash of romance. Dallis' *Judge Parker* was not developed until 1951, and first appeared in November of 1952, with the drawing by

And here, a post-operative get-together. © 1958 Publishers Syndicate.

artist Dan Heilman; again the right combination of men, material and syndicate had been found. The Minneapolis *Tribune* experimented with *Judge Parker*, running three or four days' installments each day and doing a six-week sequence in two weeks. The experiment pulled reader attention and much favorable comment, but the four-week time gap, in which *Judge Parker* would not appear at all, would probably be fatal to sustained reader interest in the end, and the strip has been run daily ever since.

Dallis is a man of intelligence and energy, both of which are reflected in his continuities. He has danced along the edge of dangerous themes, feeling that they needed attention; a hint of euthanasia in one of his *Rex Morgan* sequences caused protests from a few newspapers, and was commented upon by *Time*. Obviously, a strip attempting to portray everyday life cannot afford to show violence or grotesquerie as *Dick Tracy* or *Flash Gordon* might. But avoidance of the dangerous is not Dallis' main concern. He is equally intent on a kind of general education, which emphasis on the exotic would only hinder. There was an adoption sequence in *Judge Parker*, for example, which drew a mixed reaction from readers, a few of them feeling that it was not sufficiently sentimental. But Dallis' theme was not that all children are lovely, or that everyone should be a parent; his theme was that men and women become parents by virtue of a shared, inter-personal life, and not simply through the delivery of a baby. Another sequence in the same strip tackled the problem of a legal definition of insanity, by attempting to clarify the line between the psychopathic personality and the legally insane. (The M'Naghten rule, which is classic, states that one oriented in time, place and identity is legally responsible. Modern psychiatrists are not so sure.)

These considerations have proved fascinating to the readers. They remain faithful; they write letters. Dallis realizes that the strip's attraction is not the usual cliff-hanging suspense; what brings the readers back daily is their identification with the life of the strip, which rouses compassion in

Dallis also writes *Judge Parker*, drawn by Dan Heilman. The Judge's problems include municipal graft. © 1958 Publishers Syndicate.

The Judge's problems also include broken marriages. © 1959 Publishers Syndicate.

them and tends to confirm the notion that this kind of strip has replaced the serial and the soap opera. These strips have certain functions in common with the theater and the novel; by creating a recognizable world for the audience, they make it possible for that audience to share experiences and to feel vicarious emotions.

Dallis and Saunders were naturally not the only two men to explore the vein of naturalism. The technique did not depend on the use of professional men, or of characters in their thirties and forties. Dick Brooks's *Jackson Twins*, adolescents, exist in a world which is essentially real and thoroughly recognizable. There are no grotesques in the strip, no exotics in the true sense of the word; there are instead high schools, soda fountains, hot-rods now and then, junior and senior proms and thoroughly normal parents.

Stan Drake's *The Heart of Juliet Jones*, based on a rather unusual family situation, shot toward the top of the soap-opera field in the fifties and is a sure bet to keep its position for many years. Juliet Jones is a young woman of beauty and intelligence; she has a younger sister, Eve, of equal beauty but less maturity, and an average solid-citizen father. But the family is motherless; Juliet faces all the problems of housekeeper, mother to Eve, companion to father, and unmarried beauty— in addition to which she has been, for the last year or so, mayor of the town in which they live. All of which may sound like an overabundance of plot but is really just the beginning. In one recent sequence Juliet suffered— and recovered from— an attack of amnesia, with romantic complications; in another, Eve fell in love with a handsome French count who was unfortunately penniless and whose mother quite practically insisted that he marry a rich woman. It is typical of Drake's sense of reality that the count's mother, who might have been exaggerated as an ogress, made a rather stirring and sensible defense of her position: the count had no money, no profession, and the expensive tastes natural to his station in life— what could he do

The Heart of Juliet Jones by STAN DRAKE. Note the second panel, which has the effect of a photographic negative, and heightens the mood of secrecy, darkness, suspense, and discovery. © 1958 King Features Syndicate, Inc.

Another *Juliet Jones*, with Eve as the romantic lead. © 1959 King Features Syndicate, Inc.

Juliet Jones again, with trouble ahead for the lovers. © 1959 King Features Syndicate, Inc.

278

but marry a rich woman? Drake then demonstrated perfect command of the soap opera by having the count renounce his "station" and stand by Eve; after which the artist betrayed both his sense of contemporary mores and his own fondness for sports cars by having the outcome of the whole intrigue depend on the count's success or failure in an auto race.

Drake's is the illustrator's style *par excellence*. He has few peers as a draftsman, he positions well, and his use of light-and-shadow is among the most imaginative— even daring— in comics. All in all, his drawing is creative— other artists learn from it.

Drake's life has been full of competition; he is a former Hollywood actor, is the head of his own advertising art studio, and plays golf seriously and well. But his most competitive period is probably the present: for the past several months *The Heart of Juliet Jones* has been battling it out with *Mary Worth* for soap-opera honors. The polls go sometimes this way and sometimes that, and the rivalry does no harm; it keeps the artists on their toes and makes good newspaper copy. Drake has over four hundred and fifty newspapers now. One of them is Paris' *France-Soir*, the readership of which is estimated to be about 30 per cent violently Left Wing and anti-American— yet *The Heart of Juliet Jones* is probably its most popular feature.

Drake can be proud of himself. He has conceived and executed one of today's first-rate strips, and undoubtedly has even greater success before him.

There were a lot of thoroughly normal parents after the war, and they produced the largest crop of thoroughly normal children in the country's history. A thoroughly normal child is often beautifully illogical, which makes his parents often seem ridiculous. Stanley and Janice Berenstain, apparently afflicted by robustly independent infants, began early to make it clear that if we were not careful we would be ruled by babes.

And Hank Ketcham, finding himself the bewildered father of a small, lovable male despot, promptly created *Dennis the Menace*, the most explosively popular tot character in decades; the name and the epithet are now a part of the language.

Ketcham is another of those artists who stand at the head of a file. In one form or another Dennis is probably as familiar to as many Americans as the Katzenjammer Kids are. His name is synonymous with juvenile deviltry, yet he is capable of prodigies of affection. His harassed parents— haggard, needle-nosed father and overworked, beautiful mother— alternate between frustrated rage and unreserved love for their irrepressible tot. Dennis' rise to fame and fortune was quick, his circulation is huge, and a host of imitators has tried unsuccessfully to displace him from his present eminence. He appears as a daily panel and a Sunday page, and in all the guffawing over the boy's mischief, readers have sometimes failed to

"You heard me, Sonny! I'm not leaving until you call your mother. . . ."

A man's home is his castle. Even *Dennis the Menace* is sometimes helpful. © 1958 the Hall Syndicate, Inc.

HANK KETCHAM'S *Dennis the Menace* in a Sunday page. Dennis' targets are of all ages. © 1959 the Hall Syndicate, Inc.

notice that Ketcham draws extremely well in an apparently slapdash technique which is actually the product of careful work. (He is fond of the silhouette panel—solid black figures against a plain background, rarely used in other strips.)

Dennis is not only a major comics character; he has endorsed and modeled for any number of products for children, he appears in best-selling comic books, and hard-cover books of his adventures have sold over a million copies. Inspired by Dennis, Ketcham has created a novel playground for children, full of unusual—and colorful, and (we assume) unbreakable—play equipment.

A happy father and a fine artist, Ketcham is one of the modern greats, in recognition of which the National Cartoonists Society awarded him its Reuben for 1952.

Mel Casson's *Angel* joined the ranks of juvenile demons; and in 1958 he joined forces with Alfred Andriola to create another kind of demon, this one devilishly curved, infernally beautiful and a threat to all men— a pin-up girl named *Dilly*.

The girls had not been entirely neglected in favor of doctors, lawyers

It's Me, Dilly! by ALFRED JAMES (ALFRED ANDRIOLA) and MEL CASSON. The glamorous urban bachelor-girl, constantly coping with suitors. © 1959 Alfred James, Mel Casson.

and youngsters. Bob Lubbers had opened the proceedings with *Long Sam*, drawn to a continuity by Al Capp. Sam was the unlikely name of a leggy, bosomy hillbilly girl whose adventures ranged from the simple contretemps of refusing ardent suitors to the more complex task of escaping a band of Brooklyn science-fiction addicts disguised as Martians. Gladys Parker's *Mopsy* and Jo Fischer's *From Nine to Five* continued to reveal the inner motivations of the urban working girl, while Ted Key took another working girl, slightly more mature and infinitely more domineering, named her *Hazel* and raised her to the level of a national symbol, exclusively in the pages of *The Saturday Evening Post*. Marty Links explored the world of bobby-soxers, as did Hilda Terry. In 1957 Leonard Starr created *On Stage*, one of the countless efforts to translate the world of the theater and films to comic-strip form; none had ever succeeded for long, but *On Stage* appears to have done well.

Sports strips had always had a notoriously hard time, but one came along in this period which has done well: *Big Ben Bolt*, by John Cullen Murphy. The continuities have lately veered away from sports, but in the

A *Long Sam* by BOB LUBBERS, showing the heroine, her mother, and the little old house they live in. © 1958 United Feature Syndicate, Inc.

281

LEONARD STARR's *On Stage*. Fine drawing in the illustrator's style, reminiscent of Alex Raymond; and appropriately effective "camera angles." ⓒ 1957 the Chicago *Tribune*–New York *News* Syndicate, Inc.

sports sequences has appeared some of the best sports drawing ever to be seen in comics. Murphy himself was a protégé of Norman Rockwell and during the war a major on General MacArthur's staff. He contributed sports drawings to practically all the major magazines before turning to his strip, which now runs in over two hundred and fifty papers.

Back in the late forties there was a college boy named Spider bumbling through the panels of national magazines. He was, to put it charitably, not precisely the picture of health and good looks we all like to think of as the American Student. He was rendered blind by his porkpie hat, which lacked a certain chic; and whatever competence he had as a human being was well hidden. He was a funny caricature, put through funny paces by his creator, Mort Walker.

In 1950 Spider changed his name to Beetle Bailey and became a comic strip. For six months he struggled along with no significant rise in circulation. Walker and Sylvan Byck, comics editor at King Features, put their heads together and decided that college boys were no longer what they

A daily *Beetle Bailey*, by MORT WALKER, 1958. Three fantastic Army characters of the many who people the strip. ⓒ King Features Syndicate, Inc.

had been; too many of them had seen service, or were about to, and the old caricature was no longer very meaningful.

Beetle Bailey became a soldier. Instead of the porkpie hat, it was an overseas cap which covered his eyes. Circulation zoomed immediately. Beetle was the funniest, most ineffectual soldier since *The Sad Sack,* and he was a little younger, a little less conscious of the indignities heaped upon him, a little more resilient. Occasionally he was observed to win one of his constant battles with the topkick. He was, like many comic characters, innocence overwhelmed by superior, hostile forces; yet he was not entirely overwhelmed, and his innocence was never dimmed.

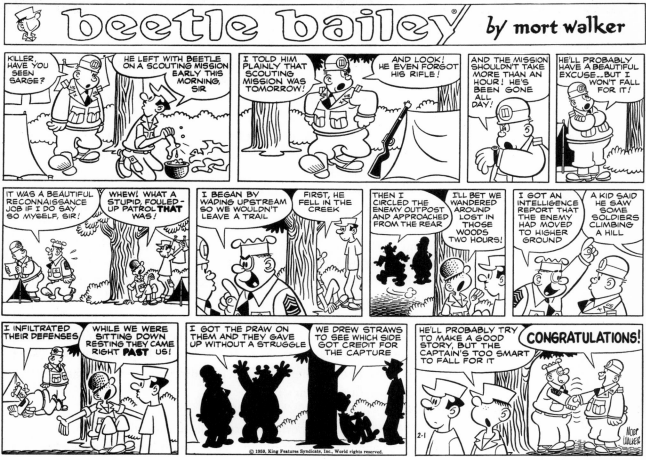

Two views of Army life— officers' and enlisted men's. Or: general impression vs. private reality. © 1959 King Features Syndicate, Inc.

This bland American Schweik exploded in 1953, becoming one of the three or four most wanted characters in comics. Hardly a city in the country could do without him. His colleagues honored Walker, as they had Hank Ketcham for *Dennis* the year before, with their annual award as cartoonist of the year. Walker was only thirty when all this happened, but he was a veteran in the trade: his first cartoon had been published when he was eleven, and he had drawn a strip for the Kansas City *Journal* at fifteen.

MORT WALKER's and DIK BROWNE's *Hi and Lois*. The thinking baby has become very popular. © 1959 King Features Syndicate, Inc.

By 1949, when he was twenty-five, he had a degree from the University of Missouri, was an ex-lieutenant of the Army and was the country's number-one gag cartoonist, having, in that year, sold more panels to top magazines than any of his colleagues.

Beetle Bailey has close to seven hundred and fifty newspapers now, but Walker has not been content with one success. He also does the gags for *Hi and Lois*, which Dik Browne draws; their collaborative effort appears in over two hundred and fifty newspapers.

This is a variant of the family strip, but done in a deliberately less sentimental style, although the basis of the strip is affection between husband and wife, rather than the traditional bickering and henpecking. Late in 1958 the artists introduced an infant, normal in every respect but one: it thought mature thoughts, which were expressed in appropriate balloons. Circulation went up immediately.

Dik Browne, who draws the strip and helps Walker write it, is a rather young old pro. He was, before he turned to the strip, New York's number-one comic advertising cartoonist. He created Chiquita Banana and the Birdseye bird, among other symbols. In a different area, he has illustrated all of Bishop Fulton Sheen's books.

Very few cartoonists, perhaps three dozen altogether, have begun their careers with one major creation and stayed with it over the decades. More often there is an exploratory period during which techniques are sharpened, a further delay while ideas are tried and discarded, an apprenticeship as another man's assistant; and always the wolf is near the door, and a cartoonist must perform a variety of tasks until his big break comes.

That variety is great, and the career of Vernon Greene, who has done the daily *Bringing Up Father* since George McManus died, demonstrates it well. (The Sunday *Jiggs* is done by Frank Fletcher.) The National Cartoonists Society recognizes seven categories of cartooning: Comic Strips, Editorial and Panel, Sports, Gag Cartoons, Comic Books, Advertising,

A post-McManus *Bringing Up Father* by VERNON GREENE. © 1958 King Features
Syndicate, Inc.

Animation. Greene has, since 1928, worked extensively in all these fields
save animation. He has often worked in more than one area at the same
time, and his curriculum vitae would read something like this:

SPORTS: 1928-9, Portland (Ore.) *Telegram*
           1930-2, Toledo *Blade*
           1934-6, New York *Mirror*
EDITORIAL: 1932-42, Central *Press*, International News
           1935-7, New York *Mirror*
           1945-50, Portland *Oregonian*
ADVERTISING: 1935-50, a variety of products for most major agencies in New
             York City
PANELS: 1946-51, *Bible Bee*, for the *Register-Tribune* Syndicate
GAG CARTOONS: 1941-4, *Charlie Conscript*, for *Pic* magazine
COMIC BOOKS: 1938-54, innumerable books, adventure and funny, for leading
             comic-book publishers
COMIC STRIPS: 1935-40, *Polly and Her Pals*, for King Features
             1938-42, *The Shadow*, for the *Ledger* Syndicate
             1954- *Bringing Up Father*
ODDS AND ENDS: Story illustrations for pulp magazines; children's books; medical,
               advertising and news photography

All of which means that Greene's work has been on view all over the
world, in many different forms, for over thirty years. Most of his colleagues have been through longer or shorter periods of diversified effort,
and the prevailing opinion that "cartoonists have it easy" is a constant
source of wonder to these men.

By now it is obvious that no two cartoonists have the same view of life,
and that they are, as men who work alone and whose continuing success
depends on the public, an independent, sometimes even truculent lot. They
enjoy each other's company, and there have always been occasional gather-
ings — like the famous dinner at Reisenweber's in 1913 — for purely
social purposes. Every few years for a long time someone suggested or-

ganizing a society, or at least an annual dinner, but before the war cartoonists were suspicious of groups and organizations: possibly each was a bit jealous of his own talent and his own success. An attempt was made back in 1927 to bring together a number of professionals, and to found a group called Cartoonists of America. One successful dinner was held, but the number of flagrant individualists on the guest list may hint at the ultimate reason for the society's dissolution: Walt McDougall was there, with Rube Goldberg, Clare Briggs, Winsor McCay, Maurice Ketten and Harry Hirshfield, and among the guests were Jimmy Walker, Judge Gary, Chauncey Depew, General Pershing, Al Smith (the Governor and not the cartoonist), David Belasco, George M. Cohan, Ring Lardner, George Ade, Irvin Cobb and Don Marquis. No such group could long cohere. Sporadic attempts were made over the next twenty years, but a natural, stubborn resistance to regimentation defeated all efforts.

During the war, though, cartoonists accepted a new role; they were called upon in large numbers to travel about the country entertaining troops. Willy-nilly, they submitted to a kind of organization. Many of the trips were planned by the American Theater Wing, and no cartoonist ever hesitated to accept an assignment. They were naturally thrown together more often, and kept running into each other in exotic places like Texas, Kansas and Illinois. A sense of contribution led to a sense of solidarity; now and then a man would mutter, "Why don't we get together more often after the war?"

The tours to bases and hospitals were a great success, and late in 1944 the American Theater Wing put together a camp show which included the talents of Ernie Bushmiller, Gus Edson, Russell Patterson, Otto Soglow, C. D. Russell and, among the non-cartoonists, Bugs Baer, Clifton Fadiman, and John Mason Brown. And sometime in the winter of 1944-5 Patterson and Rube Goldberg (who had replaced Bugs Baer as M.C.; Baer refused to fly) lay in their bunks at Quantico, Virginia, after a hard day's work, listening to Soglow, Edson and Russell make convivial sounds in the next room. Patterson suggested that the group hang together after the war; Goldberg chomped fiercely at his cigar and said, "Listen to those anarchists! They'd never come to meetings." Patterson continued to agitate, patiently and mildly; Goldberg's resistance ebbed. As the two men turned in, Goldberg said, "All right. But no more than twenty-five members." Patterson told the story later: "We'd been in bed about ten minutes when Rube raised himself to one elbow, snorted, and said, 'All right. But no more than fifty members.' After that he went to sleep. I waited for him to bring it up in the morning, but he didn't say a word about it. Then we got on a plane to go back to New York, and when we were in the air a couple of the spark plugs turned out to be faulty. Rube was a little worried. He was mangling a cigar and looking out at the engine. Every once in a while he'd look down, as though he were estimating the fall. 'Why don't you be the focal point of

THE SEVEN FOUNDERS OF THE
NATIONAL CARTOONISTS SOCIETY,
IN SEVEN SELF-PORTRAITS.

Courtesy of the National Cartoonists Society.

a society, Rube?' I asked him. 'We can send out invitations in your name.'

" 'Yeah, sure,' he said. 'Anything.' He peered out at the engine. 'There's no way to get out of this damn machine, I suppose.'

" 'Sometime when the war ends,' I said, 'we ought to call a dinner meeting.'

" 'Absolutely,' Rube said. 'How high up do you figure we are?'

" 'We'd have to get it well organized at the first meeting. Officers, by-laws, and maybe a regular meeting-place. You're the logical man to be president for the first year.'

" 'Whatever you say,' he growled. 'You think this pilot's ever flown before?' "

Thus, in a manner of speaking, was founded the National Cartoonists Society. A first informal meeting was held at the Barberry Room in New York City in January of 1946, with nine men present; twenty-three attended the second meeting, at the Coffee House in February, after which a letter went out over Goldberg's signature to practically every cartoonist in the country. For the first year Goldberg was the organization's President; Patterson its First V.P.; Otto Soglow, Second V.P.; Milton Caniff, Treasurer; C. D. Russell, Secretary. Those five, plus Bushmiller and Edson, were its founders.

CHAPTER X

Cabbages and Kings

Aɴʏ ᴄᴏɴᴠᴇɴᴛɪᴏɴᴀʟ, ʀᴇᴘʀᴇsᴇɴᴛᴀᴛɪᴏɴᴀʟ ᴅʀᴀᴡɪɴɢ says something about reality and implies a "point of view," even if the view expressed is simply that the object drawn is interesting. More often, the point is biased: there is a moral to the picture. The Renaissance *Pietà* was intended to express the artist's depth of feeling for— or even identification with— Jesus; it must also have been meant to rouse religious sentiment in the breast of the observer.

Differences in medium, technique and attitude apart, the editorial cartoon (or, equally common, the "political cartoon") shares this basically educational function. Its subject matter is more often symbolic; in a way, always symbolic. A painter in 1588 might have shown the dauntless British fisher-fleet pounding the Armada into flotsam; an editorial cartoonist would have shown Andromeda chained to her rock, labeled "England," the monster breathing fire at her, labeled "Spain," and Perseus flying to the rescue, labeled "The British Fisherman." And while the painting might ultimately have been hung in the best galleries, the cartoon would presumably have been seen by millions before the week was out, and inspired not artistic admiration (though perhaps that too) but a surge of patriotism.

The editorial cartoon may have had its origins in scurrilous caricatures circulated surreptitiously. Certainly by the eighteenth century, with Rowlandson, it had become an integral and effective part of journalism. Not that it required a journalistic outlet: Goya's Disasters of War, among the greatest of all etchings, were deliberately horrible in their impact because they were conceived by an editorializing— i.e., opinionated— mind. But one of the functions of the true editorial is to reach an audience, and it was only when newspapers and magazines came to be published regularly (or, to look at it another way, when the rise of literacy around the turn of the nineteenth century made wider circulations possible) that caricatures, visual allegories and the art of design were combined to form the beginnings of modern editorial art.

("Nobody knows why") *Nor Wherefore*, an etching by FRANCISCO GOYA, from his *Disasters of War*. An enraged, despairing protest at man's inhumanity to man, the *Disasters* were political in the truest sense of the word. Courtesy of Phaidon Press, Ltd.

Europe led America in this respect, having had the benefit of roughly a thousand years of famine, disease, war and despotism, all calculated to make men express their frustrated rages in one form or another. Most European countries— the Netherlands was an exception— lacked even the forms of democracy, and caricaturists had an obvious set of targets: the reigning monarchs and their ministers. European political cartoons to this day are more personal, reflecting that preoccupation with individual leaders, and more economically drawn, reflecting their origins in swift caricature. (It may or may not be significant that the most densely populated and carefully cross-hatched European cartoons are British, and have been since roughly 1750.)

The early American cartoons, much different from today's, derived, naturally, from the contemporary British techniques. In general they were overdrawn, crowded with figures and brutally satiric. (In general. Ben Franklin's severed snake remains a model of economy and point.) The "balloons" were squeezed in wherever possible, and the dialogue was both long and illegible. Many newspapers were at best biweeklies, and their artists had time for the rococo, if not for subtlety. There was wit, to be sure, as in Tisdale's "Gerrymander," from a Boston *Weekly Messenger* of 1812. (Tisdale was an engraver, by the way, and not a professional cartoonist.) Most of the artists remained anonymous; their positions were analogous to the unpublicized staff artists who do much of our modern newspaper illustration.

Partisan politics, with no fear of libel laws and no respect for individual dignity, gave the cartoonists their themes. Looking back, it seems to us now that the issues of those days were much more clear-cut than the labyrinthine problems of our own age. War with England, or not; high tariffs or low

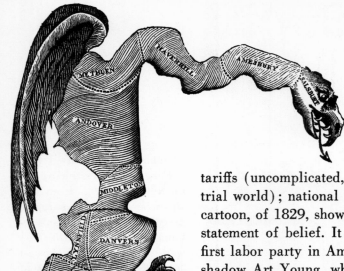

ELKANAH TISDALE'S *Gerrymander,* a public protest which added a new epithet— and a new verb— to the language. Drawn in 1812.

tariffs (uncomplicated, then, by the bureaucratic necessities of an industrial world); national bank v. local banks; free soil or slave states. One cartoon, of 1829, shows a cleaner drawing technique and a more general statement of belief. It was published by the Working Men's Party, the first labor party in America, and in both line and tone it seems to foreshadow Art Young, who came along a century later. But techniques remained largely unchanged until the Civil War, although targets varied with changing politics, and the American propensity for nicknames supplied fit subjects for caricature: the Coonskinners, the Know-Nothings, Bleeding Kansas.

(The origin of Uncle Sam as a symbol for the United States is still obscure. The name probably referred to Samuel Wilson of Troy, New York, who furnished beef and other supplies to the government during the War of 1812. His nickname was "Uncle Sam," and he stenciled his shipments "U.S.," and his products came to be known as Uncle Sam brands. The nickname was then applied to the government as a whole. Some suggest that the traditional chin-whiskered figure is a caricature of Sam Wilson; at any rate, it is the portrait of a type much caricatured later on— the conservative American farmer.)

Meanwhile journalism itself was changing, and it is likely that the evolution of the true political cartoon was due more to James Gordon Bennett than to any presumed "awakening of the national conscience" after the Civil War. Bennett was publishing the New York *Herald,* and he anticipated yellow journalism by fifty years, slanting his coverage always toward the sensational and selling his newspaper for a penny. (We forget occasionally that there were sex and murder in those days too, and the public appetite for the gory account was equal to our own.) It was a good decade for journalism. Horace Greeley's *Tribune* tried to compete with Bennett's bawdy reportage by insisting upon serious (and often garrulous and tedious) examination of the day's deeper issues; Karl Marx was one of the *Tribune's* foreign correspondents. Walt Whitman was writing editorials for the Brooklyn *Eagle.* Probably half a million people a day in New York City alone saw part or all of a newspaper, and in the 1840s that was considerable.

The effect of all this on cartooning was indirect; Bennett never hired anyone for a particular style or view of life, but he made the newspaper a staple— a regular daily necessity for most New Yorkers. High circulations made the editorial cartoon worth while as a daily feature; yet no newspaper employed a daily cartoonist for almost half a century afterward. It was one thing to spend four days on an ornately embellished tableau; it was another to do a swift six-line caricature of a famous (or infamous) figure; it was yet another to come up with a different *idea* every day; and it was a long time before newspapers were willing to gamble on the chance that one man could combine all those talents.

Meanwhile more men than ever were cartooning, and most newspapers could run a variety of visual comments as illustrations of their texts. Lincoln's rise to fame was a stimulus: here was a gaunt, lanky creature compounded of horse sense (always controversial), backwoods mannerisms,

One of the first cartoons to defend workers as a class, *circa* 1834. From the Columbia University Library.

plebeian activities (splitting rails, for example) and personal charm. He was tall, and his face, even before the beard, was striking. And of course he embodied the crucial emotional issues of the time.

He was consequently a cartoon in himself. A drawing of him included caricature, the important issues of the day and great emotional impact. By raising his brow, by twisting his mouth, by elongating his already futuristic figure, a cartoonist could express violent prejudice one way or the other.

The result was a significant and healthy change in the editorial cartoon: a tightening of the focus, a narrowing of the lens. Henceforth there would be more preoccupation with the central figure; backgrounds would remain useful as settings, but would lose their distracting importance. And an issue would be summarized concisely, rather than discussed endlessly. Economy would replace prolixity, and without economy there can be no wit. Without Lincoln there might have been no Thomas Nast.

Nast began his political cartoons with *Harper's Weekly* in the late 1860s; his greatness has always tended to obscure the superlative work of other artists of the period. Nast was an eminently serious cartoonist: his wit was grim. All right; the times were grim. But war and its aftermath generally give rise to a desire for some lightness, some escape, and it was during the 1860s that an Englishman named Frank Leslie entertained America by publishing a series of humorous magazines: the *Budget of Fun, Jolly Joker,* the *Comic Monthly* and *Phunny Phellow.* The *Budget of Fun* made a direct appeal on its masthead: "Artists and authors are invited to send to the Office of the Budget of Fun their sketches, whether pictorial or literary— marking on each its price— they will immediately receive a decision and the cash. Subjects for illustrated articles are requested— also political designs for cartoons, on all sides of politics, as the Budget of Fun will never give up to Party what was meant for Mankind."

One of Leslie's happiest acquisitions was a cartoonist who signed his work with a simple letter "N," and who has since been identified definitely (by William Murrell) as William Newman, who was one of the first artists employed by *Punch* in 1841, and who had contributed to that magazine for twenty years. Whether he came to America at Leslie's request or on his own is unimportant. Newman's work was in the old British tradition— many figures, complicated backgrounds— but his wit was sharper than that of his predecessors. And he had the good fortune to work in a decade when several first-rate cartoonists were starting their American careers. Edward Jump and Frank Beard contributed to Leslie; so did William Henry Shelton, whose "Uncle Sam's New Year's Fancy Dress Ball," of

A caricature of Lincoln, one of hundreds turned out between 1860 and 1865. This one appeared in *Harper's Weekly* in 1864.

One of WILLIAM NEWMAN's post-Civil War cartoons, from Frank Leslie's humor magazine, *Budget of Fun*.

"Our Executive Feeding Up the Southern Dragon."

1867, includes caricatures of Jump and Nast at work— a very early example of the technique called log-rolling.

Comic illustration was, in fact, booming. Names now lost to us were nationally known then: J. H. Howard, H. L. Stephens, J. Bowker, Thomas Worth, Charles Green Bush, James Wales. And others, who have remained famous, became so then: Nast, Jump, Beard and, a bit later, Joseph Keppler and the Gillam brothers. Keppler was a Viennese who had arrived in Missouri in 1867. He had founded a German humorous magazine, which failed, and when he reached America he became one of Leslie's better contributors. But he reached the heights after 1877, when he founded *Puck*— the first successful humorous weekly in this country. He loved cartooning, and spread his work— much of it in color, by the way, drawn directly onto lithographic stones— all over the magazine, inspiring assistants and competitors to contributions of their own. A Democrat politically, he was above all a European humanist in the old-fashioned sense; he hated special privilege and bigotry, and his cartoons attacked both in all the forms they took, and by whatever party they were used.

It was in the pages of *Puck* in 1884 that one of the greatest of Bernard Gillam's cartoons— and possibly the most effective that *Puck* ever ran— appeared. All through the seventies Nast had attacked the Democrats, and with reason: Tammany and Tweed were as corrupt a combination as this country has ever seen. But by the 1800s it was obvious that the Republicans

A famous view of the Upper Chamber: JOSEPH KEPPLER's "Bosses of the Senate," which ran in *Puck* in 1889.

themselves had interpreted much of the law rather loosely, to the personal profit of the party bosses. The Republican party bosses were, of course, men of substance and dignity, and their peculations were cloaked in patriotic legalisms; they were nevertheless stealing America blind, and Keppler and Gillam had at them. Gillam struck the first ringing blow during the Cleveland-Blaine campaign, with a cartoon called "The National Dime Museum," done in the old, cluttered style, but full of beautiful caricature and sensational accusation. Blaine was shown as a tattooed man, and every tattoo named one of the nefarious and probably illegal activities to which he had been a party. Many other politicians and financiers were roughly handled, among them President Arthur (the snake charmer), Samuel Tilden (in the cage) and Whitelaw Reid (the giraffe). The cartoon was printed on April 16, and the Democratic party ordered thousands of copies of *Puck* to distribute everywhere.

This was the first of a series of "Tattooed Man" cartoons; the second, printed on June 4, was in many ways better. A parody of Gérôme's "The Slave Market," it showed Blaine (as Phryne) before the nominating con-

BERNARD GILLAM launches his campaign against Blaine in *Puck*, April 1884.

"The National Dime Museum— will be run during the presidential campaign."

vention (as the Greek tribunal). In a horrified parody of maidenly modesty, Blaine hides his face; the convention is variously shocked and amused at the tattooing. Blaine was defeated, in a campaign unmatched for scurrility and mudslinging until our own day. Three separate events contributed greatly to his defeat. One was the "Rum, Romanism, Rebellion" statement. The other two were the appearance of Walt McDougall's "Belshazzar's Feast" and the publication of Gillam's tattooed men.

It was no surprise that a cartoonist could influence the course of history. Thomas Nast, the greatest of this period, had already proved it. His early years on *Harper's Weekly* were during Andrew Johnson's presidency; Nast saw him, during the reconstruction period, as a traitor to his party, and flayed him for it. (Nast was a good Republican all his life.) The early cartoons were not yet in that stark, focused style for which he was later famous; they were full of irrelevant, if attractive, detail. His style began to change when the regime changed; when Grant, his hero, became President. Nast was a crusader and something of a dogmatist; Grant was good,

By June of 1884 GILLAM was in full swing. This cartoon is from *Puck*, June 1884.

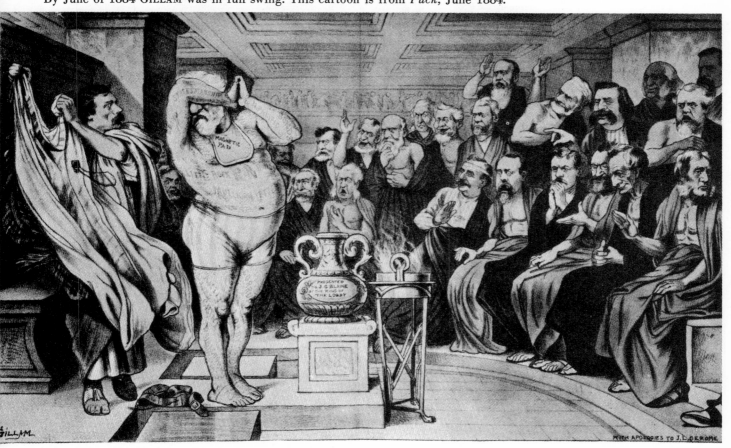

"Phryne Before the Chicago Tribunal."

"A group of vultures waiting for the storm to 'blow over'— Let Us Prey."

One of Nast's blows at Tweed: *"Let Us Prey,"* from *Harper's Weekly* of October 21, 1871.

"The Tammany Tiger loose— what are you going to do about it?"

NAST baptizes the Tiger. This cartoon from *Harper's Weekly* of November 11, 1871, is probably Nast's best-known. The tiger has been a symbol for Tammany Hall ever since.

so were the Republicans (except for traitors like Johnson), and the others were bad. Nast would never attack Grant. He needed another object, and when he found it, he produced some of the greatest political cartoons ever drawn.

You can find anything in New York City, they say; and that is where Nast found his target. The target's name was Tammany— the powerful Democratic machine in New York— and it was personified by William ("Boss") Tweed. New Yorkers had long known that their elected officials were nipping into the public funds, but no one had looked closely enough to judge the size of the bite. Tammany controlled the city and, to some extent, the governorship and state legislature. Tammany's methods were three: stealing elections, grafting, and forcing through corrupt laws.

THE MANDARIN IN THE SENATE.

NAST victimized Senator David Davis in *Harper's Weekly* of December 22, 1877. Davis had been a close friend of Lincoln back in the 1840s, when Lincoln was a circuit-riding lawyer and Davis was a judge.

Tammany was ready-made for Nast. It was Democratic; it was entrenched; it broke the law constantly and flagrantly; and it shrugged off embarrassing questions. Just before the off-year elections of 1870 Nast opened up, attacking the Tammany-backed governor; by 1871 he was in full cry, and several of his cartoons were masterpieces. There was "Tweedledee and Tweedledum." There was "Let Us Prey." There was "The Tammany Tiger Loose," perhaps his most famous single cartoon.

In one year, Nast broke Tammany. In the municipal and state elections of 1871 Tammany was swept away— though Tweed himself retained his seat in the State Senate, and though the mayoralty was not voted upon that year. Nast kept after them, in a series of what might be called Victory Cartoons. By 1873 Tweed had been arrested, found guilty and sentenced to a term in prison.

Nast now turned his attention to Horace Greeley, who had seceded from the regular Republican party and had drawn a good many fine men with him. Fortunately for Nast, the Democrats nominated Greeley to run against Grant in 1872, and Nast could defend his old hero by attacking the renegade. He was merciless. He depicted Greeley as an idealistic nincompoop, compromising with the ancient foe (the South), with Tammany, with the Catholic Church, with the Negro, with Lincoln (as John Wilkes Booth hovered in the background). Greeley was a dupe, backed by brigands. Greeley was a sentimentalist. Greeley was unfit to hold office.

Greeley lost, of course, and would have lost without Nast's opposition. But from then on Greeley was a political nothing; Nast had wiped him out, as he had Tweed, as he would Tilden in 1876. That Nast ignored the scandalous laxity of the Grant administration is not to his credit; nor that he was used by big business, which needed an appearance of vigor and righteousness. But Nast himself was never corrupt. He refused ten thousand dollars from the Republican National Committee for his services during the Hayes-Tilden election. Ten thousand dollars was a tidy fortune then, for an artist of any kind; it was a tribute to Nast's force and effectiveness.

Grant remained Nast's hero. Grant has been much maligned because his administration was weak; and it is true that he was a relatively incompetent President. But he had been a truly great general, and he was an honest man— who might not have died bankrupt otherwise. Nast might easily have chosen a worse hero. Fittingly, one of his greatest drawings was a defense of the old Grant, jettisoned by the party and under attack by the press for iniquities which were none of his doing. Nast was a fierce man. He invented the Tammany tiger and the Republican elephant, and he was the first of the great political cartoonists, and without his ferocity— in politics, in drawing, in personal loyalties— he would not have been Thomas Nast.

Peace, in the best classical style, by NAST in *Harper's Weekly*, March 31, 1877.

THE TIMES ARE RIPENING FOR A LASTING PEACE.

Beginning in the 1890s, cartoon technique moved more quickly in the direction of quick wit and immediate impact. Backgrounds tended to fade entirely; the crowds thinned out to two or three primary figures. Victor Gillam, Bernard's brother (who had, until Bernard died in 1896, signed his work simply "Victor"), and Grant Hamilton were two who furthered the new technique. *Judge* had come along in the eighties to rival *Puck,* and *Life* had been transformed from a lighthearted magazine of manners to a more outspoken representative of political liberality. The daily cartoon became, in the nineties, a feature of every large newspaper; caricatures and humorous panels appeared everywhere. William Walker and Frederick Richards, Horace Taylor and George Luks, R. L. Bristol and Eugene Zimmerman ("Zim") turned out a steady flow of cartoons better-drawn, simpler, more witty than before. One of the first cartoons to look as though it might have been drawn during the era of Franklin Roosevelt was done by Victor Gillam for *Judge* in 1900; a significant difference is that by Roosevelt's time the legend beneath it would have been unnecessary, and the fallen knight would simply have been labeled Quixote Landon.

Symbols were essential to the new technique. No artist could conceive and execute a cartoon a day if he were required also to create his own national mythology. But when the donkey was instantly recognizable as the Democratic party, the artist's task was simplified. And the lines could become fewer, bolder, less complex, more like those of caricature, which is a useless technique unless the subject of the drawing is generally known. Teddy Roosevelt, in some ways more susceptible of caricature than even Lincoln, was a blessing: a wide toothy grin and a pince-nez (sometimes surmounted by a campaign hat) came to stand for the President of the United States.

By 1900 Homer Davenport and Frederick Burr Opper (*Happy Hooligan,* remember) had begun their careers as editorial cartoonists. Davenport was one of Hearst's finds; he had been brought to New York from San Francisco in 1895, and by 1899 had immortalized himself with at least one great drawing: Wall Street's New Guardian. (The trusts, once the Spanish-American War was over, became the issue of the day.) W. A. Rogers, who was primarily a humorist, did editorial cartoons at the turn of the century; he ranked Grant Hamilton and Opper first among his contemporaries. Rogers was not alone in being versatile. From 1900 until the twenties most cartoonists did several kinds of work at once. T. E. Powers comes to mind immediately; he did editorial cartoons in the *World,* but had started as a sports cartoonist, and became best known for his *Let the Wedding Bells Ring Out,* a comic strip, in the 1910s, which appeared in the New York *Journal.* Opper's great fame was for *Happy Hooligan,* but he was doing political cartoons for Hearst well into the 1920s.

Many of the cartoonists of 1900, or of the fifteen years following, have faded into obscurity now. Powers and McDougall, Bush, Opper, Van Sant, Davenport are still remembered. Charles Macauley, who appeared in the

DON QUIXOTE BRYAN MEETS DISASTER IN HIS FIGHT AGAINST
JUDGE'S "FULL DINNER-PAIL"

VICTOR GILLAM, Bernard's brother, did this cartoon for *Judge* in 1900. The modern technique in editorial cartooning was replacing the ornate complication of the 1870s and 1880s.

HOMER DAVENPORT exposes the power behind the administration, 1899, in *"Wall Street's New Guardian."* (The real statue is of George Washington.)

New York *World* from 1904 to 1914, is forgotten; Charles Lederer, who joined the Chicago *Herald* in the 1880s, is forgotten, though his pupils and followers (John T. McCutcheon, Powers, Art Young, J. Campbell Cory) are remembered. Many tried daily cartooning but gave it up, some to become famous as panel cartoonists, like C. J. Taylor and T. S. Sullivant.

McCutcheon defies classification. From 1899 on he did editorial cartoons, satirical panels, nostalgic panels, book illustrations. John Tinney McCutcheon was his full name. He was born in Indiana in 1870, was for a time— during the teens and a good deal of the twenties— one of the three or four most popular cartoonists in the country; and yet he has left behind him the almost totally erroneous impression that he was a specialist in drawing ten-year-old Hoosiers happily fishing when they ought to be at school. Of course the one or two most famous of his cartoons created that reputation; they were perfect of their kind, and struck that low nostalgic chord always sounded by a nostalgia for something we never really experienced or at least would not really go back to now.

The kind of cartoon for which JOHN T. McCUTCHEON first became nationally famous— "*Sunday Clothes*"; and probably the kind for which he will be longest remembered. This was done in about 1903.

Comic Art in America

McCutcheon was not a limited man. He was graduated from Purdue in 1889, worked for the Chicago *Record* from then until 1901 and stayed with it for two years more after it became the *Record-Herald*. Beginning on July 1, 1903, McCutcheon belonged to the Chicago *Tribune*. He never after worked for anyone else.

The first serious turning point in his life was a world tour he embarked on in January 1898, on the dispatch boat *McCulloch*. With a reporter's luck he was aboard that ship during the Spanish-American War and turned up at the Battle of Manila Bay, whence he sent both prose and cartoons back to the *Record*. Having begun successfully, he paused to tour the Far East, touching at traditional points of romance like Shanghai and Singapore. By April 1900 (after having covered the American punitive campaign in the Philippines) he had moved west again to the Transvaal, where he joined the Boers for his newspaper. He came out of it with a whole skin, with hundreds of drawings behind him, and with hundreds of thousands of words of highly respectable prose to his credit. He reached Chicago again in August 1900 and, except for one African jaunt (for the Chicago *Tribune* in 1909–10), he did no extensive traveling thereafter.

He was obviously more than a cartoonist, but it was in the dignity of editorial cartooning that he found his ultimate satisfactions. He was, as the *Tribune's* regular and indefatigable cartoonist, the best known of all for a couple of decades. He met unusual deadlines: the Chicago *Tribune* even then ran occasional page-one cartoons in color several times in 1903 and 1904— a practice which was resumed, on a regular basis, in 1941— but the advanced technique was never too much for McCutcheon. His cartoons never needed color, incidentally. His line was expressive if bristly, and his intention was never masked. He retired with a Pulitzer Prize behind him, won in 1932, and when he died in 1949 a generation of young Midwestern cartoonists lost their master.

The Midwest was beginning to produce cartoonists of importance. Charles Bartholomew ("Bart") drew for the Minneapolis *Journal* while R. C. Bowman drew for the neighboring Minneapolis *Tribune*. J. H. Donahey displayed never-flagging wit for the Cleveland *Plain Dealer* (where he remained for forty years). Before this time many Midwesterners had gravitated to the coasts; but since 1900 no region can claim cartooning superiority over any other.

Puck was still at it, now under the reign of Joseph Keppler, Jr., who was less brutal to public figures than his father had been. One of *Puck's* contributors, J. S. Pughe, turned in a small masterpiece in 1904, when there seemed some chance that William Randolph Hearst would win the Democratic nomination for the Presidency. Hearst, champagne glass in hand, is surrounded by his comic-strip characters: the Katzenjammer Kids, Alphonse and Gaston, some Little Bears and Tigers, and so on. The cartoon has point, is well drawn and, incidentally, proves very nicely that even so early in the century comics characters were generally recognizable symbols which could be safely shown without explanatory prose.

J. S. PUGHE's intriguing peek at the future, June 1904. Hearst seemed to have a fair political future, and this might be one of the happier consequences of his success. From *Puck*.

In about 1905 a low mutter of discontent, at first barely audible, was heard about the land. Its origins were obscure; perhaps it was simply man's natural cantankerousness breaking through. Perhaps the panic of 1907 was a reflection of or justification for it. Perhaps a few sensitive and prescient observers had felt the first inklings that all was not right with labor and capital and government and foreign trade. Perhaps the growing and somewhat revolutionary labor movement was finding its voices. At any rate, cartoons began to appear which were unlike anything seen previously. They were drawn in one panel, and there was a witty point to them, but they were not funny. They were not lighthearted. They were pessimistic and sometimes vicious.

They were, to be sure, editorial cartoons. But they did not, generally, appear in newspapers, and their attitudes were not partisan in the strict Democratic-Republican sense. A good many of them appeared in *Life*; one was C. Broughton's comment on tariffs, which was a bit more discouraging than the traditional farmer-merchant cartoon. Another, and a strange one indeed for its time, was by Art Young, and was called "This World of Creepers." To most Americans it must have been obscurely disturbing, and another by Young, "Ennui," was no more cheerful. Young had always been a free-lance, and he had always been more interested in man's underlying fears and desires than in the immediate political form which they took. That interest was to make him the leader of a new generation of political cartoonists, mostly free-lance, who refused to confine their efforts to officials and daily issues, but who insisted on attacking the underlying theses of American society. They were, in short, the radical cartoonists and illustrators, and for thirty years they produced some of the best editorial art in America. Many of the attitudes they struck seem outmoded now; many do not. In a sense they were a crystallization of dissent and Bohemianism. Many were socialists, many were atheists, all were distinguished

An early, and grim, ART YOUNG, from the old *Life* in 1907. This was a departure—not anger at a political faction, but resignation and despair at the human condition.

"This World of Creepers— afraid of themselves, and of others, afraid of the Almighty, of life and of death."

ORGIE MANIACLE

ALL FOR HONOR

ALL FOR DEMOCRACY

ALL FOR WORLD PEACE

ALL FOR JESUS

EDITOR   CAPITALIST   POLITICIAN   MINISTER

Having Their Fling

A later, and more vigorous, ART YOUNG, vigorous enough to be used by the government as evidence in its trial of *The Masses* (where it appeared in September of 1917) for obstructing the war effort.

by compassion. They were obviously against monopoly, in an age when a Republican President had been forced to establish anti-trust legislation; they saw religion and war as necessary auxiliaries to capitalism, and consequently opposed them both. They were a very small but very influential minority, and for some time they were the most unpopular, but the most provocative, artists in America. Their principal outlet was *The Masses*, a socialist magazine edited after 1912 by Max Eastman and John Sloan. In the first generation of them were Young, Sloan, Balfour Ker, George Bellows, Maurice Becker, William Glackens and Robert Minor, among others.

Obviously their cartoons were not funny. They went back, in content, to another tradition: the tradition of Daumier and the radical Europeans. Two of Robert Minor's most famous cartoons are vicious blasts at war and sexual hypocrisy; and if they do not seem so shocking to us today, if we are more realistic about both, it is partly because Minor helped to make us so.

309

Art Young attacked the press, calling it corrupt; he was sued, but the suit was quietly dropped. He attacked the whole structure of American society in one cartoon (of excellent technique, by the way); it became an exhibit in court when *The Masses* was tried for obstructing the draft. When the war was over, Boardman Robinson drew a cartoon of consummate beauty and prophecy: "The Dead Hand on the Versailles Treaty."

Not all the bitterness was expressed by radicals. Luther Bradley of the Chicago *Daily News* had drawn his cynical version of the war in 1916; he was a respectable cartoonist, and was not brought to trial. And a majority of American cartoonists believed what the government professed to believe: that this was a righteous war to end all war, that the world was being made safe for democracy. W. A. Rogers kept a careful eye on Uncle Sam's interest, but was wholeheartedly behind the war effort, and his cartoons are models of carefully drawn, witty propaganda.

Generally, though, the great cartooning during the second decade of this century was anti-war. Hardly surprising, when we think that the government established a Bureau of Cartoons, in 1917, which sent out a bulletin suggesting topics— for example, Liberty Bonds, recruiting, saving food and fuel. As William Murrell observed, "When they were not doing their utmost to graphically urge any and all of the above suggestions the cartoonists, for the most part, concentrated their efforts on Uncle Sam buckling on armor, or the Kaiser with a bomb, pistol or knout."

Criticism had, in other words, been directed into very confining channels, and the old free-swinging, Nastian attitude was temporarily dead, except among the radicals.

That situation altered quickly after the war. A kind of abashed sanity returned to America; too quick to involve ourselves with Europe in 1917, we were now too quick to disengage ourselves. An age superficially characterized by the most arrant frivolity now began, and in it were sufficient targets for a generation of cartoonists.

Much of the best periodical art of the 1920s was in magazines, but by then magazine art had been transformed; it consisted of caricature (some of the best the world has known) and the "gag" panel (e.g., Peter Arno in *The New Yorker*), both of which are considered elsewhere. They are mentioned here because public taste underwent a vast and happy change in the twenties and thirties, and some credit for that change, which was reflected in editorial cartooning, must go to magazines like *Vanity Fair*, *The New Yorker* and, yes, *Time*. From 1920 to 1950 we as a nation moved painfully from naïveté through oversophistication to a reluctant maturity, and comic art, playing on two wars and a depression, was one of the moving influences.

During the war one of the more talented daily cartoonists had been Rollin Kirby, of the New York *World*. His cartoons had been a good deal less inane than those of most of his contemporaries, and it was obvious that

"Army Medical Examiner: 'At last a perfect soldier!'"

Perhaps the most aggressive anti-war cartoon ever published in this country. By
ROBERT MINOR in *The Masses* in 1915.

his use of the single figure, the symbol, was highly developed. But he came into his own after the war, during the years when soul-shattering hypocrisy and outright larceny lay like a blight upon this fair land. (Few remembered, when he was famous as an editorial cartoonist, that back in 1913 he had originated *Metropolitan Movies* for the *World*, a feature later taken over by Gene Carr and still later transformed, by Denys Wortman, into an enduring and gritty chronicle of urban life.)

Kirby was by no means a young cartoonist breaking in. When he started with the *World* in 1913 he was already thirty-eight years old. He was a native of Illinois whose mother had been a painter. At nineteen he found himself in New York studying at the Art Students League, and shortly thereafter in Paris, where he studied under the aged James McNeil Whistler. Between 1900 and 1913 he tried to make a painter's living in New York; but he found the demands of the paying public a bit too inartistic, and in 1913 took his fiery temperament and his agile brush to the *World*.

His most inspired, enduring creation was the Bluenose, a gaunt, umbrella-waving, tall-hatted, thin-lipped policeman of the free citizen's morals. Kirby was at his best when chopping away at repressive fanaticism; and one of the great ironies of editorial cartooning is that this man, who three times was awarded the Pulitzer Prize, won all three for cartoons which now seem nowhere near his best work, and no one of which concerned itself at all with the Bluenose we now identify with him. But Pulitzer Prizes are not awarded arbitrarily for, say, excellence in draftsmanship. For one thing, they are awarded in a political and social climate; any given year has its high points, its memorable occasions, its historic events to which allusion may be safely made. And then there is the method of judging. The money was left by the original Joseph Pulitzer, who gave Columbia University two and one half million dollars for a school of journalism, including just enough extra to endow annual awards for distinction in journalism, literature and education. No award for cartooning was made until 1922, when Kirby received his first. The winner is usually selected by a committee supplied by Columbia University with the carefully heeded advice of several non-Columbians who are practicing cartoonists or cartoon editors. These non-academic judges are men of high standing, and are generally drawn from several different areas of the country, in order to avoid any cry of sectionalism.

In the circumstances it is almost inevitable that a Pulitzer Prize winner will have a sneaking desire to point to another example of his work and say, "This one was better." So Kirby's famous "Thou Shalt Not" cartoon, in which the Bluenose-Puritan-Prohibitionist figure reached his *reductio ad absurdum*, remains more famous than any of the three for which he was awarded a prize; yet each of the winners has a special significance in its own year, and obviously impressed the committee of selection with its timeliness and irony. Of the three, the third, winner in 1929, is the most understandable today. The first, 1922, captioned "On the Road to Moscow," shows a darkly draped skeleton beating a tattoo on a funereal drum as an endless line of sick, ragged, crippled, homeless people stretches into the murky distances behind. The cartoon was non-political, going much deeper; we knew very little about what was going on in Russia, and one of the salient facts of the time was human misery. Kirby expressed it. In 1925 he won his second prize for a drawing of a hobo jungle occupied by Russia, Mexico and the United States, with Uncle Sam reading a newspaper which stated "48 Nations Agree upon League Peace Pact." The caption was "News from the Outside World"; the implication was that by having rejected, or been rejected by, the League of Nations the three countries concerned had placed themselves outside the pale. It was an expressive cartoon which did no good; by 1925 our citizenry was firmly entrenched in its own provincialism. The less said about Europe, about peace pacts, about entangling alliances, the better.

.1929 was something else again. This was the first time any cartoonist had received a third Pulitzer Prize; only Edmund Duffy of the Baltimore *Sun* has equaled Kirby's achievement since. Even now the cartoon explains

ROLLIN KIRBY.   New York *World.*

News from the Outside World.

Pulitzer Prize 1925.   Courtesy of the Press Publishing Co.

itself almost immediately. It is in the old-fashioned vein; there are seventeen figures plus a moneybag plus Albert Fall's reticule in the drawing, which takes us back almost to Gillam and his attacks upon Blaine. This cartoon too is an attack upon the pious righteousness of the Republican party in 1928. That the cartoon had not much effect on the 1928 election is due largely to Al Smith's being a Catholic and a Wet— the Republican candidate might carry a handicap of a good deal of corruption and even flamboyant illegality, but he did not make the mistake of offending the Yahoos.

None of Kirby's prize-winning cartoons was extremely important in itself. But the body of his work was. His ideas were not wishy-washy, for one thing; he was forthright and often angry. His drawing was vigorous, he could handle groups or a single figure with equal ease, but his net effect was to reinforce the single-figure school. The cartoon had been developing for many years, always in the direction of greater simplicity and higher symbolic value. Kirby was undoubtedly the man who gave it its decisive impetus in that direction and determined its basic character for decades to come. Kirby died in 1951 after a lifetime of uninhibited service to the *World* and then to the *World-Telegram,* and ultimately to the whole country.

No prize was awarded in 1923. In 1924 Jay Norwood "Ding" Darling won it with "In Good Ole USA," which has become famous; but he won it again in 1943 for a much wilder cartoon, far more representative of the free and cantankerous spirit that moved him when he did his best work. In 1925 the winner was Kirby; and in 1926 a truly monumental cartoon by D. R. "Dan" Fitzpatrick took the award. (It was followed by a second award twenty-nine years later!) "The Laws of Moses and the Laws of Today" is a cartoon of staggering simplicity. Its meaning was immediately and forcefully apparent; it obviously represented a deep-rooted attitude on Fitzpatrick's part. Fitzpatrick was a Wisconsin boy who appeared for a while, as so many midwestern artists did, at the Chicago Art Institute, and went on to a series of jobs in journalism which took him ultimately to the *Post-Dispatch* in St. Louis, Joseph Pulitzer's first newspaper. A man of real conviction, Fitzpatrick always had an agreement with his newspaper that he would not be forced to take an editorial position with which he disagreed. But the *Post-Dispatch,* fortunately, has been a forthrightly liberal newspaper since its inception; and Fitzpatrick is a forthrightly liberal man. There have been few conflicts between him and the *Post-Dispatch.* Time and again his cartoons have struck at the heart of some matter of national concern and confusion; time and again he has stuck his neck out, delivering an opinion directly contrary to prevalent thought in the Midwest, in the full knowledge that it would be seen and argued by millions of Midwesterners. Like most good editorial cartoonists, when he thought he had hold of good sense, he drew his cartoon and let it be published. In Fitzpatrick's case the results were almost always happy. Probably no newspaper in America has been as fortunate in its cartoonists as the *Post-Dispatch;* when Dan Fitzpatrick retired, having served for forty-four years, Bill Mauldin, another Pulitzer Prize winner, stepped into his shoes, where he has so far shown no signs of discomfort at all. In our time Fitzpatrick has shaped public opinion probably as much as any journalist. He has had a fine forum; he has been a superb advocate.

Nelson Harding and the Brooklyn *Eagle* achieved a major coup in 1927 and 1928 by taking the Pulitzer Prize both years. In 1927 Harding's drawing, very heavy and grim, showed cables originating in the League of Nations wrapped around a rude statue of Mars labeled "War" about to throw it to earth; the caption was "Toppling the Idol." In 1928 Harding reflected the country's adulation of Charles Lindbergh in a cartoon captioned "May His Shadow Never Grow Less," showing the shadow of Lindbergh's plane over a Mexican landscape as a cross with the arm labeled "Peace on Earth" and the upright labeled "Good Will to Men." (Lindbergh was on a goodwill flight to Mexico at the time, and the cartoon was published just before Christmas, so that the symbolism of the cross, the good will and the Mexican landscape combined perfectly with the maximum of meaning in a minimum of drawing.) Harding's two cartoons add up to an intimate concern for the lack of amity in the world of the late twenties, and perhaps they reflect the American desire to be left alone. Without war, without international conflict, we Americans would be left to our own happy pursuits— land speculation, stock-market speculation, the drinking of bootleg liquor; or even the more normal pursuits, like buying a home, raising a family and tending the small rectangular garden in the back yard. Harding was sensitive enough to feel that need in his public. He was not himself a sophisticated man, though he had a fine sense of humor. He was an active cartoonist until 1945, and died in 1947 aged sixty-eight.

The Brooklyn *Eagle* won the award again in 1930, but this time without Nelson Harding. Their cartoonist was Charles R. Macauley, and paradoxically he was less well known then, in the year of the prize, than he had been previously; he is all but forgotten now, except among a handful of cartoonists. The height of his popularity had been between 1904 and 1914, when he was editorial cartoonist for the New York *World.* Seizing upon Theodore Roosevelt's remark about speaking softly and carrying a big stick, he caricatured that big stick beyond all proportion, transforming it artistically into a cudgel far beyond any man's powers to carry. His use of the stick made it as much a Roosevelt trade-mark as the toothy grin or the pince-nez.

His 1930 cartoon was an after-the-fact comment on the cost of war, in this case the financial cost. The cartoon was well drawn, with the large symbolic dead horse occupying two thirds of it, and the poor burdened taxpayer, unidentified otherwise and therefore a citizen of the world, disappearing into the background. The idea is of course timeless. There is no such thing as victory or profit in war, and this was the point that Macauley made. He died in 1934, and we may be glad now that a man whose career was as long and effective as his received the profession's highest award before it was too late.

Edmund Duffy, who will always be identified with the Baltimore *Sun,* won the first of his three prizes in 1931. He was unquestionably the professional heir of Rollin Kirby. If his characterization was less subtle, his drawing was more forceful and his composition was generally simpler. There is another peculiar similarity between Duffy and Kirby: Duffy too created one figure for which he became famous— the abject, spineless, chinless Ku Klux Klansman— but none of the three cartoons for which he was awarded Pulitzer Prizes featured this creation.

Duffy was a New Jerseyite, born in 1899; he attended the Art Students League in New York, and is another of the many cartoonists who were strongly influenced by Boardman Robinson. It was not until 1924 that he moved to the Baltimore *Sun,* but it was very shortly obvious to both the man and the newspaper that they were a good match. The *Sun* had a free-swinging tradition, and Duffy was, all through his career, an angry young

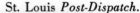

DANIEL R. FITZPATRICK.   St. Louis *Post-Dispatch.*

The Laws of Moses and the Laws of Today.

Pulitzer Prize 1926.   Courtesy of Daniel Fitzpatrick and the St. Louis *Post-Dispatch.*

cartoonist. He was with the Baltimore *Sun* for twenty-four years, leaving them in 1948 to do cartoons for *The Saturday Evening Post,* where he could restrict himself to a lighter schedule.

The statement that Duffy was Kirby's heir requires some explanation. Kirby was, in a compositional sense, midway between the nineteenth-century group cartoon and the mid-twentieth-century single-figure cartoon. It was certainly his influence, more than that of anyone else, which directed the modern cartoon into simpler form; and Duffy was the cartoonist who consolidated Kirby's first important steps in that direction. It may be too much to say that from Kirby and Duffy come the Herblocks and Mauldins of our own day; it is nevertheless true that the modern generation of cartoonists works in a tradition established by those two men.

Of Duffy's three winners, the 1934 cartoon, "California Points with Pride," is probably the best. The immediate occasion of the cartoon, now lost in history, was a pair of lynchings in California; the governor, called to account, failed to react vigorously and even made excuses for the lynchers. To a man of Duffy's fighting temperament and liberal views this was

CHARLES R. MACAULEY.   Brooklyn *Eagle.*

"Paying for a Dead Horse."

Pulitzer Prize 1930.   Courtesy of the Brooklyn *Eagle.*

unthinkable conduct for a supposedly enlightened public official, and his cartoon was the answer. His 1940 winner, displaying Adolf Hitler in the act of extending a bloody hand to the world, has much more recognizable significance for our generation; but it was a more general, less specifically angry cartoon than its predecessor. There were hundreds of cartoonists in America in 1940 who recognized Hitler's hypocrisy, unreliability and basic madness; Duffy drew a significant and powerful cartoon, but if the prize had been given only for originality of thought it is less likely that he would have won it.

There is no question but that he deserved as many prizes and honors as he could collect. He is an independent man who has never compromised his integrity for the sake of good relations with the public or with his employers. He is more than simply a commentator. He is a fighter, a destroyer. Like so many political cartoonists, he hates untruth and cruelty; he has spent his professional life chopping away at both, and it would be difficult to find a more honorable career.

John T. McCutcheon, the pride of the Midwest and probably, at least up to the 1940s, the twentieth century's best-known editorial cartoonist, finally

JOHN T. McCUTCHEON.   Chicago *Tribune*.

"A Wise Economist Asks a Question."

Pulitzer Prize 1932.

Courtesy of the Chicago *Tribune*– New York *News* Syndicate, Inc.

received the accolade in 1932, for a cartoon which was as much a panel as it was an editorial cartoon. It was simple enough: a victim of bank failure, seated on a park bench, was asked by a squirrel, symbol of prudence, "But why didn't you save some money for the future, when times were good?" and the poor innocent bystander replied grimly, "I did." The title of the cartoon was "A Wise Economist Asks a Question," and there was little more comment to be made on the waves of bank failures that crippled America in 1931.

Thus the first ten Pulitzer Prizes. There was no obvious pattern in subject matter, but there was no doubt that the most effective of the cartoons were in the modern style— a minimum of highly symbolic figures, charged with immediately apparent meanings, and placed in ironic situations. Of the first ten awards, three had gone to Rollin Kirby, two to Nelson Harding, one to John T. McCutcheon, one to Edmund Duffy, who later received two more, one to Ding Darling, who was to receive another, one to Dan Fitzpatrick, who would also receive another, and one to Charles R. Macauley.

After 1931 there were fewer repeaters; a rising generation of editorial cartoonists was displaying unusual effectiveness, and more newspapers were publishing cartoons of the highest quality. Briefly, this is how the awards ran after 1932:

1933: "The Light of Asia," by Harold Talburt, in the Washington *Daily News*. After an early career as a reporter, Talburt had become an editorial cartoonist, his basic affection being for sketching. In 1922 he was chosen by the Scripps-Howard chain to be its Washington cartoonist, and he occupied that position when he won his prize.

1934: Edmund Duffy's second award.

1935: "Sure, I'll Work for Both Sides," by Ross A. Lewis, in the Milwaukee *Journal*. This cartoon depicted violence with one foot in industry's camp and one foot in the strikers'. It was a reflection of the terrible period of labor troubles that beset us in the depths of the depression. Its message was that violence would do none of us any good, and it was undoubtedly a reassuring piece of work. Lewis was a native of Michigan who had studied at the Art Students League in New York— another of Boardman Robinson's pupils. He joined the Milwaukee *Journal* as editorial cartoonist in 1932, and it took him only three years to bring home a Pulitzer Prize.

1936: no award.

1937: "Come on in, I'll treat you right. I used to know your Daddy," by Charles D. Batchelor of the New York *Daily News*. This was the bitterest cartoon for which the award has ever been given. Like Vaughn Shoemaker's in the following year, its underlying horror lay in its terrible implication that history would repeat itself. Batchelor's technique in this cartoon was flawless; the use of a prostitute was in itself daring, and his employment of a death's head instead of normal features added the last stroke of grisly earthiness. Batchelor was born in Kansas in 1888, and worked for the

H. M. TALBURT.   Washington *Daily News*.

"The Light of Asia."

Pulitzer Prize 1933.

Courtesy of H. M. Talburt and Scripps-Howard Newspapers.

Kansas City *Star* and the New York *Journal* as well as spending ten years with a syndicate, finally being hired by the New York *Daily News*. He had already achieved some distinction as a cartoonist for his series entitled "Inviting the Undertaker," a series which is still running and is still effective. But a greater distinction by far was the fact that he won a Pulitzer Prize for a tabloid— the first time the award had been offered to one.

1938: "The Road Back," by Vaughn Shoemaker, from the Chicago *Daily News*. This was again a cartoon of warning, expressive of the theory that Europe was headed for another conflagration if anything far worse than the first. Underlying both Batchelor's and Shoemaker's warnings to the world was the hope that the United States would not again be dragged into a major war. In this, both cartoonists were ahead of the public. Any American citizen, if asked, would have expressed that same hope; but few American citizens were thinking about it at the time in anything like personal terms.

1939: "Nomination for 1938," by Charles G. Werner, in the *Daily Oklahoman*. This cartoon, almost brutal in its simplicity, reflected both sentiment and irony. The honest, sorrowful sentiment was for the passing

C. D. Batchelor.   New York *Daily News.*

"Come on in, I'll treat you right. I used to know your Daddy."

Pulitzer Prize 1937.

Courtesy of the Chicago *Tribune*– New York *News* Syndicate, Inc.

of Czechoslovakia; the irony was in the notion of awarding to a dead nation the Nobel Peace Prize at a time when surely no one else seemed worthy of it. Werner is a native of Wisconsin, born in 1909. He started his career as a typographer, but rapidly found that drawing and sketching were more to his taste. He became an editorial cartoonist with the *Oklahoman* in 1937, only a year before he brought home the prize. Later on he went to the Chicago *Sun* and then to the Indianapolis *Star*, where he still turns out cartoons of unusually high quality.

1940: Edmund Duffy's third award.

1941: "If I Should Die Before I Wake," by Jacob Burck, in the Chicago *Sun-Times.* This cartoon was published during the evacuation of Dunkirk, and was a deliberate and highly effective plea for American sympathy for the innocent victims of the European war. The cartoon has a direct appeal to sentiment, and the symbols are perfect: rubble, a child, a prayer. Burck had come to this country from Poland as a child, before the First World War. He attended the Cleveland School of Art, and then went on to New York, aiming to become a portrait painter. It was once more Boardman Robinson whose influence directed a young man into editorial cartooning.

EDMUND DUFFY.   Baltimore *Sun*.

"The Outstretched Hand."
Pulitzer Prize 1940.
Courtesy of Edmund Duffy and the Baltimore *Sun*.

VAUGHN SHOEMAKER.   Chicago *Daily News*.

"The Road Back."

Pulitzer Prize 1938.
Courtesy of Vaughn Shoemaker and the Chicago *Daily News*.

CHARLES G. WERNER.   The *Daily Oklahoman*.

"Nomination for 1938."

Pulitzer Prize 1939.
Courtesy of Charles G. Werner and the *Daily Oklahoman*.

Burck's earliest work in the field was for *The Masses*; he then went on to the St. Louis *Post-Dispatch*, and in 1938 moved to the Chicago *Times*. He had a bit of trouble after the Second World War when, during a time of political hysteria, an attempt was made to deport him because he had once gone to Moscow when the Russian government had offered him work as a mural painter. He was strongly anti-Communist when he returned to this country, but he had briefly paid dues to the Communist party, and under American law in 1955 he was subject to deportation. The support of his many friends and colleagues, plus his national reputation, plus the basic reluctance of the Attorney General to go on with the case, finally resulted in a suspension of the proceedings, and Burck has not been bothered since. His work did not suffer during this period; and there has been no sign of personal bitterness, and no diminution in the quality of his drawings, since.

1942: "British Plane," by Herbert L. Block, for NEA Service, Inc. For almost twenty years— it hardly seems so long— Herblock, as he signs himself, has been one of the three or four greats in American political cartooning. He has won two Pulitzer Prizes, and the daily level of his work has been extraordinary. Part of his fame and popularity rests upon collections of his cartoons, published with an extended commentary by the cartoonist himself; he is a most articulate man, and has done a good deal to expose the workings of the political cartoonist's mind to the general public. "British Plane" is a fine example of his early work. It consists of four figures

JACOB BURCK.   Chicago *Times*.

"If I Should Die Before I Wake."

Pulitzer Prize 1941.
Courtesy of Chicago *Sun-Times* Syndicate. © Field Enterprises, Inc.

in an obviously French street. One, a Nazi soldier, is looking grimly to the sky. The other three, French civilians, are looking at the soldier, and on their faces are tight, gloating smiles. In one cartoon Herblock summed up a whole phase of the German occupation of France. The cartoon was published in March 1941, and by the time the prizes were awarded this nation was also at war, which may have had something to do with its selection. There is no doubt that it reflected a very strong American sympathy for occupied nations in general and for France in particular. Artistically, though not ideologically, there was considerable difference between the Herblock of 1942 and the Herblock of 1954; more extended comment will be reserved for his later prize-winning cartoon.

1943: "What a Place for a Waste Paper Salvage Campaign," by J. Norwood "Ding" Darling, in the New York *Herald Tribune*. This is the wild Ding Darling at his wildest. Here is a panel so full of lines, signs and symbols, not to mention dialogue, that it takes a full two or three minutes to absorb it entirely. There are no less than eighteen signs or labels; there are two conversational balloons in comic-strip style; there are four tiny taxpayers; there are Uncle Sam, the Washington Monument, the White House and Congress. There are also millions and millions of sheets of paper, which is the whole point of the cartoon. With all that, it is rather surprising that this cartoon won the Pulitzer Prize, particularly in 1943, when heaven knows there were enough earth-shattering events taking place and inspiring editorial cartoons. It was published in September 1942, and 1942 was certainly not a year lacking in events of paramount importance. By 1943 Darling was almost a throwback: he belonged with McCutcheon and a less sophisticated, blunter, less ironic school of politics than most of the generation which was to succeed those two men. His was a kind of virtuous American indignation which saw waste in Washington as a betrayal of the war effort; which could not help contrasting the shoddy ways of bureaucracy with the lonely sorrow of a soldier's death. That there is no direct reference to dying soldiers in this cartoon is not an omission; surely behind the idea there lay Darling's own indignation at the contrast. This was the second of his prizes, and it was the last cartoon, at least up to now, to represent the old, crazy, cluttered style. Considering the time and the events, it may have been a relatively weak effort; but it was certainly executed to perfection, and it made a serious and necessary point.

1944: "But Where Is the Boat Going?" by Clifford K. Berryman, from the Washington *Evening Star*. Here again the committee of selection apparently ignored the momentous events of a world at war in favor of domestic issues, in this case the issue of direction of the war effort, more specifically of our manpower mobilization. Involving millions upon millions of men— servicemen, workers and bureaucrats— this mobilization had naturally fallen into the hands of several directors who often worked at cross-purposes. Berryman's criticism was uninhibited; he showed Roosevelt sitting nonchalantly in the stern of the mobilization rowboat while three labor leaders, a general and Paul V. McNutt all disagreed on the direction to be taken. Berryman, whose son James later received a Pulitzer Prize for a cartoon in the same newspaper, was once called by President Truman "a great cartoonist without malice." There was surely malice in this prize winner, however, but it was of an honest kind. There has never been a great political cartoon without *some* malice; it is the intellectual integrity of the artist which saves him from being merely querulous, and Berryman's integrity was never in question. Berryman died, aged eighty, still at work, having collapsed in the offices of the *Star* in November 1949.

1945: "Fresh, Spirited American Troops, Flushed with Victory, are Bringing in Thousands of Hungry, Ragged, Battle-Weary Prisoners," by Bill Mauldin, for the United Feature Syndicate, Inc. This cartoon may not have been political in the traditional sense, but the overriding event of the

JAY NORWOOD DARLING.   New York *Herald Tribune*.

"What a Place for a Waste Paper Salvage Campaign."
Pulitzer Prize 1943.

twentieth century, so far, has been the Second World War; over eleven million Americans served in the armed forces, and any cartoon inspired by them was ultimately as truly political as a party caucus in Chicago. William H. Mauldin was— and continues to be— a phenomenon, and much of what made him a phenomenon is apparent in this cartoon. In 1944 he had been assigned to cartooning for *The Stars and Stripes* on a permanent basis; these were war cartoons, but as he himself said later on, he was "editorializing" all the time. What made Mauldin great at the beginning of his career— he was only twenty-three when he won the prize, which made him the youngest ever to have received it— was not a precocious maturity or profundity, but a clarity of perception in one particular area. Mauldin was apparently aware of every argument ever adduced in an attempt to make war palatable; he was also aware that absolutely none of those arguments could stand up under any sort of logical scrutiny. Mauldin's graphic comments, all of which may be called ironic, are more than that: they are a swift, uncompromising refutation of all the hymns of glory ever raised to war. The ambition of the experienced soldier, for example, is not to wipe out a machine-gun nest single-handed, or to save his battalion in a burst of heroism, or to receive a battlefield promotion; it is very simply to avoid being shot or blown up. Mauldin's way of expressing this is to show an infantryman in a shell hole saying to another, "Th'hell this ain't th'most important hole in th'world. I'm in it."

And Mauldin knew whereof he spoke, which made him almost unique among war correspondents. Born in New Mexico, he went through high school in Arizona and entered that state's National Guard in 1940, at the age of eighteen. He had already attempted serious cartooning, but the result of his first efforts was simply a suitcase full of rejection slips. He was, however, in the habit of thinking in cartoon terms. (He had even managed to attend the Chicago Academy of Fine Arts for a year before entering the National Guard. While at the Academy, he supported himself by doing artistic odd jobs, which gave him at least a varied background.) When he entered the combat area, his assignment was not precisely that of "combat artist." He was rather a dogface like any other, who had been asked, or permitted, to turn in panel cartoons for occasional publication. (He was wounded by a shell fragment at Salerno, and was awarded a Purple Heart.) By 1944 he was a staff cartoonist, working on a permanent basis for *The Stars and Stripes*. This Pulitzer Prize winner was one of the cartoons he drew in that year.

Immediately after the war Mauldin was almost a national hero. Several of his books were best-sellers: *Up Front, Back Home, A Sort of a Saga* and others. United Feature Syndicate had signed him for newspaper publication; but it soon became apparent that something was missing. Perhaps it was the war itself; in any case, national newspaper reaction to his work was not good. Probably his savage irony, necessary when we were fighting for our lives, was less desirable and less appreciated when hostilities ceased and the public wanted simply peace and quiet. Mauldin himself sensed that, and offered many times to bow out temporarily, resting and reorganizing his talents; but United Feature Syndicate was reluctant to let him stop work. It was only in 1948 that he was able to relax and take stock. For almost ten years it was his books, plus a good deal of casual writing for magazines and newspapers, which kept him going. (In 1956 he varied his career by running for Congress in Rockland County, New York, as a Democrat, against Mrs. Katherine St. George, who was thoroughly entrenched as Republican Congresswoman from the district. Mauldin was defeated, but had the satisfaction of knowing that he had polled the largest Democratic vote— he lost in a proportion of 3–2 in a district which was normally 2–1— ever polled in the district.)

BILL MAULDIN. *Up Front.*

"Fresh, spirited American troops, flushed with victory, are bringing in thousands of hungry, ragged, battle-weary prisoners. . . ." (News item)

Pulitzer Prize 1945.

© 1944 United Feature Syndicate, Inc., by permission of Bill Mauldin.

During the winter of 1957–8, when it became known that Dan Fitzpatrick wanted to retire from his position with the St. Louis *Post-Dispatch*, Walt Kelly, Herblock and Fitzpatrick himself urged that newspaper's editor to take Mauldin on. Their advocacy was effective; Mauldin was offered a trial period of sixty days, but there was no doubt from the beginning that he would be eminently satisfactory as a replacement for Fitzpatrick. (There are few cartoonists in this country of whom that can be said.) If this discussion of Mauldin seems disproportionately long, it is not because his work is "better" than that of the many other top-flight artists in this chapter. It is rather because during two or three years crucial to America he spoke for millions of us; what Ernie Pyle did in writing, Bill Mauldin did with cartoons. There is another reason: it seems likely that Mauldin is destined for a brilliant career with the *Post-Dispatch*. Certainly his cartoon of July 17, 1958, reproduced in these pages, is deserving of the word "classic." Drawn at the height of one of the intermittent crises in a chronically dangerous Middle East, it does everything that a cartoon should do. It is direct, accusing and minatory; it is a moral lesson; and fifty years of history are enlightened by it. It is as good as many which have received Pulitzer Prizes, and it belongs in the top rank of editorial cartoons. (Extra: only a couple of weeks before this manuscript went off to the publishers, Mauldin was awarded the Pulitzer Prize for 1959. The cartoon is reproduced in these pages.)

1946: "Time to Bridge That Gulch," by Bruce Alexander Russell, in the Los Angeles *Times*. This was one of the first recognitions of a parlous state of affairs between the United States and Russia, a state of affairs which has become only more parlous as time has passed. It expressed an obvious need for moderation and intelligence in foreign affairs; there is something almost wistful about it now. Russell is a native of Angeleno, born there in 1903. He was a staff artist with the Los Angeles *Times* for many years, and also did a comic strip for the Associated Press *(Rollo Rollingstone)*. The strip was only moderately successful, but Russell's real vocation was editorial cartooning.

1947: Vaughn Shoemaker's second award: "Still Racing His Shadow," in the Chicago *Daily News*.

1948: "Peace Today," by Reuben Lucius Goldberg, in the New York *Sun*. It was bound to happen; if there was a world to conquer, Rube Goldberg would sooner or later pop up and busy himself with its conquest. There is a coincidence here. Goldberg had a degree in mining engineering, and had become famous for inventions and weird devices. The atomic bomb— not yet superseded by the hydrogen bomb— was in many ways the weirdest device of all, and it is rather fitting that Goldberg should have won a Pulitzer Prize for his comment on it. The drawing itself is Goldbergian to an extreme. There is something fantastically and dangerously hilarious about the family out in the yard; and the bomb itself is obviously not balanced. It is plainly too far over the edge, and the fact that it has failed to plunge into the abyss must be attributed to a defiance of gravity and logic which marks even Goldberg's earliest sports drawings in San Francisco.

1949: "Who, Me?" by Lute Pease, in the Newark *Evening News*. This was the best of many cartoons touching on a specific incident in American domestic life. John L. Lewis' coal miners had threatened a strike, and the government invoked the Taft-Hartley law against the miners' unions, on the grounds that a strike would cripple the national economy. Lewis flatly denied that the strike would have any harmful effect on the economy, which inspired Pease's cartoon. Pease was fortunate that Lewis was a well-known figure, as commonly caricatured as Andrew Jackson or Theodore Roosevelt in earlier eras. There was no problem of identification, and the innocence of the remark "Who, me?" contrasted in fine irony with the

REUBEN L. GOLDBERG.   New York *Sun.*

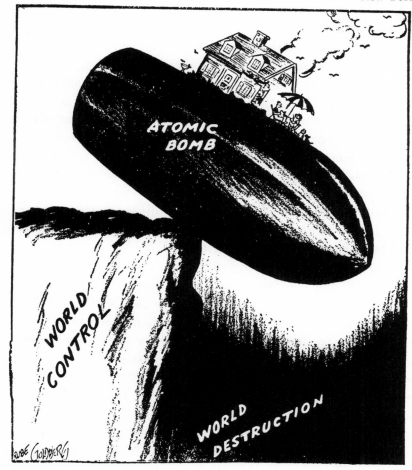

"Peace Today."

Pulitzer Prize 1948.   Courtesy of Reuben L. Goldberg.

aggressive appearance and policies for which Lewis had become famous. Pease was over eighty when he won the prize. Born in 1869, in Nevada, he had gone to the Klondike during the gold rush of 1898. He remained in the northwest— Nome and Portland— until 1912, and in 1914 he was hired as cartoonist for the Newark *Evening News*. Thirty-five years later he was still displaying imagination and artistic skills which were the envy of men half a century younger.

1950: "All Set for a Super Secret Session in Washington," by James T. Berryman, in the Washington *Evening Star*. This was one of the funniest of the Pulitzer Prize cartoons. Television had been a household institution for only two or three years, but even within that short span several Congressional committees had managed to make idiots of themselves in what looked suspiciously like a search for publicity. A terrible problem arose: on the one hand, if a committee's work were sufficiently important, its deliberations should be secret. On the other hand, no Congressman or Senator has yet been known to hide his light under a bushel, and now there was the intoxicating prospect of reaching twenty or thirty million people at once. This cartoon was Berryman's sardonic comment on the state of affairs. It is one of the five or six in the series in which no figure, human or animal, appears. The paraphernalia and the caption say all that needs to be said, and make this a masterful example of the art. James Berryman is Clifford Berryman's son and is a native Washingtonian (D.C.). His first work was for a newspaper in New Mexico, but he has remained without regional attachments, and must always be aware that the massive complexity of our federal government is peering over his shoulder.

1951: "Hats," by Reginald W. Manning, from the Arizona *Republic*. Here was a stark, powerful use of the simplest symbolism, reflecting two age-old American attributes— a distrust of diplomats, and an absolute reverence for any American boy who had given his life for his country. It was an echo of the old cry "Direct action beats legislation," but it was also imbued with a sense of terrible futility: the direct action must produce only death, and the legislation was either useless or untrustworthy by definition. Manning's position was not that of a pacifist— he has a son who was a jet pilot in the USAF, of whom he is quite properly proud. This cartoon was another frustrated cry: when would the formal machinations of supposedly civilized men finally produce some tangible result that might be measured in human lives saved? Manning had struck the right chord. He was born in 1905 in Kansas City, Missouri, but moved to Arizona when still adolescent. Before he was thirty he had gone into newspaper art, taking a job with the Arizona *Republic*. He is syndicated (by McNaught) to many newspapers; any syndicate would obviously be proud to have him.

1952: "Classified!" by Fred L. Packer, in the New York *Daily Mirror*. This is another funny cartoon, and it may be the most controversial of the whole series so far. It shows an irate gentleman facing a corps of reporters and photographers, and saying angrily, "Your editors ought to have more sense than to print what I say." There is one school of thought, dignified and conservative, which holds that the angry figure is simply a bureaucrat representing the ingrown attitudes of government officials, and that the cartoon itself is a blast at the government's perhaps excessive policy of classifying occasional and often innocuous material. There is probably more courtesy than truth in this interpretation. The angry figure bears a startling resemblance to former President Harry Truman, who was known for a tendency to speak his mind and perhaps to regret it later. He was known for many other qualities far more commendable, but it may have been that a few of his outbursts in 1951 occasioned this graphic jibe. In any case, Fred Packer's politics are his own business, and this is a good, funny cartoon. Packer was born in Hollywood in 1886, and his career resembles that of several West Coast artists. He worked for the Los Angeles *Examiner* and then for the San Francisco *Call*; then he left journalism altogether for

REGINALD W. MANNING.   Phoenix *Arizona Republic*.

Pulitzer Prize 1951.   *"Hats"*

Courtesy of Reginald W. Manning and McNaught Syndicate, Inc.

EDWARD D. KUEKES.   Cleveland *Plain Dealer*.

"Aftermath."

Pulitzer Prize 1953.   Courtesy of Edward D. Kuekes and the Cleveland *Plain Dealer*.

a while, returning to it in 1932, when he began to do political cartoons for the New York *Journal*. Shortly he was switched to another newspaper, the *Mirror*, where he performed brilliantly for years.

1953: "Aftermath," by Edward D. Kuekes, in the Cleveland *Plain Dealer*. Here is another in which a pointed opinion is expressed through dialogue and skillful drawing. The point of the cartoon has been made before, usually in political prose, but this is the finest graphic statement of it that we have had. Whatever one's opinion on the minimum voting age, Kuekes has expressed his own, and done it with great force in a simple, uncluttered cartoon. The simplicity of the cartoon is not surprising; it is one of Kuekes's firmest opinions that economy is the key to good cartooning. Kuekes was born in Pittsburgh, was brought up in Ohio, and studied, after college, at the Cleveland School of Art and the Chicago Academy of Fine Arts. He went to work for the Cleveland *Plain Dealer* in 1921, first as a commercial artist and then as political cartoonist. The *Plain Dealer*, like the Chicago *Tribune*, occasionally runs cartoons on page one; Kuekes has been thus complimented by his newspaper over two hundred times.

1954: "You Were Always a Great Friend of Mine, Joseph," by Herbert L. Block, in the Washington *Post and Times-Herald*. This was Herblock's second award, and it displayed brilliantly his maturing as a political cartoonist. By 1953 Herblock was a national figure; his work was syndicated to over two hundred newspapers through the country. His drawing had become distinctive— there was no mistaking a Herblock for anyone else's work. Herblock had come to express himself more and more freely, in writing as well as in art; one publisher has reported that it was a great chore to get Herblock to sit down and write anything but that once it was written no editing was necessary. His cartoons seem to have that same attribute. The

HERBERT L. BLOCK.   Washington *Post*.

"You Were Always a Great Friend of Mine, Joseph."
Pulitzer Prize 1954.   Courtesy of Herbert L. Block and the Washington *Post*.

excessive or redundant line is never present. His portraiture is absolutely sure; world figures are immediately identifiable, whatever their position and size in the cartoon. More than that, his sense of caricature is keen. His bespectacled, stocky Washington bureaucrat is unmistakable; so are his conservative Senators, his big businessmen, his harassed private citizens. Since his arrival at the Washington *Post* he has had the same agreement with that newspaper's management which Fitzpatrick had with the St. Louis *Post-Dispatch:* he would never be asked to tailor his own opinions to fit those of the newspaper. He never has; but, like Fitzpatrick, he has found a home with an organ whose attitudes are almost always congenial to his own. There are occasional conflicts; they are taken as evidence of journalistic independence, and the *Post* is the more respected for tolerating them. Herblock is uncompromising, and a master craftsman. He is generally called a "liberal," although he rejects the appellation on the grounds that he does not know what a liberal is. Certainly he has attacked imbecility and pomposity rather than any specific political group. If his predilection is to go after conservatives, he has nevertheless whaled away at a good many public figures usually considered liberal.. Among his books are *The Herblock Book* (1952), *Herblock's Here and Now* (1955), *Herblock's Special for Today* (1958). There is a good deal of mighty fine writing in them, and as a whole they probably represent the best collection of political cartoons that the country has ever seen.

1955: "How Would Another Mistake Help?" by Daniel R. Fitzpatrick, in the St. Louis *Post-Dispatch.* There is surely no greater tribute to Fitzpatrick's force and durability as a political cartoonist than the fact that his second Pulitzer Prize was awarded to him twenty-nine years after his first. The cartoon dates itself; Uncle Sam, bearing a rifle with six bayonets, is seen from behind, a relatively clear, whitish figure peering into a progressively darker murk against which are emblazoned the words "French Mistakes in Indochina." It was a comment on the possibility, bruited about Washington first and then about the whole country, that America would send troops to reinforce the flagging French divisions in Indochina. The Indochinese war was a true jungle-and-rice-paddy war; which is to say, it had been waged for years with little success by either side, and with a progressively deeper involvement in what appeared to be an insoluble deadlock. From 1945 on the United States had several times been forced to consider sending troops abroad. It is possible, for example, that a massive involvement on our part would have kept China from going Communist, or at least delayed the outcome of the issue until the situation had changed ideologically. In Korea we had made the decision to send troops and acted vigorously upon it; but public opinion was hardly as unanimous in approving that action as it had been in supporting the war effort after 1941. Time and again— in the Middle East, in Latin America, in Hungary, most recently in Tibet— situations had arisen in which government officials were required at least to consider the possibility of sending American troops abroad. The temptation to pull others' chestnuts out of the fire has been constant and it has been exacerbated by the strong American opposition to communism everywhere. But then what is strategically desirable may be tactically idiotic, and a great majority of Americans felt that any physical involvement in Indochina would simply be suicidal. Fitzpatrick summed up their attitude, and did it quite simply.

Three years after winning his second prize, Fitzpatrick announced that he was about to retire. A career spanning almost half a century, in which Fitzpatrick rose to an eminence unsurpassed by a political cartoonist in our time, was coming to a close. There has been no career in our history more distinguished.

1956: "Achilles," by Robert York, in the Louisville *Times*. Here is one of the most original drawings in the whole series: not a figure, but half a figure, and one drawn with a maximum of suggestion and a minimum of realism. The demi-figure, fat to the point of monstrosity, is wearing the suggestion of a loose cloak, labeled "Prosperity." From beneath the cloak protrude a pair of trousered legs; and the point of the cartoon lies in the bare feet set off by a cluster of toes behind which the heel is labeled "Farm Prices." The use of a classic symbol is, as Gerald Johnson pointed out, rather daring in a progressively more "illiterate" age. But we expect that the committee of selection, as well as a large part of the mature reading public, had no difficulty in placing the allusion. York is a native of Minnesota, where he was born in 1909. He attended the Chicago Academy of Fine Arts, and his first job in newspaper cartooning was with the Nashville *Banner*. Two decades ago he moved over to the Louisville *Times*. He may not have been surprised at winning a Pulitzer Prize, but he was surely somewhat astonished at winning it with a relatively apolitical cartoon in a hot election year.

1957: "Wonder Why My Parents Didn't Give Me Salk Shots," by Tom Little, in the Nashville *Tennessean*. This one was not political at all; it was not even truly satirical. It was instead openly sentimental and hortatory. Its burden is so poignant, and its warning so necessary, that it might serve permanently as a public-health poster. Little is a native of Tennessee, where he was born in 1898. He served as a reporter on the *Tennessean* and then became its city editor— a rather unusual background for a political cartoonist. Not many cartoonists have been able to rise to eminence in two professions, but Little has done it with a flourish.

1958: "The Thinker," by Bruce Shanks, in the Buffalo *Evening News*. This has occasionally been called, incorrectly, an anti-labor cartoon. In resorting to a variation of Rodin's protypical cogitator, Shanks retained all the power and nobility in that figure. His sympathies lie quite obviously with the man who works for a living, and his indignation is directed at the thief who will steal hard-earned money in the name of the labor movement. Corruption in the higher ranks of union leaders became a hot domestic issue in 1957, and from the very beginning there were voices warning us not to confuse the racketeer with the workingman. Shanks expressed the position cogently and seriously. He was born in Buffalo and has always lived there. His career with the *Evening News* began in 1933, and he became its editorial cartoonist in 1951. Seven years is not a long wait for a Pulitzer Prize; once more we offer congratulations to a craftsman who brought home the bacon in quick time.

1959: "I won the Nobel Prize for Literature. What was your Crime?" by William H. Mauldin, in the St. Louis *Post-Dispatch*. Mauldin's second award, less than a year after he succeeded Fitzpatrick; between them the two artists have brought three Pulitzer Prizes to the *Post-Dispatch*, and represent a total of four.

Tom Little.   Nashville *Tennessean*.

"Wonder Why My Parents Didn't Give Me Salk Shots."

Pulitzer Prize 1957.   Courtesy of Tom Little and the Nashville *Tennessean*.

BILL MAULDIN.   St. Louis *Post-Dispatch.*

"I won the Nobel Prize for literature. What was your crime?"

Pulitzer Prize 1959.   Courtesy of Bill Mauldin and the St. Louis *Post-Dispatch.*

Those were the prize winners. Any observer will find some he thinks excellent and some he would just as soon pass over; some with whom he agrees, some with whom he disagrees. In a sense, the prize system is unfair. In any of those years there were probably other cartoons as memorable. Some of the prize winners themselves, as we have noted, did better work than the cartoons for which they won the award.

The trouble is that American political cartooning is of an extremely high quality; there are probably fifty men working right now who have turned out cartoons as good as most of the prize winners. Men like William Crawford of the Newark *News*, whose forceful, boldly drawn editorial cartoons are reproduced almost every week in other newspapers than his own. Men like Hesse of the St. Louis *Globe-Democrat*, who has had what may have been the professional misfortune of competing directly with Daniel Fitzpatrick and Bill Mauldin. Or Carmack of the *Christian Science Monitor*, whose genteel, dignified expostulations have combatted stupidity wherever it appeared. Men like Poinier of the Detroit *Times* or Yardley of the Baltimore *Sun*, more a descendant of European than American cartoonists. Or men who achieved only local fame, like Billy Ireland of the

Seven favorites by seven of the great ones. Any one of these— or of dozens more by dozens of artists— might have taken a Pulitzer Prize. That they

BILL MAULDIN. St. Louis *Post-Dispatch*.

"Me? I'm the little kid you used to call a gook."

Courtesy of Bill Mauldin and the St. Louis *Post-Dispatch*.

HERBERT L. BLOCK. Washington *Post*.

"Fire!"

Courtesy of Herbert L. Block and the Washington *Post*.

did not is evidence, not of poor judgment by the board of selection, but of the astonishingly high level of American political cartooning.

DANIEL R. FITZPATRICK.   St. Louis *Post-Dispatch*.

"The Supreme Court of Something or Other."

Courtesy of Daniel R. Fitzpatrick and the St. Louis *Post-Dispatch*.

WALT KELLY.   New York *Star*.

Courtesy of Walt Kelly.

Columbus *Dispatch* or, somewhat later, Francis Dahl of the Boston *Traveller*, whose hybrids— his cartoons are usually a cross between the comic strip and the editorial cartoon— have amused New Englanders for years and who has only recently become known to a wider public through his work in *The Saturday Evening Post*, called "The Greenwoods." The list is almost endless.

Among all these editorial cartoonists John Fischetti of NEA is the only regular contributor to *Punch*, the British humor magazine. He is also— much more important, from our point of view— the most widely printed

KARL HUBENTHAL.   Los Angeles *Examiner*.

"*Speaking of Orbits.*"

Courtesy of Karl Hubenthal and the Los Angeles *Examiner*.

WILLIAM CRAWFORD.   Newark (N.J.) *News*.

Courtesy of Bill Crawford and the Newark (N.J.) *News*.

editorial cartoonist in the United States, appearing in over five hundred newspapers. He once worked for Walt Disney; he did political cartoons for the Chicago *Sun-Times* before the war; he was on the *Stars and Stripes* during the war; and over the years he has illustrated many books. He is quite outspoken in his cartoons, and this is perhaps another advantage of the syndicated cartoonist: most clients— i.e., newspapers— subscribe to more than one syndicate service, and can choose their daily offering from among three or four possibilities. It is therefore unnecessary for the syndicated man to adjust his thoughts to a newspaper's policy. (Political cartoonists rarely do so. Most of them, like Herblock, have complete freedom to express themselves, and many of them are hired by newspapers with whose policies they are in basic agreement to begin with.)

One of Fischetti's predecessors with NEA was the late Dorman H. Smith, a craftsman of the first rank, whose work was also sent out to over five hundred newspapers. Smith has been acknowledged as the most widely reproduced editorial cartoonist, over the years, in the history of the profession.

Many of the best men in the trade appear in only one newspaper, but are hardly less influential on that score. Carey Orr, whose work appears in color on page one of the Chicago *Tribune* (and whose niece Martha drew

341

"The Scepter."

Courtesy of John Fischetti and the NEA Service, Inc.

the original *Apple Mary)* is one; so are Art Wood of the Pittsburgh *Press*; Warren King, who alternates with Batchelor in the New York Daily *News*; Dowling in the New York *Herald Tribune*; Scott Long and Justus in Minneapolis; Alexander in Philadelphia; Lou Grant in Oakland; Baldy in Atlanta; Hugh Haynie in Louisville; Dobbins in Boston; Yoes in San Diego; Karl Hubenthal in Los Angeles, already mentioned as a sports cartoonist; and Ed Marcus, whose work appeared in the New York *Times* for fifty years before his retirement in 1958.

The Pulitzer Prize means a great deal to the public. Of at least equal importance to newspapermen is the award made annually by Sigma Delta

Chi, the fraternity of professional journalism. An award winner knows that he has been honored by a jury of his peers. Here are the recipients of that honor since 1942 (many of them also Pulitzer Prize Winners):

1942— Jacob Burck
1943— Charles Werner
1944— Henry Barrow
1945— Reuben L. Goldberg (!)
1946— Dorman H. Smith
1947— Bruce Russell
1948— Herbert Block
1949— Herbert Block
1950— Bruce Russell
1951— Herbert Block and Bruce Russell
1952— Cecil Jensen
1953— John Fischetti
1954— Cal Alley
1955— John Fischetti
1956— Herbert Block
1957— Scott Long
1958— Clifford H. Baldowski (Baldy).

That there are so many excellent practicing editorial cartoonists— and that we must apologize for having omitted a large number of them— is a healthy sign. Unlike sports cartooning, political cartooning has thrived in the modern world. Photographs can show us what happened, but it takes a good political cartoon to show us *why* it happened, a question which rarely arises in sporting circles. Editorial cartoonists as a whole are one of the most articulate professional groups in America. Day after day they publish pertinent, moralistic comment on a thoroughly confused world; their function is a simplification of the columnists' function, but because their medium is graphic they strike hard. When a man becomes a political cartoonist it is not simply because he wants to draw: it is also because he has ideas, and feels that he must express them. From the earliest days of the republic the cartoonist has been one of our most vociferous critics. More often than not, his warnings have been ignored; what kind of country— or world— we might have if the processes of government were more influenced by them, heaven only knows, but of one thing we are sure: the cartoonist, exposed to the public eye daily, is an honest critic, and when he has a suggestion to make, it is out of concern for the safety and health of the country that he makes it. We all take these men for granted; we open our daily newspaper, there is the usual cartoon, and we absorb its lesson without realizing that we owe thanks to the teacher. Teachers these men are, and whether they think of themselves as such or not, they are guardians of the common weal. More power and long life to them.

CHAPTER XI

Comics: The Lyric Clowns

POETRY IS A CYNICAL, VIRULENT MOUSE heaving a fresh-baked brick at an adoring cat, often under the bemused and despairing eye of a canine policeman.

If that contention could be justified briefly, there would be no need for this book. The trouble is that there is a vast area of the Inexplicable in at least half a dozen of the more successful strips. Most strips please their fans for clear and definable reasons, but these few giants of lyric irrationality require more than simple statements of approval; their fans tend to flounder a bit, to grimace and eventually to talk with their hands in an almost always unsuccessful attempt to get the point across. They have committed the gross error of yielding to a mystique. There is no arguing with a mystique.

Probably the first man who ever made sense in writing about George Herriman's *Krazy Kat* was Gilbert Seldes, whose witty and admiring treatment of the strip in *The Seven Lively Arts* remains true and a pleasure to read. The power of *Krazy Kat* is made evident to some degree by the fact that to the many intellectuals who should have a far better idea of Mr. Seldes' talents and accomplishments, he remains most famous for his advocacy of *Krazy Kat* as the one comic strip of the 1920s which was truly art.

Herriman himself is remembered almost always for *Krazy Kat*; a few connoisseurs recall the Dingbat family and Baron Bean, but most of Herriman's early work and some of his later hilarious experiments have been almost entirely forgotten. Born in New Orleans in 1881, Herriman seems never to have been far, professionally speaking, from a newspaper office; when he died in Hollywood in 1944 few obituaries recorded the fact that his first comic strip, *Lariat Pete*, had appeared in 1903 in the San Francisco *Chronicle* and many other newspapers— or that he had published full-color Sunday pages, not as a series but complete in themselves, as early as 1901. He was only warming up. By 1906 he had created his first

One of HERRIMAN's first published pages. It appeared in the Philadelphia *Sunday Press* of December 8, 1901, when the artist was only twenty years old. Courtesy of Ernest McGee.

Krazy Kat, 1930. Not snow, nor rain, nor hail, nor gloom of night stays that brick—or justice. © King Features Syndicate, Inc.

Krazy Kat, 1931. A cigar-smoking, top-hatted duck is illogical; Krazy Kat isn't. © King Features Syndicate, Inc.

major zany character: *Major Ozone, the Fresh Air Fiend,* who appeared in gorgeous irrational color in the San Francisco *Sunday Call*. With it Herriman ran a secondary strip called *Rosy Posy Mama's Girl*. It was good later on that he had learned to experiment with a second strip, which *Krazy Kat* originally was; and Major Ozone is Herriman's first sweeping bow in the direction of the *non sequitur*— or perhaps of the *sequitur ad infinitum*. Major Ozone had only one idea (as Ignatz would be a monomaniac, and the thieves later on in *Stumble Inn*, a magnificent piece of hilarity from 1926); he needed air. There was not enough air inside even with the windows open. There was not enough air outside, so close was the press of nature and humanity. At one point in 1906 Major Ozone took to a balloon. Given the importance of fresh air, there is nothing illogical in any of the Major's acts. That only an idiot would give it so much importance is a proposition we put to one side; we are overjoyed at the idea of the strip, and Herriman's drawing— not yet anywhere near his best— is plenty good enough to keep us grinning foolishly. By 1909 Herriman was doing a daily strip called *Mary* for the New York *Journal* (he was with Hearst and King Features all his life, by the way) which was nothing special as a strip but in which appeared one of the first superb touches of the Herriman magic, which Coulton Waugh very astutely noticed. A minute box within the main strip showed a small cat, about to attack a bowl of milk, looking up politely and asking "Sir?" of a dog holding his stomach in agony. The

346

A Sunday *Krazy Kat* of 1936. Puns, phonetic fancies, irregular panels, and the inevitable dénouement. © King Features Syndicate, Inc.

Krazy Kat, 1938. The brick had been in service for twenty-five years. The last panel demonstrates more logic. ⓒ King Features Syndicate, Inc.

dog is saying, "Touch it not, Kat, touch it not, somebody's doped it with fresh paint."

The pussy and the pup, obviously prototypes of Krazy and the Offissa, survived *Mary*, which only lasted a year or so. In 1910 she disappeared, replaced by the *Dingbat Family*, which later became *The Family Upstairs*. The Dingbats themselves were a great inspiration: the action of the strip revolved around not the Dingbats, but the family upstairs, who never appeared. This kind of "ricochet rococo" cannot be handled by everyone, and under its beautiful insanity lies that relief from reality which has always made us so grateful to the Herrimans, the Rube Goldbergs, the Milt Grosses.

On July 26, 1910, Herriman added a narrow strip beneath *The Family Upstairs* in which were a mouse, a stone and a Kat. Initiating a career that would last almost thirty-five years, Mouse picked up stone, heaved it at Kat, scored and left Kat paw to head. A month later the narrow strip had become independent and permanent, and in 1911 it achieved its own title, *Krazy Kat and Ignatz*. By 1913 it was simply *Krazy Kat* and had displaced the Dingbat family. People were beginning to notice Herriman, though not yet to suspect him of any genius.

Yet the magic weaving ("wivvin") had begun. The metaphysical loom on which the weaving took place was a blatant, monstrous paradox. The strip's basic population was a dog named Offissa Pup, Krazy Kat herself and Ignatz Mouse. In an astonishing reversal of nature the dog loved the cat, and the cat loved the mouse. Honest disenchantment was supplied by Ignatz Mouse, who loved nobody, and whose cynical contempt for Offissa Pup and frustrated rage over Krazy Kat were the outward signs of the true outlaw.

A pattern soon became obvious. Offissa Pup was the guardian of the doorways, the keeper of the keys, the eternal, orderly, severely moral burgher. As such, he pursued an ideal, and in this comic strip his ideal was Krazy Kat. His pursuit of her had nothing to do with the usual American pursuit of the meaty breast or thigh. Krazy Kat's gender, for that matter, was eternally in doubt. Offissa Pup was pursuing what Krazy Kat represented: perfect, unreserved love. Unfortunately, perfect love cannot exist in a confining atmosphere of rules and regulations; Offissa Pup's jail was itself a thorough negation of love of any kind. Love is an awareness of the individual; it can exist purely only in an atmosphere of pure anarchy. Ignatz Mouse was a pure anarchist, and love therefore pursued him. Krazy Kat was forever incapable of loving Offissa Pup except as he existed within the universe encompassed by her vast emotion. Her immediate, reckless love was inevitably directed at Ignatz Mouse, unpredictable, individual and a moving force upon earth. Each brick heaved in an excess of fury by a mouse who had no idea where the root of his frustration lay was to Krazy Kat a love letter. We may, if we wish, reserve all our sympathies for Krazy Kat; to love traduced, rejected, ignored, contemned. But, as Gilbert Seldes and E. E. Cummings have made clear, the ultimate object of our sympathy must be neither Krazy nor the poor, bewildered booster, Offissa Pup, the guardian of civic pride, who has, after all, the approbation of society and the knowledge that he conforms to the rules he himself has laid down. The true object of our sympathies must be Ignatz Mouse, who is doomed never to understand that (much less why) his highest rages bring the most consummate ecstasies upon his victim-lover. Krazy Kat wins. Krazy Kat survives. Krazy Kat is love; love conquers all. Love shapes its own immutable destinies, and no constable, no marauder, no public vilification can prevail against it.

This theme, in one variation after another, imbued the American comic strip with poetry for thirty years. Herriman lived in Los Angeles all this time, but made periodic trips to Coconino County, Arizona, whose loneliness, arid stretches and monolithic rock formations pleased his essentially quiet soul. But not even Coconino County could escape the touch of his magic brush; mountains were provided with balconies, battleships steamed peacefully across absolutely dry deserts, needle formations became minarets. Geological and meteorological consistency were none of Herriman's concern; he was a poet, and poets change the world while the rest of us observe it. Herriman's moon, in a dark sky, might hang like a limp cheese; it might sit like a wooden shoe; it might hover like a bowl upside down,

Krazy Kat, 1942. An essay in pure frustration, with Krazy trapped by love. © King Features Syndicate, Inc.

disgorging heaven only knows what beneficence upon the earth below. Herriman carried this unconcern for reality to what may seem like an extreme; at one point he wrote to his employer, William Randolph Hearst, suggesting that he, Herriman, was being overpaid, and that perhaps a reduction in salary was in order. Hearst naturally wrote back that Herriman must concern himself only with the comic strip, leaving financial details to Hearst himself.

Herriman's drawing style reflected perfectly his basic attitude. His frames, on the Sunday pages, were rarely in orderly sequence. They lay at angles to one another; they disappeared; they reappeared where they were not needed. Similarly, the identifying name of the strip might appear where it belonged, the top line; then again it might bob up somewhere in the middle of the strip; and as often as not the words Krazy and Kat were separated by several panels.

We have accused Herriman of abjuring reality. And yet what makes him great, and what made his strip great, was an awareness— no one knows how he came by it— of the truth that escapes most of us all our lives. Most of us yearn for the truth of love, and those who swore by *Krazy Kat* probably found some little bit of it in the strip. But most of us are afraid to face love in everyday, prosaic terms— the awful responsibility of giving oneself entirely! Fantasy is the perfect way to find it. We laugh without blushing; we make a small private obeisance; and we are charged with none of the embarrassment that good, solid, hardheaded, right-thinking American citizens must inevitably feel when face to face with an emotional absolute.

When Herriman died in 1944 his editors knew better than to search for a successor. Here, if ever, was a marriage of the man and the material. It was poetry— i.e., thought— that made *Krazy Kat* great; and no other human being could have been expected to think like George Herriman. In the truest sense of the word he was a genius. Between him and the universe of men there was a kind of love affair, and the allegory he gave the world was unique. With him the world took on a new dimension; without him it was reduced to reality. There will be no more *Krazy Kat*, and we are all of us the losers; but how much we have gained because he existed at all!

For a few years after Herriman's death, fantasy and the intellect lay relatively neglected. Crockett Johnson's *Barnaby* carried the full load (more about him later), and syndicates seemed reluctant to commit themselves to anything outside the safely traditional categories of family, adventure and slapstick of the human variety.

As always, however, there was a beady-eyed alchemist lurking in a shadowed corner of the world of art meditating his own special magic and waiting for an opportunity to bewitch an unsuspecting public. This man was not a recluse; he was very much of the world, and reacted vigorously to its foibles and idiocies. His name was Walter Crawford Kelly; and at Herriman's death he was thirty-three years old, with several active and dubiously successful careers already behind him.

Kelly was born in Philadelphia, but moved to Bridgeport, Connecticut, as an infant and was there educated. Having done casual reporting for the Bridgeport *Post* as a high-school student, he stayed on with them as a reporter, writer and part-time artist. He had a fling during the depression as an investigator for the Bridgeport Welfare Department, but in 1935 his love of cartooning reasserted itself and he moved to Hollywood, where for the next six years he was an animator with the Walt Disney Studios. He lived through some hectic and productive years on the West Coast— but they were productive for Disney and not for Kelly. By 1941 he was back east.

He spent part of the war as a civilian with the Army's foreign-language unit, and, oddly enough, it was there that he first fell in love with the Georgia dialect. (He never saw Okefenokee Swamp until 1955.) In 1942, among many of his odd labors, he drew animal comics (in comic-book form) for the Western Printing and Lithographing Company in New York. In the first issue there was a five-page episode called "Albert the Alligator" in which there appeared a possum named Pogo, who looked not at all like the Pogo who later became famous. Pogo appeared again briefly in the same medium in 1943, 1944, 1945, 1946— by which time both he and Albert had evolved considerably toward what they are today.

Kelly had also evolved considerably toward what he is today. He had never been one to neglect the world around him and now he would begin his indirect assault upon it. The first few issues of *Albert and Pogo*, a one-shot comic book which replaced *Animal Comics* in which the five-page episodes appeared, ran to about half a million copies. The first appeared in 1946, the second in 1947. After the appearance of the first few editions of *Animal Comics*, when it was apparent that this publication was dead, a survey was made to find out why it had collapsed. Kelly himself cornered children and asked them questions. And the answers all added up to the same thing: "That comic book didn't have no action in it. Nobody shot nobody. It was full of mice in red and blue pants. It stunk."

In 1947–8 occurred two events which provided turning points in Kelly's so far checkered life. First, the newspaper *PM* folded. *PM* had been a stronghold of radical (or independent) journalism and of free journalistic experimentation. Among its comic strips had been Crockett Johnson's *Barnaby*, *Claire Voyant* and *Patoruzu*, a South American import, which showed elements of fantasy. (Many of *PM's* experiments were not, of course, limited to the comics page.)

PM might have gone, but its spirit lingered on. In June 1948 half a dozen men of good will, including some of the best journalists in New York, founded the New York *Star*, which would succeed *PM* on the inde-

pendent left wing of the New York newspaper spectrum. Kelly had been doing commercial comics, but his reputation both as a man and as an artist was too good and too widespread for him to go long unnoticed, and he was shortly offered a job as art director, political cartoonist and editorial adviser to the New York *Star*. He accepted.

Two phases of his career were now almost in conflict. As art director he ordered himself to produce a daily *Pogo* comic strip; as political cartoonist it was necessary for him to produce a daily editorial cartoon. This was the summer and fall of 1948, an election year. Harry Truman was running against Thomas E. Dewey, and the *Star* was unequivocally anti-Dewey. Kelly's cartoons, representing Governor Dewey as a Mechanical Man, caused some stir in New York, ripples of which reached the hinterland. Granted that the *Star's* circulation was limited, Kelly was still coming into at least local prominence; it would not be long before he achieved national fame. Unfortunately the *Star* lasted only until January 28, 1949. Kelly lost not only his berth as a political cartoonist, but also his one outlet for *Pogo*. When the *Star* folded, *Pogo* was homeless. On the other hand, he had made such a mark in the world of comics that the *Pogo* comic book, put out by the Dell Publishing Co., was revived about this time. It was first issued in 1949 as *Pogo Comics*, Issue Number One. The press run was half a million copies.

Kelly had been to see syndicate people. Many of them professed to be amused but were absolutely sure that the general public (as opposed to highly perceptive syndicate editors) would not understand this strip. One editorial director, a woman, insisted that her syndicate was no longer interested in animal strips— using these words: "We're not buying any of those duck strips."

When the break came it was from outside. In the spring of 1949 syndicate president Robert Hall asked Kelly to drop around. Hall himself liked *Pogo*. Moreover, he thought the public would like it. Hall could give the strip an immediate start in the New York *Post*. The strip did start in the *Post* in May 1949. Only three or four papers took the strip during that first period. During the summer of 1949— and summer is a notoriously slow period in any mass-circulation medium— *Pogo* attracted a few readers, but his career was not spectacular. Hall had faith in the strip; Kelly was less optimistic. In the fall, however, a few editors took the strip. It held up well. Kelly said at the time that as Pogo picked up newspapers "his fans increased."

They increased not only in number but in enthusiasm. Intellectuals with friends who had not yet caught on to *Pogo* began to gloat, secure in the knowledge that they were "insiders." Kelly himself, relatively unimpressed, went happily about his business, amusing himself vastly with the Georgia dialect and with the ludicrousness of human foibles in animal form. Issues Two and Three of *Pogo Comics* appeared. In 1951 Issues Four, Five, Six, Seven and Eight of *Pogo Comics* were published. The total press run was two and one half million.

The success story after that was spectacular, but, like many success stories, it is less interesting in itself than the man or the product. After slightly more than a year's syndication, *Pogo* was appearing in 126 American newspapers. It was, according to a poll by *The Saturday Review of Literature*, in seventh place in popularity among comic strips. By 1952 it was estimated that it had thirty-seven million readers in over 225 newspapers. By 1954 the number of newspapers was 415; by 1956, 450; by 1958, over 500. Some fifty million people enjoyed *Pogo* every day. But the end was not yet. Simon and Schuster published *Pogo* in book form — sometimes collections of strips and sometimes original work done by Kelly. Beginning with the original *Pogo* in 1951, some ten or a dozen

Howland Owl and Churchy la Femme in the practice of nuclear horticulture. © 1950 Post-Hall Syndicate, Inc.

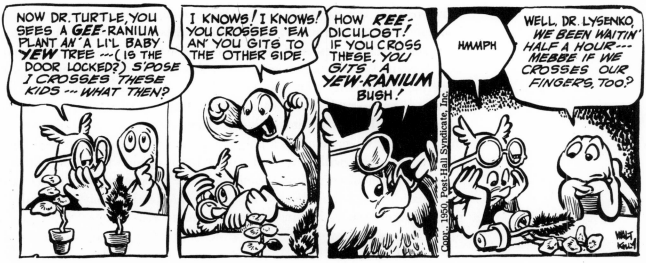

Howland Owl, Beauregard, and Pup Dog warming up for the Orpheum. © 1950
Post-Hall Syndicate, Inc.

volumes have been published, with titles like *Pogo Papers, Incompleat Pogo, Potluck Pogo, The Pogo Sunday Book.*

One of the titles was *I Go Pogo,* reminiscent of one of the more automatic and hypnotic political chants in American life. *I Go Pogo* was the little possum's entry onto the political scene. Like many incongruities, this one was quickly seized upon by certain incongruous elements in American life, such as college boys. Pogo was a candidate much against his own will — his friends had pushed him into it— but he did not lack for supporters. Political rallies were held on campuses; one of the most noteworthy was in Harvard Square. Kelly himself appeared briefly on behalf of his candidate, but something was missing. Perhaps it was a big-city political organization. In any case, Pogo was not elected to public office, which is just as well; it leaves him free to express himself without the restraints necessarily imposed by responsibility to an electorate.

Well, what was all this nonsense? Who was Pogo, to begin with? He is the central figure in the strip; he has been described by Kelly himself as "the reasonably patient, soft-hearted, naïve, friendly little person we all think we are." But Kelly's mythical Okefenokee is inhabited by well over one hundred other creatures, ranging from Albert the Alligator, urbane, cigar-smoking, a ladies' man, down to the "low types" like Chil' Bug and Boll Weevil. What is so amazing about this fauna is not its size but its variety of personality traits. No two of Kelly's animals or insects can be confused. Each stands alone, each has his own way of speaking, his own mannerisms. This is an incredible gallery. And Kelly does incredible things with it. When he needs a political allegory, somewhere in those one hundred creatures will be a symbol of tyranny; somewhere a symbol of resistance; somewhere a dupe; somewhere the innocent victim of society's machinations. And the allegory need not be political; it may be social, it may be purely domestic. Miz Beaver, for instance, is the perfect example of the harried housewife, eternally at her laundry, eternally in search of her wandering "tads."

354

Of course it would be wrong to assume that all the fantastic and hilarious Kelly characters stand for something. Most of them exist to make us laugh; that is their primary function, which is as it should be. On the other hand, a good many intelligent observers have gone a little bit too far in exonerating Kelly from the charge of thoughtfulness. It is partially true, as Murray Kempton observed in a review, that Kelly "quite obviously peddles his wares for children, bright children, but children." It is also partially true, as David Dempsey wrote in a New York *Times* book review, that Kelly "is not really trying to say much of anything— he is simply restoring comic-strip art to the position of non-social, apolitical, unmythological and self-contained humor which it abdicated some years ago." These statements and others like them set *Pogo* squarely in the *Krazy Kat* tradition, with heavy emphasis on the use of English, incongruity and a dark, illogical logic which pervades the whole strip.

On the other hand, Kelly has things to say. He may say them in fun— his goal is always the laugh— but they are nevertheless by his lights true and often important. One of the early sequences in *Pogo*, in which Dr. Howland Owl, compounded of arrogance and stupidity, attempted to make an atom bomb, was much more than a simple play on pomposity; when the laughter died down the reader might realize that he had been exposed to several telling jabs at scientific egotism, atomic secrecy, foreign affairs and ultimately, by some weird process in which Kelly broadens our minds in spite of ourselves, at the laboriously evolved seventeenth- and eighteenth-century scientific method itself. Surely the trial of Albert the Alligator for having eaten a pup dog, another classic sequence, was not unrelated to certain idiocies current in the higher circles of the American government; it is to Kelly's everlasting credit that he was aware of the seriousness of these currents some four or five years before they finally came to a head. Kelly has concerned himself with international good will, with world peace; but his primary concern has always been laughter.

And when we think of the humor, we find the real Kelly. When Albert

Pogo is not all vaudeville; its hero often approaches wisdom. © 1957 Walt Kelly.

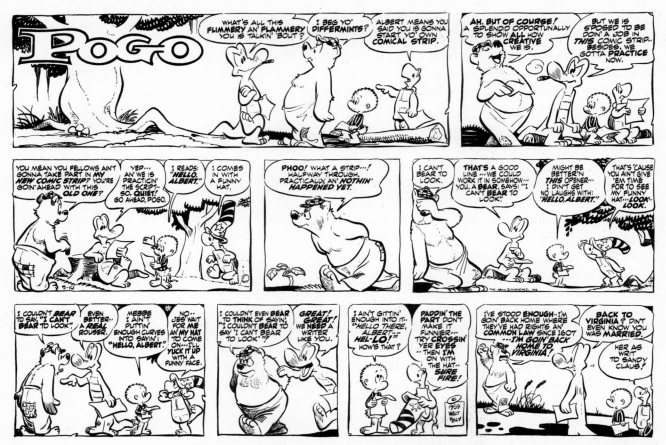

Thespis in the swamp; there is madness in The Method. Language here o'erleaps itself. © 1959 Walt Kelly.

the Alligator, clad, for the purposes of espionage, in fierce chin whiskers and an equally fierce set of rectangular spectacles and a hat that looks as though it came out of a burlesque show of the early 1920s, sees his reflection, his reaction (cigar puffing away) is "Dog my cats! A handsome man looks good in anything." Having changed to a straw hat, and in the process of serenading Miss Mlle. Hepzibah, a rather comely skunk, these are the lyrics he chooses: "I was eating some CHOP SUEY/with a lady in ST. LOUIE/when I sudden hears a POUNDIN at the door."

Kelly's knowledge of languages should not be underestimated, though it is by no means the whole story of Pogo. He was, we remember, a civilian employee in the Army's foreign-language unit during the war. Noting later that Kelly was a linguist, an *Editor and Publisher* in 1952 pointed out that "some of Pogo's special appeal may be in some of the almost hypnotic awareness of the dialogue, a synthesis of Elizabethan English, French, Negro and Freudian dialects, heavily interspersed with puns." There is no question but that this dialogue helps to create *Pogo's* particular mystique. There are touches of Perelman in the language (for example, taking metaphor literally). And Kelly is quite capable of creating an American type with a few lines of dialogue. Phineas T. Bridgeport, for example, the bear whose speech is always printed in circus-poster type, is the epitome of American showmanship. The swindling, card-playing mouse with the heart of gold is another perfect type, and his reminiscences of "Kansas City in 1928" are those of a particular species of American which includes W. C. Fields and every medicine-show operator in this country's history.

Kelly himself, as we might suspect, is a jovial man with a sharp eye for hypocrisy and pomposity. In some respects, his modesty knows no bounds. Tall and heavily built, he describes himself as "impressively flabby." Accurate data on the man are hard to obtain. Reports have drifted in, however, describing him as cheerful, humanistic and generous; he is married and has four children; in addition to the heavy schedule demanded by a daily and a Sunday comic strip, he has taken it upon himself to deliver a variety of speeches, some fifty to seventy-five every year in all parts of the country, on topics of local, national or cartooning interest. Energetic and gregarious, he was chosen cartoonist of the year for 1952 by the National Cartoonists Society, and was elected to the Society's presidency in 1954. It was during his term as president that the issue of censorship came to a head, and it is largely due to the efforts of Kelly (with Milton Caniff, who was chairman of the Society's ethics committee) that the comics world— chiefly the world of comic books— cleaned its own house, and that no legislative restraints, always abhorrent to American journalists, writers and artists, were imposed.

Kelly is, in a sense, a libertarian, possessed of a rich sense of fantasy. He seems aware that humor is the enemy of regimentation; that fantasy is the enemy of tyranny; and that the artist, whatever his medium, is the born, sworn enemy of complacency, stagnation and repression. He is no more "political" than Krazy Kat— ultimately Krazy encompasses all of politics and then some; he is simply more immediate, in the same great tradition.

In April 1942 the irrepressible and venturesome *PM* presented America with yet another surprise, this one stunning to the intellectuals. Its name was *Barnaby*, and it was drawn by Crockett Johnson, and within a year it had called forth a critical accolade unmatched by anything since *Krazy Kat*. (When it first appeared in book form, the following supplied extensive blurbs for the book jacket: William Rose Benét, Louis Untermeyer, Rockwell Kent, Norman Corwin and Ruth McKenney. Dorothy Parker was moved to remark, in a piece directed openly to Crockett Johnson, "I think, and I'm trying to talk calmly, that Barnaby and his friends and oppressors are the most important additions to American Arts and Letters in Lord knows how many years." Johnson was sufficiently appreciative to draw a special portrait of Mr. O'Malley to be printed with the note. O'Malley's

Destiny was occasionally on O'Malley's side— or perhaps Barnaby's. Copyright by Crockett Johnson.

remark was typical: "Mrs. Parker is a woman of rare discrimination, m'boy.")

The title role in this strip was played by a small, extremely winsome boy, burdened with normally obtuse parents and possessed of a fine, level head himself. But it was not Barnaby who enthralled the intellectuals; it was the aforementioned Mr. O'Malley.

Mr. O'Malley was Crockett Johnson's answer to Barnaby's request for a fairy godmother. He entered the strip via Barnaby's window, and his first words identified him as a last survivor of the species confidence man, as formerly found in the environs of Omaha, Nebraska, and Kansas City, Missouri. He was a fat little fellow as Irish as poteen, as talkative as a

The Fairy Godfather at work, in a shattering display of ineptitude. Copyright by Crockett Johnson.

O'Malley reminisces, in the best club-car manner. Obviously a man of infinite resource and varied experience. Copyright by Crockett Johnson.

stand-up comic with an option falling due and as brash as an actor's agent. Withal, he was no taller than Barnaby. Yet he filled the panel. When he arrived, presumably in a flashing glitter of small pink wings (they grew out of the region of his shoulderblades), he took over the scene entirely. Others might serve to move the action, to supply a hint of realism and, even more important, to supply an occasional leg of lamb and, most essential, a clear Havana cigar. This clear Havana cigar must not be neglected. When necessary, it served as O'Malley's magic wand. That events transpired rather in spite of this wand than because of it must be considered the fault of malign forces: elves, gnomes and leprechauns. It is not on record that any of these Havanas was ever ignited, but it is quite obvious that O'Malley refreshed his supply periodically, and it was stated unequivocally at one point that Mr. Baxter, Barnaby's father, maintained a supply of the best for visitors.

O'Malley was, as Ruth McKenney said, the most immoral character in all of the comics. He was the most egotistical, the most innocently arrogant, the most cocksure and— if we set aside a few favorable accidents— the most ineffectual. But his sheer, naked egocentricity, his unmitigated greed, were fascinating. Here was a being who could talk his way into or out of practically anything, in the accents of a master proprietor of a most successful shell game. His appetite for delicacies, including all manner of leftovers, was enormous; and there seemed to be no useful article or furnishing in the Baxter household to which he did not feel that his position gave him a sovereign right. His friends, too, were either disagreeable or inefficient. Chief among them were Lancelot McSnoyd, surely the most unpleasant leprechaun ever conceived, and Gus the Ghost, who wanted only peace and quiet, who fainted at the drop of a hat and who had never in his life (?) done a successful job of haunting.

The adventures of this ill-assorted group, including Barnaby himself and later a friend his own age named Jane, were an instant success. Johnson's drawing technique enhanced the fascination of the strip; he used only medium or thick lines, white space and solid black, and he achieved

Gus the Ghost, another magnificent failure, really cut out for the quiet life. Copyright by Crockett Johnson.

great economy by drawing in only what was absolutely necessary and leaving the rest to the reader's imagination— which, it is agreed, might already have been a touch strained. The drawing is actually more expressive of Barnaby himself than of anyone else in the strip. Barnaby is purity: childlike, trusting innocence. Never in the entire course of the strip did Mr. and Mrs. Baxter evince the slightest tendency to believe in O'Malley's existence; nor did they credit Gorgon, the talking dog, with any of the powers which were so evident to Barnaby. Barnaby is the pure ray of light against which adult reality and ghostly self-assertion throw their grotesque shadows.

Even the fact that the balloons were set in type, rather than handlettered, adds to the simplicity of the strip; that fact also leads us to an examination of Crockett Johnson, creator of this fantasy. His real name is David Johnson Leisk; he is a writer and illustrator of children's books; he is a typographer also; he lives in Rowayton, Connecticut; and he is called Dave by good friends. He has never been counted among the world's most outstandingly industrious men. He never did lettering well, for example; it was, to him, simply a laborious job. As a typographer he had a natural bias in favor of set type; what more natural than that he should reduce the time Barnaby took by probably one third, by the simple expedient of putting type rather than lettering into the balloons. Certainly the innovation did not bother his audience. *Barnaby* was an extremely successful strip wherever it ran, though it never achieved the high circulation of the more popular strips. O'Malley was no respecter of his employers; at one point, during the war, he came up with a perfect solution to the paper shortage. This was nothing more or less than the total elimination of comic strips. Statistics, he pointed out, indicated that ninety-six per cent of the readers read the comics. Would it be worth while to print the rest of the newspaper for the other four per cent? Of course not. The newspapers themselves would suspend publication; the presses could be sold for scrap— O'Malley's imagination ran riot.

What doomed *Barnaby* finally was Crockett Johnson's disinclination—to which he had and has a perfect right— for steady, day-in-day-out, monotonous creation. Within a few years he had turned the strip over to Jack Morley and Ted Ferro. Morley is an excellent artist, and there is practically no difference at all between his renditions and Johnson's; Ferro is a prolific and imaginative writer. The collaboration was a happy one— up to a point. It is possible that, like many collaborations, this one foundered on the rock of emphasis; was the drawing or the writing more important? At any rate, the strip began to slip. Probably it had lost that indefinable something which can only be supplied by the creator of a work of art and is generally missing in the work of his students. In an attempt to salvage the strip as a property Johnson took it back entirely, but it was too late and Johnson himself was not that seriously interested. One by one, newspapers dropped the strip. By 1954 it was gone. One of the most fanciful and entertaining of comic strips had lived a brief, explosive life, and would probably not be seen again.

Barnaby contrasted starkly with *Krazy Kat*, and yet its appeal was to the same kind of audience. The only real element of fantasy in *Krazy Kat* was the simple fact that animals spoke a relatively intelligible tongue. Beyond that, the glory of the strip lay in Herriman's drawing ability and in his tender, loving view of the world. But *Barnaby* contained a frankly supernatural element. It also contained more or less real people, and its animals were only incidental. Walt Kelly would take the poetic strip back to the world of animals; but a man named Charles Schulz would take it even further into the world of children, and would dispense with the supernatural.

In a profession well crowded with screwballs and eccentrics, Charles Schulz— as a man and not as a cartoonist— is something of a rarity. The fraternal literature of comic art (newsletters and such) abounds in anecdotes, some of which are true, some of which are apocryphal and many of which are racy. Legends of one cartoonist or another and his predilection for wine, women and song are not hard to come by. Dozens of cartoonists have achieved fame solely on the basis of the inferior quality of the cigars they smoked. Small groups of traveling artists have been known to awaken in the wrong city entirely. The rich and famous have been variously insulted, flattered and cajoled into releasing large quantities of food and drink, all this by conniving, fun-loving cartoonists. There have been no major scandals, but the general level of mischief has been high, and the banshee might rightly be considered a cartoonist's muse. But Charles Schulz defies all tradition.

He does not drink. He does not smoke. He does not swear, even at syndicate editors. He was born in 1923 in Minnesota, and is already a resounding success; yet his demeanor, clothes and environment remain modest. He is a lay preacher with a non-denominational group called The Church of God. He is very happily married and the father of four children. For years his hobbies have been golf, bridge, reading and listening to classical music. He loves his work and does not employ an assistant. A paragon: no eccentricities, no neuroses, no seething hatreds beneath the calm exterior.

By the wild logic of the comic-strip industry this man might be expected to turn out a strip replete with action, horror, mayhem and gore. But by a kinder, more human logic which occasionally makes itself felt even in man's most bizarre activities, Charles Schulz is the creator of *Peanuts*, which won the National Cartoonists Society's Reuben in 1956 as the comic strip of the year, and which has insinuated itself thoroughly into the daily routine of millions of readers.

Furthermore, Schulz cannot remember ever wanting to do anything else; he has always wanted to draw a comic strip. He began well: when he was still an infant a relative nicknamed him Sparky, after Billy DeBeck's famous Sparkplug. (Why a baby should be named for a horse is one of the few mysteries in Schulz's life.) He attended no academies or institutes,

The Adventures of Charlie Brown, with a typical dénouement. © 1958 United Feature Syndicate, Inc.

Winter sports among the reckless small fry. © 1952 United Feature Syndicate, Inc.

but took a correspondence course with Art Instruction, Inc. His work impressed them, and after the war he joined them as a cartooning instructor. He stayed for five years, free-lancing all the time. Much of his work appeared in *The Saturday Evening Post*, and among it was a series of panels he did for them depicting the strangely devious and sophisticated ways of what was apparently a group of three-, four-, and five-year-old children. These minuscule characters and their often intellectual didoes shortly became a weekly panel in the St. Paul *Pioneer-Press*.

Schulz seems to have had good luck with the U.S. Mails; he sold a strip idea, based on that panel, to United Feature Syndicate by mail. The idea was original; the strips were simple, and the gags were often uproariously funny. When they were not funny they were intriguingly offbeat. Possibly to the surprise of the syndicate, in no time at all a *Peanuts* coterie had formed; and within two years the strip was quietly roaring through the nation's newspapers.

What makes the strip so successful has been the subject of a good deal of speculation. A common remark is to the effect that these small fry react in the manner of adults, but that is highly inaccurate. Most often they react like children, but children possessed fully of the mid-twentieth-century culture. Their names give no real clue to their personalities, with one exception. The hero of the strip is Charlie Brown; two other male players are Schroeder and Linus; there are three young ladies, Patty and Violet and Lucy; and then there is the one exception, the aptly named Pigpen. These are not ordinary children, nor is their dog an ordinary puppy. Charlie Brown is possibly the most sensitive child ever to appear in a comic strip: he is capable of a Shakespearean variation in mood. It is important to note immediately that one of Schulz's great talents is expressing those moods accurately by means of no more than two or three lines— the eyebrows, perhaps, or the mouth, or the angle of the head.

As the strip's protagonist, Charlie Brown is much put upon. He is in most respects the leader of the little band; but he is in some respects totally ineffectual. His triumphs are few, his tragedies many. Does it rain, and does the ball club leave the field for a warmer, dryer setting? Charlie Brown alone, in a misguided burst of courage and team spirit, patrols the outfield, up to his knees in swampy rainwater, talking it up and pounding

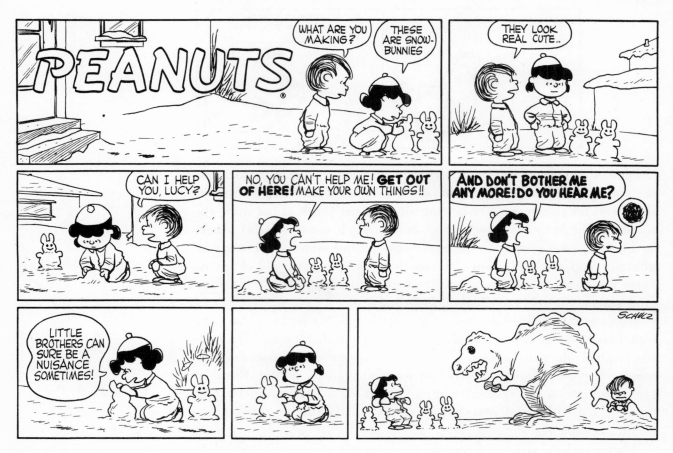

A Sunday *Peanuts*, with Lucy and Linus; or "Linus' Revenge." © 1958 United Feature Syndicate, Inc.

his mitt. Does a young lady fish for a compliment? Charlie Brown, occasionally quite articulate, will mangle one phrase so badly that the lady leaves him flat, at which Charlie presents to the world the features of utter frustration and despair. (When twenty members of the National Cartoonists Society went to Washington in May 1956 by joint invitation of the Treasury Department and the Department of Defense, Schulz was among them. All the cartoonists— and many, many others— had assisted the government in the sale of U.S. bonds, and during the festivities each of them was asked to give a brief chalk talk. When it was his turn Schulz explained that his drawing would not have much to do with the sale of bonds, but would pertain to baseball. As he sketched, he explained that

Charlie Brown as a representative of the best in free enterprise. © 1951 United Feature Syndicate, Inc.

Charlie Brown normally played the sewer position on the ball club. He was posted in an unlikely spot, and his function was to see that the ball did not go down the sewer.)

But Charlie is by no means the whole strip. The girls are much more than precocious women. They epitomize traditional femininity: they are by turns catty, lovable, unctuous, grasping and winsome, and they are *always* independent. They can accept even indifference from the boys, possibly because they know that an opportunity to outdo their competitors will soon arise— it is generally Charlie Brown who is outdone, in athletics, or outwitted, in conversation.

Charlie Brown as master of the manly art, with a happy ending. © 1951 United Feature Syndicate, Inc.

Schroeder is another phenomenon. He is a musician, a pianist, and what makes him so remarkable is that he is a thoroughly accomplished pianist. Beethoven is his idol, though the occasional scraps of written music which appear in the strip may not always be Beethoven's work. Schroeder's preoccupation with music, like that of a few other great artists, precludes an interest in the fair sex, which naturally drives Lucy and Violet crazy. But Schroeder's love is his art, and his victories and defeats are always artistic. Linus, by far the youngest of the gentlemen in the cast, is famed for another kind of affection: like millions of other infants, he is firmly attached to a blanket. The removal of that blanket for any reason at all brings on a severe emotional crisis, a state of affairs often taken sadistic advantage of by the girls. Linus has the makings: if he can survive his early neurosis, he will become another Charlie Brown; if he sublimates it, he may become another Schroeder. (The use of psychiatric jargon is not out of place. All these children save Linus seem up to date on trends and opinions in child psychology, and occasionally express themselves in no uncertain scientific terms, usually to complain that a basic axiom has been violated.) Pigpen rounds out the troupe of boys, and, as his name implies, he is immutably dirty. (One attempt was made to clean him up. It failed.) Pigpen is not very bright, either, and provides a startling and refreshing contrast to Charlie Brown and Schroeder, who are usually clean if not elegant.

There is the cast of *Peanuts*, and Charles Schulz is the man who created them, and the combination seems to be irresistible. Except for the puppy, Snoopy, who often seems to have an intelligence superior to that of his playmates, Schulz has steered clear of animals; and there is certainly nothing supernatural about any of his characters. (In a series of panels called "It's Only a Game," which ran from October of 1957 to January 1, 1959, Schulz showed a perfectly natural— and very funny— comprehension of adults, by exposing their snarling idiocies as they took games too seriously.) In a sense, *Peanuts* is the logical humanization of the "intellectual" strip. But in another sense— once we accept the fact that these children are playing with ideas and will occasionally use a big word— there is nothing intellectual about this strip at all. It is funny. It is a kid strip, and one of the best ever. It ranks with *Krazy Kat* and *Barnaby* and *Pogo* because of the mystique: that certain something which hooks a reader and will not let him go. There is no explaining magic, which may be why we all love magic, and for millions of us *Peanuts* has it.

One comic strip or another has often been accorded the admiration of the eminent. That E. E. Cummings should lavish praise upon *Krazy Kat*, or that President Eisenhower should declare a fondness for *Mutt and Jeff*, is no surprise. But when two public figures as disparate as Calvin Coolidge, who never said anything about anything, and Oliver Wendell Holmes, Jr., who made frequent and trenchant pronouncements on matters of the great-

"Came de skwuzz witt de cabooses"

A tender maternal scene from *Hiawatta*, by MILT GROSS. From *Hiawatta*, copyright 1926 by George H. Doran. Reprinted by permission of Doubleday & Co., Inc., and Mrs. Milt Gross.

est moment to all mankind, declare publicly for the same comic artist, we must pause to note the circumstances.

The pause is refreshing: the artist was Milt Gross. His public was not limited to Presidents and Supreme Court justices. Even those who disdained to read the funnies were caught up by the magic of his books, most of which appeared during the twenties. Over much of his work now there has drifted a jazz-age haze; readers, and even some of Gross's personal friends, harken back to the twenties as soon as the man's name is mentioned. Yet his career as an artist had begun in 1913; one of his great creations, *Dave's Delicatessen*, was wholly a product of the thirties; and when he died in 1953 he had earned fame in still another profession— scenario writing, in Hollywood.

Most cartoonists have arrived in New York City after a certain amount of struggle, traditionally from some small town in the Midwest. Milt Gross had the inestimable advantage of having been born in New York, in the Bronx, in 1895. He went to a perfectly ordinary public school in the Bronx, where one of his classmates was a local cutup named Arthur Flegenheimer, who, when he reached maturity, changed his name to Dutch Schultz. But school held few attractions for Gross, and when he was twelve he wangled his first job. It was in the art department of the New York *Journal* and he was office boy for Tad Dorgan. There was little more he could have desired. Tad even had a nickname for him— Davenport, after the great pen-and-ink artist Gross was trying to emulate. There was plenty of work; a good many of the *Journal's* artists were regularly late with their creations, and Gross found himself ghosting and retouching for them. By 1913, when he was eighteen years old, he was a staff artist for the American Press Association. This lasted until 1915, when he went to the New York *Evening Journal*. There he created his own strip, his first strip, called *Henry Peck, A Happy Married Man*. He was all of twenty-two years old and was making a small living, but he was doing what he would always like to do best, drawing and satirizing. He made the mistake of asking Brisbane for a raise; Brisbane turned him down; Gross quit. He shifted to animated cartoons, producing a few of his own features for the Bray Studios; but shortly he was back at newspaper work, this time for the New York *World*, where his first great creations began to appear: *Banana Oil* and *Count Screwloose from Toulouse*. During the war he was a private in the infantry, but after the war he went right back to the *World*. His greatest successes were immediately ahead of him: *Nize Baby* and *Hiawatta* (these were books), and a little later *Dave's Delicatessen* and *Grossly Xaggerated*, of which latter the most popular feature was *That's My Pop!*

Like all highly original comic talents Gross's is hard to explain. Perhaps a clue was supplied by his old friend Ernie Bushmiller, who once described him as a man totally without guile. This guilelessness is not to be confused with naïveté, but it is true that there was something of the in-

"*In de liss a cluzz 'No cheeldren'*"

Life among the savages, by MILT GROSS. From *Hiawatta*, copyright 1926 by George H. Doran. Reprinted by permission of Doubleday & Co., Inc., and Mrs. Milt Gross.

The frontispiece to *Nize Baby.* Somehow this drawing is particularly funny because it has practically nothing to do with the book that follows. Reprinted by permission of Mrs. Milt Gross.

MILT GROSS's treatment of another classic. The horseshoe is, of course, upside-down. From *Nize Baby.* Reprinted by permission of Mrs. Milt Gross.

nocent about Gross. And perhaps it was that innocence which enabled him to poke wide-eyed fun at the world's stupidities, as Count Screwloose did; to maintain a gentle integrity, as the proprietor of *Dave's Delicatessen* invariably did; or to show us a small boy's constant pride in his constantly erring father. It was he, after all, who advised Bushmiller, in about 1931, that little Nancy should be kept on in *Fritzi Ritz*; she was ingenuous without being ingenious, and Gross liked her.

His first thrusts at a goofy humanity were delivered by *Count Screwloose*. This was a Sunday page, and the plot was simple and unvarying: Count Screwloose inhabited an asylum called Nuttycrest, and each week he a) found a way out, b) observed humanity at its normal activities, and c) returned to Nuttycrest, a saner spot by far. This is almost trite; it is simply the old joke about the escapee who returned voluntarily. It was Gross's talent which made of this more than just a gag, more than just a comic strip, more than just a variation on a theme. *Count Screwloose* was, in the world of comic art, an event. It generally appeared in nine panels, and no one of them lacked its own touch of the ridiculous. Count Screwloose's escape, for one thing, was always accomplished as if by inadvertence; an inmate of the asylum, believing himself a judge, raps his gavel on an unbalanced plank, propelling Count Screwloose into the air and over the wall. Or another inmate, formerly a butcher, puts his heavy thumb on one pan of a balance while Screwloose, who was sitting in the other pan, sails through the air from the violence of the weighing. Once outside, Screwloose always found assorted mayhem— a practical joker, an unsanitary cook, a lonesome gangster, a recently divorced melancholy. Screwloose himself, less than half the size of the other figures in the strip, bobbed up here and there among the panels, to witness the most flagrant of the imbecilities. And in the last panel he was safely back at Nuttycrest, always in the company of a dog named Iggy who thought himself Napoleon. There, for no reason at all, except possibly to express his great joy at having found a haven, Screwloose broke into a dance, offered Iggy a bone, or performed some other token gesture, as he sang out in high glee, "Iggy, keep an eye on me!"

It was beautiful slapstick. Gross was already drawing as he did for the rest of his life: the protruding eyes, the oddly assorted hats, the paunchy supernumeraries, and the violent, totally unrestrained action. Yet *Screwloose* is most rewarding when it is studied carefully. Each panel had its own imaginative touch. In one, where the focal figure was a chef, there appeared on a kitchen table a hat under glass, in the manner of roast breast of guinea hen. In another, where a cat was being chased by that same chef, a rather stirring scene took place in a corner of the panel, almost unnoticed in the rush of action: a mouse, standing on a small can, harangued four of his fellow mice on the desirability of belling the cat. The harangue consisted of one scalloped balloon (a "thought" balloon) in

A typical *Looy Dot Dope*, displaced by other GROSS creations; he had more ideas than he could keep running at one time. Reprinted by permission of Mrs. Milt Gross.

which the cat appeared with a bell around its neck. A casual reader might miss the small subscene entirely; it was a totally unnecessary but engagingly zany touch. In another *Screwloose* a gangster in fear of his life a) took a bath in a suit of armor, b) ate grass (well salted) because he did not trust his cook's food, c) traveled through the city streets in a most conspicuous armored car, d) arrived at a rendezvous through a secret passage the exit to which was a large oven in an old-fashioned stove, and e) explained to a pretty girl reporter that he was a gangster because he wanted to enjoy the comforts of life; he wanted to come and go as he pleased. Iggy, keep an eye on me!

This was the first burgeoning of what his colleagues always referred to as Gross's genius. (Apparently, it was impossible to dislike the man. He was not only guileless; he was modest, generous, and genuinely interested in his fellow man.) He was a satirist, all right, but his satire was directed at humanity and not at any one segment of it. He began in 1913, remember, when it was not yet *infra dig* to poke sometimes malicious fun at Dutchmen, farmers, Negroes, Jews, and even(!) Englishmen. But there was never a trace of malice in anything that Gross ever drew. And when, in the twenties, he began to publish his dialect stories, the result was unadulterated fun for everybody.

The titles themselves provoke the beginnings of a belly laugh: *Nize Baby* (1926), *Hiawatta with No Odder Poems* (1926), *Dunt Esk* (1927), *De Night in de Front from Chreestmas* (1927), and *Famous Fimmales Witt Odder Ewents from Heestory* (1928). It was *Nize Baby* which established Gross as a national figure. This saga of the Feitlebaum family and their disturbed and disturbing neighbors (nowadays they would be called neurotic) not only convulsed newspaper readers everywhere, but drew a personal letter, almost abject in its admiration, from Justice Holmes to the artist. ("Iggy, keep an eye on me!" had incidentally swept the nation in much the same manner. Children all over the country screamed it at each other, much as a later generation would shout, "Look, Ma, no hands!")

If *Nize Baby* was Gross's prose masterpiece, *Hiawatta*, which was pub-

The frontispiece to *Famous Fimmales Witt Odder Ewents from Heestory*. GROSS's revision of Darwin. Reprinted by permission of Mrs. Milt Gross.

369

Count Screwloose from Toulouse in action. Note the candle in the window. Reprinted by permission of Mrs. Milt Gross.

lished in the same year, was his poetic triumph; and the illustrations for it were even funnier. All in all, *Hiawatta* was the greater work of art, and with *He Done Her Wrong*, Gross's graphic masterpiece, which came along in 1930, can stand as the peak of his achievement.

Hiawatta was a good deal more than simply a rendering of Longfellow's classic in Yiddish dialect. Yiddish was no longer simply Yiddish, for one thing; it was a corrupt and expressive urban language. There was a double incongruity: that a European dialect should be used for a proto-American poem, and that its urban accents, rhythms and idioms should be applied to the forest primeval. Gross was anticipating, and even he may not have known it. In the thirties and more particularly in the forties, chiefly through the incidental influence of entertainers, a good many translations of Yiddish phrases entered the English language: break a leg, drop dead, you should live so long. Gross was simply fifteen years ahead of his time, and he had chosen to assimilate two of the most widely disparate cultures possible. The result was an exercise in parody which went beyond parody, into the realm of jolting laughter; and the author's inspired drawings added the final lunatic note. *Hiawatta* is still a pleasure to read, and the laughter now is no less convulsive than it was in 1926.

Satire and parody were Gross's meat. His inimitable *He Done Her Wrong* is both, and it came directly out of his experiences in Hollywood,

A Sunday *Dave's Delicatessen*. The victualer in repose. Otto and his family are possibly the most horrendous group ever to appear in the funny-papers. Reprinted by permission of Mrs. Milt Gross.

A daily *Dave's Delicatessen*. The extraneous final panel shortly became a feature in its own right. Reprinted by permission of Mrs. Milt Gross.

a city which seems to bring out the satirist in a good many of us. He had worked with Charlie Chaplin on *The Circus*, and had done screenplays based on *Nize Baby*. When he returned to New York, presumably astonished by his first brush with Hollywood, he began an undertaking unique in American literature: the creation of a novel without words. *He Done Her Wrong* contains hundreds of outlandish and monumentally funny drawings. It is not simply a satire on the Hollywood adventure film; it jabs away at the stock situations and emotions of American melodrama. (It is worth noting that Gross was, all his life, in love with the Gay Nineties, and that the nineties were certainly a melodramatic era, on stage and off. Surely his flair for the heightened emotion, for the intensely dramatic scene of consummate unimportance, was one of the qualities that made all his strips and all his observations on life so enduringly funny.) *He Done Her Wrong* is lavishly stocked with homicides, grand passions, chases, and villain, hero and heroine; it also contains a wholly bewildering cast of totally incidental innocent bystanders, much like the unrelated insanities drawn wantonly into odd nooks and crannies of *Count Screwloose*. There is literally not a word of text in the book; as it is a novel without words, so it is a silent film transferred to paper. It remains unique.

Gross maintained his connections in Hollywood, even moving to the West Coast. When the *World* folded in New York, King Features snapped him up, and during the thirties he created for them *Dave's Delicatessen* and *That's My Pop*, working on comic strips with one hand, so to speak, as he turned out scenarios with the other. *Dave's Delicatessen*, the earlier of these two creations, was a strip based in some alchemical manner on a real Broadway delicatessen called Dave's Blue Room, whither Gross often repaired with two of his closest friends, Ernie Bushmiller and Bob Dunn. Gross and Bushmiller had been close since the early twenties, and Dunn worked with Gross for years, doing much of his drawing. (Dunn is now Jimmy Hatlo's right hand, and has also turned out strips of his own.) Both Bushmiller and Dunn are large, lusty extroverts, and the scene must have been fascinating: three noisy gourmands, gesticulating happily over their corned beef and letting their flights of imagination carry them farther and farther from reality. Many of those flights were the origins of sequences for *Dave's Delicatessen.* One of those sequences concerned a shady operator trying to sell Dave a houseful of excelsior; one imagines Gross leaning forward earnestly and asking, "What would you do if you had a house full of excelsior and you had to sell it to Dave or go to jail?" and Bushmiller and Dunn chomping into pickles, thinking fast, and coming up with a thousand and one confidence games the goal of each of which was the disposal of several tons of excelsior. None of Gross's previous comic-strip work had involved so many problems of continuity. *Count Screwloose* was a full page, but each page was complete in itself. Gross obviously had no trouble with continuity. He was a scenarist, and he had written *Nize Baby,* and he was already working on *He Done Her Wrong.* But the continuing sequence added a new dimension to his newspaper work; though his preference was for the gag, the quick comment, the epigram, he was quite at home doing a strip which required daily continuity.

But in the late thirties he went back to the panel with *Grossly Xaggerated.* These panels were subtitled "Could I Write a Book" or "That's My Pop," and the latter became so much a catch word that the title of the panel is often given incorrectly, as simply "That's My Pop." One theme carried "That's My Pop" from beginning to end: the gleeful pride of a small boy in his father's nefarious doings. Was a chicken thief caught by an automatic camera? That's My Pop! When a display bed in a store window was advertised "Once you get in you won't want to get out," the combined efforts of the store manager and floor walker were insufficient to remove one literal-minded bum from its comfortable mattress: That's My Pop! These went on day after day, and Gross's powers of invention seemed limitless. The drawing had not changed much; Pop had the same sausage nose, the same protruding eyes (with the pupils touching in the center) as many of the victims and villains in *Count Screwloose.*

The drawing itself deserves a word. There is a similarity, partly accounted for by Bob Dunn, between Gross's work and Jimmy Hatlo's, and between both of those and Al Fagaly's drawing in *There Oughta Be a Law.* It is a style basic to the funnies, with a good many of the older conventions retained: the little hop of surprise, the lines of wavy motion, the flying drops of water or perspiration, and the small figure (Screwloose, or the cat in "Could I Write a Book," or the youngster in "That's My Pop") whose comment sets off the scene illustrated. Working toward burlesque from this style, we run into Bill Holman, George Lichty and Reamer Keller. Working toward reality, we might pass through Charles Wellington, Fontaine Fox, Loy Byrnes's *Spunkie,* to Leslie Turner's version of *Captain Easy* or even Roy Crane's Sunday strips featuring Rosco Sweeney. From there to the illustrator's style is only one step. There has never been a deliberately funny strip done in a straight illustrator's style, and the satirical or parody style would naturally be fatal to an adventure strip.

A *Grossly Xaggerated* of 1937. GROSS's drawing hardly changed over the years— fortunately. Reprinted by permission of Mrs. Milt Gross.

373

Gross is another fine example of the marriage of style and content; just enough reality is evident to identify people and places for the reader, but the law of gravity is not necessarily immutable, and the foibles of men and women are exaggerated beyond any reasonable extreme.

Gross was still living in California, and still working on scenarios, when he died in 1953. He left a wife and three sons. He also left a reputation, not only as one of the century's great comic artists, but as a man who had combined the professional and personal virtues. He was original, forthright and independent, but there was no trace of arrogance in him. He accepted his success, was happy in it, and made no further mention of it. He did what he could for his fellow artists, and he brought years of mirth to his fellow men. His colleagues, asked to describe him, shrug helplessly, shake their heads, and say, "He was a great guy," using that unoriginal phrase because there are not sufficient words to explain the man properly. To all of them he was much more than a great guy; he combined a brilliant career with absolute honesty and generosity to all men. No ego, no tantrums, no feuds. Just Milt Gross.

In the year 1958 a young Canadian pianist named Glenn Gould came to New York to give a recital. One of his selections was a particularly demanding set of variations by Johann Sebastian Bach. Because these variations required much agility and perfect position, Mr. Gould used a piano stool which could be adjusted in the pauses: up, down, right, left. The New York *Times*, in its review, remarked that Mr. Gould had supplied a thirty-first Goldberg Variation— the Rube Goldberg variation.

No reader of the *Times* over the age of fifteen could have missed the reference. Of all the phrases he has added to our language, Rube Goldberg has contributed none more significant than his own name. As an adjective, "rubegoldbergian" may yet enter our dictionaries.

Because of his inventions, of course. Neither art nor science has ever

RUBE GOLDBERG's mangling of his early observations as a sports cartoonist. The result: an Invention, a satire, and relative immortality for the artist. Courtesy of Rube Goldberg.

PROFESSOR BUTTS CHOKES ON A PRUNE PIT AND COUGHS UP AN IDEA FOR AN AUTOMATIC TYPEWRITER ERASER. RING FOR OFFICE BOY (A), WHO COMES RUNNING IN AND STUMBLES OVER FEET OF WINDOW CLEANER (B). HE GRABS FOR HAT-RACK (C) TO SAVE HIMSELF. HAT-RACK FALLS AGAINST BOOKS (D) WHICH DROP ON RULER (E), CAUSING PEN (F) TO FLY UP AND PUNCTURE BALLOON (G) WHICH EXPLODES WITH A LOUD REPORT. TRAINED MONKEY (H) MISTAKES REPORT FOR GUN THAT IS THE SIGNAL TO BEGIN HIS VAUDEVILLE ACT AND HE STARTS PEDALLING LIKE MAD. THE RUBBER TIRE (I) PASSES OVER PAPER (J) AND ERASES MISTAKE MADE BY SLEEPY STENOGRAPHER WHO IS TOO TIRED TO DO IT HERSELF BECAUSE SHE HAD SUCH A LONG WALK HOME FROM AN AUTOMOBILE RIDE THE NIGHT BEFORE. IT IS ADVISABLE TO HAVE YOUR OFFICE OVER A GARAGE SO YOU CAN GET QUICK SERVICE IN CASE OF A PUNCTURE.

Another nightmare for the Patent Office, this is GOLDBERG's attempt to make life easier for the working girl. Courtesy of Rube Goldberg.

seen such outlandish contraptions; fortunately, the American public has. For a time Professor Lucifer Butts, the perpetrator or victim of many of these crimes against cause-and-effect, was one of the best-known academicians in the United States.

The inventions were a logical development: Goldberg had been an engineer and was known to have a profound contempt for simplicity and for the laws of nature. For decades these parodies of the Industrial Revolution (they were certainly that; Goldberg was kidding our mechanical civilization) appeared singly; then for years they did not appear at all; and then in 1959 a book was published which bore a suspicious title, *How to Remove the Cotton from a Bottle of Aspirin, and Other Problems Solved*, and an even more suspicious author's name, Rube Goldberg. The book consisted of three extended inventions— extended beyond all bounds of space, time, velocity and human behavior. The book was hilarious.

Perhaps not so oddly, it is Goldberg's contention that after all the years of sports and editorial cartooning, comic-strip work, book illustration and advertising art, he will be remembered by a grateful and giggling posterity for his inventions. Which is very possible. And for once the joke would be on Goldberg.

Thus the work of six men whose hold on their audience was or is at least partly inexplicable and whose comic strips don't seem to fall into any of the traditional categories. *Krazy Kat* is certainly not an animal strip, nor is *Pogo*; *Barnaby* is not a supernatural strip; *Peanuts* may be a kid strip, but it is like no other kid strip; and Milt Gross's work is different from anything else in the history of comics. And there are others whose work is equally funny and equally habit-forming. There is Al Capp; there is Bill Holman, whose *Smokey Stover* is often as funny as anything else drawn; there is Stan MacGovern, whose *Silly Milly* wowed readers consistently for as long as he drew it. These men— and many others scattered throughout this book— have taken the comic strip back to its beginnings. They have, to use a cliché, put the comic back in the strip. And oddly enough most of them have something to say about this world and the characters who people it. That may be the funniest thing of all.

Military science to the rescue. Ultimately that football defied all known laws of flight and trajectory. From *How to Remove the Cotton from a Bottle of Aspirin* by RUBE GOLDBERG. Copyright 1959 by Reuben L. Goldberg. Reprinted by permission of Doubleday & Co., Inc.

"As football soars into outer space military observers try to agree on its identity. The Army says it is a satellite from an unknown country. The Navy insists it is a flying saucer. The Air Force says it looks like a football but withholds its final decision. As the object loses altitude the Pentagon holds a cocktail party to await developments."

BRIEF EPILOGUE

No predictions. A peek at the future is de rigueur in most reviews of the past. Histories of naval armament, or of shoes, usually end with a few severely delivered injunctions, minatory or hortatory: "The destroyer is obsolete," or "The wing tip is here to stay." But that is Science; this is Art. At the moment it looks as though the adolescent strip is on the rise, the Western strip declining, the mystery or detective strip stabilized, and the fantasy, or free form, strip in another frenzied period of prenatal moiling. The family strip— and, by extension, the kid strip— are surely here to stay. Sports cartooning is in a parlous state. Editorial cartooning is becoming more and more important in what looks like an epoch of declining literacy. Yet who can say? Suburban newspapers have been folding and metropolitan newspapers have been merging, all of which may presage serious changes in the world of comic art. And the public, that great beast, is always changing its mind, usually for no obvious reason. For all we know the thirty-day serial will come back, and editors will trim down their comics pages. Conversely the editorial page, often the funniest section of a newspaper, may disappear entirely, to be replaced by a series of cubistic panels depicting world events. What is past can be observed; it can be praised or damned or ignored. The future can only be awaited.

No apologies, either. There have been very few hypercritical remarks in this book, and there is practically no destructive criticism. The reader may wonder, and even cavil, at the author's apparently inexhaustible affability. But with comic artists there is a predisposition to good will that amiably blunts criticism in advance.

One regret remains, however: the omissions. The responsibility for determining the cast of characters and emphases is wholly the author's; no one within the industry could reasonably have been expected to assume any such function. Up to about 1930 pretty much everything of importance has been touched upon, because history has already made many of the necessary judgments. But since 1930 there has been so astonishing a proliferation of cartoon techniques in this country, with a consequently enormous increase in the number of practitioners, that a full roll call is impossible. Whole areas of graphic art have been slighted. Book illustration deserves a volume of its own; advertising and education have been only lightly touched upon; the greeting-card industry, which now runs to hundreds of millions of dollars a year and places more emphasis on humor all the time, has hardly been mentioned. Where, for example, is Robert Osborn, whose book and magazine illustrations— and indeed whose prose

— *rank him among the real humorists of the time? Where is R. O. Blechman, a young artist whose Christmas cards, drawn originally for his private use, have become among the most popular in the industry and whose* The Juggler of Our Lady, *originally a small, very witty book, has now been animated by Terrytoons? Where is Jules Feiffer, whose leering analyses of neurosis have established him as a comic artist? Where, for that matter, are a hundred gag cartoonists whose work appears regularly in national magazines; or a couple of dozen young comic-strip artists whose creations, seemingly viable, have added new spice to our Sunday supplements? And the scores of talented men whose anonymous efforts keep the comic-book industry alive; where are they?*

The answer is that they are in other books than this, some of them unwritten. In twenty years, when history has made new judgments, an aficionado will record them. Our own generation has no cause to complain. In comic strips, the period of the giants ran from 1894 to the First World War, and much of the material is still available to us. The second great period ran from the first war to the depression, and its better strips are still running. The third period ended with the Second World War and may be properly called contemporary; and it is hardly unreasonable to assume that we are now at the beginning of— or perhaps halfway along in— a fourth period, characterized by wit, sophistication and science.

Entertainment and edification are the goals of comic art, and we have probably had more than we deserve. For the most part it comes to us in small daily or weekly doses; we forget to be appreciative. This book is offered in tribute— to the hundreds of creative talents who have made American comic art what it is, and to the American public, which— sometimes with indifference but most often with enthusiasm— has taken those men to its vast bosom, accepting with unabashed fondness this mischievous offspring of our culture.

A fitting farewell, this is RUBE GOLDBERG'S comment on Rome, mankind, and the march of civilization. Drawn by Rube Goldberg and reproduced by permission of the publishers, the Vanguard Press, from *Rube Goldberg's Guide to Europe* by Rube Goldberg and Sam Boal. © 1954 by Rube Goldberg and Sam Boal.

National Cartoonists Society

REUBEN WINNERS

1946 — Milt Caniff

1947 — Al Capp

1948 — Chic Young

1949 — Alex Raymond

1950 — Roy Crane

1951 — Walt Kelly

1952 — Hank Ketcham

1953 — Mort Walker

1954 — Willard Mullin

1955 — Charles Schulz

1956 — Herblock

1957 — Hal Foster

1958 — Frank King

This is the Reuben, conceived by Rube Goldberg in a dazzling moment of white-hot creativity, wrought with tender incredulity by William Crawford, and awarded annually by the National Cartoonists Society to the cartoonist of the year. Courtesy of The National Cartoonists Society.

INDEX OF TITLES

(Italic numbers refer to pages on which illustrations appear)

INDEX OF PERSONAL NAMES

(Italic numbers refer to pages on which illustrations appear)

ABOUT THE AUTHOR

STEPHEN BECKER'S *first novel,* The Season of the Stranger, *was a Harper Find in 1951. His short stories have appeared in* Harper's *Magazine and in* Best Short Stories of 1954. *Among his many translations from the French are* The Colors of the Day *by Romain Gary and* Faraway *by André Dhôtel. His second serious novel,* Juice, *was published in 1959.*

He attended Harvard College, did a year of graduate work at Yenching University in Peking, China, and lived for several years in France. In 1954 he received a Guggenheim Fellowship for creative writing. He now lives with his wife and three children on a small farm near Bedford, New York.